Hell
Put
to
Shame

ALSO BY EARL SWIFT

Hell
Put
to
Shame

**THE 1921 MURDER FARM MASSACRE AND THE
HORROR OF AMERICA'S SECOND SLAVERY**

Earl Swift

MARINER BOOKS
New York   Boston

HarperCollins books may be purchased for educational, business, or sales promotional use. For information, please email the Special Markets Department at SPsales@harpercollins.com.

FIRST EDITION

Designed by Jennifer Chung

Map by Kevin Swift

Library of Congress Cataloging-in-Publication Data has been applied for.

ISBN 978-0-06-326538-7

24 25 26 27 28 LBC 5 4 3 2 1

For Laura LaFay

Contents

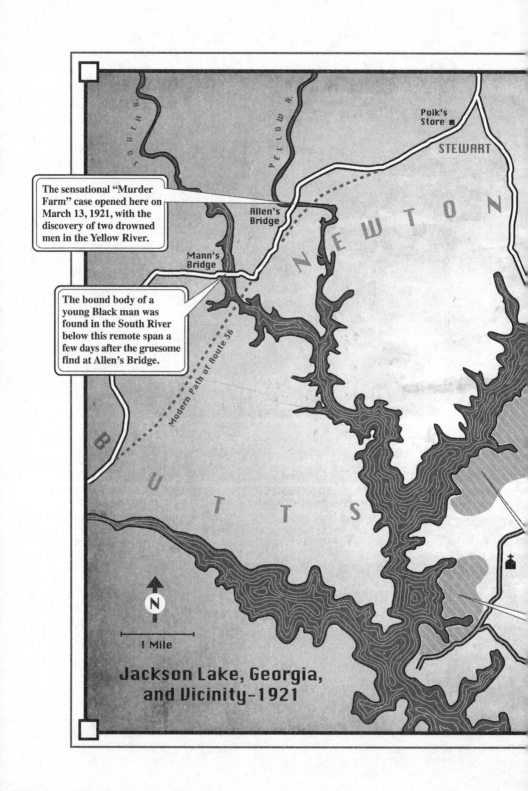

The sensational "Murder Farm" case opened here on March 13, 1921, with the discovery of two drowned men in the Yellow River.

The bound body of a young Black man was found in the South River below this remote span a few days after the gruesome find at Allen's Bridge.

Polk's Store

STEWART

NEWTON

Allen's Bridge

Mann's Bridge

SOUTH R.

YELLOW R.

Modern Path of Route 36

BUTTS

N

1 Mile

Jackson Lake, Georgia, and Vicinity—1921

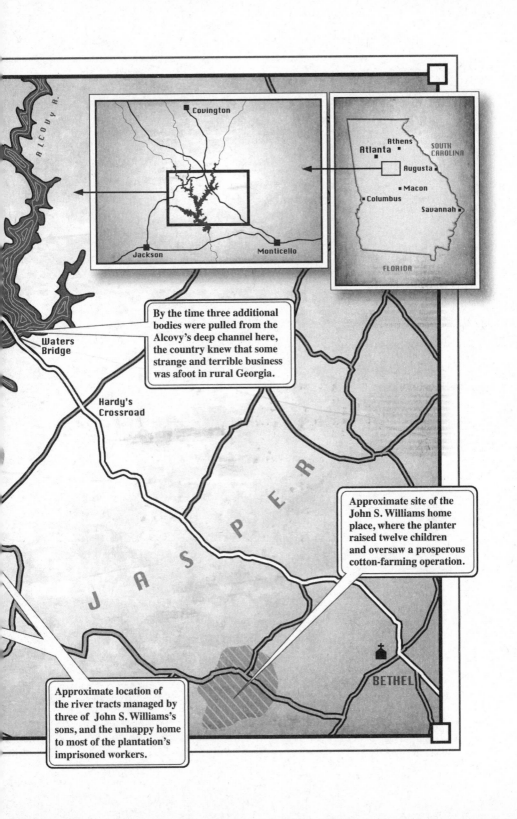

Covington

ALCOVY R.

Atlanta
Athens
SOUTH
CAROLINA
Augusta
Macon
Columbus
Savannah

FLORIDA

Jackson
Monticello

Waters
Bridge

By the time three additional
bodies were pulled from the
Alcovy's deep channel here,
the country knew that some
strange and terrible business
was afoot in rural Georgia.

Hardy's
Crossroad

JASPER

Approximate site of the
John S. Williams home
place, where the planter
raised twelve children
and oversaw a prosperous
cotton-farming operation.

BETHEL

Approximate location of
the river tracts managed by
three of John S. Williams's
sons, and the unhappy home
to most of the plantation's
imprisoned workers.

PART ONE

Wire and Chain

Prelude

THEY MOVED ROUTE 36 in the years after the killings. Now the road runs straight where it used to dogleg through Newton County, an hour's drive southeast of Atlanta, and most travelers don't see that it was ever otherwise. Orphaned stretches of the old highway linger here and there, most of them dwindled to rough trails—hardwoods and high weeds pressing their flanks, yearling pines braving their unpaved crowns, thick weaves of vine plunging their remote twists into midday dusk.

Leave anything for long in the Georgia heat and rain and, sure as the sunrise, nature will reclaim it. It does not take long.

You have to look hard for one piece of the original roadbed, where it veers from modern blacktop into jungle at the county's southern tip. Its passage into the trees has knitted shut, season by season, over a lifetime of disuse. A sign once warned off the curious; when it fell away, the opening had shrunk so small, so easily missed by passing traffic, that hanging a new one must have seemed a waste of effort.

The road beyond is an abstraction, a shallow groove carpeted in pine needles. But if you dare push through the tangle into the gloom, and follow the ghost of old Route 36 on its curving path among the trees, you soon reach the South River—and what's left of the span that bore the abandoned highway to the far bank.

Mann's Bridge squats on rusting pylons a few feet over the drink, its wood-plank floor stripped away, its box-truss skeleton venturing only halfway across the water. Its bones are pitted, flaking, and brittle with age. It receives few visitors, this fossil of horse-drawn days. Barely visible from the modern concrete bridge a thousand feet downstream, it's paid little mind by anyone.

Yet here, unknown to most folks in Newton County and unmentioned by those aware of it, an event of powerful repercussion occurred. One winter's Saturday night in 1921, an automobile chugged up the old highway to stop in the span's middle, and one of its occupants dropped to the water below. Then, as now, the South River was shallow at the bridge, its bottom only eight to ten feet down. But when a man is bound by wire, with a hundred-pound sack of rocks chained to his neck, water need not run deep to do its work. Dark with tannins, clouded by mud, it swallowed him up. A minute later, it was back to running smooth and slow.

On the same night a mile from here, where old Route 36 crossed another river, two different men, likewise trussed with wire and chain, were thrown off Allen's Bridge, now all but vanished. In the space of a few nights, three more men were pitched off a third bridge five miles to the northeast.

Many others died in the surrounding countryside, all of them Black and all at the hands of what seemed an unlikely killer. His arrest and trial would spawn front-page headlines from coast to coast about the virtual prison he ran on a plantation one county over, and about what lay behind the farm's prosperity and the murders, both—a form of slavery that had survived in the South for generations after Appomattox.

Each day's paper brought new details of the slaughter, new glimpses of the brutal months and years the victims endured before meeting their ends. The revelations tore at America's faith in its own virtue. They undermined its sense of modernity, challenged its grasp of history—resurrected sins thought dead and gone, put to rest by the Thirteenth Amendment. Provoked wonder: How could such things happen here, in the Empire State of the South? How could they happen now, amid the inventive dazzle of the twentieth century? How could they happen at all?

A century on, you might ask the same questions. The whole business remains incredible, the more so because it has so faded from memory. No roadside marker calls it to mind out on the new Route 36. No town square monument honors the dead. Nothing commemorates the drama that brought a pernicious but largely unseen form of indentured servitude to widespread attention—and, by dragging it into the light, perhaps helped to hasten its decline.

Neither do we have tangible reminders that Georgia's governor at the time, a man vilified for his role in an earlier murder case, earned some measure of redemption through his response to these killings. Nor that, while doing so, he allied with two African American activists who rank among the twentieth century's ablest generals in the long and continuing battle for racial justice.

About the only memorial to those clamorous days is here, in an out-of-the-way corner of a sparsely populated county in central Georgia, at the end of an abandoned dirt road, at the decrepit remains of Mann's Bridge.

It seems too tranquil a setting for the lessons it offers. That the past lurks close. That we haven't learned as much as we think we have. That maybe we never do.

Crickets and birdsong fill the air. Fish leap. The bridge's old metal bakes hot in the sun.

The river swirls like syrup around its legs.

A JANUARY WEEKDAY at the U.S. Post Office and Courthouse in downtown Atlanta—today the home of the Eleventh Circuit U.S. Court of Appeals, but in 1921, a busy warren of federal offices. Two special agents of the United States Department of Justice's Bureau of Investigation, the forerunner of today's FBI, were working at their desks on the third floor when up walked a Black man named Gus Chapman.

Thirty-nine years old and worn for his age, Chapman told the agents that he had been living in Atlanta the previous spring when he was picked up on a loitering charge. Fined five dollars, unable to pay it, he was facing hard labor on the chain gang when a young farmer approached him in the jail. Come home with me, he said, and you can work out your fine there. You'll be happy you did. It'll be like a home to you.

And so Chapman accompanied Hulon Williams home to Jasper County, in the cotton country forty miles southeast of the city, and to a sprawling plantation owned by Williams's father. He quickly saw that "Mr. Hulon" had oversold its charms. Chapman received no pay. He was forced at the end of a gun barrel to work from dawn to well past dark. He was forbidden to leave the premises under threat of death. He was locked up at night in a bunkhouse crowded with other prisoners, and whipped for any infraction, real or imagined. The Bureau agents recognized the conditions he described. Gus Chapman had been held in peonage.

That word has fallen out of use, and today is unknown to many Americans, if not most. But throughout the late nineteenth and early twentieth centuries, peonage claimed lives by the thousands and ruined untold others. It tore men from their wives and children, stole sons from their mothers, and helped fuel the Great Migration of southern Blacks to the industrial cities of the Northeast and Midwest in the years on either side of World War I.

Chapman was typical of its victims. In one of its many forms, a man, usually Black, would be arrested for a trifling or trumped-up offense. Vagrancy—that is, having no job, or at least no ready proof of one—was a favorite, as was loitering. Conviction was pretty much automatic, and almost always carried a fine and fees beyond his means. A third party would then step forward to pay the fine in return for the prisoner's labor until his debt was repaid. If, before he settled his account, he was prevented from leaving, that prisoner was a peon, trapped in what amounted to debt slavery. Ginned-up bills for his food and housing might be added to his fine, effectively turning a short jail term into a life sentence. His working and living conditions were often hellish. And if he tried to run, he'd be hunted down like an animal.

Chapman knew that firsthand. The previous July, after three months on the farm, he had slipped away by night and struck off to the east. Roughly a dozen straight-line miles across forest and cottonfield, he found himself cornered. The farm's owner, John Sims Williams—"Mr. Johnny" to his field hands—dragged him home and threatened to kill him. Chapman pleaded for his life until Williams softened. He decided instead to beat the prisoner with his fists, treat him to a savage whipping, then order him to chop firewood in the rain until the sun went down.

The memory of that beating, and Mr. Johnny's assurance that if he ran off again he'd be killed like a snake, dissuaded Chapman from another flight for more than four months—until, on or about December 1, 1920, he again snuck off the Williams place in the dark. This time he made it to Atlanta. He'd been in hiding since.

Others had not been so lucky. Chapman told the agents that he knew of peons killed at the Williams place, and that he had witnessed one of their deaths. A prisoner nicknamed Blackstrap had run away the previous spring and was recaptured after several days on the lam. Back at the plantation, he was draped over a gasoline barrel, his hands and feet held by other field workers, and whipped by Mr. Hulon with such fury that he begged for the torture to stop, begged for the pain to end; cried and begged even as Mr. Hulon handed a revolver to another farmhand and ordered him to shoot.

These Williams people were dangerous, Chapman told the agents. He lived in fear they would track him down in Atlanta. If they found him and took him back to Jasper County, it would be to kill him.

It so happened that Gus Chapman was not the only peon to steal away from the Williams plantation and seek out Special Agents Adelbert J. Wismer and George W. Brown. A second man had been bailed out of jail by Mr. Hulon in February 1920 and had been held against his will until his escape the following September. He evaded capture, ghosting into neighboring Newton County and reaching its seat, Covington, before turning west to Atlanta.

The record is vague on whether James Strickland spoke to Wismer and Brown before or after Chapman, but their visits came within weeks of each other, and the accounts they gave the agents dovetailed in their particulars. In exchange for the $5.25 fine that Mr. Hulon paid the jailers, Strickland worked from daybreak to night, without pay and under guard; Mr. Johnny, Mr. Hulon, and Hulon's brothers, LeRoy and Marvin, carried pistols, as did two trusted Black hands who served as the plantation's field bosses. Strickland was locked up at night with other men "bought" from the jails in Atlanta, Macon, and Monticello, the Jasper County seat.

Like Chapman, he described seeing a fellow peon murdered. Strickland had not been on the farm long when a worker named Iron Jaw—who also went by Long John, and whom still others knew as Smart John—took off running. The Williamses hunted him down, brought him back, and whipped him. Three of the Williams boys took turns getting their licks in. On a Saturday morning not long after, the peons were building a hog enclosure, and Iron Jaw was dispatched to retrieve a coil of wire for the fence. He was unable to carry it, or was making a mess of rolling the wire—the exact nature of his offense wasn't clear, but whatever the case, Mr. LeRoy decided he had earned another whipping. LeRoy was well into giving it to him when Iron Jaw asked him to stop. When Mr. LeRoy did not, Iron Jaw told him he would rather die than be treated so.

Mr. LeRoy asked him: You want me to kill you, sure enough?

Yes, came the reply.

Mr. LeRoy shot him in the arm, then asked: You really want me to kill you?

Iron Jaw nodded. Mr. LeRoy shot him dead.

He turned to Strickland, standing a few feet away, and asked: Do you want some of this? The gun, he meant.

No, Strickland recalled saying. I don't want none of it.

Wismer and Brown took it all down. Though Congress had outlawed peonage in 1867, it had endured in the hardscrabble back blocks of the rural South, and it was among the agents' duties to investigate reports of its presence. It wasn't the sort of work they savored. Victims were often too terrorized to say much, white juries tended to side with white defendants, and even if the government won a conviction, the penalties faced by the accused were meager. Still, the Bureau had other business in that part of the state, so on February 18, 1921, the agents drove to Jasper County.

From their office they wove through a booming city of electric lights and elevators, grand movie and vaudeville houses, and office towers reaching higher than songbirds flew. They drove boulevards clogged with Model Ts, streetcars, and slow-rolling drays, past smoking factories and the tenements of the poor. Atlanta, the capital of the New South: a city of smarts and bustle and cosmopolitan style to match most any in the East.

Out through its suburbs of fine homes they passed. Soon the houses fell away, and the cotton rose, and they were in the country.

It was another Georgia out there. It was another century.

2

—

THE JOHN S. WILLIAMS HOME PLACE occupied 325 acres of rolling field and forest, split by a narrow, unpaved farm road off an almost equally primitive highway about eight miles northwest of the county's center at Monticello. The spread bore little resemblance to the plantations of classic southern fiction. The main house was wood-framed, modest in size, and plain in design, its two forward-facing gables linked by a wide porch. Like other Jasper farmhouses of the day, it had neither electricity nor running water; a privy was one of several outbuildings scattered about the yard. Across the road stood a few tenant shacks, open fields of cotton and corn, and pastureland stretching away to the north.

The place was not home to the julep-sipping rich, either. Cotton farming was a backbreaking, financially uncertain line of work. Plowing was still powered by mules. Seeding and harvesting were done by hand, under a searing Georgia sun. Plucking the fluffy blooms from the sharp bolls that encased them sliced and shredded tender skin. A turn in the weather could ruin a crop, and no matter how ideal the conditions, the cotton plant leached nutrients from the soil, eventually exhausting it.

Early in 1921, those difficulties were sharpened by two developments. The price of cotton had dropped by almost two-thirds in the past few months, from forty cents a pound the previous July to less than fourteen at Christmas. And an even greater threat loomed in the form of the boll weevil, a long-snouted beetle that migrated into the United States from Mexico in the 1890s and had advanced through the South in the years since. The insect laid its eggs in ripening bolls; its larvae devoured the cotton inside. The results were ruinous, and seemingly impossible to stop. Even wealthy planters were at sixes and sevens in dealing with the threat.

So it was no picture of wealth or grandeur that greeted the agents as they braked the car on the rutted lane below the Williams house. This was a rough and dusty place, wholly devoted to hard labor, its only touch of finery a platoon of carefully tended rosebushes out front. As they came to a stop, the agents saw three Black farmhands walking from the direction of the house. They called them over and learned that Mr. Johnny was not home. The men introduced themselves as Johnnie Williams, John Brown, and Clyde Manning. Both agents recognized Manning's name: Gus Chapman had identified him as one of the plantation's field bosses and as the man who kept him locked up at night. When Chapman ran away the first time, it was Manning who caught up with him first and held him for Mr. Johnny.

Wismer and Brown explained that they were there to conduct an investigation into conditions on the farm and asked a few questions. The men were unwilling to say much in front of one another, so the agents took them, one by one, behind an equipment shed that the hands called the gear house. The first was Johnnie Williams. He confirmed one piece of Gus Chapman's report: Clyde Manning was, indeed, a field boss—he carried a gun and guarded the hands brought to the farm from jail. The agents asked him about Blackstrap's death. Johnnie Williams said he knew nothing about it.

Manning was the next field hand they led behind the little building. He was a short, broad-chested man, coal black in complexion, twenty-six years old. They asked whether he was paid for his work. He said he was— twenty dollars a month. We have information, the agents told him, that you are a boss over the niggers for Mr. Williams, and that you keep them locked up at night.

Shocking though it is today, such language was not unusual in the South of a century ago, even from officers of the federal government. The N-word was omnipresent, among the educated as well as the ignorant, the rich along with the poor. And one need not be southern-born to throw the slur around. Wismer was from Michigan and had a law degree from the university in Ann Arbor.

No, sir, Manning said. I ain't no boss.

Well, now, Agent Brown said, if Mr. Williams is guilty of peonage, and you're the boss and you're helping him and you keep it a secret from us, that would make you as guilty as the one telling you to do all that.

Manning denied he was keeping secrets.

We have information, the agents said, that a man named Gus Chapman ran off and that Mr. Williams, you, and another farmhand went after him and brought him back.

No, sir, Manning said. I didn't do anything of the kind.

They asked about Blackstrap's death. Manning claimed ignorance.

Getting nowhere, they excused Manning and led John Brown behind the shed. As his partner conducted the interview, Wismer wandered back to their automobile. He was chatting with Manning and Johnnie Williams from the front seat when a big, seven-passenger Chandler touring car pulled up. Out stepped John S. Williams.

He was a tall man, broad-shouldered and sinewy, with a well-trimmed mustache, graying hair cut short on the sides and back, and a face and neck chapped and creased by fifty-four years of life in the weather. He introduced himself to Wismer as Brown emerged from behind the gear house, and the agents explained the reason for their visit: to investigate reports that Williams had violated the laws of the United States pertaining to peonage. Williams voiced no objection to having the agents on his land. On the contrary, he invited them to explore the place, said he'd be glad for them to make any investigation they felt necessary. But he was confused on one point. What, exactly, did they mean by *peonage*?

Brown attempted to define the term. If Williams bailed prisoners out of jail and worked them on his farm, he said, under some conditions it might be peonage. Well, if that's true, Williams replied, just about every farmer in the county is guilty of it. The crime was in the details, the agents explained. It depended on what happened after he put the prisoners to work. If he kept them there and didn't let them leave, then that would be working them against their will, and *that* would be peonage. We have information that that's what you've been doing, they told him. That you keep your workers locked up at night.

Not true, Williams said. Nobody is locked up.

The agents asked him about Gus Chapman: Did he once have a man of that name working for him?

Yes, Williams replied, he did.

Had Chapman run away from the farm?

Yes, Williams said, he had.

We have information that you, Clyde Manning, and another farmhand captured Chapman and brought him back, the agents told him.

Williams did not hesitate. I did, he said.

Brown turned to Clyde Manning. "You just told us a lie, didn't you?" he asked. Manning said nothing.

This Chapman fellow had come from the Atlanta lockup, Williams told them, and ran away after he assaulted Manning's wife, Rena. Williams and his "boys" chased him down, intending to hand him over to the authorities for prosecution. Chapman had begged so hard, Williams said, that he decided not to turn him in. Sometime later Chapman again took off. He had not returned.

Williams said he paid Chapman fifteen dollars a month for his labor, which contradicted the peon's statement that he had received just a handful of change from Williams over the whole of his seven months on the farm. Such inconsistencies aside, it was an oddly cordial conversation. Williams conducted himself as a man with nothing to hide. He seemed eager to help.

The agents had a list of farmhands Chapman and James Strickland had said would corroborate their accounts of the conditions on the plantation. They told Williams they wanted to speak with those men, as well as his sons Hulon, LeRoy, and Marvin. They're up on the river, the planter told them. I'll be happy to drive you there.

Away to the west of John Williams's home place, three rivers ran southward to meet at the edge of Jasper County. They form the rough shape of a pitchfork. The South River, the fork's leftmost tine, descends sixty miles southeast from its headwater streams in and around Atlanta. The narrower middle tine, the Yellow River, runs golden brown with sediments from the town of Lawrenceville, northeast of the capital. And the right tine, the Alcovy River, begins east of Lawrenceville and snakes seventy miles southward. The three fuse to form the Ocmulgee, one of Georgia's principal streams; think of it as the pitchfork's handle.

In 1911, the Central Georgia Power Company completed a hydroelectric dam across the Ocmulgee a few miles south of this confluence, and a decade later water had piled up behind the obstruction, had jumped the old riverbanks for miles upstream and spread wide over bottomland once covered with timber and cotton to form a vast impoundment called Jackson Lake. Today, that lake is ringed by waterfront homes and boathouses, and on sunny summer weekends its sparkling surface is dotted with fishing skiffs and pontoon boats. In 1921, however, the lake was still digesting the red-clay soil and forest at its fringes. Its water was a turbid stew of mud and dead vegetation, and its stagnant coves served as breeding pools for mosquitos carrying malaria. Many a farmer not displaced by the lake's rising water had quit the area to escape its unwholesome effects.

John S. Williams had done the opposite. He had been buying land since soon after moving to Jasper County in the 1890s, his early acquisitions concentrated at and near what would become his home place. But as the lake filled, he shifted his buying to properties on its shore. In 1916, he bought 145 acres from a prominent family there, the Leveretts. Over the following two years, he added the adjoining "Stone place," measuring 123 acres, and the 200-acre "Steele place," also bordering the original parcel. And in May 1919, he acquired 282 nearby acres from Doyle Campbell, the solicitor general, or prosecutor, of the local court.

These purchases gave Williams more than a mile of frontage along the lake. The family did the bulk of its farming on these outlying tracts, overseen by three of the planter's sons: John Hulon Williams, twenty-eight years old; LeRoy Lane Williams, twenty-five; and Marvin Harris Williams, twenty-two. And on this balmy Friday, with the temperature edging toward sixty degrees, it was to these river tracts that Williams and the two agents set off in the Chandler.

Their first stop, roughly five miles from Williams's home, was the farm Hulon managed on the Campbell place. Brown told Williams he hoped to speak with two farmhands, Claude and Clyde Freeman. From the car they could see several men working in a field, and Williams said he believed that Brown would find at least one of the Freemans among them. Leaving Wismer and Williams in the Chandler, the agent strode toward the group. He was intercepted by Hulon Williams. Brown explained who he was and what he wanted, and Hulon confirmed that at least one of the workers was, indeed, a Freeman. When they reached the group, however, the man in question turned out to be Clifford Freeman, who had gone unmentioned by Chapman and Strickland. Brown told Hulon this was not the man he wanted to see.

Hulon walked him back to the car and climbed in behind him, and the party drove on to Hulon's house. It sat on high ground overlooking a shallow valley, and they could see a cottage down at the bottom, perhaps three hundred yards off. Not so far down the slope stood a second small house, painted red. When the agents announced they wanted to see where the farmhands slept, Hulon led Brown down to the faraway cottage.

The agent saw straightaway that the building was the home of a single family, rather than the crowded and locked peon bunkhouse that Chapman and Strickland had described. So, once back at the car, he collected Wismer, and both government men hiked down to the red house. This time, they found what they were looking for. The cottage had two doors that swung open from opposite sides and met at a center jamb. The jamb formed the end of a partition that ran through the interior to the back wall, splitting the structure in two: they stepped through the door on the right, and found that it bought them entry into just half the place. That half was divided into two rooms—a living area containing a bed and a cot up front, and a smaller kitchen in the rear. The left door opened onto the other side of the partition, a single space stacked with a dozen or more rough plank bunks. Two windows—actually, glassless holes—lit one wall. The agents saw that heavy wooden shutters mounted on the house's exterior covered the openings, and that sticks of lumber could be dropped across the shutters and into cleats on either side to lock them shut from the outside.

A hole had been bored through each of the front doors, and another through the partition, so that a chain could be snaked through all three and secured with a padlock on the building's right side, thereby caging anyone on the left. The partition was built of planks spaced two or three inches apart, so that nothing in the rude dormitory went unseen. The agents also noticed something else on the premises: equipment for resoling shoes with the treads of old tires. They learned that Clyde Manning's Uncle Rufus, who lived here on the river farms, was trained to use it.

After examining a few other outbuildings, the agents repeated their wish to speak with Clyde and Claude Freeman. The Williamses told them the men were likely a mile away, give or take, at Marvin Williams's farm on the Steele place—so again the four climbed into the Chandler, Brown riding shotgun, and followed a rough dirt track that wound through the trees lining Jackson Lake's shore. Before long, the path turned so muddy that the car could go no farther, and they continued on foot until they came upon Marvin and LeRoy Williams, along with several farmhands, burning off the woods at a field's edge.

The agents could see that LeRoy was carrying a revolver in his pocket. Brown faced him. We have information, he said, that you killed a man, one of your Black workers, last year. LeRoy replied, with evident calm, that it wasn't true. He hadn't killed anyone. Well, that gun of yours, Brown told him, that looks bad. I could arrest you for that right now. LeRoy said that he had a permit. He was allowed to carry the gun as long as he didn't conceal it.

One of the Williamses pointed out Clyde Freeman in the field, plowing behind a mule. A cluster of Black farmhands was plowing several hundred yards beyond. Brown announced that he wanted to speak to the workers in private. He left Wismer with their hosts and hiked first to the more distant group, where he interviewed three men. They said nothing of use. But in those exchanges, the agent detected fear—the hands were tongue-tied by it, loathe to say anything about Mr. Johnny or his sons. The same was true of Clyde Freeman, whom Brown stopped to speak with on his way back. He refused to utter a word about the family or the conditions on the farm.

When the agent rejoined his partner and John Williams, the three backtracked to the Chandler and motored to the home place. Whether on the drive or at some other point when they were alone with the planter— the record, again, is unclear—the agents raised the subject of Blackstrap's death. Williams denied that any such killing had taken place. Wismer asked if anyone else had been killed on the farm. Yes, Williams replied, a hand named Will Napier. His son Hulon had killed him: Napier was coming at Hulon with a knife, so Hulon shot him in self-defense. Wismer asked whether he had reported the incident to the county authorities. No, Williams told him. He had not.

Arriving back at his house, Williams offered his further cooperation. I may have violated the peonage laws, he allowed, but if I did, I didn't mean it, and I'll never do it again. He wouldn't get any more workers from the jails, he promised. Almost all of them were gone, anyway—most of the men he and his sons had bailed out had moved on. He was willing to let the few remaining go, provided they repaid what he'd spent on them.

Wismer and Brown said their goodbyes and left to tackle other business. They had frustratingly little to show for their visit. Of the interviews they conducted with the farmhands, only one—that with Johnnie Williams—had produced any information at all, and it wasn't particularly compelling. About the only solid evidence they had found was circumstantial: the red house at Hulon's place. And that, unfortunately, had been unlocked and unoccupied at the time.

The Williamses were almost certainly working peons. But building a case for federal prosecutors to take to a grand jury would require a great deal more evidence, including witnesses willing to testify against the family. The agents knew they could not count on local law enforcement to help gather such evidence—sheriffs and jailers played key roles, after all, in turning prisoners into peons. They were on their own. To advance the investigation, it would be up to them to interview the farmhands at a place, and in a circumstance, in which they felt comfortable enough to talk. Until then, the case was stalled.

3

IT MIGHT SEEM THAT FINDING and stamping out peonage should not have been a difficult process. The practice had been central to the South's economy for decades. In one form or another, it was ubiquitous in Jasper and the surrounding counties—so much so that even a half-conscious observer would find it hard to miss. And in many a courthouse, it was considered business as usual; local officials, serene in their authority, did not bother to hide their complicity in the process.

Those officials were protected by long tradition. In the first two years after the Civil War, Georgia and other states of the old Confederacy had enacted a web of new laws engineered to keep newly freed African American citizens under heel and in the fields. The Black Codes, as these interlocking statutes were dubbed, made an end-run around the Thirteenth Amendment, which outlawed slavery and involuntary servitude except as punishment for convicted criminals. Though they made no mention of race, the new laws gave Blacks a choice: to be locked up, or ground down in conditions evoking the terrible past.

First, the states enacted laws making unemployment a crime. Vagrancy statutes, deployed almost exclusively against Black people, criminalized joblessness, no matter how brief, and irrespective of whether the jobless were actively seeking work. Violators were funneled into the criminal justice system and into hard labor as convicts. The employed, meanwhile, had reason to cling to the jobs they had, no matter how disagreeable and exploitative they might be.

Vagrancy laws were so broadly written that on any given day, just about any poor person qualified for arrest. Georgia's statute of 1866 labeled as a vagrant anyone "wandering or strolling about in idleness, who is able to work, and has no property to support him; or any person leading an idle, immoral, profligate life, having no property to support him." A later Florida definition was even more of a catch-all, targeting gamblers, jugglers, "common pipers and fiddlers," drunks, brawlers, hangers-on at whorehouses and tippling shops, "persons who neglect their calling or employment and misspend what they earn," and those "wandering from place to place able to work and who are without means."

In Georgia, vagrancy could get you a year. And enforcement of the law was stiffened or relaxed, as needed. "At harvest time cotton farms experienced an acute need for a large work force," historian William Cohen observed, "and it was precisely at such times that the police became most active in discovering vagrants."

Second, contract laws worked hand-in-hand with vagrancy statutes to compel Black workers to stay put and busy: the measures required them to sign agreements keeping them at work for a single employer for a year or more. Oftentimes, these documents virtually guaranteed that a laborer would end the contract period in debt to his employer, thereby compelling him to sign a second contract that would sink him further into a state of dependence.

Not happy with the terms of a contract? If you were a Black man hurrying to find work, you were in no position to dicker. Odds were, you couldn't read the document, and thus had to accept your would-be employer's account of what it said. Because you were without education or training, you had little hope of holding out for better work. And if you didn't sign, you might well be reported to the sheriff for vagrancy.

Contract laws grew sharper teeth with so-called prima facie clauses, which made it an automatic crime to leave a job while in debt to one's employer. In declaring that failure to repay an advance was, on its face, evidence of fraud, the southern states criminalized debts that should have been a matter for the civil courts, and threatened Black residents with additional charges, fines, and jail time should they dare walk off the job. A worker in debt became a peon, whether or not he was coerced with the threat of violence—the prospect of incarceration did the trick. And some contract-enforcement laws went to ridiculous lengths: Florida's made "willful disobedience of orders" a crime, along with "wanton impudence."

Finally, the southern states created laws that, while they seemed to target whites, were actually devised to keep Black people in bondage. Dubbed "enticement" statutes, these laws prohibited any employer from luring away workers already under contract—by offering more money, better working conditions, or, in the words of the Georgia statute, "in any other way whatever." In nine of the eleven states of the former Confederacy, such enticement was treated as a criminal offense.

With the arrival of federal troops to enforce Reconstruction, most of the Black Codes were set aside. But with Reconstruction's premature end, southern states resurrected them in modified form, along with their unstated but widely understood goal: to preserve white supremacy and the plantation economy. They were diabolically effective. As the great Black writer and civil rights activist W. E. B. Du Bois put it: "The slave went free; stood a brief moment in the sun; then moved back again toward slavery."

The form of peonage that the agents investigated at the John S. Williams plantation developed alongside another, better known system of forced labor embraced by the southern states in the wake of the Civil War. Convict leasing, as this other system was known, saw state governments lease their prisoners to private-sector businesses. The operator of a coal mine or steel mill or railroad, say, would pay the state a nominal fee per month for a prisoner's labor, and would work that prisoner as hard as he saw fit—which, as often as not, proved to be very hard, indeed. Legions of leased convicts died of disease, starvation, exposure, and exhaustion. Still others were beaten to death by their private-sector bosses in the name of boosting productivity. Many a man convicted of some petty offense thus received a death sentence, and no sooner had he been buried at the work site than his employer could ask the state for a replacement, for the same trivial monthly fee. The states, eager for the income, were happy to supply fresh blood.

Convict leasing stoked southern industry for decades, until public outcry shamed the states into stepping back from such officially sanctioned brutality. Georgia did away with it in 1908. In its place, the states locked their convicts in prison farms or put them to work building and maintaining highways and other public works. Though this new system could be almost as barbaric, it at least promised some small measure of accountability: if a prisoner lived to complete his sentence, the state let him go.

But the private exploitation of prisoners did not end with the demise of convict leasing; it merely shifted from state control to local. In Georgia, civilians like Williams could show up at a county jail or courthouse, pay the fines and court costs of a Gus Chapman or James Strickland, and leave with him. In theory, the farmer or businessman got a laborer on the cheap. The prisoner evaded the known deprivations of the chain gang, on the wager that his lot would improve under the care of his supposed benefactor. In practice, however, the prisoner was cast to the wind. Officials rarely tracked the inmates they handed over, or took steps to ensure that their rights were safeguarded. In some cases, they didn't even bother to record the names of the men who took them away.

All too often after that, the victim's debt to his new boss grew, rather than shrank, so that no matter how hard or long he worked, he could never dig himself out. And while the state was technically uninvolved in the arrangement, its contract laws kept peons bound to their enslavers. If an inmate tried to leave before settling his account, he faced prompt arrest.

Not many got away. As a rule, men working peons were not bashful about using violence to keep them from running. Conditions were often meaner than in the worst of the South's prisons and chain gangs. In fact, they could be worse than in full-on slavery—for while a slave of old was considered valuable property, worth caring for, a peon had no such status. His exploiter's investment began and ended with the piddling fine he paid the jailer. He could work or abuse a peon to death, then simply return to the jail for an equally cheap replacement.

How many victims did the system claim? With the casual approach to record-keeping in the counties, there is no way to say. The National Association for the Advancement of Colored People came to believe that bonding convicts from jail into peonage was routine throughout the Cotton Belt, from the Atlantic coast into East Texas. It likely ensnared tens of thousands.

Other forms of debt slavery existed alongside this model. Recent immigrants from Europe were lured to Florida from the Northeast to build Henry Flagler's famed over-ocean railroad linking the Keys, and before earning a paycheck had to work off the cost of their trip south. If they managed that, they still found themselves marooned on the islands, besieged by malaria, hunger, and physical abuse, while surviving on provisions advanced from the company store. Meaning that, once again, they would soon owe more money than they could ever expect to earn.

Meanwhile, untold numbers of Black peons labored in remote migrant camps scattered among the pine forests of Georgia, Alabama, and Florida, drawing sap from the trees to brew into turpentine. Forced to buy their food, clothing, and medicine from on-site commissaries, they too rapidly sank into a quicksand of debt. Many did not survive the experience. An infamous North Florida boss regularly beat or worked his peons to death, kept others in bondage for years beyond their sentences, forced women into prostitution, and raped children. One unfortunate peon serving a six-month sentence was ostensibly freed after seven months, and encouraged to pick up a fresh pair of trousers from the camp store on his way out. Before he could get away, he learned he'd have to work off the cost of those pants. Eight years later, he was still trapped.

Then there was the most widespread form of peonage, which, again, at first inspection might seem innocuous. Sharecropping called on a tenant farmer and his landlord to share the costs and benefits of raising a crop together. The landlord supplied the land; the tenant, or "cropper," supplied his labor. At harvest time, the farm's yield would be sold, and the earnings split between them.

Trouble was, the tenant had to wait until season's end to collect his earnings, and to get by in the meantime, he needed advances on his share of the proceeds. "The landlord either has a plantation store or has arrangements made with the nearby village or small town store to credit the Negro and charge the account to the landlord," as Louisiana native J. D. Sayers explained to readers of the *New York Evening Post* in 1921. "In the majority of cases the Negro is uneducated and unable to keep an accurate account of what he buys. He simply trusts the landlord."

If the cropper was lucky enough to have an honorable landlord, he'd be treated fairly, be billed accurately, and—assuming he worked hard and produced a good crop—reach the year's end in the black. That's how the system was supposed to work. Unfortunately, honor and fairness were hard to come by. A great many landlords overcharged their tenants for the year's supplies. "If the Negro has bought five bacon middlings for 40 cents a pound he is charged up with fifteen or so, and at a much higher price than the regular store price," Sayers wrote. "He may have bought a barrel of flour, but he must pay for two or three at extortionate prices. He may have ploughed in rocky fields bare-footed to save having to buy more than one pair of shoes, but he finds at the end of the year his memory has played a trick and he has really, according to the store account, enjoyed the luxury of two pair or three pairs of healthy priced shoes. His wife may have gone through the year with two cheap calico dresses and find in December that she has, in fact, dressed quite sumptuously during the year—according to the infallible store record."

Landlords often shortchanged their tenants on the earnings from their crops, as well. An NAACP investigator illustrated how the year-end accounting could vary in a 1919 story for *The Nation* comparing the experiences of "two Negro share-croppers, one of whom rented from a white landlord and the other from a colored one":

Both made fourteen bales of cotton, and each was entitled to seven bales as his share. For convenience the first farmer will be known as *A*; the second as *B*.

In A's family were seven members, two of them infants. In B's there were five, all adults. A's landlord took all his cotton seed and declared that he had sold the cotton at fourteen cents per pound, although cotton in the open market was at that time selling at twenty-eight cents. A received $490 and was presented with a bill for supplies of $853, leaving him in debt the following year to the extent of $363, which was reduced to $340 when his landlord with great magnanimity "allowed" him $23 as he "is a good nigger and needs encouragement."

B sold his cotton, and with the seed received $1,214.50 for it, to which was added $187.50 for 150 bushels of corn which he had raised in addition to the cotton. B's bill for supplies for the year was $175, although he received more supplies and of a better quality than A. He thus cleared $1,227, while A came out $340 in debt. A's landlord went to B's and told him that he had to change his method "or we won't be able to handle these niggers around here."

In most cases, the tenant got no itemized report of his spending and income: he would simply be given totals. But even a detailed breakdown offered him little grist for challenging the numbers, because questioning a white man's word in the South of 1921 could get him killed. "Since . . . no Negro can leave a plantation until his debt is paid," the NAACP investigator wrote, "the owner, by padding the accounts of Negroes to the point where the 'balance due' always exceeds the value of the crop, can assure his labor supply for the following year."

So indebted, a cropper was no partner with his landlord; he was a prisoner. "No doubt many workers drifted from freedom to peonage often in their lifetimes, never realizing that they had crossed the line," historian Pete Daniel noted. "The result was "a labor system that preserved the larva of slavery in the evolution of freedom."

In 1907, Special Agent A. J. Hoyt, who had long investigated peonage and racial intimidation cases for the Department of Justice, estimated that one-third of the owners of large spreads in Georgia, Alabama, and Mississippi were "holding their negro employees to a condition of peonage, and arresting and returning" any who bolted.

Having invented this system, southern states were not inclined to discard it; setting things right fell to the federal government. In March 1867, Congress enacted a statute to forever abolish peonage in any U.S. state or territory. The "holding of any person to service or labor" through debt servitude was "hereby declared to be unlawful," the statute read, and anyone who dared engage in or abet the process courted one to five years in prison, a fine of up to five thousand dollars, or both. Despite its timing, the measure wasn't adopted with the South or recently freed slaves in mind. Peonage was known to be widespread in Mexico, and the law addressed worry that the practice was taking root in the adjacent U.S. borderlands.

Which might explain why the statute languished, untested, for more than thirty years. It wasn't until April 1898 that a federal grand jury indicted a wealthy planter in northeastern Georgia on five counts of peonage. William Eberhart, the jury charged, had used the threat of violence to force Black men and women to work for him to settle their debts. Worse, he had arm-twisted his victims into binding their children to the same fate: One had five, aged two to eleven, who were contracted to work as virtual slaves into adulthood. Another peon was ordered to pinion his young son to the ground while Eberhart beat the boy bloody.

His trial came to an abrupt end in January 1899, when the federal judge overseeing the case decided that he should not hear it—that "industrial serfdom," as the *Savannah Morning News* called it, was more appropriately a state matter, and thus the bailiwick of the Oglethorpe County Superior Court. Eberhart was a popular and powerful man thereabouts. The county declined to take up the case.

Despite that disappointing outcome, publicity surrounding Eberhart's prosecution thrust peonage into the public eye and uncorked a gush of federal investigations throughout the South. Scores of indictments followed, and while many ended in acquittals, some defendants pled guilty and paid fines. A few cases established important legal groundwork. In 1901, for instance, a Georgia turpentine operator was prosecuted for chasing down two fleeing workers and returning them to peonage. A federal court found him guilty and sentenced him to four years in prison. On appeal, the U.S. Supreme Court reversed the verdict, but found that the peonage statute was constitutional and could be used against individuals as well as states, counties, and other political entities.

In the midst of all this, peonage captured the interest of a remarkable investigator named Mary Grace Quackenbos. An independently wealthy New York lawyer and advocate for the downtrodden, Quackenbos took on several clients whose relatives had gone south for work and had not been heard from since. She went undercover to assess conditions in the turpentine camps, sometimes in disguise and always at great personal risk, and returned with affidavits detailing the industry's abuses.

Her findings prompted the Department of Justice to undertake its own fact-finding mission in 1906. Assistant Attorney General Charles W. Russell embarked on a four-month tour of the South to get a feel for just how widespread debt servitude remained, and to lend his expertise to the prosecution of the cases he encountered. He found that state laws were the chief mechanisms used to keep peons in servitude—laws that might not have been "originally passed to enslave workmen," but which, "in view of the use to which they are put, need amendment in order that they [cannot] be so abused."

Contract laws with prima facie clauses, for example, were used "before juries and the local public to hold the peons up as law-breakers and dishonest persons seeking to avoid their 'just obligations,'" Russell wrote, "and to convince patriotic juries that the defendants accused of peonage should not be convicted for enforcing, still less for threatening to enforce, the laws of their State."

Measures such as Florida's all-inclusive vagrancy statute made a mockery of the Thirteenth Amendment, he wrote: "If a State can make a crime within the meaning of this amendment whatever it chooses to call a crime, it can nullify the amendment and establish all the involuntary servitude it may see fit."

In three well-publicized reports, Russell urged "that an incessant fight be made against peonage in every district in which it is to be found," and that the Department of Justice assign to the job "only men from whom 'eternal vigilance' about such things may be expected." That was a backhanded reference to the uneven and long overdue response of law enforcement to a scourge that was claiming thousands of victims in plain sight.

Russell also raised an issue that would frustrate federal investigators for a generation to come: That peonage prosecutions were all well and good, but they did nothing to combat compulsory labor that involved no debt. As it was, an employer could hold people captive, work them past exhaustion, pay them nothing, and beat them nearly to death, and the federal government could do little to stop him unless the workers happened to owe him money. Why? Because while the Thirteenth Amendment outlawed slavery, it contained no language enforcing the ban. There was only the 1867 statute specifically pertaining to peonage.

Russell recommended that "the real intent of Congress" be made law—that "the definition of legal peonage be made broad enough to include the holding of persons in servitude whether in liquidation of an indebtedness 'or otherwise.'

"It might even be well to abandon the use of the word 'peonage,'" he wrote, "and pass a law forbidding involuntary servitude and all attempts at it, as well as aiding, etc.; in other words, to pass a statute repeating the thirteenth amendment with appropriate penalties for all who undertake to disregard that amendment."

It didn't happen. All through the first decade of the new century, the Department of Justice continued to bring cases against peonage operations, but it was a scattershot effort, and many of the victims it liberated were not Black people (who accounted for the vast majority of peons) but white immigrants contracted to work in turpentine camps and on railroad gangs by employment agents in the big cities of the Northeast.

Then, in 1911, a peonage case in Alabama pitted the federal statute against the prima facie clause in that state's contracting law. The U.S. Supreme Court found the Alabama law unconstitutional. The presumption of guilt baked into the clause, it ruled, contravened the Thirteenth Amendment as well as the peonage statute. In the wake of that seeming knockout punch, several southern states struck the prima facie clauses from their criminal codes.

Georgia was not among them. Its contract law continued to punish a peon who fled from captivity as "a common cheat and swindler." And truth be told, the decision did little to stem debt slavery there, in Alabama, or anywhere else. What's more, the practice endured despite another Supreme Court decision three years later finding that Alabama's "criminal surety" system—the very style of peonage alleged on the Williams plantation—was a violation of the Constitution.

Years passed. Peonage faded from newspaper headlines and public attention.

Until February 1921, when two special agents of the Bureau of Investigation stopped by the Williams place in Jasper County.

4

—

THE INVESTIGATION REMAINED STYMIED when, four weekends after the agents'
visit, a young boy made a disturbing discovery a few miles to the west,
as he played at Allen's Bridge in Newton County. The narrow steel span
crossed the Yellow River about a mile north of where it broadened into
Jackson Lake. Even by rural Newton's standards, it was in the middle of
nowhere. The nearest settlement, Stewart, was not much more than a
backcountry crossroads, and it was a good two miles away.

That Sunday morning—March 13, 1921—the boy noticed something
jutting from the river's middle, and in the bridge's shadow: a shoe, and in
that shoe, a foot. He ran for help. Among those who answered was Carl
Wheeler, eighteen years old, who scared up a boat and, with his father
and a neighbor, reached the foot. They found that a complete body lay
submerged beneath it. When Wheeler tried to move it, he realized that it
was lashed to a second set of remains.

They pulled the dead to the riverbank. Two Black men lay before them,
hands tied with wire behind their backs, then each man's hands to the
other's, so that they lay back to back. A trace chain, usually used to harness
a mule to a plow, was wrapped around their necks and knotted to a short
length of rope. At the rope's end was a heavy sack of rocks.

Sheriff Bonham L. Johnson was summoned. He found the dead men
in fairly decent shape, considering they'd been underwater. They were
well-built fellows, both fairly young, both wearing shirts and blue overalls.
One was very dark and weighed about 150 pounds. The other, meatier,
weighed a bit more, was a few inches taller, and had a lighter "ginger-cake"

complexion. Had he known them in life, Johnson reckoned, he could name them.

The chain around their necks was held in place with wire and left little room for movement. The sheriff picked up the sack of rocks and estimated its weight at seventy-five to one hundred pounds. The Yellow was running lower than usual, explaining why that foot had broken the surface. Weighted and bound as they were, the bodies had not come up. The water had gone down.

Johnson was joined by C. T. Hardeman, a physician who lived nearby and did sideline duty as a county coroner. He examined the corpses and found one to be that of a man in his early twenties, the other two or three years older. One of the men, he saw, had worked a hand loose of his bindings and had wrapped his free arm around his fellow victim.

Dr. Hardeman decided that the men had been thrown from the bridge alive—the condition of their necks and tongues, along with their bulging eyes, signaled they had drowned, though he chose not to conduct a full-on autopsy to inspect their lungs. They had been in the river, he estimated, for a week to ten days.

Sheriff Johnson had only recently been elected Newton County's top lawman, but at forty-two years old, he had spent most of his adult life in law enforcement, first as a policeman in the county seat of Covington, and later as the town's police chief. It took no deductive leap to recognize that his rural jurisdiction was host to a major crime. It wasn't that two Black men had been found dead; that, sadly, was routine enough in the Georgia of 1921. The manner of their deaths, though—that was extraordinary. That would excite attention.

Sure enough, in the short time it took Dr. Hardeman to convene a coroner's jury to weigh the physical evidence at the scene, word of the discovery flashed up and down the road that passed over Allen's Bridge. It linked Jackson, the seat of Butts County, to the south, and Covington, away to the north, and from those towns and the villages and farms between came carloads of the curious, until the bridge and the Yellow River's banks were crowded with hundreds of onlookers.

And so the coroner's jury, once assembled, did its work before an audience remarkable for this out-of-the-way place. Muted by the sight of the bloated bodies on the riverbank and the serious business at hand, the throng watched as the jury affirmed the doctor's opinion that the men had been alive when they hit the water, and that they likely had been flung from the bridge. This was murder.

The panel was unable to conjure a motive for the crime, however, and found no evidence on which to base identification of the dead. Dr. Hardeman polled the people looking on: Did anyone recognize these men? None stepped forward. So, lacking a better way to preserve the bodies until more evidence could be gathered, the sheriff and coroner oversaw their careful burial in the riverbank.

Little chance existed that the story would be buried with them. Before the day was through, word had reached the region's newspapers. The next morning—Monday, March 14, 1921—the gruesome discovery in the Yellow River was news across Georgia and much of the South. The *Atlanta Constitution* ran a brief item on its second page. "Newton County was thrown into excitement Sunday," it opened, "when it was learned that the bodies of two young negro men, tied hand and foot, fastened together with a trace chain and heavily weighted with rocks, had been discovered in the deep water of Yellow river at Allen's bridge, near Stewart."

The most interesting part of the story might have been its ending: "Absolutely no trouble has occurred in this county recently to which the death of the two negroes, who are believed to have been about twenty years of age, might be attributed, and people in this vicinity are completely mystified over the occurrence. It is thought probable that the negroes came from Jasper county, as no Newton county negroes are reported missing."

In the Atlanta office of the Bureau of Investigation, the story landed on the desks of Special Agents Wismer and Brown.

5

IF IT SURPRISES MODERN READERS that the discovery at Allen's Bridge made the next day's papers, what with the rustic state of communications and travel in the Newton County of a century ago, it must come as nothing short of astounding that those first bulletins speculated that the dead came from Jasper. For one thing, no one in law enforcement, let alone the news business, knew who they were. And for another, Jasper was a good ways off. Although Jackson Lake separated the two counties, it did so along its Alcovy River branch, the easternmost of the three rivers that met in the reservoir. By car, the nearest bridge over the river and into Jasper was five miles away. Butts County, on the other hand, was only a mile and change down the road that crossed Allen's Bridge. If one accepted that the dead did not come from Newton because no Black residents had been reported missing there, common sense dictated that Butts was far more worthy of investigation.

But journalists had reason to mention Jasper, and the reason was Sheriff Johnson. He told reporters that not only were no Black men missing in Newton County, there had been no race trouble there. A wire service report noted, however, that "a month ago . . . he learned of some race trouble in Jasper County." The dispatch added that "whether these negroes belong there has not been determined."

It was no secret that Jasper had become a focus of federal inquiries into peonage. The U.S. attorney for Georgia's Northern District, Hooper Alexander, was riding herd on at least four investigations there, including the inquiry into John S. Williams. Even the county's longtime sheriff, William F. Persons, was under federal scrutiny—not for peonage, but a crime not far afield of it, that being that Persons was suspected of having falsely arrested a man as part of a scheme to enslave him. Jasper had also witnessed a lynching not long before. In October 1919, a Black preacher and schoolteacher named Eugene Hamilton was set upon by a mob said to number sixty men. Convicted of attempted murder after an attack on a white farmer, he was already locked up and facing a ten-year prison sentence. The farmer's friends promised to "get" Hamilton, just the same. They kept their word.

Sheriff Johnson was not alone in speculating that Jasper County might be the wellspring of this latest trouble. As soon as they read of the killings in the newspaper, the federal agents realized that Allen's Bridge was an easy drive from the John S. Williams plantation.

From a 1932 Bureau of Investigation case summary:

> Knowing the small regard for the life of a negro held by certain of these planters who practiced peonage, and considering the proximity of these points where the bodies were found to the plantation of John S. Williams, the Special Agents of the United States Bureau of Investigation set afoot some inquiry for the purpose of ascertaining whether these bodies were those of negroes from the Williams plantation.

Agents Wismer and Brown no doubt realized that if the victims were peons on the Williams place, their deaths were more than a coincidence: the agents' questions might have unwittingly triggered this violence. The two thus had a personal stake in seeing that justice was done. They had to wonder, however, whether Jasper County was up to the job. The government men had a better understanding than just about anyone of the county's troubled reputation—after all, their work had helped to create it. Beyond that, they likely knew that an indictment against Sheriff Persons, in a case that had grown out of their office's investigation, was imminent. In fact, a federal grand jury in Atlanta would hand it down that very week. It would charge that Persons caused the false arrest of Robert Lee Griggs, a Black farmhand who had recently worked for the sheriff's thirty-four-year-old nephew, Harvey K. Persons. Griggs had quit the job and left for Atlanta against the nephew's wishes. A short time later, the Atlanta police were notified that a Jasper County arrest warrant had been issued for Griggs, charging him with assault with intent to murder. Sheriff Persons took custody of the man, dragged him back to Jasper, and released him into his nephew's custody. The warrant was bogus. The arrest was illegal. The grand jury would decide the whole business was a subterfuge designed to force Griggs into involuntary labor.

The agents' concerns were not restricted to the sheriff. On the day they had visited the Williams farm, they first paid a courtesy call to Doyle Campbell, Jasper's prosecutor, to alert him to their activities. On hearing they planned to drop in on Williams, Campbell told them that he had a personal and business relationship with the planter. In May 1919, Williams had paid him two thousand dollars for the big riverfront parcel that he, his family, and his farmhands still called the Campbell place. Five months later, Williams had borrowed five thousand dollars from Campbell, securing the loan with the deed to his home place. These transactions, the prosecutor assured the agents, would have no bearing on his official performance. He pledged his full cooperation.

Still, the overlapping conflicts raised questions about the county's willingness and ability to pursue the case with vigor. And if the county could not be relied upon, alternatives were limited. The federal government lacked jurisdiction in the matter, as most murders were state offenses. Their best bet, the agents realized, might lie with Georgia's governor, Hugh M. Dorsey, whose office at the capitol was a short walk across downtown Atlanta from the federal courthouse.

Governor Dorsey had limited pull as well. He had no power over local officials, including county sheriffs; though he had identified the need for a statewide police force free from local biases and entanglements, the legislature had not seen fit to give him one. Wismer and Brown decided to brief him on the situation, all the same. And, indeed, on sharing their suspicions about Williams, the agents found the governor was "considerably interested," as the Bureau put it later, "and offered to cooperate in every practicable way."

Meanwhile, business leaders in Covington, smarting over the publicity the killings would bring to their city and all of Newton County, circulated a petition calling on Dorsey to offer a reward in the case. He did not need much encouragement. The governor recognized that the strange particulars of the murders at Allen's Bridge, especially the way the bodies had been bound and weighted, suggested the involvement of several perpetrators. So on Wednesday, March 16, he offered rewards totaling $1,750 for information leading to the arrest of the killers—five hundred dollars for each of the first two taken into custody, and $250 each for the next three.

The development was overshadowed within hours by more grim news out of Newton County. A short distance downstream from Mann's Bridge over the South River, and little more than a mile from Allen's Bridge, a passerby spotted a pair of feet jutting from the water. Locals pulled up the body of a single Black man, tied with wire like the others, a trace chain wrapped around his neck, and a heavy bag of rocks tied to the chain. The bag's weight had kept his head and chest down near the bottom, so that he floated almost vertically in the river's shallow channel.

Mann's was a county line bridge. Its middle, like the river's below, marked the border between Newton and Butts. Once authorities decided that the body was on the Newton side of the divide, they organized a coroner's inquest on the riverbank for the next day. Its findings, like those of the Yellow River inquest four days before, were meager. The victim had been thrown from the bridge and drowned. He had been in the water for about two weeks. He appeared to be a few years older than the two men pulled from the Yellow, but his body yielded few other clues to his identity.

Except, perhaps, for one detail: he wore shoes that had been freshly resoled with the rubber tread from automobile tires. The *Atlanta Constitution* noted this "peculiar circumstance," adding that the two men found earlier in the week wore similar shoes, and that all the tire casings were "apparently of the same make."

This body, like those before, was buried in the riverbank, awaiting further clues. But for the next several days, not one presented itself. The investigation crept to a standstill. Besides the federal agents' suspicions, only the men's shoes linked the Newton County murders to anyone. The agents, however, had apparently overlooked mention of the shoes in the news coverage, so their hunches were all they had.

The Justice Department official overseeing their work, U.S. Attorney Alexander, expressed frustration with the situation in a conversation with reporters two days after the third body's discovery. "It is no doubt true that the coroner's jury in Newton County have not sufficient evidence as to who committed the murder," the *Constitution* quoted him as saying. "But I am morally sure, and I have no doubt that half the people of Newton County are equally sure, as to where the Negroes came from, and why they were slain." He called the situation "a challenge to the conscience and civilization of the state."

His remarks sparked an immediate fuss in Newton, whose people took them as an accusation that they knew who the guilty were and had conspired in a cover-up. Alexander countered that he'd been misunderstood— that he meant only that many in the county, and in Jasper, too, likely had suspicions about who'd done the killing, but no evidence to back them up.

Meanwhile, Sheriff Johnson chased a dead-end tip that Black men had engaged in a shoot-out near Allen's Bridge earlier in the month that could be connected to the river deaths. Governor Dorsey received an equally errant lead that the Ku Klux Klan was behind them.

Then, five days after the third body turned up, came a break.

It arrived in much the same way the case had started: a Black man walked into the Bureau of Investigation offices to report that he had fled Jasper County out of fear for his life, and that the reason was John S. Williams. Eberhardt Crawford, sixty-three years old or thereabouts, told the agents that he was among the hundreds who had massed at Allen's Bridge immediately after the bodies were pulled from the Yellow River two Sundays prior. He witnessed the coroner's inquest and the jury's unsuccessful search for evidence that might provide names for the dead. More to the point, he was among those watching who had been asked whether he knew who the men were. Crawford had told the officials that no, he did not—then added that if they were from Jasper, it could be that some of the hands on the Williams place might know them.

It was an innocent comment. Crawford had lived not far from the Williams home place for decades, and knew that his neighbor owned a lot of land along the lake. Everyone in that part of Jasper County was aware that Williams employed a lot of Black farmhands, too, and the general impression was that he did not use them gently. Innocent or not, the remark reached the ears of John S. Williams. That night, the planter appeared at Crawford's front door to demand an explanation for his comments at Allen's Bridge. It was a threatening exchange, Crawford told Wismer and Brown. After Williams stormed off, Crawford—"knowing of the reputation of Williams," as the Bureau later put it—convinced himself that his caller would be back, and it wouldn't be to talk. He fled the house, leaving his grown nephew sleeping inside. Within hours, several men appeared outside his place and opened fire into the building. When Crawford dared to return, he found his house shot to pieces and his nephew hiding in the privy, one hundred feet across the yard.

Crawford offered another detail that caught the agents up short. The two men pulled from the Yellow River had been wearing unusual shoes. They were soled with rubber from automobile tires.

A scattering of purely circumstantial details now coalesced into a single, compelling argument for focusing attention on the Williams plantation: the timing of the deaths, so soon after the federal agents' visit to Jasper County; the fact that no one in Newton County had been able to identify the dead men, suggesting they came from elsewhere; Williams's intimidation of Eberhardt Crawford; and the shoes the victims wore, which recalled the investigators' own observations on the farm.

Wismer and Brown arranged another meeting with the governor, this time taking Crawford with them.

The press caught wind of the session, but gleaned only vague accounts of what transpired behind the governor's closed doors. The *Constitution* learned enough to report that the mystery of the drowned men "was believed to be near a solution" thanks to the appearance of a Black man declaring that "an attempt had been made to murder him a few nights ago, causing him to leave Jasper county." The visitor's story, the paper added, was "said to involve well-known citizens of that county." The *Savannah Morning News* sniffed out pieces of the conversation, too. "So lurid was the story told by the old negro," the paper advised, "and so closely does it dovetail in with criminal incidents under investigation, it has seriously arrested the attention of the governor of the state."

Indeed, that March 21 meeting marked a turning point. When he heard Eberhardt Crawford's story, Hugh Dorsey decided to bring the full weight of the state to bear in investigating and prosecuting the atrocities in Newton County, and in exploring what might lie behind them in Jasper. He chose to contact the presiding judge of the Stone Mountain judicial circuit, which included Newton, and its solicitor general, Alonzo M. "Lonnie" Brand, and to urge them—direct them, really—to place the case before a grand jury.

With that, Dorsey tossed aside one of the central planks on which he had run for office: keeping the executive branch out of the judicial system's business. He also began a journey that, whether he intended it to or not, might redeem his reputation in the eyes of history.

Partway, at least. The governor had a lot to atone for.

6

EIGHT YEARS BEFORE, while serving as Atlanta's chief prosecutor, Hugh Dorsey had steered a case remembered for mob violence and lawyerly misadventure, and as one of the most flagrant examples of judicial anti-Semitism in American history. Leo M. Frank, a Jewish transplant from New York and the manager of an Atlanta pencil factory, had been charged in the death of thirteen-year-old Mary Phagan, one of his employees. This, despite strong indications that another man was responsible. On the way to winning a conviction, Dorsey suppressed exculpatory evidence, manipulated testimony, and misled the jury by insinuating that Frank was deformed and depraved.

"If Leo Frank is hanged," a frustrated defense attorney told the judge, "I'd rather be dead and rotting in my grave than in Hugh Dorsey's place. His conscience will drive him crazy, distracted, and to God only knows what ends. And it will be no less than his just deserts."

Frank had, in fact, hanged, at the hands of a mob inflamed by Dorsey's prosecution. The trial made the lawyer both a hero to thousands of Georgians and an international pariah. He was far more complex than his public image suggested—he was no rampant bigot, by the low standards of his day—but it was the Frank case that propelled him into the governorship and for which he is best remembered today.

Dorsey was born in 1871 in Fayetteville, these days a southern suburb of Atlanta. His father, a lawyer, moved the family to the capital when Hugh was eight, serving for a year as a municipal judge before settling into a long and lucrative private practice. After a boyhood spent in both private and public schools, Hugh enrolled in the University of Georgia to study liberal arts, with a heavy load of Latin and Greek.

He was an unhealthy-looking young man—short and slight, with lank, rapidly thinning hair, a sallow complexion, and prominent, liverish bags under his eyes. He was not overburdened with charisma, either. But Dorsey compensated for his lack of easy grace with determined effort. In college, he had his hand in a tangle of extracurricular activities—theater, debate, a literary society, and a fraternity dedicated to glorifying Robert E. Lee and the Lost Cause. He emerged from his coursework a fluid writer and an excellent public speaker.

He continued his ambitious range of social and intellectual engagements into adulthood. After a year of law school at the University of Virginia, he won admission to the Georgia bar in 1894 and joined his father's law firm; there he found time, while juggling a heavy load of criminal and civil cases, to play a central role in several Atlanta social clubs and the city's Young Democrats, to work on numerous political campaigns, and to accept regular invitations to speak on the glories of the Confederacy. He was named to the city's water board, served as trustee of its biggest hospital, and was a viable candidate for his own municipal judgeship after just a few years' practicing law.

In short, Hugh Dorsey was an up-and-comer, though not entirely comfortable in the role. In an age of political bluster and florid oratory, here was an unromantic, no-nonsense technocrat, repelled by glad-handing and disdainful of the insincere niceties that encouraged support. He probably wouldn't have stood a chance in politics had the Atlanta Circuit's longtime solicitor general not died in office in 1910; the straight-arrow Dorsey was appointed to fill the unexpired term. Earnest and organized, a skilled and aggressive courtroom litigator, his "efforts to faithfully discharge the onerous duties of the office," as he put it, earned him reelection in 1912.

But however adept he was at managing the city's titanic caseload, Dorsey suffered several headline-grabbing defeats before the bench. In the summer of 1912, he prosecuted socialite Daisy Opie Grace for the attempted murder of her husband, whom she admitted shooting during an argument in their Atlanta home. Eugene Grace, left paralyzed from the waist down, disputed his wife's insistence that his injury was accidental. The jury sided with Mrs. Grace.

Not long after, Dorsey lost a second seemingly surefire case. Mrs. Callie Appelbaum was staying at Atlanta's Dakota Hotel with her husband, Jerome, when early one morning the sound of gunshots brought other guests and the night clerk running. They found Mrs. Appelbaum in the hallway, disheveled and wailing. They found the late Mr. Appelbaum with fresh holes in his arm, neck, and left temple. Dorsey argued that Mrs. shot Mr. after a long night of arguing. The defense countered that he committed suicide, despite state's evidence that the shots had been fired from at least thirty inches away.

When Mrs. Appelbaum took the stand, she testified that her husband had pushed a pistol into her side and told her she had five minutes to live. She fainted and woke to find him bleeding on the floor. "Gentlemen," she told the jurors, "I swear to you that I am as innocent as an angel in heaven of this act, and I only wish I could know, to satisfy myself, how his death came." They believed her.

The papers feasted on these defeats, and nourished sneaking doubts about Dorsey's fitness for his post. The upshot is that on April 25, 1913, when the verdict came in the Appelbaum case, the solicitor general badly needed a win.

The very next day, Mary Phagan died.

And Hugh Dorsey had the case that would define him.

So much has been written about the subsequent investigation and trial that we'll here restrict ourselves to the highlights. Mary Phagan, a couple weeks shy of her fourteenth birthday, caught a streetcar downtown that Saturday morning to see the city's much-anticipated Confederate Memorial Day parade. On the way, she stopped at the pencil factory to pick up her earnings. Leo Frank handed her an envelope containing $1.20 in his second-floor office.

Mary was next seen before dawn on Sunday, when a night watchman found her in the factory basement, lying facedown on a floor of sawdust, cinders, and earth. A garrote of cotton fabric was knotted tight around her throat. The back of her head was bashed. Her underwear was ripped and bloody. Police made a further discovery while moving Mary's body: two notes hidden beneath her, scrawled in pencil. They were rife with misspellings and confused syntax, but seemed to blame the killing on the night watchman. Whoever authored them, it appeared, wanted the police to believe that Mary herself had dashed them out while under attack.

Detectives ventured to Frank's house to bring him to the scene. The factory manager appeared nervous as he was dressing, they would later say, and several times remarked that he wanted a cup of coffee. Down at National Pencil, Frank was shown the crime scene and gave investigators a factory tour. Throughout, the detectives reported, he appeared agitated and jittery. Frank's obvious discomfort and his status as the last person known to have seen Mary alive spurred the police to take him into custody. Over the following days, the Atlanta papers decided that a rich Yankee Jew made a fitting villain for such a heinous crime and whipped themselves and their readers into a feeding frenzy. With the case every day generating multiple "extra" editions, Dorsey commandeered the inquiry from the police.

Soon there emerged a key witness: the factory's janitor, Jim Conley, a Black man with no shortage of jail time in his past, a fondness for whiskey and gambling, and the opposite of an alibi—he had been seen skulking about the factory's entrance at about the time Mary Phagan stepped inside to pick up her pay. Mounting evidence argued that Conley, not Frank, killed the girl. His statements to the police were inconsistent and wildly improbable. He told officers he was illiterate. When it was found that he did know how to write, he told them he knew nothing of the notes under the body. When it became clear that he had written them, he changed his story again: Frank had asked him to write them the day before the killing. No, actually, he had not been at the factory the day before—he went into work on the day of the murder, and Frank ordered him not only to write the notes (which Frank dictated) but to help him move Phagan's body to the basement.

His ever-changing story did not make a suspect of Jim Conley. On the contrary, he became the state's primary weapon against its chosen defendant. The final version of his account had Frank cornering the girl on the factory's second floor, killing her accidentally while trying to defile her, and enlisting Conley to help dispose of the evidence. The conventional wisdom among his white listeners held that no ignorant Black laborer had the imagination to make up such a tale. Conley had to be telling the truth.

Atlanta's new courthouse was under construction, so the trial commenced in a former city council chamber on the ground floor of the old city hall. Its windows opened onto busy downtown sidewalks that filled with hundreds of spectators unable to get seats—and this outdoor gallery demonstrated noisily for Frank's conviction even before jury selection began. Every comment that left Dorsey's lips was greeted with applause. Every argument from Frank's lawyers was jeered.

Dorsey presented his star witness as a "trusty old Negro" of the Uncle Remus mold. Conley came through for him. Not only did he provide his heavily edited account of the killing under oath, but he insinuated that Frank often devoted his Saturday afternoons at the idled factory to all sorts of debauchery with lady callers of dubious repute, and claimed the boss had disclosed that he was "not built like other men." No sooner had the defense refuted these claims (with a doctor's testimony that the defendant was physically normal) than Dorsey suggested, none too subtly, that Frank was actually homosexual. Over thunderous objections from the defense, and despite a parade of witnesses who challenged Dorsey's narrative, the solicitor continued to refer to Frank's alleged physical deformities, supposed perversions, and fondness for young flesh. The crowd outside went wild. When Dorsey left the building each evening, he was cheered by hundreds, sometimes thousands, of admirers. When he arrived for each morning's session, the mob hailed him as a defender of southern womanhood.

Finally came Dorsey's closing argument, an epic nine hours long and spread over three days. He attacked Frank for not facing Conley in a police interview room when given the chance ("Never in the history of the Anglo-Saxon race, never in the history of the African race in America, did an ignorant, filthy Negro accuse a white man of a crime and that man decline to face him"). He mused about Frank's Judaism while scoffing at the defense's assertion that anti-Semitism was at the heart of the case. He intimated that the defendant was a lecherous beast: "Gentlemen, there's no telling what a pervert will do," he told the jury, "when he's goaded on by the unusual, extraordinary passion that goaded on this man, Leo M. Frank, when he saw his opportunity with this little girl in that pencil factory." And he framed Phagan's death as the martyrdom of a chaste southern belle who "gave up her life in defense of that which is dearer than life."

He wound up the speech as midday approached. "Your Honor, I have done my duty," he told the judge. "There can be but one verdict, and that is: 'We the jury find the defendant, Leo M. Frank, *guilty!*'" At that moment, the bells of a nearby Catholic church started to chime the noon hour, and Dorsey bellowed "Guilty!" after each peal until the ringing stopped.

The jury was out for less than two hours. Frank did not hear the verdict—the judge, fearing the mob outside could turn violent, arranged for the defendant's absence. It was probably a good call. With the announcement that Frank was guilty, a hurricane's roar erupted from the thousands gathered on the street. Hats flew into the air. Women wept. Dorsey stepped from the building into a tumult. "The solicitor reached no farther than the sidewalk," the *Constitution* reported. "With hat raised and tears coursing down his cheeks, the victor in Georgia's most noted criminal battle was tumbled over a shrieking throng that wildly proclaimed its admiration. Few will live to see another such demonstration."

The next day, in a session kept secret from press and public, the judge pronounced sentence. Frank would hang.

The defendant immediately petitioned the court for a new trial, on the grounds that the evidence did not support his conviction, that the jury was swayed by outbursts inside and outside the courtroom, and that anti-Semitism had influenced his fate. His lawyers attacked Conley as "a criminal of the lowest type" whose initial statements to police were "spread out over the whole territory of asininity." They denounced the detectives who helped shape his testimony, and Dorsey for sneaking his invented "perversion evidence" into the record. The trial judge aired his own doubts: "I am not certain of this man's guilt," he said. "With all the thought I have put on this case, I am not thoroughly convinced that Frank is guilty or innocent." But the jury had been convinced, he acknowledged, so he denied the petition. The verdict would stand.

Frank took his appeals through the state court system. He was denied twice by the Georgia Supreme Court in 1914, but the prosecution sustained a string of setbacks, too: A forensic scientist studying hair strands collected near Frank's office, and used by the prosecution to establish that Mary Phagan had been killed there, announced they did not come from the girl—and added that Dorsey knew as much, but kept it to himself. Several key witnesses for the state then recanted their testimony, saying detectives had pressured them to deliver it. Among them was a young man who had testified that Phagan complained of Frank's advances. The boy now recalled that when he had an attack of conscience and sought Dorsey out, the prosecutor snarled at him: "Just stick to that."

A sharp-eyed lawyer for the defense, on reexamining the infamous notes found with Mary's body, was able to prove that the paper on which they were written came from the basement, thus making a lie of Conley's assertion that it was from a pad in Frank's desk. In March 1914, the *Atlanta Journal*, whose rabid reporting did Frank no favors during his initial trial, published an editorial pleading that he get another, and arguing that his execution would "amount to judicial murder." Other prominent Georgia newspapers followed suit.

Ah, but the editorial also roused a sleeping giant. The *Jeffersonian*, a weekly paper out of eastern Georgia, unloaded on the *Journal* for trying to "blast the future of a thoroughly brave and efficient Solicitor General." Its publisher was Thomas E. Watson, one of the most powerful and problematic figures in Georgia history. Brilliant but unbalanced, Watson had started his career as a Populist campaigning for the little guy, Black or white. He had served in Congress, as the Populist ticket's vice presidential candidate, and twice as its standard-bearer. Unfortunately, over the years he morphed into a raving bigot whose unhinged screeds against Jews, Catholics, and Blacks made the Ku Klux Klan sound dainty. Despite or because of that, he wielded tremendous influence on rural Georgians. His support had helped elect the last several governors.

Watson opened a sustained barrage on the Frank appeals, often stoking the darkest predispositions of his readers. "His pure little Gentile victim is dust in the grave," he wrote, while the "Sodomite" and "beast who took her sweet young life basks in the warmth of Today." He issued not-so-veiled threats that if "Frank's rich connections keep on lying about this case, SOMETHING BAD WILL HAPPEN." And while tearing down the condemned man, he elevated Dorsey, whom he called "the fearless, honest and victorious Solicitor" and "the sort of Georgian that the people delight to honor" and "dignified, thorough, urbane and statesmanly."

"Honor to Hugh Dorsey!" he wrote in his monthly *Watson's Magazine*, for having "triumphed over Big lawyers, Big detectives, Big money, and Big newspapers in Georgia.

"And because an enthusiastic people caught up this young hero in their arms, *after he had fought the good fight and won it*, we are accused of saturating the court-room with the spirit of mob violence!

"*It's an outrageous libel on the State of Georgia!*"

The italics and capitals are all his.

Frank's appeals continued, Dorsey fighting them at every step, until they reached the U.S. Supreme Court. The justices voted 7–2 against hearing the case. A faint hope remained: The Georgia Prison Commission could recommend clemency to the governor. This did not break his way, either, despite a letter from the trial judge admitting that "after months of continued deliberation I am still uncertain of Frank's guilt."

But Governor John M. Slaton, troubled by what he had heard and read of the case, opened his own investigation. He invited both sides to present arguments at a hearing in his office—a remarkable session that stretched over two days in mid-June 1915, and for which Dorsey prepared a speech that ran fifty-three typed pages. Days before his term as governor was to end, Slaton concluded that the evidence against Frank was sketchy and that his trial had been a circus. He commuted his death sentence to life in prison.

The news did not go down easy in Atlanta. A howling crowd of thousands marched on the governor's home in Buckhead, north of the city. Slaton had to summon the Georgia National Guard, the only instance in American history in which a state executive has declared martial law for his own protection. Hand-to-hand combat ensued at the edge of his lawn. The soldiers came perilously close to opening fire.

Slaton explained his decision to commute a few days later. "Two thousand years ago, another governor washed his hands and turned over a Jew to a mob," he wrote. "For two thousand years that governor's name has been accursed. If today another Jew were lying in his grave because I had failed to do my duty, I would all through life find his blood on my hands and would consider myself an assassin through cowardice."

His critics were unswayed. Mobs burned Slaton in effigy, and a pipe-wielding thug attacked him at the inauguration of his successor, Nathaniel E. Harris. Only the quick reflexes of a national guard officer saved both governors from maiming or death. Slaton and his wife embarked on a months-long tour of the West and Hawaii, and found that threats to their safety still abounded on their return.

Tom Watson's reaction was predictably deranged. "We have been betrayed!" he railed in the *Jeffersonian*. "The breath of some leprous monster has passed over us, and we feel like crying out, in horror and despair, 'Unclean! UNCLEAN!'

"When John M. Slaton tosses on a sleepless bed, in the years to come, he will see a vivid picture of that little Georgia girl, decoyed . . . by this Satyr-faced New York Jew: he will see her little hands put out, to keep off the lustful beast: he will hear her cry of sudden terror; he will see her face purpling as the cruel cord chokes her to death—and *John M. Slaton will walk the floor, a wretched, conscience-smitten man, AND HE WILL SWEAT BLOOD!*"

If the system could so fail them, Watson argued, Georgians had to be prepared to exact justice of their own. "The next Leo Frank case in Georgia will never reach the Courthouse," he wrote with more than a hint of menace on August 12, 1915. "THE NEXT JEW WHO DOES WHAT FRANK DID, IS GOING TO GET EXACTLY THE SAME THING THAT WE GIVE TO NEGRO RAPISTS."

A few days later, the mob came for Leo Frank. Twenty-odd prominent citizens of Marietta, Phagan's hometown, drove to the state prison farm at Milledgeville, broke in, kidnapped Frank, and hauled him back across the state to Marietta. Daybreak found them on the outskirts of town. The caravan pulled off the road and, with little ceremony, dropped a noose around Frank's neck and hanged him from a tree.

A thousand or more gawkers ventured from town to eye his corpse. Many posed for pictures. "There were a number of women in the crowd," the *Atlanta Georgian* reported. "It was noticed that several of them carried babies in arms."

—

HUGH DORSEY REVEALED LITTLE TO THE PRESS about his meeting with the federal agents and Eberhardt Crawford. But in deflecting their questions, he made the point that the killings at the Newton County bridges were not uncommon crimes—that, however beastly, they were typical of a state in which race relations had reached "a disgraceful stage." He knew of some Black citizens who had been forced to stay in their homes and work for next to nothing, and others intimidated to the point that they had to flee. "We have a Negro working right here at the capitol building who is a victim of treatment of the most brutal type," the governor said. "He still bears gashes about the hands and arms where he was slashed with a knife by a man from whom he attempted to run away.

"No indictment has been returned against the man for attacking the Negro, but instead, the man secured an indictment against the Negro and succeeded in having him given a chain gang sentence on the claim that he was five dollars in debt to him. When the case came to our attention, we got the Negro out on probation, and gave him employment here at the capitol." Many such refugees in Atlanta were "in constant fear of their lives."

Eager to make good on his promise of help to agents Wismer and Brown, Dorsey invited them back the following afternoon to meet with a panel of citizens that included two Atlanta clergymen—Baptist minister M. Ashby Jones and Cary B. Wilmer, rector of St. Luke's Episcopal Church—to go over what was known about the murders and figure out how to propel the investigation forward. The preachers were particularly interesting members of this brain trust. Both were members of the

Commission on Interracial Cooperation, started two years before by white Atlanta liberals, several of them churchmen, to improve conditions for Black southerners and foster forbearance, if not harmony, in their relations with the white majority. The ministers had not always seen eye to eye with Dorsey—Wilmer, for example, had been a noisy advocate for the commutation of Leo Frank's death sentence—but their inclusion underlined the governor's apparent belief that the drowned men were victims not of an isolated crime, but an almost standard practice.

The other citizens at that March 22 meeting might have included Lonnie Brand, Newton County's prosecutor. What is certain is that Dorsey was in contact with Brand and Stone Mountain Circuit Judge John B. Hutcheson, and that he convinced them to convene the Newton County grand jury to hear the case. The investigation, once trapped in a jurisdictional limbo and hamstrung by a paucity of evidence, now broke into a gallop. Meeting in Covington the next morning, the grand jury issued subpoenas for four Williamses—Mr. Johnny and his sons Hulon, LeRoy, and Marvin. It further summoned the "negro farm hands known to have been recently on the Williams plantation," in the words of the Bureau of Investigation, "including all of those negroes who had been interviewed by the Special Agents upon the occasion of their first inquiry at the Williams farm." By day's end, deputies had served John S. Williams. They'd also delivered subpoenas to two farmhands, Clyde Manning and Clyde Freeman, and taken them into custody. The plantation's other Black workers were nowhere to be found.

Manning and Freeman were taken to the sheriff's office, where they joined Frank Dozier, a slightly built seventeen-year-old who had done a brief turn as a peon on the Williams place before his escape the previous year. Since then, he had lived in hiding in Covington. The three were separated and a lengthy interrogation began, the questions coming from Wismer, Sheriff Johnson, and Special Agent Edward S. Chastain, a more seasoned member of the Bureau who stepped in to replace George Brown.

Manning and Freeman denied any knowledge of lawbreaking at the plantation. Not so Dozier, who unspooled a story all too familiar. He had been arrested for vagrancy in Macon, sentenced to thirty days in the city stockade, and hit with $20.75 in fines and court costs. Hulon Williams had appeared in town and offered to cover the price of getting him out, provided that Dozier went to work for the family; the farmer promised to pay him thirty-five dollars a month. But once on the plantation, Dozier found himself locked up at night, beaten frequently, and whipped for the slightest of missteps. When he fell off a mule and broke his leg, one of Williams's sons—fuming that Dozier was so lazy he couldn't be bothered to stay on the animal's back—threatened to kill him. He seemed angry enough to do it.

Like Gus Chapman and James Strickland, Dozier offered a vivid description of the whippings he and other peons routinely endured. The Williamses would strip the victim and drape him over an oil drum turned on its side, with his fellow workers holding him by the head and feet while the blows came down. His punishers used whatever tools happened to be handy—leather belts, bridles, trace chains; he took off his shirt to show the scars left by the lashings. Dozier also said he had heard that LeRoy Williams shot a man named Iron Jaw or Long John during one such whipping. He'd heard that Clyde Freeman fetched wire to tie up Iron Jaw's body before it was sunk in "the pond," one of Jackson Lake's slack-water coves edging the river tracts. He catalogued other cruelties suffered by prisoners bailed out by the Williamses—among them, having to help train the family hounds to chase down anyone who tried to escape. Sunday mornings, he said, the peons were forced to take off running until the dogs brought them down—reinforcing Mr. Johnny's assurance that if they tried to run for real, they would not get far.

Dozier's account gave the Bureau three eyewitnesses offering compelling testimony that John S. Williams and his sons oversaw a particularly savage peonage operation. Problem was, they were all *former* peons—they neither were on the property during the agents' February visit, nor knew what had happened there since.

So the investigators turned next to Clyde Freeman. The Williamses worked two classes of Black farmhands, and Freeman belonged to the luckier. His family and the Mannings, all cousins to each other, lived in small cottages scattered about the plantation, and were paid wages or earned shares of the income from the crops they raised. Their labor was augmented by that of the unfortunate "stockade Negroes" the Williamses "bought," as needed, from the jails in Atlanta, Macon, and elsewhere. Clyde's father, John Freeman, had moved Clyde, his younger brothers Claude and Clifford, and his four other siblings to the farm when Clyde was twelve. He was now twenty-five. He'd rarely left the property over those thirteen years, save for a five-month stint in the army. He could not read. He could not write his own name.

At first, Freeman evaded their questions, but "after a number of hours agreed to give the Special Agents the facts," the Bureau later said. With one proviso: he feared that "if he were to tell all that he knew and should ever be released, he would be immediately killed by Williams." His interrogators promised to protect him. If he cooperated, he need never go back to Jasper County.

Freeman knew next to nothing about the death of Blackstrap, he told them—only that he had run off the previous year with another peon nicknamed "Little Bit," and the Williamses had tracked them down. Little Bit had returned to the farm. Freeman had not seen Blackstrap since. He had much more to say about the killing of Iron Jaw. LeRoy Williams had shot the man twice at point-blank range, and Freeman had witnessed it from three or four steps away, along with three peons—Charlie Chisholm, James Strickland, and another whom everyone knew as "Foots." After Iron Jaw died, LeRoy Williams ordered Freeman to strip the clothes from the body. Freeman balked, telling Mr. LeRoy he was scared to touch a dead man. At that, Charlie Chisholm and Foots pulled off Iron Jaw's clothes, carried them to the edge of the pond, and stuffed them under logs sunk in the shallows. Marvin Williams told Freeman to fetch some wire, which he pulled from hay bales. Charlie Chisholm then used it to lash the body to a heavy log, rolled it to the water's edge, hoisted it into a rowboat, carried it to the pond's middle, and dumped it overboard. Iron Jaw sank out of sight.

Freeman's most relevant contribution was of more recent vintage. Shortly after agents Wismer and Brown had called on the Williamses, prisoners bonded from the jails began to disappear. Three of them—Lindsey Peterson, Will Preston, and Foots—vanished at the same time, he said. Another named Johnnie Green went missing. Charlie Chisholm, who had been at the Williams place long enough to become a trusty—a peon given more responsibility and freedom than most—was gone. Mr. Johnny told those remaining that he released the men, that they had gone home. Freeman had doubts about that. He suspected that Williams had taken the three who left together—Peterson, Preston, and Foots—and put them in the river.

He couldn't be sure, he said. He was offering just an opinion. He wasn't the man who could tell all of what happened.

Who is the man, the lawmen asked, who can tell all?

Clyde Manning, Freeman replied. I think Clyde knows all about it.

Evening settled, and Sheriff Johnson and the agents decided to take a break from the interview to drive Freeman and Manning out to Allen's Bridge. The graves there were opened, the bodies of the two drowned men exposed. Ten days had passed since their discovery, and if the coroner's estimate was at all accurate, they now had been in the water or the clay riverbank for something like three weeks. The time had worked on them; Sheriff Johnson noted that they were in far worse shape than the last time he saw them. Even so, Freeman readily identified them as Lindsey Peterson and Will Preston. He had more than their disfigured faces to go on. He recognized their shoes: Rufus Manning had half-soled them with tire tread just before the men left the Williams place.

Manning watched, silent, as Freeman made the identifications. The party returned to Covington, where Manning was locked in the jail and Freeman returned to the sheriff's office for whatever additional details he might offer. He named all the hands present on the plantation when the agents visited. He confirmed that Clyde Manning was a field boss who kept those at the home place locked up at night. And he told of the last time he saw Lindsey Peterson and Will Preston alive: A few Saturdays back, Mr. Johnny was up at the river tracts, and he told Peterson, Preston, and Foots to drive some hogs that were penned there down to his house. One of Williams's younger sons, fifteen-year-old James Luke, helped the men get the hogs through the woods and out onto the road. From there, the three farmhands struck east toward Mr. Johnny's. Freeman had not seen them since.

The agents turned their attention to Clyde Manning. They had made brief attempts to open him up throughout the day—had asked whether he knew Blackstrap, or whether some farmhands had gone missing, or how the men wound up in the water below Allen's Bridge. Manning had insisted he knew nothing. Now they sat him down in the sheriff's office and hammered at him. Later, some would suggest they did it literally— that he was roughed up, that a rope was put around his neck, that he was threatened with worse. The lawmen denied it, and so did Manning. The worst he got was some cussing, he would later say, and "they didn't cuss me considerably."

As a matter of fact, Sheriff Johnson was struck by how mild an approach the two federal agents took with the prisoner. They told him they knew he'd been lying. Suggested that he knew, as well as they did, that he couldn't maintain such dishonesty. Over and over, they came back to that: The time had come to tell the truth. Stop the lying, Clyde. You can't keep this up. They were relentless, but they never laid a hand on him.

Whatever the case, in the early morning dark of Thursday, March 24, Clyde Manning cracked. He might be able to tell them something, he said, if they could protect him from Williams. Mr. Johnny had told him not to talk, and would kill him for sure if he found out that he had.

You don't have to worry, the investigators told him. You're safe now. Mr. Johnny can't hurt you.

Reassured, Manning began his story.

8

—

WHATEVER THE AGENTS AND SHERIFF JOHNSON expected to hear from Clyde
Manning, it was not the statement he gave them once assured that he
need never return to the Williams plantation. The field boss began simply
enough: "The first Negro I remember being killed was Bill Napier," he
said, referring to the farmhand supposedly shot while wielding a knife.
"Hulon Williams killed him.

"The next one killed was Blackstrap. Charlie Chisholm killed him. Hulon Williams was whipping Blackstrap and Charlie Chisholm was holding his head. Hulon quit whipping him and said, 'Kill him,' and Charlie
Chisholm shot him with Hulon's pistol." Like many of the whippings, this
happened at the home place, in a small carriage shelter next to the gear
house. "Charlie Chisholm was standing on the left side of Blackstrap and
shot him one time in the head," he said. "He raised up on his knees for a
minute and fell over. This was cotton picking time last year," on a Sunday.
Manning saw it himself. Gus Chapman was there, too, along with farmhands John Brown and Johnnie Williams, both of whom the agents had
interviewed during their visit. Mr. Johnny watched the whole thing.

"It was about the middle of the evening when Blackstrap was killed,"
Manning said. Just after, Hulon set off for his house on the river tracts,
telling Manning and Gus Chapman to cover the body, so the two grabbed
some empty oat sacks from the gear house and draped them over the slain
peon. Later that night, Hulon returned in his Ford, bringing peons Johnnie Green and Will Preston with him. Those two and Gus Chapman
loaded the body into the car, and Hulon, Green, and Preston drove off

toward the river. "I did not see where they put Blackstrap," Manning said. "Willy Preston and Johnnie Green told me they put him in the pond."

His delivery was quiet, steady, almost clinical in its detachment. The agents kept detailed notes, trying to faithfully capture Manning's turns of phrase as he now shifted to the events of the past several weeks: Mr. Johnny knew that Johnnie Williams had spoken to the agents, and "three or four days after they were down there, Mr. Williams sent Johnnie Williams to the pasture to drive the cows off the seeds" recently sown down that way. "He never came back."

That same day, Mr. Johnny asked peon John Brown, whom his fellow hands called "Red," whether he wanted to go home—told him that if he did, he'd drive him to the railroad station and put him on a train. "John Williams and Red got in the car and left together," Manning said. "I have not seen or heard of Red since." John Brown came from the jail in Macon, he added. He had worked for the Williamses for about three years.

The agents interrupted Manning's statement to show him a cap, shoes, and a trace chain taken from the bodies recovered in Newton County. He'd seen Lindsey Peterson wear a cap like that, Manning said. The shoes looked like those he knew Foots to wear.

Manning resumed his monologue. Others vanished after the agents' visit, he said. A farmhand known as "Big John." Another called Little Bit. Artis Freeman—no obvious relation to Clyde Freeman or his kin on the farm—who left on a Saturday, just after the midday meal. "Johnnie Green left Sunday after Artis Freeman left Saturday. Lindsey Peterson, Willy Preston and Foots left Saturday night, the same Saturday night that Artis Freeman left and before Johnnie Green left the next morning."

On the Saturday in question, everyone was working up on the river tracts, on the Campbell place, "when John Williams told Lindsey Peterson, Willy Preston and Foots to drive the hogs down to the house that evening and he would carry them to the train that night." He told Johnnie Green to come down to the home place Sunday morning, and he'd take him to the station, too. He would let them all go.

Up to this moment, Manning had described the disappearances as un-explained events—men simply "left." Now came a shift. "The ones I know was killed was Johnnie Green [and] Willie Givens," he told the agents. "Mr. Williams told me that he wanted to do away with them. Then he told me he wanted me to kill Johnnie Green.

"I told him, 'I hate to do this.'"

Williams's response, according to the Bureau's summary of the case, presumably taken from notes of the interview: "All right, if you hate to do it. It means your neck or his. Just whichever you think the most of."

Manning would relate this exchange many times in the weeks and months to come, with only slight variation. In the version that has achieved the most consistent quotation, Williams approached him a few days after the federal agents' visit with the words: "Clyde, it won't do for these boys"—meaning the plantation's peons—"to go up yonder and swear against us. They will ruin us. We will have to do away with them."

Manning, shocked, answered, "Mr. Johnny, that is so bad, I don't want to do it." To which Williams replied: "If you don't want to do it, it is all right—it is your neck or theirs. If you think more of their necks than you do of your own neck, it is yours."

The exact wording is beside the point. Clyde Manning was telling Sheriff Johnson and Special Agents Wismer and Chastain that John S. Williams had solicited the murder of Johnnie Green. He forced Manning to commit the crime with the threat of death if he did not.

Manning's next sentence left no doubt as to how it had turned out: "The killing was down in Williams's pasture."

Johnnie Green's last few hours on Earth, as described now by Clyde Manning: On Saturday, February 26, eight days after the agents called on the farm, John S. Williams told Johnnie Green that he had business the next morning in Jackson, the seat of Butts County. Johnnie should come down to the main house early, and he would take him to the train station there and let him go. Next morning, Green was standing ready outside the house. Mr. Johnny told him he had a chore for him first—to go down into the pasture about a quarter mile below the house and fix its wire fence.

Manning knew little about Johnnie Green but his name and that he was jailed in Macon before coming to the farm. He was otherwise a blank, a man with only a ghost of a recorded past, and the same was true of pretty much every peon at the Williams place. They were all young, most of them in their early twenties—unmarried, far from their homes, and pitched into jail and debt slavery before they established work histories. Had the agents consulted the 1920 census, they would have learned that Green was present on the farm the previous year, that he was Georgia-born, twenty-one or twenty-two years old, and that he could not read. But that was the limit of the official record. On paper, he barely existed.

Manning, Green, and Mr. Johnny walked down to the pasture, Manning carrying an axe and a hammer. They halted beyond the sight of anyone else on the property. There, Mr. Johnny told Green that he'd heard he had plans to talk to the government, to try to have the Williams sons' "necks broke." He turned to Manning and said: "Hit him."

Manning, wielding the axe, did as he was told. "After I knocked him down, Williams told me to hit him again," he said. "We just left him there and went on back to Williams's house. This was just after sun-up.

"Then, about the middle of the morning, Willie Givens came and John S. Williams asked him if he didn't want to go over to the store. [Willie] told him, 'Yes.' [Williams] asked me if I did not want to go, and I said, 'Yes.' He told me to get the axe so I could cut a foot log, so we could cross the creek.

"Williams told me he was going to walk on in front and I was to walk behind, and when we got to the woods I was to hit Willie and not make no miss lick"—not miss his target—"and if I did, he would not miss me."

Givens was even more of a cipher than Green. He was eighteen or nineteen years old and unmarried. Like Green, he had been held on the plantation for at least a year. Beyond that, he left no trail. Even his surname was a guess: the census listed it as "McGivens."

"We were going through the same pasture where we took Johnnie Green," Manning said. "When we got to the woods, I hit Willie in the neck and he fell. I didn't hit him no more. We turned and walked back to my house, where I stopped and lain across the bed. Williams went to his house. He told me that he didn't want to hear anything or he would take his shotgun and do the [same] to me." That night, Manning said, he and Mr. Johnny returned to the pasture and dug shallow graves for Green and Givens. "We covered them up and put some pine straw over it. Just put them in like they were." He was sure he could find them again, if the agents chose to go looking.

As the session continued and Manning relaxed, he returned to the departures he'd already mentioned, this time offering a more complete version of what happened in each case. Johnnie Williams had not simply left, never to be seen again. Rather, he was the first to die after Mr. Johnny had delivered his "your neck or theirs" ultimatum. One evening Williams told Manning he wanted him to kill Johnnie. The next day, the peon was chopping wood when Williams had him stop, saying he needed him and Manning to tackle some work down in the pasture. Once the three had descended the long slope from the farmhouse, the planter confronted Johnnie—asked why he had told on him to the government men, why he'd told them a passel of lies.

Confused, Johnnie said he told the agents nothing. The boss wasn't listening. He turned to Manning and ordered him to take the axe and brain the man. Johnnie Williams's confusion turned to horror, disbelief, panic. He backed away from Manning, begged him not to swing that axe, cried to Mr. Johnny: please, no, don't do this.

Manning hesitated. John S. Williams looked at him. Are you going to do as I said?

Please, Mr. Johnny, the peon cried. Don't make Clyde kill me.

Because if you're not, Williams said, give me the axe.

Manning knew that if he did that, two farmhands would die in the pasture that morning. He swung the axe and hit Johnnie in the head.

Next came Red and Little Bit. Mr. Johnny asked if they wanted to go home, and they both said yes, so he had them come at night to the home place; along with Manning and Chisholm, they climbed into the Chandler and set off for the train station. Out on the main road, headed toward Covington, Mr. Johnny pulled the car to the shoulder and turned off the engine. Manning and Chisholm tied the men's hands with wire, then tied them to each other. They looped a trace chain around their victims' necks. They tied a heavy iron wheel from a cotton press to the chain.

They set off again. A short drive farther, they came to the steel-truss Waters Bridge spanning the Alcovy River, broad and deep and muddy red. Mr. Johnny stopped the car halfway across. Red and Little Bit were in a panic—weeping and begging, promising anything. Mr. Johnny calmed Little Bit by whispering that he was just trying to scare Red, and wouldn't hurt either of them. Little Bit evidently believed it right up to the moment Manning and Chisholm pushed them over the railing.

He had more to say about Big John, too. Mr. Johnny had summoned him to the river tracts with Manning and Charlie Chisholm to dig what Big John was told was a well. The three men took turns with the shovel. The hole was about two and a half feet deep, with Big John digging deeper, when Mr. Johnny handed Chisholm an axe. Big John stayed in that hole.

Artis Freeman really had gone off with Mr. Johnny, just the two of them, Manning said, and he honestly had no idea what became of him. All he knew was that Mr. Johnny was alone in the car when he arrived back at the plantation. Later the same Saturday that Artis left—February 26— Peterson, Preston, and Foots ran the hogs down to the home place, and afterward John S. Williams told them he would take them to the train. So they got into the Chandler with Manning and Chisholm and off they went in the darkness. This time, Williams did not stop on the Waters Bridge; they crossed it into Newton County, and drove on for perhaps a mile before he eased the car to the shoulder and killed the engine. Manning and Chisholm tied the three men—Peterson and Preston first, with wire, back to back, a trace chain around their necks, and knotted to the chain a short piece of rope connected to a bag of rocks, already filled, that Manning had found on the car's floorboards when he climbed in. He and Chisholm next tied up Foots, who was sitting in the front seat, next to Mr. Johnny.

The men wept. They told Mr. Johnny they changed their minds, that they didn't want to leave, that they never wanted to leave. They begged him to let them stay. Their fear rose as the binding went on—and it went on for about half an hour, there on the roadside. Again, Mr. Johnny steered the car back onto the highway. He drove on to the west, to the highway's fork at Stewart, and turned onto the road running south to Jackson. And two miles down, the cotton and corn at the highway's sides gave way to trees, and then they were at the Yellow River, stopped in the middle of Allen's Bridge. And Manning and Chisholm wrestled the terrified men across the wooden deck to the railing.

Foots watched from the car. They drove a mile farther down the road, to the South River, and stopped in the middle of Mann's Bridge. Mr. Johnny ordered everyone out. Once on his feet, Foots had a request. "Don't throw me over," he told them. "I'll get over." They helped him to the top of the banister and let him sit there for a few moments. Then, with a cry of, "Lord, have mercy," he flung himself off.

It was the day after the killings at the Yellow and South Rivers that Johnnie Green and Willie Givens died, Manning said. Still, the carnage didn't end. Paranoid as he was, John S. Williams grew uneasy about Charlie Chisholm. On the following Saturday he told Charlie he would let him go, that he would drive him to the train.

Chisholm surely knew what was coming, but he climbed into the car. Out on the main road, Mr. Johnny told him he had heard about all his damn talk, and that he had something to show him. And Chisholm must have resigned himself to his fate, because he let Manning tie him up with wire that Mr. Johnny had placed under the Chandler's seats. He let Manning tie two sacks of rocks to him, at his neck and his ankles, and let the two of them drag him to the railing at the Waters Bridge. Manning held him by the head and Mr. Johnny by the feet, and he went over without much fuss.

Manning's story wasn't finished. One day the following week, he said, he was in a hilltop field at the Campbell place with Mr. Johnny and a lot of farmhands, and Mr. Johnny sent them all away but Fletcher Smith, twenty-eight or twenty-nine years old and about the last bailed-out prisoner left on the farm. Williams dispatched Manning down the hill to get some tools, along a route that put the planter and Fletcher out of sight behind a swell. On his way back, Manning heard a gunshot, and on reaching the field found Fletcher dead on the ground, a hole in his head, and Mr. Johnny standing a few feet away with a shotgun in his hand.

At that, Manning ran out of murders to describe. The investigators sat stunned. They had started the day hoping to identify the three bodies in Newton County, as well as those responsible for their deaths. Instead, they had heard about eleven murders in the past month—from the mouth of an accomplice and eyewitness—and further corroboration that other, older killings merited investigation. Manning's account was shocking. It was grisly. And once it went public, it was sure to outrage the people of Georgia, the South, and the country at large. The most startling element of the story was that Williams ordered Manning to kill under threat of death. It was one thing to suspect that John S. Williams was aware of what had happened to the men found below the bridges. It was quite another to hear that the planter had planned, directed, and participated in the mass murder of his workforce.

This, after all, was a churchgoing Christian, a steady and supportive member of his Baptist congregation. A patriot who had sent four of his boys off to fight in the World War, and whose oldest, William Augustus, or "Gus," distinguished himself in the field, earning Britain's esteemed Military Cross. This was a doting father to his eight other surviving children, who ranged in age from two to twenty.

He was a successful planter, said to be one of the wealthiest in Jasper County—not as well-to-do as many thought, but still, the owner of roughly eleven hundred acres, enough to dwarf New York's Central Park. And he had come by it through patience, sweat, and hardship, for John S. Williams was self-made: he'd been born poor in West Georgia's Meriwether County just after the Civil War, spent his childhood in Jasper, struggled as a young farmer in nearby Monroe County, then moved back to Jasper and assembled his plantation piece by piece and crop by crop over twenty-seven years.

This was a man long married to the former Lucy Alice Lane, and thus bound to one of Jasper's first families. Lanes had farmed the county since the 1830s, had sent their men off to fight for the Confederacy, and since had wielded growing influence in state and local affairs.

By all indications, John S. Williams was a distinguished citizen and admired member of society.

And, most important, he was white.

PART TWO

The Murder Farm

9

THE VAST MAJORITY OF AMERICANS, it seems fair to say, had received the news of Leo Frank's lynching six years before with revulsion and alarm. Newspapers throughout the country condemned it in the strongest terms. Typical was an editorial in the *Richmond Times-Dispatch*, which labeled the perpetrators "a pack of wolves" and their act "the most vicious blow that has been struck at organized government in this country in a century." The *Louisville Courier-Journal* demanded that Georgians prosecute the lynchers or confess their collective guilt. The *Birmingham News* judged the crime enough "to make every Southerner hang his head in shame."

The *New York Age*, one of the most influential Black weeklies in America, wrote off Georgia as beyond salvation. "The great majority" of the state's people were "ignorant and primitive, the slaves of their prejudices, unable to control their passions, unwilling to abide by the law, if the law stood in the way of popular clamor," it charged—"a people living under a form of government and a standard of citizenship for which they were not yet fitted."

Frank's death served "one great purpose," however: "It has served to fix the eye of the nation upon this bold fact, that Georgia and several of her sister states are not civilized, in the modern sense of the word. And this is something which innumerable lynchings and burnings of colored men, women and children have failed to do."

Outrage ran high within Georgia, too. Governor Nat Harris vowed to hunt down those responsible. Former governor Slaton declared that every person involved "should be hanged, for he is an assassin." But also among the citizenry were untold thousands who supported the lynching with grim satisfaction, as justice done—who sided with Tom Watson's pronouncement that "the Law forfeited this man's life, for a horrible crime, and he has paid. That's all. *Now let outsiders attend to their own business, AND LEAVE OURS ALONE.*"

And in that response lurked political opportunity. The press had already speculated that Hugh Dorsey might attempt to parlay the Frank case into a political bid, and in the months following the lynching, he made a pilgrimage to Hickory Hill, Watson's estate outside Augusta, to explore the idea in earnest. He emerged with the kingmaker's endorsement of his candidacy for governor, and quit his post as prosecutor in July 1916 to campaign.

His platform consisted of a single issue, drawn straight from his experience with Slaton in the Frank case. He stood for the sanctity of jury verdicts, and against interference with them from governors or anyone else. Such interference undermined the public's confidence in the judicial process, he maintained, and that doubt provoked lynching. Remove this meddling, and Georgians would no longer be eager to take justice into their own hands.

It was, at best, a disingenuous position. Georgia had led all the states in lynching for years, and precious few of its hundreds of mob murders had come in response to any form of outside interference in jury decisions. The majority of lynchers claimed their victims before they had a chance to stand trial, thereby preempting any verdicts with which to interfere. Another large share of the killings occurred after juries had already convicted the accused and passed sentence. Still others saw mobs seize defendants from lawmen while their prosecutions were underway. Lynchings weren't crimes committed to ensure that justice was done, or to correct justice thwarted. They reflected the mob's belief that justice wasn't enough.

While hardly a racial progressive, Dorsey was clear-eyed about lynching's evils. They had been impressed on him not only by his jurist father and devoutly Methodist mother, but by his exposure to the subject throughout his adult life. Two earlier governors, in particular, had provided him with models of executive courage and forthrightness. In 1892, when Dorsey was a college student, then-governor William J. Northen denounced lynching as criminal vengeance and urged the General Assembly to pass laws to safeguard the state, as well as its people. "These self-constituted judges and executioners are more than murderers," he said. "They have not only taken human life without authority or excuse, but they have put before their fellow citizens an example, which, if followed to any extent, would speedily end in the dissolution of society itself."

That would have been hard to miss for a student of the law. A few years later, Dorsey had served in the state militia and pulled a stint as aide-de-camp to then-governor William Yates Atkinson. He no doubt knew of the governor's passionate opposition to lynching. Like Northen, Atkinson appealed to the legislature to stiffen the state's response to it. He also waded into a massive lynch mob in 1899, pleading with its members to halt their planned assault. He failed, but his righteous daring left an impression.

Beyond that, Dorsey had been living in Atlanta during the race riot of 1906, the city's darkest moment since the Civil War. Fanned by fabricated newspaper reports of Black-on-white rapes and assaults, thousands of agitated whites rampaged in the streets that September, viciously attacking every African American they saw. They pulled men off streetcars and beat them to death, murdered tradesmen in their shops, wrecked and looted Black homes and businesses, and strung the bodies of luckless innocents from telephone poles. In the days that followed, Dorsey's city was dumbstruck and horrified by its own capacity for random cruelty, for gleeful violence, for collective madness.

So Dorsey knew better. Thing was, his platform gave him a way to trade on his role in the Frank affair without mentioning it explicitly. Watson spelled out the ploy in an August 1916 *Jeffersonian* column: "There are some honest men who ask, '*Why should Dorsey be elected Governor on the Frank case?*' Nobody seeks to elect him on the Frank case. His enemies drag that case in: his friends don't.

"But we say this: It is *the test* that proves the Man. Often one crisis, one emergency, one law-case shows what a man is. . . . The Frank case did the same thing for Hugh Dorsey. *It proved him*, as by fire!"

That resonated with Georgians still outraged by the Slaton commutation. With Watson beating the drum on his behalf, Dorsey launched a series of speaking tours around the state at which he time and again hammered on his central message in his trademark dry, no-nonsense style. "There isn't much 'color' to a Dorsey oration, but there is a wealth of fact and wisdom and subject for thought," the *Constitution* observed. "He talks slowly, almost in a monotone—and his voice seldom rises or falls. He speaks in words of one syllable. Simplicity is the keynote of his oratory. His speech is crowded with thought, free of verbosity.

"He is brief, business-like, 99 percent efficiency."

That report included a scene that captured Dorsey's sometimes brusque conduct on the campaign trail. Riding a train in the state's far south, he "was seated toward the front of the car, going over some records. A sleek, well-fed, prosperous-looking man dressed in tweeds recognized the candidate and fell into the empty seat beside him, introducing himself in the breezy manner of one accustomed to expecting a hearty welcome from office seekers.

"Dorsey looked up briefly from his work, took the stranger's hand, grasped it tightly, said he was pleased to know him, then curtly asked if he would excuse him, as he was busily engaged at the time with his papers, to which he turned in dismissal of the man. The latter sat back astonished."

Dorsey faced three other candidates in the 1916 Democratic "white primary," which, as its name suggests, barred Black Georgians from taking part. Given the unyielding grip that the then white supremacist party had maintained on southern politics since Reconstruction, winning the primary meant winning the office. Dorsey's entry effectively ended the contest. He drew huge crowds and enjoyed a hero's welcome in every part of the state.

The masses didn't seem to mind that his strategy of keeping the Frank case out of his campaign did not survive the run to election day. In early September 1916, Dorsey charged that his rivals, who included Governor Nat Harris, had entered into a conspiracy against him, and that this cabal was led by none other than John Slaton. As evidence, he produced a letter the former governor had written months before, in which Slaton dismissed Dorsey as standing "practically no chance" because he was "lacking in every qualification that a governor should possess.

"I do not believe that any man can be elected governor of Georgia with a scaffold for his platform," Slaton wrote, "and with that platform written in blood."

Dorsey insisted that his campaign was actually based on "earnest and exalted principles," and that Slaton and his fellow conspirators were bent on dragging the Frank case into the contest. They were allied, he hinted, with forces that fought to keep Frank from the gallows—presumably, Jewish forces. Slaton responded that Dorsey was displaying "a reckless disregard of truth."

If anything, the dustup helped the candidate. Dorsey carried more than twice as many counties as his three primary opponents combined. In the general election that November, he destroyed his Republican rival with more than 96 percent of the vote.

10

MARCH 24, 1921: WITH DAYBREAK, SHERIFF JOHNSON and the federal agents drove Manning back out to Allen's Bridge. It had been just hours since he stood by as Clyde Freeman identified the dead buried there, but the lawmen thought it prudent to get a second identification from one of the last men to see the two alive. Once again, the makeshift graves were opened, the bodies exposed. Manning didn't require much time. "That is Willy Preston on the side next to the river," he said. "That is Peterson, on this side."

They drove on to Mann's Bridge, where the investigators started to open the grave in the riverbank a week after it was dug. Manning told them they need not finish the job, that he knew whose remains lay there. "That is Foots," he told them. "We put him off the bridge there, in the river."

Up in Atlanta, the governor's mail that day included a letter from forty-four citizens of Jasper County, who wrote that they had followed newspaper reports of the findings in the Yellow and South. "Our spirits revolt at such a terrible crime," the letter declared, "and if any of our citizens are responsible for it, we are not aware of it; furthermore we invite the fullest investigation and shall co-operate in every way with federal and State authorities in discovering, arresting and punishing the guilty parties, whoever they may be."

The signature of one prominent Jasper citizen was missing from the document, but he was busy the next county over. John S. Williams testified that he had not seen the bodies pulled from the rivers and could not say for sure they were his employees, leaks from the grand jury meeting in Covington revealed. Regardless, he would happily spend his own money to find the people responsible for the killings and bring them to justice.

He had done nothing wrong, nothing at all, and stood ready to help the grand jury in any manner it deemed useful. His testimony was so convincing that some jurors wanted to clear his name as soon as he left the room. A majority decided that the panel should hold off doing so, however. That judgment was soon rewarded: after their trip to the bridges, the sheriff delivered Clyde Manning to the courthouse.

He begged the grand jury to protect him. Then, for the second time that morning, Manning detailed each killing. His words, delivered in the same subdued monotone he had used in the sheriff's office, hit the jury like a cyclone. That afternoon, the panel returned a true bill of indictment in just one of the three Newton killings, thereby preserving the county's ability to seek indictments in the other two cases should the prosecution fail to win a conviction in the first. Manning and John S. Williams "did unlawfully and with malice aforethought kill and murder Lindsey Peterson," it charged, "by tying a chain about the neck of said Lindsey Peterson and weighting the body with a certain sack full of rocks and drowning the said Lindsey Peterson in Yellow River."

Sheriff Johnson took Manning to the Fulton County Jail in Atlanta, a massive stone fortress that well earned its nickname—the Tower. Clyde Freeman was held there as a material witness. Williams was arrested and jailed in Covington. Newton and Jasper Counties slumbered through a quiet, anonymous night, their last for months to come.

The rest of the world learned of Manning's confession the next morning, when the story broke in newspapers across Georgia and in the *New York Times*. Based on leaks from the courtroom and interviews with Sheriff Johnson, the articles laid out the bare and terrible facts: Eleven men, not three, had been killed. Black farmhands had been held in virtual slavery on the plantation. A white man was responsible for killing would-be witnesses in an ongoing federal peonage inquiry.

The story took fuller and far more sensational form later in the day, when reporters were allowed to talk with Manning at the Tower and he repeated much of his confession in the same matter-of-fact tone. "I knocked four Negroes in the head with an axe in one week and buried them in a pasture back of Mr. Williams's barn," he was quoted as saying. "Why did I do it? Because the boss said he wanted to get rid of them Negroes and that if I didn't make 'em disappear he'd kill me, and I knew he meant what he said.

"I don't know how many Negroes there are in the river, but I helped Mr. Williams drown six, including Charlie Chisholm," Manning reportedly said. "Me and Mr. Williams took him to the river one night and pitched him off the bridge after we weighted him down. Charlie begged hard, but Mr. Williams said: 'Let's throw him over and have it over with.'

"We took the other five to the river at night, after getting them out of their houses, and chained 'em down with rocks and threw 'em in," he said. "Yes, sir, they all cried and begged and some of 'em asked to be knocked in the head before being thrown in, but Mr. Williams wouldn't do it and wouldn't let me do it. We just threw them off the bridge and rode back up to the plantation." Manning regretted his role in the killings, he told reporters, "but there wasn't nothing else I could do. The boss told me if I didn't do as he said, I would be the next dead Negro around there."

To the *Atlanta Georgian*, Manning added an intriguing bit of personal history—his own father had been murdered on the Williams farm years before. Will Manning had worked for one of Sheriff Persons's brothers before going to work for Williams and moving his family onto the home place. When Clyde was in his mid-teens, he said, his father was ambushed—shotgunned at night and found dead the next morning. He didn't think Mr. Johnny was responsible, but he wasn't so sure about his sons.

The *Georgian's* reporter was fascinated by the man's demeanor. One hundred years later, it's well understood that the kind of flat emotional affect Manning displayed can be traced to a number of factors—post-traumatic stress, brain injury, depression—one or more of which he doubtless suffered in abundance. None of this was common knowledge among newspaper journalists of the day, however. "In all of this story, the most remarkable fact is the coolness with which Clyde Manning tells of the series of crimes," the reporter wrote. "He displays absolutely no feeling as he tells of the slaying. He volunteers no information and withholds none. Apparently, he is what would be called a 'good nigger,' in that he does what he is told to do, answers any questions 'white folks' ask him, and doesn't try to talk if 'white folks' don't ask him questions."

Williams, meanwhile, was doing some talking of his own. Transferred from Covington to join Manning in the Tower, he offered a jailhouse interview in which he blamed his arrest on his neighbors. "I want to say that I am entirely innocent in this case and I am sure that I will come clear if it is ever tried," he told a reporter from the *Georgian*. "I believe the charges against me were brought by members of the family of Miss Em Leverett, who owns a farm adjoining mine."

That would be Emily W. Leverett, the sixty-eight-year-old widowed matriarch of a farm bordering one of the river tracts. The Williams and Leverett clans had been skirmishing for years over property lines and livestock, he claimed. Miss Em had "tried to get something on me and my boys," and her own three grown sons had been "carrying pistols for several months" with menace on their minds. "They have tried to get me in three courts and have failed, and Miss Em has threatened that she would get me before the federal court."

The feud had grown especially heated the previous fall, Williams said, when one of the Black men employed by the Leveretts killed a farmhand working for the Williamses—an incident that no one else on either side would recall, and that he apparently forgot to mention to the federal agents back in February. The Leveretts had also accused his sons of reporting a liquor still to county authorities, he said, "and a shooting scrape almost resulted." Williams further divulged that he had exchanged blows with David Leverett, Miss Emily's forty-eight-year-old son, after which the family vowed to bring peonage claims against him.

"I had nothing in the world to do with these killings and I'll show them I did not when I am tried," Williams told the *Georgian*, insisting that he could not confirm that the dead men even worked for him: "I have never seen any of the Negroes who were found chained and weighted in the

Yellow River. I told the grand jury . . . that I was ready to look at them and say whether or not they were any of the Negroes who worked on my farm. The grand jury was willing for me to look at them, but the government men would not let me do so. I don't know whether they were my Negroes or not."

Note the *my*.

In conversation with the *Constitution*, Williams offered a more pragmatic defense. "If I had killed the Negroes, I wouldn't have carried them fourteen miles away to dump them in a river, but would have placed them in the river near my farm, where I know the depth," he said. "Manning's statement is a positive lie."

Asked about his boss's comments, Clyde Manning was dismissive. "I know the Leveretts," he said, "but they haven't got anything to do with this. Mist' John, he's the man that did it."

That same afternoon—Friday, March 25, 1921—Governor Dorsey met again with state attorneys, Newton County prosecutor Lonnie Brand, and the federal agents, all of whom recommended that the next obvious step in the investigation was to corroborate Manning's story. As he was the sole cooperating witness, they had best find and recover the victims' bodies and decide whether the evidence supported his confession. The task posed risks, however: Any party venturing into Jasper County might have to contend with Williams's many friends there, along with his three grown sons. Clyde Manning would be especially vulnerable, as would the entire case should any harm befall him.

Dorsey suggested that Sheriff Johnson assemble a posse of deputies and trusted civilians to accompany and protect the field boss. So, early the next morning, Johnson pulled Manning out of the Tower, bundled him onto a train, and took him to Covington, where they were joined by a posse of twenty men. In a convoy of five cars, the group drove to the Waters Bridge, where Jasper's Sheriff Persons waited with eight of his deputies.

Newspapers reported that a national guard company stood at the ready in Jackson, in case the Newton County delegation met resistance. That proved unnecessary: with Persons's vow to help his counterpart on the grim errand that had brought him to the county line, Johnson commanded enough muscle to meet most any challenge. The small army paused at the bridge's midpoint so that Manning could show the sheriffs where he and Williams had heaved three men over the banister, and where in the Alcovy he believed they remained. "Them Negroes are down there," he told them. "Ain't no chance for them to be anywhere else, with all those stones around their necks and feet."

They left a few men to drag the river bottom while the rest drove on to the Williams home place. It was about ten o'clock when Manning directed the party into the pasture down below his house, and, in the words of Sheriff Johnson, walked "straight as a martin to his gourd" to one of the graves hidden there. "Here's one, boss," he announced. He dropped to his knees and clawed at the dirt until, just a few inches down, he reached a body. He contemplated the sight for a moment before telling the sheriff: "This is Johnnie Green." A month underground had taken its toll. "The body was in horrible condition," the *Constitution* reported, "but the negro went about his identification in a calm business-like way."

As the posse exhumed the remains, Manning dug the toe of his shoe into loose soil a few yards away. "Here's another, boss," he told Sheriff Johnson. "Just like I told you." Diggers got to work clearing dirt from a second shallow grave. With little or no hesitation, Manning strode to what he promised was yet another. In short order, three bodies were lying topside. All had suffered devastating blows to their skulls. Special Agent Wismer, standing in the pasture before the three, contemplated the mud-caked corpse of Johnnie Williams. It had been just five weeks since he interviewed the peon. But for that brief conversation behind the gear house, he might not be standing here, and this pitiable young man might not be decaying before him. "No picture more horrible could have been painted by Poe," the *Constitution* declared.

Once Manning identified the bodies of Williams and Willie Givens, the three dead peons were lowered back into the ground and recovered, to await a coroner's inquest scheduled for the next morning. The group returned to the cars and drove to the river tracts, where Manning led the way to Big John's grave. As it was emptied of dirt, the peon was revealed to be slumped in the hole he'd been digging when he died. He, too, bore a terrible head wound. "Charlie Chisholm killed Big John," Manning was quoted as saying at the scene. "Hit him on the head with the back of an axe. I saw him hit him.

"Mr. John had the axe. Charlie was digging and Mr. Williams told him to let Big John dig. Charlie got out of the hole. Big John got in. Williams touched Charlie with the axe handle, and [Charlie] took the axe and hit Big John." The party took time out to search a just-built, still-empty cottage near the hole, and turned up an axe, shovel, and mattock. The axe was stained with blood. "Those are the tools used in killing and burying Big John," Manning told the sheriff.

From there he directed the party into a field at the crest of a high hill. All could see that it was plowed and planted with corn, the first green shoots of which had broken the soil. It seemed that searching for a grave in ground so altered might take hours, if not days. Again, Manning did not falter. He pointed out a patch of earth indistinguishable from any other spot in the field, and a body soon appeared beneath the shovels.

Fletcher Smith, Manning told those around him, "worked for Hulon and LeRoy Williams. He was killed about two weeks ago. He was the last Negro killed. Mr. John Williams killed him. Shot him with a double-barreled shotgun right at dark."

Sheriff Johnson confirmed that Smith had suffered a wound to the head. With that, the full import of the day's digging came into focus. The dead were exactly as and where Manning had described. He'd been a convincing witness from the start—calm, consistent, and self-incriminating—but today, his credibility had ratcheted further skyward with each uncovered body. "I can't see anything else to it than that Manning has told the truth," the sheriff commented to a reporter. "He has corroborated with sufficient evidence everything he said about the dead bodies of Negroes." And this simple, uneducated, dirt-poor Black man, his story freshly backed by the rotting remains of his friends, insisted that a white Georgian of influence was behind it all—an assertion, outrageous and unthinkable and close to blasphemous on any other day, in any other circumstance, now presumed to be fact.

"Now, boss, the other three bodies are in the Alcovy River underneath Waters Bridge," Manning told the sheriff, stressing again that "they ain't coming up unless you bring them up." At this, the party left the Williams spread, bound for the river. It was late afternoon by now, and word that five bodies had been found on the Williams plantation was spreading fast through Jasper County. Monticello was said to be in a fever.

At the Waters Bridge, the posse learned that the crew left behind to drag the Alcovy had achieved partial success: With a borrowed boat, deputies had rowed back and forth beneath the span, towing a grappling line from the stern, and within a half hour snagged something on the bottom. Hauling up the line, they found they had snared a single decaying corpse, tied hand and foot and weighted with rocks at the neck and ankles. Not long after, they snagged a second heavy object, but as they lifted it through forty feet of water it came loose. They had been unable to rehook it.

The recovered body was stretched out on the riverbank, where Manning identified it as that of Charlie Chisholm. "Mr. Williams got uneasy about the way Charlie was acting and made me get him," he told the reporters gathered around. "So we weighted him pretty good at both ends, and *splash*—that was the end of Charlie."

Sheriff Johnson called a halt to the day's work. They would return in the morning for the other two bodies. He took Manning back to the Tower. During the ride, he asked a question of his prisoner that would prove central in the days and weeks ahead: Why, once the killing started, didn't he run? "He said he was told to kill the Negroes. He was also told that if he attempted to get away they'd get him and kill him," the sheriff later recalled to a reporter in Atlanta. "He said he knew it meant death to him not to do what he was told, or to try to make his escape. And that was the reason he didn't leave."

11

WHEN THE SUN WENT DOWN THAT SATURDAY, newspapers in Atlanta and Macon were racing to nail down a story that seemed sure to further bruise the reputation of Jasper County: reporters had learned of the awkward relationship between Williams and prosecutor Doyle Campbell.

It didn't come as news to many in Jasper, where land deals fed conversation, and farmers had a pretty firm understanding of what their neighbors owned and how they fared at harvest time. Besides, anyone could stop in at the Monticello courthouse and, in minutes, find the pair's transactions recorded in the county deed books. Neither did it surprise Special Agents Wismer and Brown—they had heard about Campbell's sale of his river property and his loan to Williams from the prosecutor himself.

But the forty-year-old Campbell, who had held office since 1916, found himself the subject of intense scrutiny from the out-of-town press. He told reporters that the land Williams put up was worth three times the money he borrowed. He wasn't beholden to Williams, in other words—the opposite was true. "There is no foundation for the ugly rumors regarding this transaction," he said.

Truth was, though, that there existed other, continuing grounds for worry that Jasper County might be conflicted in pressing the case. The newspapers sniffed out that Williams was cousin to Sheriff Persons (and indeed, they had great-grandparents in common). There was the fact that Persons himself faced trial for a crime that bordered on peonage. And it didn't help matters when the county's presiding judge blocked the governor's efforts to round up Williams's sons Hulon, LeRoy, and Marvin, whom Dorsey knew were implicated in the killings of Blackstrap, Iron

Jaw, and possibly others. Dorsey had arrest warrants for the three issued in Atlanta. Afterward, he called Judge James Park of the Ocmulgee Circuit, the Superior Court district of several counties that included Jasper, to ask that he have the sons taken into custody and delivered to the Fulton County Tower. The judge declined, explaining that, as he read the statutes, any legal arrest warrants would have to come from him.

That ran counter to Dorsey's own understanding of the law. Just the day before, his assistant attorney general had advised him that "a warrant could be sworn out in Fulton County for the arrest of [a] defendant in Jasper County," and that the warrant could be "executed in Jasper County by the Sheriff of either Fulton, or Newton, or any other County." In a second telephone conversation, Judge Park told the governor that he had been to Monticello and assured by "reliable informants" in the town that no evidence linked the sons to the homicides now under investigation. That was good enough for him.

To the newspapers, Judge Park further argued that any defendant arrested in Jasper would be perfectly safe in the county jail and need not be transported to Atlanta. "That a few persons violate the law constitutes no reason why a whole county should be condemned," he wrote. "It would be unfair to the good people of that county that I should add further to their cup of sorrow by ordering anticipated prisoners to the Atlanta Tower, even if I had the authority, without investigation and due process of law."

Prosecutor Campbell did his best to calm the situation. On learning of the six bodies turned up by Sheriff Johnson's posse, he called Judge Park and urged that a special term of its grand jury "be convened at the earliest possible moment to investigate this matter." And that Saturday night he called the governor, telling him "that I am exceedingly anxious to cooperate with the law-abiding citizens of Jasper County in order that justice may be done." He asked Dorsey to send the state's attorney general, Richard A. Denny, to assist in any prosecutions. "The people of Jasper County are outraged at the rumor which has been circulated through the newspapers that we are unwilling to investigate this matter," Campbell declared, "and I do not believe we have been treated fairly."

Perhaps not. Nevertheless, with the new day—Easter Sunday, March 27—it was clear to all that Newton County had chased the case with greater urgency, and that this had cast Sheriff Persons and Campbell into supporting roles to Sheriff Johnson and Lonnie Brand.

Early that Easter morning, Sheriff Johnson returned to the Waters Bridge with a detachment of deputies and launched two boats equipped with dragging lines into the Alcovy. The party had an audience. Provoked by news of the previous day's discoveries, more than two hundred people watched from the bridge and riverbanks. "So crowded was the bridge," the *Constitution* reported, "that traffic became almost impossible and automobiles were parked on opposite sides as the dredging was in progress. The onlookers were horrified over the gruesome sight of the body of Charlie Chisholm lying in shallow water near the bank, where it had been left by the deputies for the coroner's inquest."

For five hours the boats circled beneath the bridge in the Alcovy's main channel until, at noon, one of the lines hooked onto a heavy object thirty to forty feet down. With a lot of grunting and hollering, the men in the boats hauled it to the bank. "The people ran from the bridge to aid the searchers, all crowding along the bank until it became necessary to have them moved away," the *Constitution* told its readers. "Then the dredge was slowly hauled in by the deputies, and from the yellow water came a heap—the figures of two men bound together with chains and wire, and so decayed identification was impossible. The crowd gathered around the bodies, some of the men peering over the shoulders of others and almost fighting for a position."

In this manner did most of humanity make its first and last acquaintance with John "Red" Brown and the man known as Little Bit, whom investigators would eventually identify as one John Benford or John Vinson. Their bodies, still chained by their necks and roped to the heavy iron wheel, were left in the shallows to await further examination.

A few miles away, another throng of onlookers had materialized at the

Williams home place, where Jasper County coroner Thad Cheek and his jury began its inquest over the dead in the pasture below the main house. With Sheriff Johnson present to answer questions, the jury witnessed the reopening of Johnnie Williams's grave. "Such a stench was created when the body was removed," the *Georgian* reported, "that disinfectants were brought and placed in it so the jury could remain near it to hold inquests on the bodies in the other two graves, less than thirty feet away."

Dr. Robert F. Cary, a Jasper physician, testified that the young man's skull was fractured, and that he was likely struck with a blunt object. He had been dead, the doctor said, ten to twenty days. Armed with details of Clyde Manning's confession from the sheriff, the jury found that Johnnie Williams met death from an axe wielded by Manning at the order of John S. Williams. The panel drew similar conclusions about the other two killings in the pasture, then departed for the river tracts. The roads leading to the killing fields were clogged with gawkers and their automobiles.

When the jury finished its work in the hilltop cornfield where Fletcher Smith lay, it offered its verdict in the death of the three men in the Alcovy River. John Brown and John "Little Bit" Benford, the panel ruled, had been killed by Clyde Manning and Charlie Chisholm, with John S. Williams's assistance. Charlie Chisholm was dispatched by Manning and Williams, acting together. In short, Manning was judged responsible for most of the deaths, with Williams as his accomplice. When the jury was finished, the Jasper jail warden took the bodies, heaped in a wagon, to the county paupers farm, where prisoners placed each in a plain pine coffin and buried it in an unmarked grave. "Another chapter in the most horrible murder case in Georgia's history was ended," the *Constitution* said of the day.

And a new chapter was beginning. Newspapers across America were now taking notice, their interest piqued by the weekend's gruesome discoveries. Readers from Honolulu to Los Angeles to Baltimore found the story prominently displayed in their local dailies. Georgia business, civic, and social leaders were "stunned by the swift developments of the last few days," the *Kansas City Star* reported on its front page. "At first there was a feeling of sympathy for Williams when Manning made his charges, but since the tide has changed. Anger and indignation have taken hold of the citizens who have witnessed every statement of the negro farm hand borne out by investigations."

The case laid bare a "brutish lapse into primitive savagery," one Cincinnati paper breathlessly observed, and the recovered bodies provided "incontrovertible evidence of unspeakable pagan barbarism in the midst of Christian enlightenment." The *Knoxville Sentinel*, serving a state with its own long history of peonage and race crime, held all Georgians to blame: If they had "always assumed the proper and righteous attitude to this cowardly and greedy peonage thing," the paper judged, "the conditions that have been uncovered in Jasper County could not have developed."

Georgia's newspapers, having chased the news out of Monticello for days, professed horror, shame, and disbelief on their editorial pages. The *Constitution* called Manning's confession "an alleged statement of fact that, in point of sheer fiendishness and revolting brutality, rivals a Bluebeard romance!" *Georgian* columnist James B. Nevin postulated that Jasper County had enabled the crime. The killer "had to believe he could 'get away with it' before he even imagined the possibility of undertaking it," he wrote. "And back of the somebody who reached that conclusion must have been a long, disheartening and mean community history of hatred and indifference to the negro as a negro."

"It hurts us to think that we have gotten to such low depths," the *Macon Telegraph* wrote. "We knew we had murdered negroes one at the time, but we shudder with all the disgust that can rise within us to find that the slaughter pen has been turned into a wholesale establishment and that the bloody work is being done overtime."

"The fact that the men killed were, in some if not all cases, negro ex-convicts has nothing to do with the case," the *Savannah Morning News* instructed, as the victims "were human beings and entitled to the protection of the laws; and the laws are a joke unless it is made plain that no man, however powerful he may be or may think he is in his own community, whatever his wealth is, can become lord of lives and end them when and as he pleases." The paper held out hope that it could be "established beyond all doubt that the white man accused is not guilty," but warned that if a jury found otherwise, "nothing short of the limit penalty of the law will satisfy law-abiding Georgians."

Some of the coverage shared a new journalistic shorthand for the murders and their investigation. In papers the country over, *Georgia v. John S. Williams and Clyde Manning* became known simply as the "Murder Farm" affair.

12

IF HE WASN'T AWARE OF THE SITUATION in Jasper and Newton Counties before the weekend expeditions to recover the victims, James Weldon Johnson certainly understood that something significant was taking place there by Monday. He was expected to react publicly to such news, but he was particularly well positioned to do so now: Though he lived and worked in New York, Johnson was well acquainted with the geography of central Georgia. He knew quite a lot about Hugh Dorsey, too. Over the course of his forty-nine years, he also had developed an unhappy expertise in the violence, abuses, and daily injustices suffered by Black people in America, especially in the South.

And that does not begin to address the qualifications Johnson brought to the table. Of all the Americans who left a mark on the early twentieth century, few, if any, were graced with such an embarrassment of diverse talents as this educator, lawyer, songwriter, poet, novelist, journalist, diplomat, and civil rights activist. Such were his gifts that he not only excelled at all of his chosen pursuits, he often did so in defiance of the color line. He was the first African American to attempt, let alone master, much of what he did.

Later in Johnson's life, the *New Yorker* would observe that "many consider him the best-known Negro in America." If he wasn't, he was high in the running, and his works were known to legions unfamiliar with the man himself. Consider that he was the coauthor of "Lift Every Voice and Sing," regarded as the Black national anthem; a founding influence on the Harlem Renaissance, the flowering of Black arts and culture in New York following World War I; and a celebrated writer of poetry, fiction, memoir, and history. Not least, he was the first Black chief of the National Association for the Advancement of Colored People, a post he had held for a little over three months when the Murder Farm made national news.

That Easter Monday morning, Johnson telegrammed a college classmate, now an Atlanta University professor, requesting that he "send all copies *Atlanta Constitution* containing pertinent information" about the case. That same day—March 28, 1921—Johnson thrust the NAACP into the affair by wiring three telegrams the Association shared with the press. The first, to President Warren G. Harding, urged that the Department of Justice launch "a thorough investigation . . . of peonage conditions in Jasper County, Georgia" and asserted that the case was "not an isolated one but is indicative of similar conditions which exist in most Southern states.

"The entire economic future of the South and of America are affected by this system," Johnson wrote. "[Thorough] investigation and punishment of those guilty of perpetuating this system, whatever the cost to the United States, must be made. We urge you to issue such an order."

His second telegram, to U.S. Attorney General Harry M. Dougherty, echoed his entreaty to the president, and called for the entire machinery of federal justice to be devoted to the case. The third was to Hugh Dorsey. Johnson implored the governor "to use every effort to bring to justice the murderers of eleven Negroes," and to thoroughly flush out "this vicious system of economic exploitation and debt-slavery which is so prevalent in other parts of Georgia as well, and which is so great a menace to the well-being of Georgia, the South and America."

Johnson and other Association leaders expressed horror at every new detail they learned of the killings. At the same time, though, they recognized that the Murder Farm provided them with a weapon: Here, at last, was an example of peonage that laid bare the inhuman, even deadly, character of the practice. Here was a case that put faces on both victims and perpetrators, and threw hard light on an evil unseen and only vaguely understood by most Americans, if they knew of it at all.

Johnson ended his telegram by putting the crime in its rightful, unignorable context. "Next to lynching," he wrote, "there is no greater cause of unrest than this vicious system."

Sure enough, the sentence garnered attention, and the telegrams earned press coverage from coast to coast. But the most remarkable reaction they produced came from Dorsey, who answered Johnson with a telegram of his own—an act that strayed from standard procedure for southern governors of the day.

"I assure you," Dorsey wrote, "that all true Georgians deplore the awful tragedies recently brought to light, and I am leaving no stone unturned to put the 'wheels of justice' in motion, and hope to bring about the conviction of the guilty parties.

"The Governor, as you know, has no jurisdiction," he added. "All he can do is to try to bolster up the officials elected by the people."

Johnson's biography is so eventful that it defies easy distillation. He was born in Jacksonville, Florida, in June 1871, to a Bahamian mother and a New York–born father, she a schoolteacher, he the headwaiter at a fashionable beachfront hotel. His boyhood was comfortable and thoughtful, by the standards of Black life in the South, and he grew up to be curious, intellectually restless, artistic, and genteel. After finishing the eighth grade—at which point public education for Blacks came to a halt in Jacksonville—Johnson attended both high school and college at Atlanta University. He distinguished himself not only as a top student but as one of the Black institution's star athletes; he was said to be the first Black college pitcher to master a curveball. He also worked as a student teacher in rural Henry County, Georgia, during two of his undergraduate summers. Henry adjoined Newton and Butts, and Johnson, who got around mostly on foot, got to know the lay of the land well.

Graduating in 1894, Johnson returned to Jacksonville and an appointment as principal of his alma mater. Although it remained a grammar school, he convinced its graduating eighth graders to stick around for another year of instruction, then a second, then a third. Adding a grade per year, he transformed the place into a high school, the first for Blacks in Florida. When school officials realized what he had done, they made the change permanent.

His school duties failed, however, to keep Johnson sufficiently busy in mind and spirit. Interested since boyhood in writing and publishing, he pooled his savings and borrowed money in 1895 to start an afternoon newspaper, the *Daily American*—reputedly the first Black daily in the United States. Initially successful, it fell victim to competition from Jacksonville's white dailies. The presses stopped after eight months.

Undaunted, Johnson devoted his after-school hours to another long-standing interest: law. He studied under the tutelage of a local attorney, who, after six months, allowed him to draft most of the firm's court filings. After eighteen months, his mentor suggested that Johnson was ready to sit for the bar exam. Jacksonville's legal community turned out for the show, a grueling, two-hour interview before a panel of seasoned lawyers. When he answered every question that came his way, one of the panelists muttered, "I can't forget he's a nigger, and I'll be damned if I'll see a nigger admitted to the Florida bar." The man was spared the sight only by stalking out of the room, because minutes later, Johnson became Florida's first Black attorney.

He did not practice law for long before a new passion gripped him. With his musically genius younger brother, John Rosamond Johnson, he set out for New York in the summer of 1899, hoping to peddle a comic opera they had worked on for a year. The opera didn't get any takers, but the pair met the principals of the New York stage, including a Black vaudeville actor, producer, and songwriter named Bob Cole.

Back running his school that fall, Johnson began tinkering with poetry. He published his first piece in *The Century*, a national magazine—a coup made all the sweeter when Rosamond set it to music and it won surprise popularity. The experience guided their songwriting partnership for years to come—Johnson would write lyrics in the form of poems and Rosamond would craft the accompanying music. That winter, they joined forces on a song to be sung by schoolchildren at a Jacksonville celebration of Abraham Lincoln's birthday. Johnson worked out the lyrics in a single evening. "The song was taught to the children and sung very effectively," he would recall, "and my brother and I went on with other work."

But "Lift Every Voice and Sing" had staying power. "The schoolchildren of Jacksonville kept singing the song; some of them went off to other schools and kept singing it; some of them became schoolteachers and taught it to their pupils," Johnson wrote years later. "Within twenty years the song was being sung in schools and churches and special occasions throughout the South and in some other parts of the country.

"My brother and I, in talking, have often marveled at the results that have followed what we considered an incidental effort, an effort made under stress and with no intention other than to meet the needs of a particular moment. The only comment we can make is that we wrote better than we knew."

Returning to New York that summer, the Johnson brothers formed a partnership with Bob Cole and churned out the first in a string of wildly successful songs for the Broadway stage. But big-city success did not immunize Johnson from the dangers of being Black in the turn-of-the-century South. Back in Jacksonville in May 1901, he was spotted in a city park in the company of a light-skinned woman and surrounded by an enraged gang of white soldiers. The timely intercession of their commander saved him from lynching—but it was close.

The following year, he quit teaching and moved to New York.

In 1904, while accepting an honorary degree at Atlanta University, Johnson met a storied professor there: William Edward Burghardt Du Bois, the brilliant and uncompromising champion of full citizenship for Blacks, who the previous year had published his landmark essay collection *The Souls of Black Folk*. Johnson reckoned it "had a greater effect upon and within the Negro race in America than any other single book published in this country since *Uncle Tom's Cabin*."

Easier to like on the page than in person, the acerbic, austere, and militant Du Bois was a fiery bookend to the courtly Booker T. Washington, the founder of Alabama's Tuskegee Institute and the leading Black spokesman of the day. He had no patience for Washington's gospel of accommodation in dealing with the white majority—the strategy of emphasizing African American education in trades and farming, and of working toward economic independence ahead of any drive for equal rights. Washington preached that Blacks would eventually earn equality by demonstrating they deserved it.

Du Bois considered him submissive, too eager to please whites, a sellout. Were Black people not human beings, and entitled to life, liberty, and the pursuit of happiness as surely as whites, without any such demonstration? Were they not Americans, and therefore entitled to all of the rights—including the vote—that their fellow citizens enjoyed?

Their differences opened a yawning divide in the struggle for civil rights. Washington's influence was at its peak, however, while his rival was just getting started. A year into his acquaintance with Johnson, Du Bois would be among the organizers of the Niagara Movement, a conference of Black lawyers and intellectuals united in their demand for racial equality. The alliance would lay the ground for the creation of the NAACP four years after that. Du Bois would be the only Black person among its leaders, and become the editor of the Association's monthly magazine, *The Crisis*. In time, he and Johnson—who would come to align with him in ways neither man could have predicted—would vie with Washington as Black spokesmen and advocates, and surpass him in lasting influence: tracing the origins of the civil rights campaigns of the 1950s and 1960s leads back to them.

But first, in that summer of 1904, Johnson was approached about organizing a Republican club for Black New Yorkers, which led to his partnering with his brother and Cole to write a campaign song for Theodore Roosevelt. The candidate judged it "bully good," which ushered yet another career change: the president appointed Johnson U.S. consul to Puerto Cabello, Venezuela, a pioneering assignment for a Black man, with a charge to assist visiting Americans and keep an eye on the port's international commerce.

The posting left him with enough free time to write a novel, *The Autobiography of an Ex-Colored Man*. Published anonymously in 1912, the book is now regarded a classic—a rumination on "passing" for white, on the indignities faced by Black people in general, and on the challenges weathered by the growing African American middle class, featuring a cast of smart, cultured, and ambitious sophisticates. Absent were the kindly Negro sages, folk-wise mammies, and comic rascals that populated most literary depictions of Black life. For many readers, it was revelatory.

Eventually, Johnson won a promotion and a new posting in Corinto, Nicaragua, which injected him into the middle of a revolution. He handled the assignment with aplomb. In fact, through a combination of fast talking and stagecraft, he saved the port city from rebel takeover. He married Grace Nail, herself a civil rights advocate, who braved Corinto's intrigues by his side. And he continued writing poetry; one piece, "Fifty Years," became the title poem of his first collection.

Johnson was promised another promotion and posting to the Azores, but with Woodrow Wilson's ascension to the presidency, he was denied both. He quit the consular service and in short order got another shot at journalism: in October 1914, he was named a contributing editor to the *New York Age*, with the task of filing a weekly opinion column titled "Views and Reviews." And here he completed his writerly turn, begun with his novel, from entertainer to prosecutor for equality.

Taken together, the columns amounted to "a colossal rebuttal against the absurdity of American race prejudice," wrote Sondra K. Wilson, the late Harvard historian and executor of Johnson's literary estate. "He used his power as a writer to present race prejudice as such a foolish and absurd thing that even those who practiced it should have been compelled to see that it was ridiculous."

Johnson campaigned in his early columns for the defeat of Woodrow Wilson, whom he believed to be the enemy of Black America: "If there is a colored man in the United States who really believes that Wilson intends to do anything to help the Negro," he wrote in September 1916, "he is a man who needs a few more brains to make him half-witted." He predicted that the Great Migration of southern Blacks to the industrial cities of the North, already underway, would only swell. "If the white people of the South dream that the Negro, because he is silent, does not resent, does not keenly feel the bitter injustice to which he is so often subjected, they are mistaken," he declared in another 1916 column. "The Negro remains there because economic necessity compels him to do so. And whenever economic conditions open for him elsewhere, he will leave."

Georgia consistently earned Johnson's attention, for the simple reason that it offered a steady supply of atrocity and outrage. No state lynched more of its citizens. None was more a prisoner of its racist past. None offered so much promise bundled with disappointment, horror, and grief. In Johnson's view, the fact that Tom Watson wielded power there was evidence of the state's moral bankruptcy. "Let us say to Mr. Watson that the South may continue lynching Negroes for rape and for murder and for theft and for owning a prosperous farm and [for not] being 'respectful' to white men," one 1915 column read, "but let him remember that by the Eternal Laws the South will pay for it. Let him look around and see that the South is already paying the debt of sin that began with the first load of slaves that was landed at Jamestown. She stands today bound in the chains of prejudice, cowed under tyrannous public opinion, half-benighted and wholly impecunious, while the rest of the country is enlightened, free and prosperous."

Alongside Du Bois's editorials in *The Crisis*, Johnson's *Age* columns became required reading for Black and white intellectuals the country over. However different their personalities, the men shared the view that their art was inseparable from their politics. "I stand in utter shamelessness and say that whatever art I have for writing has been used always for propaganda," as Du Bois put it. "I do not care a damn for any art that is not used for propaganda." Johnson believed that even if he did not write explicitly about race, his words contributed to the fight: Black literature and art demonstrated "intellectual parity by the Negro," and were sure to elevate his people's status.

It so happened that one of his regular readers was Joel Spingarn, a white philanthropist and the NAACP's chairman of the board, who detected in Johnson a figure of potential value to the Association. That fall, Spingarn wrote to him with a job offer. He caught Johnson by surprise. But "it at once seemed to me," he would recall, "that every bit of experience I had had, from the principalship of Stanton School to editorship on *The New York Age*, was preparation for the work I was being asked to undertake."

And so James Weldon Johnson, having already proved himself an estimable talent at virtually everything he'd tried, became a professional activist for civil rights. He joined a still-embryonic organization that operated on a shoestring budget and a skeleton staff, out of a pair of cramped rooms in lower Manhattan. Despite its name, the Association was far from national: It had sixty-eight branches in the northern and midwestern states, and just a handful in the South—and one of those was a tiny outpost in Key West. It had no others in Florida, and no presence in Tennessee, Mississippi, or the Carolinas.

That was partly by design, as some of the group's directors worried that expanding into the South might force the NAACP to soften its positions. Johnson, granted the title "field secretary" and charged with expanding the membership, felt otherwise. "It was my deep conviction that the aims of the Association could never be realized only by hammering at white America," he recalled. "Regardless of what might be done *for* black America, the ultimate and vital part of the work would have to be done by black America itself." And the South was where most of Black America lived.

Besides expansion there were dollars and cents at stake: the former slave states "could furnish members and resources to make the Association a power." So, soon after starting work in January 1917, Johnson embarked on a lengthy recruiting trip through the land of cotton—to Richmond, Norfolk, and Raleigh, to Atlanta, Augusta, and Savannah, and down to Jacksonville and Tampa. On his way southward, he met with

Black leaders in each city and laid the groundwork for community meetings to follow. On the return journey, he revisited each and spoke to those gatherings. The odyssey birthed thirteen new NAACP branches and saw membership balloon by more than seven hundred.

The new Atlanta branch seemed particularly promising. Johnson was most taken by one of its firebrand organizers—a twenty-three-year-old recent graduate of Atlanta University named Walter F. White. "I saw him several times," he wrote, "and was impressed with the degree of mental and physical energy he seemed to be able to bring into play and center on the job in hand." It was impossible to overlook something else about the young man that would prove useful to the NAACP: he was fair-haired, blue-eyed, and so light-skinned that he could pass for white.

Shortly after Johnson returned to New York, the Association's secretary—for all intents and purposes, its chief operating officer—quit to enter the army. Johnson was named acting secretary. A short while later, he was recruiting in the Midwest when he learned of a lynching in Memphis, and made his way to the city to investigate. A sixteen-year-old white girl had vanished while on her way to school, he learned. She was found days later, decapitated, in a wooded river bottom near her home. Two Black woodcutters working in the area were arrested on suspicion.

Detectives disinterred the girl's body, hoping that the last thing she looked upon would be preserved on her eyes; such was the state of forensic science in May 1917. Her pupils were photographed and the images magnified to show "an object that appears to be the upper part of a man's head," the *Memphis Scimitar* reported. "The forehead and hair seem to be plainly visible, but the features are indistinct." Police nonetheless claimed that they could detect a resemblance to one of the woodcutters.

In an all-too-common development, a mob snatched the prisoner from lawmen escorting him to trial and burned him alive before an audience of thousands. Visiting the scene, Johnson had an epiphany that resonated within and without the NAACP: that achieving racial justice involved "the saving of Black America's body and white America's soul." His unflinching account of the crime, published in *The Crisis*, was the first in a decade-long series of NAACP reports aimed at saving those bodies, and those souls, by displaying the horrific details of such savagery to the world.

The Association did not have long to wait for the next horror show. In late May 1917 and again five weeks later, the meatpacking city of East St. Louis, Illinois, was consumed by rioting, sparked by an influx of Black workers (and strikebreakers) from the South. White mobs beat Black men, women, and children to death in the streets, set fire to the town's Black quarter, and shot residents fleeing their burning homes to cries of "Kill them all!" Police and the state militia did nothing to help. Thousands of refugees streamed across Mississippi River bridges into St. Louis.

While Du Bois investigated the massacre, Johnson mulled some sort of public demonstration to protest the summer's madness, as well as an earlier lynching by fire cheered on by a vast crowd in Waco, Texas. He decided on a silent march. On July 28, 1917, a Saturday, children dressed in white led ten thousand protesters in a parade up New York's Fifth Avenue to the beat of muffled drums. As the parade passed, marchers distributed flyers explaining their purpose. "We march because we want to make impossible a repetition of Waco, Memphis, and East St. Louis by arousing the conscience of the country, and to bring the murderers of our brothers, sisters, and innocent children to justice," they read, in part. "We march because we deem it a crime to be silent in the face of such barbaric acts."

It was the largest mass protest by Black Americans to date, and Johnson was well pleased with the attention it drew to the cause. But before he could mark his eighth month on the job came another riot, this one in Houston and involving troops of the army's all-Black Twenty-Fourth Infantry Regiment. Enraged by rough and openly racist treatment by Houston police, and alarmed by a rumor that white mobs were descending on their camp, about 150 soldiers mutinied, armed themselves, and marched on the city on the night of August 23. By the time they covered the two miles into town, five policemen, four soldiers, and eleven white civilians were dead or dying, and at least eleven others lay seriously wounded.

Johnson took the view that the cause of the trouble was more white Texans than Black soldiers. The Association launched a legal campaign to defend the men that was destined to last for years. It largely succeeded, but not before thirteen of the soldiers were hanged.

All of which is to say that Johnson's first few months with the NAACP were eventful. That fall, he urged the Association's board to create a position for the impressive young Atlantan he met on his foray to the South. The directors had qualms about Walter White's youth, but agreed to bring him aboard. Johnson invited White to New York to become the Association's assistant secretary. White, too, had reservations. He held a promising job in insurance, and the NAACP post did not pay nearly as well. At his father's urging, however, he accepted the offer, and assumed his new role in January 1918.

Walter White's racial makeup was all but indecipherable. "One felt a strange, even comic, feeling at the sound of his name and the sight of his extremely white complexion while hearing him described as a Negro," the Jamaican-born poet Claude McKay recalled. "It violates my feeling of words as pictures conveying color and meaning." Of White's thirty-two great-great-great-grandparents, just five were African American.

He had always identified as Black, however—an identity, he would later say, that was cemented during the Atlanta riot of 1906, when his father handed the twelve-year-old a rifle and the two prepared to defend their home against an advancing white mob. The rioters turned away, but not before the young Walter was imbued with a new certainty about himself and his place in the world: he was a Negro, and proud of it.

He first put his complexion to use for the NAACP twelve days after he joined the national staff, when a Black sharecropper was roasted alive by a mob in Estill Springs, Tennessee. Dispatched to the town—"as remote from the outside world as though it had been in Tibet"—White insinuated himself among the perpetrators and found them eager to talk with a seemingly sympathetic stranger.

But it was his next investigation, in the late spring of 1918, that established the short, slight, easily overlooked White as an indispensable weapon. On the evening of May 16, a white planter in Brooks County, on Georgia's border with the Florida panhandle, was shot twice through an open window of his home. Hampton Smith died instantly. His pregnant wife was wounded, as well.

Smith had a long-standing reputation as a harsh taskmaster of his tenant farmers and Black hands, some of whom were peons bailed out of local jails. One of them, Sidney Johnson, reportedly worked off his obligation and demanded that the boss pay him for his continued service. Smith refused and the two argued. A few days later, Johnson failed to show up for work, and Smith went to his cabin for an explanation. Johnson told him he was sick. Smith responded by beating him, and Johnson, it was said, answered with threats. So when the shooting occurred, suspicion immediately centered on the Black man—though the white rabbles formed to exact vengeance for the killing did not restrict themselves to actual suspects. Enraged by rumors that Mrs. Smith had been raped, and further incensed by talk that several Black conspirators had planned Smith's death, they went on a rampage in Brooks and neighboring Lowndes County.

Within three days, they chased down and killed several people with no obvious connection to the attack. Will Head and Will Thompson were snared separately and lynched before a day had passed. The morning after their deaths, Hayes Turner, in whose house Johnson was rumored to have plotted the shooting, was captured and locked up in the town jail in Quitman, the Brooks County seat. When the sheriff and court clerk tried to move him to a larger jail in nearby Moultrie for safekeeping, a vigilante band intercepted the trio, seized Turner, and strung him up. His body hung alongside a country road for days.

The next victim was Turner's nineteen-year-old wife, Mary. On learning of his death, she "made unwise remarks . . . about the execution of her husband," the *Macon Telegraph* reported, "and the people in their indignant mood took exception to her remarks, as well as her attitude, and without waiting for nightfall, took her to the river where she was hanged and her body riddled with bullets." Grim as that account was, it came nowhere near to describing the horrors actually visited upon Mary Turner. The papers reported that mobs later killed two others, including Sidney Johnson—who, according to the *Telegraph*, had been hiding out in a swamp before he was shot by authorities.

Walter White arrived in the area "shortly after the butchery and while excitement yet ran high," as he'd later write. He learned that not six, but at least eleven people had been lynched, and perhaps as many as eighteen— and that the local papers had sanitized their accounts of one killing, in particular.

From White's report in *The Crisis*:

Mrs. Turner made the remark that the killing of her husband on Saturday was unjust and that if she knew the names of the persons who were in the mob that lynched her husband, she would have warrants sworn out against them and have them punished in the courts.

This news determined the mob to "teach her a lesson," and although she attempted to flee when she heard that they were after her, she was captured at noon on Sunday. The grief-stricken and terrified woman was taken to a lonely and secluded spot, down a narrow road over which the trees touch at their tops, which, with the thick undergrowth on either side of the road, made a gloomy and appropriate spot for the lynching. Near Folsom's Bridge over the Little River a tree was selected for her execution—a small oak tree extending over the road.

At the time she was lynched, Mary Turner was in her eighth month of pregnancy. The delicate state of her health, one month or less previous to delivery, may be imagined, but this fact had no effect on the tender feelings of the mob. Her ankles were tied together and she was hung to the tree, head downward. Gasoline and oil from the automobiles were thrown on her clothing and while she writhed in agony and the mob howled in glee, a match was applied and her clothes burned from her person. When this had been done and while she was yet alive, a knife, evidently one such as is used in splitting hogs, was taken and the woman's abdomen was cut open, the unborn babe falling from her womb to the ground. The infant, prematurely born, gave two feeble cries and then its head was crushed by a member of the mob with his heel. Hundreds of bullets were then fired into the body of the woman, now mercifully dead, and the work was over.

In a story he wrote a decade later for the *American Mercury* magazine, White recounted his conversation with a local storekeeper. The man told him that Hampton Smith "never paid his debts" and "wasn't liked much around here," but that his death had inspired the mobs to "show niggers that they mustn't touch a white man, no matter how low-down" he might be. "Little by little he revealed the whole story," White wrote. "When he told of the manner in which the pregnant woman had been killed he chuckled and slapped his thigh and declared it to be 'the best show, Mister, I ever did see. You ought to have heard the wench howl when we strung her up.'"

White found no evidence that Mrs. Smith had been raped—the "usual crime" cited for lynching had not figured in the killing, despite persistent reports to the contrary. He also learned that Sidney Johnson had not sought refuge in a swamp, but had holed up in a home in Valdosta, the region's commercial center and the seat of Lowndes County. A posse surrounded him there and killed him in a brief shootout. Afterward, the crowd castrated Johnson's body with a sharp knife, roped it to a car, and dragged it through Valdosta's business district and over miles of dirt road to a spot near the Smith farm, where they burned it to a blackened lump.

Before his pursuers found him, White wrote, Johnson told several visitors that he alone was responsible for shooting the Smiths. None of the others lynched knew of the crime until after the fact, and some had no connection to it whatsoever.

White did not sit on this information. Weeks before his report was published in the September 1918 issue of *The Crisis*, he took his findings to Hugh Dorsey.

BY THE TIME HE MET WITH WALTER WHITE, nearly three years before the Murder Farm killings came to light, Hugh Dorsey was more than halfway through his first term as Georgia's chief executive. The job's two-year duration was just one of its quirks. Another was that after winning election in November of an even-numbered year, a governor-elect did not take office until late the following June, and his outgoing predecessor had to endure lame-duck status for the same seven-plus months. Dorsey had thus assumed office in late June 1917—a confusing moment in state governance, as America had entered World War I just two months before, with the associated disruptions to Georgia's labor force and economy.

The new governor devoted much of his inaugural address to his campaign's central plank, but then quickly broadened his administration's priorities. In his first "State of the State" speech, he urged Georgia legislators to boost spending on Black education, pointing out that although African Americans accounted for about 45 percent of the population, their schools received only about 3.5 percent of the state's outlays. He wrestled with a budgeting system out of the Dark Ages and with undisciplined spending that constantly threatened Georgia with insolvency. And notably, he beat the drum for an end to lynching. "If this is not done, it is very probable that federal intervention will not be long delayed," he warned in his second annual message to the General Assembly. "Without awaiting federal action, I submit, it is the duty of Georgia to take drastic steps to deal with this question."

His meeting with White, convened at the governor's request, came on July 10, 1918, a week after that second "State of the State" address. His visitor handed him a typed report crowded with additional details of the monstrous crimes in south Georgia. Mary Turner's body was "riddled with bullets from high-powered rifles until it was no longer possible to recognize it as the body of a human being." The slain mother and child were "buried about ten feet from the tree" under which they died; at the head of their makeshift grave was "a whiskey bottle with a cigar stump placed in the neck."

White also named fourteen members of the mob that killed Will Head and Will Thompson on the first day of the slaughter. The leaders, he reported, were both from Quitman—a cotton broker and an undertaker who had boasted of his role in the violence. Other lynchers included a postal clerk, a furniture company employee, an auditor for Standard Oil, five farmers, and four of Hampton Smith's brothers. "A spirit of unrest exists in both Brooks and Lowndes Counties which will undoubtedly affect the labor situation in that community," his report concluded. "It is my information that over five hundred Negroes have left the community since the lynching. Many more, because of property which they own and crops which they have now in process of cultivation, are unable to do so at the present time, but are planning to leave as soon as they can dispose of their land and gather their crops. At this time when the production of food means so much towards the success of the Government in the war such a condition is serious."

Dorsey's reaction to the information evidently impressed White. He would later call him "a man genuinely eager to stop lynching," but hamstrung by "restrictive laws against which he had appealed in vain." But the governor's response to the rampage had, to that point, been inconsistent and confusing. On May 22, three days after Mary Turner's death, he authorized rewards of five hundred dollars each for the first five lynchers apprehended and delivered to the Lowndes County sheriff. That same day, he declared that a state of insurrection gripped Lowndes and Brooks, and deployed a company of the Georgia National Guard to Valdosta to restore order. "While it is the desire of the authorities to exercise the powers of martial law mildly," his proclamation read, "it must not be supposed that they will not be vigorously enforced as the occasion arises." That put an end to the bloodshed.

Alas, Dorsey's determination wavered in the days that followed. The Colored Welfare League of Augusta sent him a resolution decrying Mary Turner's slaying, and urging him to "exercise of all your legal power against this horrible and barbarous act." Dorsey chose instead to criticize the league's resolution as "silent concerning the unspeakable outrages apparently committed by members of your race, and which undoubtedly precipitated" the carnage. Lynching was "an evil which can only be effectively suppressed by removing the aggravating cause," he wrote. "Whenever the law-abiding element of the negro race shall convince the lawless among them that such crimes will not be tolerated anywhere, and that the guilty parties will not be shielded or sheltered, but will be delivered to the officers of the law, such unspeakable crimes . . . will no longer occur to stir race prejudice and resentment beyond immediate control."

What prompted such a reversal? Perhaps he was looking out for himself. His decision to send troops into Lowndes County, however well justified, had been politically risky, and he was just months away from campaigning for a second term as governor. It was one thing to nudge his state toward a consensus against lynching. It was quite another to maroon himself too far ahead of the electorate.

Moreover, Dorsey may have been struggling to reconcile two opposing belief systems: the one with which most white Georgians of his generation had been raised, in which lynching was a hideous but understandable response to provocation, most often the "usual crime"; and a second, more modern view, holding that mob murder was never justified and almost always racially motivated. As he had not yet had his meeting with Walter White when he wrote to the Augusta group, he was likely unaware of the depredations Mary Turner suffered. But he knew that a woman had been killed for speaking against the mob—not for having committed any crime, usual or not, but for simply criticizing her husband's murder. He knew, too, that she had infuriated her killers by threatening to pursue legal action against them—by placing her faith in the very system he claimed to hold dear. Any way you looked at it, there was no justice, rough or otherwise, in Mary Turner's death. She and her baby were innocent victims.

The essential point is that no matter how positive his exchange with Walter White, the governor was unreliable on matters of race in the summer of 1918; what's more, he would remain so. That September, the NAACP's new secretary, John R. Shillady, wrote Dorsey about another lynching, this one claiming a Black escapee from the chain gang accused of assaulting two white women. He was chased down by local Black men and delivered to the sheriff. When the lawman and two deputies arrived at the county jail with the suspect, an armed mob wrested the prisoner away and killed him.

Shillady reminded the governor what he told the Colored Welfare League of Augusta: that if Black people got tough on crime and turned in wrongdoers from their own ranks, lynchings would stop. This latest death exposed that as untrue. It also reflected the incompetence or criminal complicity of local law enforcement in a great many mob murders.

Dorsey doubled down on blaming the victims. "I condemn lynching and am doing all that I can to prevent it," he wrote, before concluding: "I believe that if the negroes would exert their ultimate influence with the criminal element of their race and stop rapes that it would go a long way towards stopping lynchings."

By then his immediate political aspirations were safe. That same month, Dorsey was unopposed for the Democratic nomination for a second term.

14

MONDAY, MARCH 28, 1921: Limited though his powers were, Hugh Dorsey had been busy with the Williams case over the Easter weekend. His meetings with Newton County's Lonnie Brand, the state's own legal team, and his counselors in the clergy had produced the beginnings of a strategy. Williams and Manning should be tried separately, and it made good sense to try Williams first, as the state could rely on Manning as its key witness. He would testify against Williams, and then—because he was apparently unafraid to implicate himself—his own testimony could be flipped against him if and when he came to trial. The prosecution need rely on Williams for nothing.

Dorsey wondered how he might, as he had put it in his telegram to the NAACP, "bolster up the officials" of Newton and Jasper. This was, after all, a murder case against a white man accused of killing Black people. Only a few such cases had gone to trial in the past forty-four years—since the state adopted a constitution, still the law in 1921, that reintroduced racial apartheid at the close of Reconstruction. Convictions had been vanishingly rare. To Georgia's shame, untold numbers of white-on-black killings had been ignored or, at the least, unpunished, over those years. Hundreds of Black men and women had been lynched without repercussion. The record demanded that the state go after Williams with all the might and ferocity it could muster.

Dorsey conferred with state attorney general Denny about drafting solicitors general from the state's other judicial circuits to create a sort of prosecutorial all-star team, aimed at helping Lonnie Brand in and out of the courtroom. The AG doubted he had the authority to do that. Dorsey asked whether he had the power to hire a high-powered private-sector lawyer to help argue the cases. No, Denny reportedly told him, he probably did not.

Sending Denny himself, or Assistant Attorney General Graham Wright, would be simple enough, provided either could free up his calendar. But the governor considered another possibility, besides: What if he could find an ace lawyer for the prosecution, but whose fees were paid by private parties?

While Dorsey pondered that question, Brand appeared before Judge Hutcheson of the Stone Mountain Circuit to hurry the case onto the Newton County Superior Court docket. He pushed for a Thursday start for the trial—as in the coming Thursday, March 31, three days away. Monticello lawyer Greene F. Johnson, newly hired to represent Williams, objected that that was hardly enough time to prepare a defense. Judge Hutcheson agreed.

Which raised the prospect of waiting for months. Both the judge and Lonnie Brand "rode" the Stone Mountain Circuit, which consisted of five counties. The judge would hear and Brand would prosecute cases for a term ranging from days to weeks in each county, then move on to the next. Once Newton's current term ended—and the schedule called for that to happen in a matter of days—they would not return to the Covington courthouse until midsummer. Well, a disappointed Brand told the court, if they didn't schedule trial for the coming week, they would have to wait until July. Hutcheson made no reply. Greene Johnson would later say he left the courtroom believing he had months to prepare his case.

If he misread the exchange, it was something that didn't happen often. The forty-seven-year-old Johnson had a statewide reputation as a skilled trial attorney, particularly in murder cases. He had defended 154 clients charged with capital offenses, the press reported. Not one had hanged. In fact, in twenty-five straight years of lawyering, from his admission to the bar in 1895 until just the previous year, Johnson had never seen a white client spend a day on the chain gang or in the penitentiary.

Although he had passed his entire career in a rustic backwater, that kind of performance did not come cheap. That very same Monday, John S. Williams handed over his plantation to Johnson and his partner of seven years, Covington lawyer Charles Chester King. The planter had oftentimes put up his properties to secure debt—witness his loan from Doyle Campbell—but this was a full-on deed transfer, not a mortgage. He was relinquishing his land, and thus his livelihood, as payment "for the legal services to be rendered said party of the first, by parties of the second part," as the paperwork said. Those services were valued at five thousand dollars.

The transaction was complicated by a loan that Williams had taken out earlier in the month, when he hocked his river tracts to the First National Bank of Monticello for a little over six thousand dollars, or something like ninety-four thousand in today's money. Why he needed to raise cash at that point is unclear. He took out the loan eight days before the first bodies were found at Allen's Bridge, well before one might think he needed it.

That loan would have to be settled before Johnson and King could do anything with the land themselves. Regardless, as of that afternoon, Williams was no longer a wealthy planter, though the press would continue to label him as such.

He was no kind of planter at all.

On that same Easter Monday, the investigation was taking a weird and convoluted turn. Throughout the day, a rumor swept through Jasper and the surrounding counties that a Black uprising was afoot—that organized bands of African Americans planned to wipe out Jasper's white population in reprisal for the Murder Farm atrocities. Aiming to counter the threat, an army of heavily armed whites crowded into cars and drove in from Newton and Butts. What with the carloads of rubberneckers who likewise descended on Jasper, hoping for a glimpse of the crime scenes they had read about in the papers, the narrow roads to the Williams home place and river tracts were clotted with traffic.

Alerted to rumors of an uprising the night before, the authorities had grasped by sunup that talk of Black payback was just that. The only gathering of African Americans in the vicinity was discovered near the Waters Bridge, where a prayer meeting was underway on the lakeshore—a meeting, it developed, that had been encouraged by unidentified Jasper whites to fuel the rumors they themselves had started. The authorities were confident they knew who those whites were, and that the Williamses were involved in organizing what the press would label a hoax.

That term shortchanges what Hulon, LeRoy, and Marvin Williams were actually up to—engineering a complicated plot to pin the killings at Allen's Bridge (and by implication, at the sites of the other four drownings) on a gang of mysterious Black assailants, while at the same time igniting a race war to swing public opinion in their father's favor. The scope of the effort came into public focus the next day—Tuesday, March 29—when the Newton County grand jury took up the matter.

Called to testify was a young white farmer named Floyd Johnson, who said that nearly two weeks before, he had found a note addressed to him planted outside his house "between his plow stock and a bunch of honeysuckles." The note instructed him to falsely claim that he had been in Newton County one night in late February and had encountered several cars occupied by Black men stopped on Allen's Bridge. He was to say that three of the men drew pistols on him and led him "to one of the Ford cars, and that there was two dead niggers in the back seat all chained up, and as they stood there, the three men still held their pistols on him, and they dropped the niggers off the bridge into the river."

That's the way Floyd Johnson described the note's contents in a sworn statement he gave to the Newton County court clerk. One intriguing aspect of his account is that he said he discovered the note on Thursday, March 17—just a day after the third body, that of Foots, was pulled out of the South River at Mann's Bridge, and eight days before Clyde Manning fingered John S. Williams as a killer. Even at that early stage of the investigation, it seems, the Williamses were looking for ways to deflect attention from their father.

The note asked him to swear that after dumping the bodies, all of the men on the bridge climbed into their cars and pulled away, leaving him to flee the scene. "That was what was on the note," his statement read. "The note also said for me to meet [the note's senders] on next Thursday night, which was the 24th of March, [at Allen's Bridge] and bring the note with me. . . .

"I did go to the Allen Bridge at that time, and carried the note, and I saw a Chandler car and [Hulon] and Marvin Williams, and they asked me if I had the note. I said yes. They asked me to give it to them, and I did so, and they . . . said they would give me $500 if I would swear [to] what was in the note; and I asked them when would they give it to me."

This meeting would have occurred hours after Manning testified before the Newton County grand jury, and the very night of their father's arrest. The young man's testimony continued into even stranger territory. The brothers, he said, told him that the next day he was to sound the alarm that he'd seen and heard Black prowlers outside his house. He was to seek the help of a neighbor, J. T. Stubbs, and ask him for a ride to the Williams farm. There, in the presence of Mr. Stubbs, he was to tell Hulon and Marvin about the prowlers and about what he had supposedly seen on the bridge, "just like they didn't know nothing about it." From there, they apparently imagined, the plot would take on a life of its own. In exchange, the Williamses promised they would meet him back at Allen's Bridge on Sunday night—Sunday the twenty-seventh, which they had no way of knowing would be the day the last two of the eleven dead peons would be dragged from the Alcovy's bottom—and they would give him two hundred fifty dollars, with the balance coming "after [a] while."

Johnson did as he was told. The following night, he went to his neighbor's house "and got him to carry me to the Williams place," he said under oath. On finding no one home at Hulon's house, they drove on to John S. Williams's home place, where Hulon and Marvin waited with their mother. "And I told them this story just like they didn't know nothing about it," he said. "I went back with Mr. Stubbs to his home, and staid [sic] there all night."

Two days later, on Easter Sunday, Floyd Johnson told his older brother Walter what he had done. Walter hustled him into his car and drove him to Covington, where he related the whole business to lawmen. So when the rumors of an uprising sprang up, officials in Newton had a fair idea that they were related to this improbable scheme.

The Williams brothers had been industrious. In addition to soliciting Johnson's fantastic story, they had apparently planted other notes warning white farmers that Black marauders were on the way. One such note, the *New York Times* reported, was found by Newton County resident Will Cook on his front porch and advised him to "look out for the niggers." According to the *Atlanta Constitution*, investigators believed the notes to white farmers were to be amplified by "runners . . . dispatched in several directions, crying that the colored people were gathering to start a racial war." And if that wasn't enough to spark a counteroffensive, lawmen believed the Williams sons were prepared to stage raids on white homes and farms to solidify the impression that Blacks were on the rampage.

With Floyd Johnson's confession, the plot disintegrated before it had a chance to do damage. The grand jury accused the three Williams men of conspiring to foster white hostility for Newton's African American population and sympathy for their father, but leveled no formal charges against them.

The family countered the accusations with a trusted and admired source of its own: Gus Williams, the eldest of John S. Williams's twelve children—the war hero, now a physician living an hour's drive west of the plantation in Henry County. He declared to reporters that the allegations were "the latest attempt to arouse public sentiment here against us," and that the first inkling his brothers had about the plot and their supposed involvement "was when I told them the other night about rumors I had heard in Covington.

"The truth about the situation is this: [Floyd] Johnson came to my mother's house the day after father had been arrested and told of meeting a car filled with Negroes on the Allen Bridge over the Yellow River. He stated that he had seen two black bodies in the car and that the

Negroes had told him if he told anyone they would kill him. At the time they told him this, he said, they held their guns on him, and since he has been sleeping with his gun. He told my mother that he had decided to come voluntarily to her and tell of the occurrence, because he wanted to help my father.

"And now," Dr. Williams fumed, "they tell me he has confessed in Covington before the grand jury that it was all a 'frame-up.'" He insisted that his father had nothing to do with the murders.

While the Newton County grand jury picked through evidence of the race war conspiracy, Solicitor General Doyle Campbell visited Hugh Dorsey at the capitol to chart Jasper County's prosecution for the eight killings in its jurisdiction. Joining them: state Attorney General Denny, Assistant Attorney General Graham Wright, Special Agents Wismer and Chastain, and the head of the Bureau of Investigation's Atlanta office, Vincent Hughes.

The conference, which went on for hours, made plain that Dorsey was assuming command of the state's case against John S. Williams. He insisted that any federal peonage trial wait until after the state exhausted its efforts to convict the planter of murder. He decreed that Graham Wright would be sent to Jasper to assist in investigating the case there and presenting it to the county's grand jury, and that Wright and Campbell should seek indictments against the three Williams sons, as well as their father. He made clear that Williams and Manning should go to trial first in Newton County—and "at the earliest possible moment," as the *Macon News* put it.

That was no hyperbole. That afternoon, the governor wired Judge Park of the Ocmulgee Circuit to convene a special session of the Jasper Superior Court and seat a grand jury to consider indictments there on April 11. That signaled that he expected Clyde Manning, the chief witness against Williams, to be available in thirteen days—which is to say, he counted on the first Newton trial to be wrapped up by then. "The governor is acting in the murder farm case with very little actual legal authority," the newspaper observed. "Nevertheless, he feels that a duty of the highest moral sanction rests upon him, and that the people of the state are looking to him to leave no stone unturned to bring the guilty to judgment."

The *News* offered a neat summation of how he intended to see that through: "Governor Dorsey's idea is to have Williams tried first on one murder indictment. If there is a conviction and death sentence in that case, and if Attorney [Greene] Johnson, a very able and influential lawyer of Monticello, who represents him, makes a motion for a new trial and carries it up to the higher courts, it is the governor's idea to have Williams tried immediately on murder indictment No. 2, while the first appeal is pending. Then, to have him tried on murder indictment No. 3; to have him tried in Jasper County on as many murder indictments as the grand jury may see fit to return; and to keep on trying Williams ad [seriatim], so to speak, so that there will be the fullest possible prosecution of the charges against him."

That evening, Judge Hutcheson and Lonnie Brand pulled into Atlanta for their own conference with the governor. Meeting at the executive mansion, the trio went over the Newton County case in detail, Dorsey offering advice borne of his years as a prosecutor. Sever the cases, he again suggested, and tackle Williams first. After the meeting, Brand told reporters that he expected to be ready for trial within three weeks.

Judge Hutcheson apparently felt it shouldn't take nearly so long. The following day—Wednesday, March 30—the judge informed both Brand and Greene Johnson that John S. Williams would stand trial beginning the following Tuesday. The judge would not call a special term of the Newton County Superior Court, he added. Because this particular case was of such importance, he had decided instead to extend the present term by a week. He ordered the county staff to summon one hundred potential jurymen to the courthouse. The news must have come as a rude shock to Greene Johnson. Rather than months to prepare a defense, Williams's attorney had six days.

Within hours of the judge's announcement came a surprise raid on the Williams plantation. Worried that Hulon, LeRoy, and Marvin Williams still lived on the premises, and that they might pose a danger to potential witnesses there, U.S. Attorney Hooper Alexander obtained subpoenas for every Black person on the farm to be delivered to the Tower for safekeeping. Wasting no time, federal agents Wismer and Chastain and Newton's Sheriff Johnson left Covington in three automobiles, telling no one of their plans. They arrived at the Williams place late in the afternoon, expecting to find nineteen or more farmhands and cooks. When they canvassed the cottages, however, they found just two men and three women. A tour of the plantation's fields turned up no others. "A thorough search of all the surrounding territory was made for the missing negroes," the *Covington News* reported, "and it was finally decided that they had fled."

They brought the five back with them. Later, appearing before the Newton County grand jury, the workers were asked to partially disrobe to show the bruises and scars of their mistreatment. Gashes in their flesh, the souvenirs of repeated whippings, were deep, obvious, and unsettling to behold. When asked how they had received the injuries, the witnesses replied that they had been beaten by John S. Williams and his sons.

In New York, James Weldon Johnson and the NAACP were busily preparing for John S. Williams's trial, too. The Association prepared letters to its thirty largest branches in the North and West, calling on their memberships to demand a governmental war on peonage. "You have, of course, seen in the press the revelation of the horrible conditions under the peonage system in Jasper County, Georgia," Johnson wrote in one such letter, to the Los Angeles branch. "This is one of the most revolting stories that has [ever come] to light and makes the blood of every decent citizen boil with indignation. This condition is true throughout the south. If we act quickly we can force an exhaustive investigation of southern peonage states and the punishment of perpetrators of the system."

To that end, he called on each of the branches to plan "a monster meeting of protest" for April 10 "or during the week beginning on that date"—the first week the new Congress would be in session. Its purpose: "to arouse public sentiment to the point that aggressive action will be taken against the vicious evils of peonage!" He also asked that members deluge the president and attorney general with indignant telegrams. Johnson's similar letter to the Philadelphia branch ended: "Do not hesitate to serve notice that unless action is taken, colored voters and fair-minded white voters will remember those men in public office who refuse to do their utmost to make situations like those in Jasper County impossible."

Johnson also prepared to shotgun-spray American labor unions with requests that they pressure Washington to get serious about peonage. Who had more skin in erasing forced labor in America than its labor unions? At the same time, Walter White was writing to the Black members of seven state legislatures in the North, urging that they introduce resolutions calling on Justice officials to "institute a rigorous and exhaustive investigation of peonage" and hunt down its practitioners. "The Georgia horror has aroused nation-wide condemnation," he explained, "and we must strike while the iron is hot." Within days, lawmakers in New York, Ohio, Pennsylvania, and West Virginia replied that resolutions were in the works.

Newspaper reporters down in Jasper County, meanwhile, continued chasing down any and all details about the Williams family, life on the farm, and the killings themselves. Perhaps the most important new insight was that Judge Park's "reliable informants" had been correct when they told him that the three Williams sons were not directly implicated in the eleven murders. Hulon, LeRoy, and Marvin were out of the county at the time: John S. Williams had sent the trio on a purported land-buying trip to Texas within a few days of the federal agents' mid-February visit to the plantation. He didn't call them back until three weeks later, after Fletcher Smith's death ended the killing spree. "Business is picking up," his telegram to his sons read. "Come home."

In her first comments since her husband's arrest, Lucy Lane Williams told the *New York World* that John S. Williams was the finest man on the planet, and that she found it inconceivable that he could have done the things with which he was charged. The paper got a comment from Clyde Manning's wife, Rena, too. "If Mr. Williams told Clyde to do it," she said, "then Clyde done it."

Dr. Gus Williams, cementing his role as his family's propagandist, made a claim to the *Constitution* that he and others would repeat often in the coming days: that during their February visit to the plantation, the federal agents had told farmhands "they should be making more money and working only eight hours a day." Afterward, he said, his father "decided to let all those dissatisfied leave. He even gave the Negroes who owed him money enough funds to get them out of the county and cancelled their debts."

The doctor also branded reports that the farm's peons were crowded into a locked bunkhouse at night "damn lies." He said this while meeting with reporters at his father's house, from which several tenant cottages were visible in the fields. "You don't see any stockade around here, do you?" he asked, using a contemporary term for a jailhouse. "The Negroes were not made to sleep together in such a place, but stayed in these houses that you can see from here."

Had reporters inspected the river tracts, they would have come upon the little red building with its simple but effective locking system. A visit to one of the tenant houses within sight of the porch—the cottage in which Clyde Manning lived—would have turned up a similar arrangement. But in the rush to get news into print ahead of the competition, the journalists often took comments such as the doctor's at face value, and failed to seek corroborating sources. The press thus peppered its stories with unconfirmed, and often inaccurate, details. The *New York Times* told its readers that the body count thus far might be mere prelude to discoveries yet to come—that "more, even as many as forty" victims might lie in the area's rivers. That might well have been true, but it was sheer guesswork; officials had found no evidence to support such a number.

The *Savannah Morning News* was among several papers to suggest that John S. Williams had come to Jasper County twenty-seven years before when "his home and other buildings on his plantation in Monroe County were destroyed by fire," the implication being that he was "burned out" for mistreating his Black workers. Maybe that was true, and maybe it wasn't; we don't know, because the papers didn't chase the lead further.

The *New York Call* and a few other papers reported that when Williams was confronted by newsmen in the Tower, "tears streamed down the great lined face, and he screamed: 'Let me alone! Please leave me alone!' his eyes roving wildly." If true, that would have been a rare display for Williams; other newspapermen described him as seemingly unfazed, even carefree, about his situation.

And why not? He had lost his farm, and sitting in jail was no small inconvenience, but before long he would surely be free to rebuild. His alleged victims were Black, as was his accuser. The jury, drawn from rural Newton County, would be white as a matter of course, and most likely a good number of its members would be farmers like himself. Who were they going to believe?

15

THE NAACP HAD COME FAR SINCE THE ARMISTICE. In his first year as secretary, John R. Shillady sought to professionalize its business practices, and saw its revenues almost triple. Thanks to James Weldon Johnson's efforts in the field, the Association grew at a furious pace, from 9,282 members in 1917 to nearly 44,000 by the end of the following year. It would more than double that number in 1919.

Following both men's lead, the group waged an increasingly pitched battle with the Ku Klux Klan. After decades of dormancy, the so-called white knights had reawakened in 1915 and spread their pox through the South and Midwest. The NAACP also launched a campaign against one of the inspirations for the Klan's revival: D. W. Griffith's *The Birth of a Nation*, the first epic of American cinema, which glorified the Reconstruction-era KKK, demonized Black men as criminal brutes, and traded on the supposed prevalence of the "usual crime." The NAACP attacked the film as vicious slander—Shillady called it "an undisguised and unjust appeal to race prejudice"—and spurred its branches to organize successful protests and boycotts in several cities.

Shillady's most dramatic contribution came when he committed the Association to study lynching in a bid to fact-check the myriad myths and excuses enshrouding the practice. He dispatched two researchers to the Library of Congress to review newspaper reports of lynchings over the previous three decades. "The facts are well known to students of public affairs," he wrote in the foreword of the resulting booklet—*Thirty Years of Lynching in the United States, 1889–1918.* "It is high time that they became the common property, since they are the common shame, of all Americans."

Over the thirty years, at least 3,224 people had died at the hands of lynch mobs, the study showed. African Americans accounted for more than three out of every four victims; in Georgia, they made up 93.3 percent of the total. The report served up real news when it focused on the alleged offenses prompting the killings. Of Black victims, just 19 percent were charged with or suspected of rape—the "usual crime," in fact, was not so usual after all—and another 9.4 percent were lynched for lesser "attacks upon women." Those numbers did not necessarily mean what they suggested, the text advised, because "in a number of cases where Negroes have been lynched for rape and 'attacks upon white women,' the alleged attacks rest upon no stronger evidence than 'entering the room of a woman' or brushing against her." Furthermore, lynchings for assaults on women, sexual and otherwise, had declined over the thirty years. Lumped together, they now accounted for fewer than one in five cases, nationwide. The age-old excuse that mobs murdered in defense of chaste white womanhood was a lie.

The NAACP spread the news far and wide, while the bulk of its work unfolded with far less public notice. It supplied money, lawyers, and expertise to Black victims of false arrest, segregation, "Jim Crow" seating on public transportation, civil service disputes, and obstacles to voting. It lobbied for equal access to theaters, restaurants, and public accommodations. Shillady, Johnson, and Walter White testified before Congress about the KKK and about reducing the congressional representation of states that blocked Black voting. The Association labored in the back rooms of Congress and numerous statehouses to block retrograde legislation, including measures to bar intermarriage. It campaigned against political candidates it considered hostile.

Nowadays, we tend to think of the civil rights movement as a product of the 1950s and 1960s. In truth, the NAACP was waging a bare-knuckles campaign for African American rights years before Martin

Luther King Jr. was born—a radical campaign, by the standards of the day, and one in which its officers faced the risk of death whenever they ventured into those parts of the country that needed them most. As dangerous as the later movement was to its leaders, it came nowhere near the deadly risks of racial activism in the teens and 1920s. Back then, a trip into rural Georgia or Alabama thrust an Association operative beyond contact with the outside, civilized world—minus ready telephone access, lacking the protection later afforded by state police and the FBI, and without the moderating presence of a national news media poised to beam images of southern lawlessness into living rooms from coast to coast. Life or death might depend on the whims of a local sheriff, who, all too often, looked the other way during lynchings—if he wasn't, in fact, party to mob violence himself. The NAACP's leadership took on its assignments with clear eyes and astounding courage, just the same.

"People used to say in those years gone by, 'I do not like to read *The Crisis*, it depresses me; it makes me sick,'" Johnson recalled in a speech a few years later. "That was exactly our aim. We meant to make America sick of its sin, and so we put up to the American people the raw, naked, ugly, brutal facts. We attempted to hold the mirror of America as it was before the nation's eyes that it might see itself a sinner among the nations of the world.

"And so we agitated, and held public meetings, and called conferences, and sent investigators into the South, and learned the actual facts about the individual cases of lynching. And so gradually, year after year, we worked on public opinion, awakening it, quickening it, until there was some perceptible effect."

That campaign grew ever more restless, ever more brazen, as American troops returned from Europe. Among their number were tens of thousands of Black soldiers who "over there" had enjoyed a degree of social and political acceptance that was utterly new to them, and who came home with newfound understanding of how their lives in the United States ought to be. Back on U.S. soil, those soldiers found themselves targeted for violence because they had dared wear the uniform of their country. Du Bois captured the moment in a *Crisis* essay, "Returning Soldiers," that appeared in the April 1919 issue. It opened with a long recitation of America's racial abuses and concluded:

> Under similar circumstances, we would fight again. But by the God of Heaven, we are cowards and jackasses if now that that war is over, we do not marshal every ounce of our brain and brawn to fight a sterner, longer, more unbending battle against the forces of hell in our own land.
> *We return.*
> *We return from fighting.*
> *We return fighting.*
> Make way for Democracy! We saved it in France, and by the Great Jehovah, we will save it in the United States of America, or know the reason why.

All the while, as the NAACP campaigned, the Great Migration continued to drain the South of its agricultural workers. By some estimates, 10 percent of the South's Black population fled the region between 1910 and 1920, with the peak coming during the war. The effects of this exodus on the southern economy were already critical by the Armistice. In combination with the falling price of cotton and the arrival of the boll weevil, the loss of cheap labor threatened to bleed away the region's primary source of income. With increasing frequency, the Association received reports of Black workers prevented from leaving southern farms. Local laws threatened arrest to those who made a run for it, and individual farmers devised schemes to keep their cotton pickers put. From their perspective, debt servitude worked like a charm.

Black migration had no less dramatic an impact on the northern cities that absorbed it. Chicago's African American headcount more than doubled, from 44,103 in 1910 to more than 109,000 a decade later; Detroit's multiplied seven times over. These and other cities strained to house and employ the arrivals. With the postwar homecoming of thousands of blue-collar white workers, competition for jobs became heated.

So tensions mounted between the races, in the South because Blacks were leaving, and in the North because they were showing up. The stresses exploded in the summer of 1919, when a series of white-on-Black race riots tore through cities of the Midwest and Mid-Atlantic, as well as the South. "The colored people throughout the country were disheartened and dismayed," Johnson later wrote. "The great majority had trustingly felt that, because they had cheerfully done their bit in the war, conditions for them would be better. The reverse seemed to be true." Johnson coined a name for this outbreak of violence, by which it is still known today: the Red Summer.

In early May, three African Americans were killed and eighteen wounded in Charleston, South Carolina, in a riot touched off by whites. Two months later in Longview, Texas, marauding whites attacked several Blacks and set fire to part of the town's Black neighborhood, prompting intervention by the Texas National Guard. A few days after that, on July 19, rumors that a Black man had been collared for the rape of a white woman touched off a white rampage in Washington, D.C., that lasted four days and saw members of the military join in the violence. Even while that disturbance was unfolding, a celebration for returning Black troops was marred by a bloody fray in Norfolk, Virginia.

At July's end, the biggest riot of the summer engulfed Chicago, after a Black child swam into a stretch of beach traditionally reserved for whites and was stoned to death for his mistake. For nearly two weeks, fighting and fires raged on the city's South Side. Dozens died, and a thousand African American homes were reduced to ash.

Then, in Omaha, Nebraska, the reported rape of a white woman led thousands of local whites—already aggrieved by an influx of Black southerners to the city, and whipped into a bloodlust by race-baiting newspaper stories—to surround the courthouse where a Black suspect was in custody. When police refused to hand him over, the mob went berserk, storming the building, setting it ablaze, clubbing police with bats, even hanging the mayor from a trolley pole; he was close to death when he was cut down by rescuers. The suspect, Will Brown, was eventually seized by the rioters and shot to death; his body was burned and dragged through the streets. It took an army occupation to restore order.

As alarming as these eruptions were, the riot that most captured the NAACP's attention took place in the cotton country of Phillips County, Arkansas, along the Mississippi River in the state's southeast. There, Black sharecroppers had seen their earnings unchanged despite a leap in the price of cotton. They unionized and hired a white lawyer in a first step toward forcing financial transparency from their landlords. On the night of September 30, about one hundred of them were meeting at a small church when a pair of white deputies and a Black trusty showed up outside.

Some of the Black farmers inside were armed. Shots were exchanged. Who fired first was never pinned down, but one of the deputies died and the other was wounded. When news of the shooting reached whites in the nearby town of Elaine, they declared open season on the county's African Americans. Hunting parties gunned down scores of men, women, and children. They chased fleeing Blacks through forests and swamps, shot them in their houses, killed them in the cotton fields. White men streamed into Phillips from surrounding counties to join the blooding. The governor eventually called on federal troops to restore order. They did some gunning, too, and arrested hundreds of Black people who had, to that point, eluded death.

Estimates of the African American toll ranged to well over two hundred—an accurate count was complicated by the county's scattered settlement. Even before the shooting stopped, white officialdom had concocted a tried-and-true explanation for the violence: the Black farmers had been part of an armed insurrection aimed at wiping out the county's white landowners and taking their farms.

In swooped Walter White, bearing credentials as a reporter for a Chicago newspaper. He found that the massacre was really a cover for what amounted to peonage. The sharecroppers in Phillips County, like those throughout the South, had been kept in a state of debt servitude through creative accounting and outright thievery. The new union threatened to unmask the racket.

White's exposé did not provide much solace to the Black victims. Of those arrested, seventy-nine were charged with murder and insurrection. Twelve were sentenced to die in the electric chair by juries that took minutes to decide their fates, in courtrooms packed with armed white hordes. Another sixty-seven defendants were given long prison terms. The NAACP launched a vigorous, four-year campaign for justice in Phillips County. The fight reached the U.S. Supreme Court, which ruled that the sharecroppers had been denied due process, because their trials were influenced by the presence of threatening mobs—a reversal of its decision not to intervene in the Frank case. All of the prisoners won release.

His time in Elaine, White would later say, brought one of his closest brushes with disaster. While walking to an interview with the sheriff and some of the arrested farmers, he was intercepted by a local Black man, who warned him that he had been found out and would be ambushed at the jail. White snuck his way to the railroad tracks and aboard one of the two daily trains leaving town. As he bought a ticket from the conductor, the man objected that he was leaving Elaine "just when the fun is going to start."

"What kind of fun?" White asked.

"There's a damned yellow nigger down here passing for white," the conductor said, "and the boys are going to get him."

"What'll they do with him?"

"When they get through with him," the man replied, "he won't pass for white no more."

The Red Summer claimed one victim especially close to home. In August 1919, officers of the NAACP's branch in Austin were hauled into court to answer charges that the Association was doing business in Texas without a state license or charter. The move appeared to forecast an attempt to shut down all of the state's thirty-one branches, comprising more than seven thousand members. If it succeeded, the same would surely happen throughout the South. Shillady hurried to Austin to offer state officials a primer on the group's activities.

On arriving, he found that neither the governor nor the attorney general was available to meet with him. But in a conference with underlings at the AG's office, he was told that the state's interest in the Association had been set off by that same old bogeyman—white reports that Black locals were stockpiling rifles and ammunition for a planned uprising. Shillady patiently assured his hosts that the NAACP opposed such action and would boot any member or branch attempting it. As he was leaving, he was served with a subpoena and hauled before a "court of inquiry," an openly hostile star chamber convened to determine what he was doing in town. Shillady maintained his poise in the face of such questions as "If you're a nigger lover, why don't you go and stay in a nigger hotel?" The inquisition dragged on for hours.

The next day, while on his way to a meeting with an officer of the Austin branch, he noticed he was being followed. Still, there was little hint of what was to come: Shillady was returning to his hotel in the bright light of midmorning when he was jumped on a downtown sidewalk by six to eight men, including a county judge and a local constable. They beat him senseless. The judge, who injured his fists in the attack, later said the group had "evidence" the secretary was stirring up trouble among Austin's Black population, and decided "to give him a good thrashing on general principles."

Shocked and battered, Shillady fled the city. When word of the assault reached the national office, board chair Mary White Ovington telegrammed the Travis County sheriff and Texas governor William P. Hobby, asking what they were doing to bring the offenders to justice. A deputy sheriff replied that Shillady had been "received by red blooded white men," and as they "did not need any of his kind (negro-loving white men) we have sent him back home to you."

Hobby's response was even more outrageous. "Shillady was the only offender in connection with the matter referred to in your telegram, and he was punished before your inquiry came," the governor wrote. "Your organization can contribute more to the advancement of both races by keeping your representatives and their propaganda out of this state, than in any other way." In a speech he gave a few days later, Hobby declared that he believed "in sending any narrow-brained, double-chinned reformer who comes here with the end in view of stirring up racial discontent back to the north where he came from, with a broken jaw if necessary."

One of Houston's two airports is named for this man.

"What democracy, what respect for law and order, what common decency can be left in Texas when officials of the state, from the governor on down, have no regard for the one or the other?" James Weldon Johnson wrote of the attack. "Of course, the white people of Austin and every other Southern community are trembling in their shoes over the fear of Negro uprisings. And why shouldn't they tremble? God knows, if I were a Southern white man with anything resembling a conscience I would not be able to sleep at night, knowing the injustice which I and my race had done the Negro.

"But the white people of Austin and other Southern communities are not going to be able to still those fears by beating up either white men or black men who are taking a stand for fair play and justice. If anything, such actions will only hasten the very thing of which they fear."

Johnson met Shillady's train at Penn Station. "His face and body were badly bruised; moreover, he was broken in spirit," he later recalled. "I don't think he was ever able to realize how such a thing could happen in the United States to an American, free, white, and twenty-one. He never fully recovered spiritually from the experience."

To Walter White, Shillady seemed a shadow of himself: His "deterioration which followed from the crushing blows on his head was pitiful to watch. His great gaiety and warm smile disappeared. The superb efficiency which had been his was replaced by an indecisiveness as though he were paralyzed."

While the NAACP explored taking the attackers to court and the governor's misdeeds to Congress, Shillady spiraled in mind and body. That November he was given a paid leave of absence to recuperate, but his health continued to slip until he resigned in the summer of 1920. Johnson was named acting secretary while the Association searched for a new leader. Months passed, during which it became clear that although Johnson had done more to nurture the NAACP into a truly national organization than any other officer, and had amply demonstrated his toughness, intelligence, and competence in four years as field secretary, the board hesitated to install a Black man as the executive of an organization dedicated to Black advancement.

Not until November 1920, amid growing discontent in the branches, did the board appoint Johnson to the post. He introduced himself to readers of *The Crisis* in January 1921, the same month federal agents in Atlanta became acquainted with John S. Williams. "I enter upon my new work as secretary with a full realization of the importance of the task before me," he wrote. "There is no greater cause than ours—it is a fight for the rights which belong to all free men. For eleven years we have been building the efficient machine for sustained and organized effort; with loyalty, steadfast courage and unity the goal before us will be achieved."

Hugh Dorsey, meanwhile, continued to mystify his observers at the NAACP. During his second inaugural address in June 1919, he again advocated "taking immediate steps to suppress mob rule in Georgia." And when southern governors met in conference in Savannah the following January, he sent telegrams inviting prominent Black Georgians to attend the session to discuss race relations. All but powerless to address racial violence in the state's rural backcountry, he regularly prodded its sheriffs for accountings of their efforts to prevent it.

Was Dorsey a friend to African Americans, or not? In person, as Walter White had found, he came across as sincere in his hopes for racial harmony and fairness. In his public pronouncements, he sounded practical, if not full-on progressive. But in his correspondence, as Shillady had discovered, he was often an apologist for the status quo.

It's possible that Dorsey remained as uncertain of his feelings and beliefs as he looked. Robert W. Thurston, a historian who has deeply explored the governor's life and career, believes he was wrestling with a conversion experience—that Mary Turner's death continued to haunt him, that it gnawed at his understanding of "civilization," that it shook his lifelong faith in white superiority. That, unseen by the public and over the length of his second term, Dorsey was making a steady turn toward enlightenment.

If so, it was a metamorphosis he planned to continue in private. The state constitution allowed an incumbent governor to seek reelection just once. A two-time winner had to wait four years, or two election cycles, before he was eligible for a third term. Dorsey made no secret of his desire to return to his legal practice, and a life out of the public eye, when his stint as governor ended.

But another political opportunity presented itself. In the summer of 1920, Georgia's upcoming race for the U.S. Senate had attracted two well-established Democratic candidates, both unacceptable to many party regulars. The incumbent, Hoke Smith, a former governor who had overseen the disfranchisement of the state's Black voters in 1907, had been out of step with his Democratic colleagues at critical points over the past year. Even more vexing was his announced opponent, Tom Watson.

The former kingmaker had broken with Dorsey shortly after the governor's first election. In the years since, he had fallen on hard times. Federal postal officials barred his *Jeffersonian* from the mails as seditious and obscene, forcing Watson to suspend its operation in 1917; Dorsey's reelection would have been an iffy proposition otherwise. Then, in quick succession, Watson's two adult children died. He turned to drugs and drink and descended into an unglued despondency. Party leaders were not worried about losing the Senate seat to a Republican; rather, they were troubled by the notion that the wrong Democrat was sure to win.

Unless, that is, voters had a third option. Prominent Democrats leaned on the governor to declare his candidacy. Seeking wider advice, Dorsey convened more than one hundred friends and political allies at the governor's mansion for a debate on the idea. The attendees voted 3–1 that he should enter the race. Later that day, he announced that he would.

Hoke Smith called Dorsey's entrance a "flank attack," and worried that "while he cannot hope to be elected himself, he can seriously help Watson in the fight with me." Watson wasn't thrilled with the new competition, either. "I have constructed many things in my life, and some of them I am proud of; but in the construction of Hugh Dorsey as governor of this state, I did a thing of which I am thoroughly ashamed," he said late in the campaign. "The man is full of perfidy; he bulges with ingratitude; in his veins there lurks the poison of a [water] moccasin."

Stumping across the state before spirited crowds, with the *Constitution* reporting that he was riding a massive wave of popular support, Dorsey came to think he had the race won. "I say to you," he told an Atlanta audience, "that I am just as certain to be commissioned to represent the Empire State of the South in the upper house of the next Congress as the sun is to rise after primary day."

He was mistaken. Tom Watson, reduced though he was, shellacked the field. Dorsey placed a distant second.

He was now officially a lame duck. With nothing to lose, politically speaking, he was free to follow his conscience for his remaining seven months in office—and, though few knew it, his conscience had shifted considerably in the years since Mary Turner's death. At the same time, he received almost daily reminders that Georgia had yet to experience a similar change of heart. One came in mid-January 1921, when a report reached his office that the Ku Klux Klan was attempting to force Black people from their farms in several Georgia counties. In the Rock Bridge District of Gwinnett County, northeast of Atlanta, armed Klan members had visited several Black farmers in the dead of night to order them out of the area. Dorsey responded by wiring the county's sheriff. "This is an outrage," he wrote, "and I beg that you will go into this district this afternoon and tonight with ample force not only to protect these negroes, but for the purpose of making such a display as will deter these worthless white people from continuing their campaign of terror."

The sheriff replied a few days later. "Pursuant to your telegram, I have gone to the place directed by you and have made an investigation of the trouble credited to the Ku Klux Klan," his letter read, "and I find it is the general belief that it is not the Ku Klux Klan, but some lawless element in the community there causing the trouble. As best I can find out, the Ku Klux Klan is also conducting an investigation for the purpose of ascertaining who the parties are in order that the law may be vindicated." The letterhead paper on which the sheriff's words appeared included the seal of the KKK and the endorsement of its Cameron Klan.

That same month, agents Wismer and Brown walked into the governor's office with news out of Newton and Jasper Counties.

16

COME THURSDAY, MARCH 31, 1921, Hugh Dorsey was still pondering how he might boost the prosecution's firepower in the courtroom. With just five days to go before the first trial opened, he decided that his idea to appoint a special prosecutor to help Lonnie Brand was a good one. And while he could not hire such a prosecutor himself—that is, pay the lawyer's fee from the state's coffers—he could ask private citizens to cover the cost.

When reporters caught wind of this plan, both the governor and Brand denied that they were up to any such thing. It soon came out, however, that in addition to having Assistant Attorney General Graham Wright on the prosecution's team, Dorsey had negotiated with attorney William M. Howard of Augusta to help out. Howard's was a well-known name throughout the state: He had served seven terms in Congress, from 1897 to 1911, gaining a reputation for oratory and legislative finesse, until a candidate backed by Tom Watson beat him in the 1910 Democratic primary.

On Howard's departure from Congress, President William Howard Taft had appointed him to the U.S. Tariff Board, calling him "very able, level-headed, and judiciously minded." He'd also been a regent of the Smithsonian Institution and a founding trustee of the Carnegie Endowment for International Peace, one of the world's foremost think tanks. He had spent the last eight years in private practice in Augusta. In short, at sixty-three, Howard was a formidable addition to the team—"a man with no superior in the profession," the *Savannah Morning News* trumpeted, "for presentation of a case to the jury and an analysis of testimony."

He and Dorsey had a past, too. Six years before, Howard had represented Leo Frank in the appeal of his death sentence. When Governor

John Slaton heard arguments on whether he should spare Frank from the gallows, it had been Howard arguing for, and Hugh Dorsey against. Howard charged that Frank was the victim of police incompetence and prosecutorial mistakes, if not misconduct. The case against him reeked of doubt. Jim Conley was surely the real killer of Mary Phagan.

Evidently, he was convincing.

At one point during that June 1915 hearing in the governor's office, Dorsey had been in mid-argument when Slaton interrupted him to permit a local pastor to present a petition urging mercy for the defendant. The pastor was Cary B. Wilmer—the same Episcopal minister who, with Rev. M. Ashby Jones, would later occupy prominent slots in the Commission on Interracial Cooperation, and who would advise Dorsey on how to prosecute the Williams case. What's more, it was the reverends Wilmer and Jones to whom Dorsey turned to raise William Howard's fee as special prosecutor. In his scramble to ensure that justice prevailed in the Williams trial, Dorsey now sought help from his opponents in the case that made him governor.

When he announced Howard's appointment to the state's team, Dorsey noted that the arrangement had to be agreeable to Lonnie Brand. The solicitor general's own remarks to the press suggested that was a given. "My interest in the case is only that of an official of the state, but owing to the unusual circumstances surrounding the charges against Williams, I felt that additional counsel should be employed to assist me at the trial," Brand said. "I therefore asked Governor Dorsey to designate Assistant Attorney General Graham Wright, and told him, after the subject had been suggested to me, that I would welcome any further assistance he might care to provide."

Dorsey's intervention did not stop there. He had come to view Clyde Manning's situation as especially vulnerable. Here was the state's chief witness and, presumably, a defendant as well, with no one guarding his interests in either role. The governor urged that Manning be given extra protection in the Tower. He also wired Sheriff Johnson that he understood that Manning's mother, India, remained on the Williams farm and was "scared to death," and asked that she be brought to the Tower for protection. The request came just in time for another sweep of the plantation by federal agents still on the lookout for potential witnesses. They returned to Atlanta with several, India Manning included.

Most memorably, Dorsey called together several well-heeled private citizens to ask that they underwrite Clyde Manning's legal representation. Prominent among them was W. Woods White, an Atlanta insurance executive, philanthropist, and a living rebuttal to the notion that the white South was a monolith of racist crackers. He was a devout Presbyterian known as a friend and benefactor to ex-convicts, a principal in the international YMCA, and a key organizer of the Y's first Atlanta branch for African Americans. With White leading the way, the group agreed to put up the money for Manning's defense, "feeling especially under the peculiar facts of the case that the interests of justice demand that [he] have the benefit of competent counsel," as he said when he announced the arrangement. The group invited like-minded Georgians to help shoulder the cost.

That load was bound to be considerable, because White and company retained a heavy hitter for the job—Atlanta's E. Marvin Underwood, a former assistant attorney general of the United States, past general counsel for the U.S. Railroad Commission, and once a partner in the city's largest and most prestigious law firm. He was destined for a federal judgeship later in his career.

Clyde Manning, little more than a slave for all of his twenty-six years, illiterate and penniless, ignorant of the world beyond a few roads and farms in western Jasper County, would be represented by one of the best lawyers in the country.

In the last few days before trial, both sides hunkered down to fine-tune their cases. Federal agents grilled Manning in the Tower, going over every detail of the killings. Greene Johnson held a lengthy jailhouse session with Williams. He also filed a motion for a change of venue, to move the trial from Newton County—and almost immediately withdrew it, saying he felt sure that an impartial jury could be empaneled and that his client would be safe standing trial there. On Sunday, April 3, he toured the plantation to see for himself, for the first time, where the crimes allegedly occurred.

The *Constitution* offered its best guess on how the defense would proceed. Johnson would "seek to prove that Manning's confession, involving the planter in the murders, has not been substantiated." Further, when the bodies were pulled from the Yellow River, "no money was found in their pockets, and it is plausible that the defense may attempt to prove that the negroes came to their death at the hands of a gang of blacks. The motive advanced would be robbery." Williams's four oldest sons and the owners of neighboring farms would take the stand on his behalf, reporter Marion Kendrick wrote, while word in the courthouse was "that the defense has several mystery witnesses, who will be introduced near the close of the trial."

When asked directly, Johnson declined to map out his strategy, "except to say that in general we will enter a complete denial of Manning's charges." He could say no more, he explained, because he knew "nothing of the state's case except what I have been able to gather from the newspapers and current reports." A lawyer "cannot tell what course he will adopt until he hears the evidence of the other side. We may work out in advance a general idea of how we will proceed, but we frequently change the line of procedure in the midst of the trial of a case." From there, Johnson veered into a justified complaint about how little time he had to organize his defense. "It is very doubtful whether we will be ready for trial next week," he said. "It is no light matter to prepare for trial of a case of this character, with so many possible ramifications.

"I have been engaged in Newton Superior Court practically every day since Williams was indicted, and have not had the opportunity to examine any witnesses for the defense, nor even to go fully into the case with my client." He'd just been excused from his regular court duties, he added, and expected to spend every remaining minute preparing for the battle ahead.

He made these remarks at about the time the newspapers were uncovering the first slim details of earlier deaths on the plantation—of Blackstrap, Iron Jaw, and possibly another peon, as well. The *Constitution's* Kendrick reported that when the Jasper County grand jury convened on April 11, Solicitor General Doyle Campbell would have enough evidence to charge Hulon, LeRoy, and Marvin Williams with these older murders—evidence placed in his hands by Hugh Dorsey, who had received it from the federal agents. If the three men were arrested in Jasper before or during the Newton County trial, Johnson said, he would appeal to Judge Park "to obtain their release as witnesses in Covington."

Lonnie Brand, meanwhile, spent the eve of the trial at the Piedmont Hotel in Atlanta, in conference with Assistant Attorney General Graham Wright and William Howard, detailing the evidence and figuring out how best to present it. He had a lot less to say than Johnson about the coming fight. "Not only have the physical facts of the case against Williams been corroborated," he told reporters, but his prosecution would not rest solely on Clyde Manning's testimony.

"All of our evidence," he said, "will be substantiated by the testimony and affidavits of white people."

The same day—Monday, April 4—James Weldon Johnson went to the White House to visit the new Republican president, Warren G. Harding. He had met with candidate Harding at the former senator's Ohio home before the election, and with President-elect Harding shortly before his inauguration. In those sessions, Johnson had explained the work of the NAACP to a man who, in his estimation, knew "absolutely nothing about the race question," and came across as a "rather timid politician" and "a man of very little imagination and seemingly of very little human sympathy," to boot.

Harding had expressed support for virtually all of the Association's positions, but balked at making them his own. Still, as president he was game to keep a conversation going. So Johnson again sat down with him to discuss the beleaguered state of Black America, and how Harding might enact measures to relieve the situation. He handed the president a memorandum that reiterated his points. It opened:

> The National Association for the Advancement of Colored People earnestly requests the President to include in his message to Congress, convening April 11, a recommendation that it take action to end lynching, the most terrible blot on American civilization.
>
> It earnestly urges that a wide and thorough investigation of peonage conditions be made by the Department of Justice. The recent disclosures in Jasper County, Georgia, reveal conditions that are unspeakable, but the Jasper County conditions are not isolated. There are similar conditions in nearly every southern state, especially in the Mississippi Delta region. The Federal government has full power to investigate, punish and abolish peonage.

Johnson's lobbying bore fruit. Harding did, in fact, condemn mob violence in his first address to Congress a week later, telling its members they "ought to wipe the stain of lynching from the banners of a free and orderly representative democracy." What's more, six months later he delivered a second speech advocating expanded civil rights for Black Americans—in Birmingham, Alabama, no less.

As for a Justice probe into peonage, well, that was already well in hand, at least in Georgia—and even as Johnson met with the president, he and the NAACP's other leaders suspected that they themselves might have set the investigation into motion. The previous fall, the Association's national staff had amassed leads on numerous cases of alleged peonage in the South. On October 2, 1920, Walter White had traveled to Washington to meet with Assistant Attorney General William C. Herron. They talked for two hours, during which White pled the case of the imprisoned sharecroppers from Phillips County, Arkansas, which naturally raised the subject of debt slavery. As White remembered the conversation later, he "demanded an investigation ... and the punishment of those persons who were practicing peonage," and presented Herron with the Association's collected notes on the subject.

Herron, looking over White's paperwork, told him that one of the leads looked promising—a peonage allegation out of Zebulon, Georgia, to the southwest of Jasper County. He told White he would order the U.S. attorney for the Northern District of Georgia—Hooper Alexander, in Atlanta—to open an investigation into the case. He also asked that the NAACP pass along additional peonage tips as it found them.

In January 1921, Alexander announced that a federal grand jury had indicted three men on peonage charges in Henry County, and that he was opening a statewide investigation into the crime. "Comparatively little effort is being made by proper officers to end those conditions," he said, hinting that collusion between criminal farmers and local law enforcement was afoot. "Ninety percent of our people would utterly deplore and condemn what is going on, but something more is demanded of a civilized people and their government than mere sentiment." Agents Wismer and Brown worked under Alexander, of course. The federal prosecutor made those comments at about the time the Bureau of Investigation was hearing the first about John S. Williams.

From all indications, the Williams farm was not mentioned in the leads supplied by White. Yet the timing seemed more than coincidence to the Association. It was well within reason that instructions from Washington to look into the Zebulon case, or others, elevated peonage as a priority in Alexander's office and, by turn, among the Bureau's Atlanta agents. In a March 28 telegram to NAACP board chair Mary White Ovington, Johnson wrote: "Have reasons to believe present investigations Jasper County due to matter presented to Department of Justice by Association. . . ."

White was especially keen to understand the genesis of the Bureau's interest in Williams. On March 29, he wrote to Herron to ask whether he could be "good enough to advise me if there is any connection between the facts which we presented . . . on peonage conditions in Georgia with the later statement by Hooper Alexander of Georgia and the investigation and prosecution of Jasper county, Georgia peonage cases." He also asked a lawyer friend in Washington to back-channel the same question to the assistant attorney general. The DOJ declined to answer. Herron's office replied that "a number" of the cases the Association had brought to its attention had been "carefully investigated by the Bureau of Investigation, but owing to the confidential nature of the work, you [cannot] be informed as to the name of the cases, or the action taken, at this time."

White nonetheless came to feel confident that the case had started with him, and the Association would go on to issue a press release strongly hinting just that. The NAACP could claim additional influence in the Williams affair, too: Members of the Atlanta branch passed along word that either Gus Chapman or James Strickland had sought their help while on the run back in January. The members did not specify which fugitive peon they spoke with, referring to him simply as "the man who furnished the material on which the investigation was begun," but said they had steered him to Hooper Alexander, who presumably handed him off to the Bureau of Investigation. The bottom line, the Association believed, was that its everyday, behind-the-scenes work to combat peonage was yielding dividends.

Inevitably, Johnson's visit with the president raised hackles in Georgia. The *Cordele Dispatch* complained that Harding had been "closeted in the White House with a New York negro who had come to demand that peonage in Georgia be investigated." It continued: "If the white people of Georgia have to be arraigned and made to do their duty towards their negro population by a New York gentleman of color who stirs the new republican president into action with his reports of a down trodden, persecuted and butchered negro race in Georgia, then we have come to a poor state of affairs."

Standard cracker fare, to that point. Not for long. "This is wholly an affair for Georgia and Georgians," the editorial concluded, "not the business of a New York negro who wants to find out what it means to swing all night by the road side from a tree limb—and who is encouraging that sort of racial relations by his conference with the president."

Johnson caught wind of the editorial not long after its appearance. "These are not the words of a rational human being but the bellowings of a mad animal," he wrote in his *Age* column. "Every peanut-brained southern bully suffers under the hallucination that the race problem can be settled by swinging somebody from the limb of a tree.

"Even if the 'best' white citizens of Cordele did swing me from the limb of a tree," he declared, "they would not settle it; they would find the race problem just as troublesome the next day as it was before."

PART THREE

The Majesty of the Law

17

THE FIRST TUESDAY IN APRIL dawned sunny and fair in Covington, so much so that, by shortly before nine, it felt more like summer than early spring, especially to the reporters down from New York to cover what was expected to be the first of many trials of John S. Williams. On the town square, several hundred farmers and local tradesmen clad in overalls and shirtsleeves clustered around the requisite Johnny Reb monument, discussing their neighbor's behavior and the price he might pay for it. A spotted dog sunbathed on the pavement in front of the Newton County Courthouse, a handsome Second Empire structure dominated by a soaring, domed clock tower—an outsize building for so modest a place, and the focus of much local pride. Parked automobiles choked the streets framing the grassy square and lined curbs in the surrounding neighborhoods. Stores and cafés bustled. The town's two hotels were booked solid.

In Judge Hutcheson's second-floor courtroom, some three hundred whites filled every chair, aisle, and windowsill on the main level an hour before court was to begin; about two hundred Black spectators crowded into the much smaller gallery, the segregated balcony at the room's rear. Hugh Dorsey had worried in recent days about the safety of Clyde Manning and other Black witnesses, and had signaled his intention to call in the national guard, if need be, to maintain order. Judge Hutcheson had deemed military force unnecessary, choosing instead to rely on a squad of newly sworn deputies. They were enough. "From the beginning," noted the *Covington News*, "the remarkable feature was the orderliness of the spectators."

Up in Atlanta, Sheriff Johnson and a deputy escorted Williams onto an early-morning train. The party's route and travel times had been shared with few; even so, as they rolled southeast through a succession of small country towns, crowds of Black men, women, and children appeared alongside the tracks, straining for a glimpse of evil. "Just throw me out among them," Williams reportedly half joked, half boasted to his chaperones, "and you'll see them scatter."

When the train arrived at Covington, the three transferred to a waiting car for the short ride to the courthouse. The throng on the sidewalk was so dense that deputies had to elbow a path to the front doors. All fell quiet as Williams passed through. He paused to speak to several friends, and, according to the *Constitution*, "appeared unconcerned over the fact that he was entering the court to watch his attorneys battle for his life." As he climbed the stairs inside, he told other acquaintances: "I'll come clear. Don't you worry."

Packed as the courtroom was, it took a while for everyone to realize that Williams had squeezed his way to a seat up front. He spent a few minutes speaking in whispers with Greene Johnson, interrupting himself now and then to greet an approaching friend, before his wife, Lucy, arrived with two of their daughters, her uncle, and two of her brothers. Williams stood and embraced her for a long moment. Dr. Gus Williams followed her in, shook his father's hand, and took a seat beside him. Notable for their absence: Gus's brothers Hulon, LeRoy, and Marvin. "Williams stroked his chin and at times played with his dark brown mustache," the *Constitution* reported, "his eyes remaining fixed for many minutes on the ceiling of the room." Now and then he shifted his gaze to the Black faces in the gallery.

Judge Hutcheson assumed the bench. At sixty, he was two years into his tenure as a Superior Court judge, after an interesting and varied past: newspaper editor in his small hometown, Jonesboro, south of Atlanta; the town's two-term mayor; its longtime prosecutor; and lawyer in private practice. Thin, with a long face and prominent brow, Hutcheson could seem a dandy—he favored old-fashioned, high and stiff shirt collars, and wore his longish hair parted close to center—but on the bench was the picture of common sense and directness. He was widely admired for his keen legal mind.

Quickly settled, the judge explained that one hundred potential jurymen were on hand. The court would call the candidates forward in groups of twelve, subject them to a few cursory questions to determine whether there was legal reason they could not serve, and replace those for whom such reason was found to exist. When four complete panels of twelve had been assembled, the lawyers for the prosecution and defense would work their way through them, interviewing one candidate at a time and excusing those they deemed problematic, until a single jury of twelve men acceptable to both sides had been seated.

With that, the first group of twelve appeared before the judge. He asked if any had served on the county's grand jury in its present term or had another legal excuse for not serving. Five of the twelve were released, and another five summoned to replace them. The first panel ready, a second set of twelve men was called. Two were dismissed. And so it went, through the third and fourth panels, until the grittier, tedious business of actual jury selection could begin.

The first panel was recalled and took its place in the jury box. Lonnie Brand rose. Doughy, double-chinned, and wearing rimless eyeglasses, he looked more like a kindly shopkeeper or jolly country preacher than the Stone Mountain Circuit's prosecutor. He was no pushover, however: years before, a gunman had attacked this former mayor of Lithonia, Georgia, in his law office; Brand had relieved the man of his gun, then of a knife, and held his assailant for the sheriff despite stab wounds to his shoulder and hand. The state was ready to proceed, he now told the judge.

Greene Johnson, who had stepped out, hurried back into the courtroom to announce that the defense was not, and to move for a continuance. He recounted the exchange of eight days before, when Brand had attempted to schedule the trial on practically no notice—and how, when Judge Hutcheson agreed with Johnson's objection, Brand had complained the case would be held over until July, to which the judge said nothing. He left court that day convinced the case would be heard in the summer, Johnson said.

Instead, he was being asked to defend his client just twelve days after his indictment, and that indictment listed a date for the offense—March 19—that was clearly inaccurate, insofar as Lindsey Peterson's body had been fished from the water nearly a week before that date. He had been given little time to confer with the defendant, Johnson said, and no access whatever to Clyde Manning, the codefendant. He therefore did not know when Manning claimed the killing of Lindsey Peterson actually occurred. And without knowing that, it was impossible for his client to offer an alibi.

Looking back from a century later, one has to sympathize with Greene Johnson, because the style of rural jurisprudence in the Georgia of 1921 would never pass muster today. The trial was, indeed, rushed into being. Johnson had, in fact, far too little time to prepare an adequate defense. Pretrial discovery, now a foundation of judicial procedure, was not yet standard—it would not become the law of the land, in fact, for another forty-two years.

Brand was unmoved by Johnson's argument. Georgia law did not require the prosecution to specify the date of an offense, he argued, so the indictment's reference to March 19 was immaterial. And with three able lawyers on the job—Johnson was assisted by his partner, Charles Chester King of Covington, and William H. Key of Monticello—there was no excuse for not being ready. The judge agreed. He denied Johnson's motion.

Rebuffed in his bid for more time, Johnson demanded to know how Brand had acquired private-sector help in the person of William Howard, and who was paying his fee. He asked that Howard take the stand and divulge who had hired him. Judge Hutcheson granted the request. Once sworn in, Howard said he was retained by Hugh Dorsey, though the governor had told him at the time that neither his office nor the state treasury had the money to pay him. Instead, a group of private citizens "interested in the welfare of the state" had agreed to do so. He did not personally know these men, Howard said; the governor had mentioned some of the names, but he could not recall them.

"Were the names of any of the men the governor listed residents of Atlanta?" Johnson asked. It was a cagey question: as a rule, rural Georgians resented interference in their affairs from the state's largest city. They certainly wouldn't care for "secret prosecutors," as Johnson labeled them, pulling strings from on high.

Howard: "I think they were."

Johnson took his implication of big-city meddling up a notch. He asked Howard whether any of these unnamed underwriters were members of the NAACP. Howard replied that he knew of no connection between the men and the Association, but the seed had been planted. Not only were some of these interlopers from Atlanta, they might well be (by the standards of Newton County) pro-Black radicals.

Johnson next called on Assistant Attorney General Graham Wright, asking how *he* had become part of the prosecution team. Wright testified that he had been assigned the role by the governor, that he was serving as a representative of state government, and that he was paid as such. No private-sector money was coming his way.

Lonnie Brand spoke up: "Do you want to talk about *my* connection with the case?" The courtroom erupted in laughter, prompting Judge Hutcheson to gavel the crowd to order. "I don't want this to happen again," he warned. "This is not a minstrel show."

Johnson turned now to E. Marvin Underwood, asking who had employed him to represent Clyde Manning and requesting that he respond under oath. Brand objected: Underwood, he pointed out, was a defense attorney, and not part of the prosecution. Johnson countered that Underwood had, just the day before, attended the conference of prosecution attorneys at the Piedmont Hotel. The judge instructed Underwood to take the stand, saying he was committed to seeing the case "tried in the open" and "fair to the defendant and fair to the state."

Sworn in, Underwood testified that he was hired by W. Woods White, with his fee raised by subscription and guaranteed by a citizens' group. He acknowledged his presence at the Piedmont Hotel powwow. "I went to conference as attorney for Manning for several reasons," he said. "One, to find out when Manning was to be tried." He offered no opinions at the meeting, he said, and was afforded no insight into the state's case against his client. In fact, he learned only what Manning had told investigators so far.

Johnson questioned whether his attendance was appropriate. "Then, as a lawyer for Manning, a codefendant with Williams under the indictment, you entered a conference with state's attorneys for two hours?" he asked.

"Yes," Underwood answered.

"That's all," Johnson said. He asked for a recess so that Howard and Underwood could contact those who had hired them, and return with fuller accounts of the out-of-town maneuverings that had brought them to the courtroom. Judge Hutcheson granted the motion and, after a short break, Howard returned to the stand. He had spoken by telephone with Governor Dorsey, he said, and learned that Atlanta ministers Cary B. Wilmer and M. Ashby Jones had authorized his employment. He did not know the names of others who had contributed to his fee. Underwood had been unable to reach W. Woods White, but listed the members of the citizens' group whose names he remembered. They included the reverends Wilmer and Jones. So enlightened, Johnson moved that each prospective juror be questioned as to whether he was at all connected to anyone named as contributors. And so, each candidate was grilled about his links to the reverends and the Commission on Interracial Cooperation. The first panel of twelve produced just two jurors who passed muster with both sides. Ten members of the second panel also fell by the wayside. With two panels dismissed and just four jurors chosen, Judge Hutcheson declared a recess for lunch.

While his lawyers huddled, John S. Williams was allowed to eat a picnic meal with his family in a courthouse anteroom, their first private time together since his arrest. He had three pieces of pie for dessert. Whatever stress he felt about standing trial, it didn't seem to affect his appetite.

When the judge gaveled the proceeding back into session, the lawyers turned their attention to the third panel of twelve; this time, both sides agreed to three farmers. As the fourth group filed in, those watching must have wondered whether it could possibly deliver the five souls still required. Suprisingly, it did: The seated jury consisted of a Covington grocery store clerk, an automobile dealer, a barber, a merchant from the small town of Oxford, a drugstore employee, and seven farmers—an outcome that caused several northern newspapers to nervously observe that the jury looked rigged to favor the defendant. In truth, as Georgia historian Timothy Pitts has pointed out, the panel reflected the county from which it was drawn: Newton was home to 2,439 farms in 1920, and just fourteen manufacturing concerns. Residents not engaged in agriculture were few.

Of the original one hundred jury candidates, the process had chosen, excused, or rejected sixty-two. Judge Hutcheson directed the remaining thirty-eight to leave the courtroom and not return. "Another defendant is to be tried at this term," he explained, "and any man who hears the evidence given under oath disqualifies himself as a juror in the case against the other defendant, and we may need you.

"The sheriff will, therefore, see that any man who remains in the courtroom and whose name is in the jury [pool] is arrested and taken to jail to await the order of the court."

The day's business concluded at 2:45 p.m. Williams was locked in the Newton County Jail for the night. So was the state's star witness: Clyde Manning had been brought on the afternoon train from Atlanta, along with Clyde Freeman and several other potential witnesses snatched up from the plantation.

That evening, Gus Williams met with reporters gathered outside the courthouse, and again insisted that the whole affair was a miscarriage of justice. "I can safely say that I have not seen a single employee abused while working on our farm," he said. "The Negroes always had plenty of food and were paid fair wages. Of course, most of them lost what they made in 'skin games,'"—they gambled it away—"but we couldn't help that. All the Negroes have their 'skin,' and they'll be found playing on any farm in the state.

THE MAJESTY OF THE LAW

"The Negroes that were carried before the grand jury came from convict camps before being employed on our farm, and it is possible they were mistreated there. Anyway, they didn't receive all those scars and gashes while working for us." True, his brother Hulon had killed a Black worker, but that had been self-defense. Contradicting his father, the doctor said the slain man was "later buried in a cemetery and a license was secured for his burial, so the killing must have been reported."

The newsmen were curious about his brothers' absence. Williams answered that he did not know why Hulon, LeRoy, and Marvin had failed to attend the day's session. "The last time I saw them was Friday. I was at the farm Saturday, but did not go down to their places." He had heard rumors that they had fled the state, which he dismissed as "false, so far as I know."

Then he returned to his original point, that the Williams plantation was a kind, wholesome place where workers were treated well: "Why, I have received letters and telephone calls from I don't know how many Negroes who used to work on our place, and they always ask to be taken back.

"Only last night, I had a Negro to communicate with me regarding his return to the farm," he said. "I am satisfied my father will come clear. As the trial progresses, everyone will come to the same conclusion."

18

THE TRIAL'S SECOND DAY BEGAN, as had the first, with the courtroom filled to capacity and John Williams threading his way down the crowded aisle to take his seat. Again, Hulon, LeRoy, and Marvin failed to appear. The defendant, talking quietly with reporters before the judge's entrance, said he did not know why his sons were absent, but that he expected them to show up during the day's session.

Judge Hutcheson gaveled the trial to order promptly at nine, and five minutes later the jury filed in. As the first order of business, the prosecution called its witnesses to formally establish their presence and to sequester them out of earshot of any testimony. All appeared at the front of the courtroom—the two federal agents, several Black farmhands, Sheriff Johnson, and Williams's neighbor, scapegoat, and punching bag, David Leverett. The most important of the bunch, Clyde Manning, stood, as the *New York World* described him, "soot black, insignificant" before the court. He was visibly nervous, looking one moment at the floor and the next to the ceiling—striving, it seemed, to avoid meeting eyes with Mr. Johnny, who sat with his lawyers a few feet away.

With the witnesses sequestered, the business of the Newton County Superior Court of the Stone Mountain Circuit, State of Georgia, was ready to begin. The state called Special Agent George W. Brown. Prosecutor William Howard had just started his questions, and Brown had just launched into a description of his February 18 trip to the Williams plantation, when Greene Johnson objected: The agent went to the farm to investigate a peonage complaint, a crime for which Williams was not on trial. Surely, therefore, Brown's testimony was inadmissible. Howard countered that the agent's investigation established a motive in the case, in that Williams was attempting to destroy evidence of his peonage operation by eliminating potential witnesses. Had the agents not pursued the peonage complaint, the crime for which he *was* on trial would not have happened.

So began a long series of objections from the defense, most aimed at isolating the killing of Lindsey Peterson from other murders on the farm. It was, and is, a judicial standard to exclude testimony and evidence that speaks to offenses other than those for which a defendant is on trial. But Howard's argument that the agents' visit set into motion the events that led to Peterson's death was convincing. Judge Hutcheson allowed Brown to continue, overruling the defense for the first of fourteen times before lunch.

With Howard guiding him, Brown described pulling up outside the farm. "When we first arrived—that is, Mr. Wismer and I—Mr. John S. Williams was absent," he testified. "A Negro, Clyde Manning, a Negro by the name of Johnnie Williams, and a Negro by the name of John Brown were at home, at the home of Mr. John S. Williams."

When Williams did arrive, he made no objection to their presence, Brown said. "I told Mr. John S. Williams that we had information that a Negro by the name of Gus Chapman, who had worked on his place, had run away, and that he and Clyde Manning and another one of the Negroes on his place had captured Gus Chapman and brought him back to his place."

"Mr. Williams told me that was the truth. He told me they captured him up near Monticello on the railroad track." Brown did not, at that point, bring up the fact that he had also asked Manning about his capture of Chapman, and Manning had denied any part in it. Williams "stated on the night before the Negro left, he had tried to assault the wife of Clyde Manning—or that was his information," the agent said, "and that the Negro ran away on that account, and that he went with Manning to catch the Negro, in order to bring him back and have him prosecuted."

Whether Brown knew of it is unclear, but this was a cover story Manning cooked up after helping Chapman make his first escape, in the summer of 1920. Chapman had been locked into Manning's cottage, which was split down the middle like the little red house on Hulon Williams's place, with peons on one side of the partition, and Manning and his wife, Rena, on the other. Chapman had come to the partition late at night and, whispering, begged Manning to let him out. Manning had done so. Afterward, recognizing that he had to explain Chapman's disappearance to Mr. Johnny, he claimed that the missing peon had attacked Rena and fled.

"Then, when we got through with that, Mr. Williams asked us about going to the other farm, and we told him we wanted to go," Brown testified. "And he said that he would be glad to go with us, and he taken us then in his automobile from his place, first to the farm of Hulon Williams." He described the red house in detail—the system for securing the twin front doors with a chain, the window shutters that locked from the outside. He didn't have a clear recollection of the overall size of the building, but guessed that it was "at least thirty or forty feet long" and perhaps twenty-five wide.

From there, Brown said, Williams drove the agents to the farm managed by LeRoy and Marvin, where they found the two "burning off the woods" and where the agents informed them of the complaints they had come to check out. "And one of these was, I remember distinctly, to Mr. LeRoy Williams: that he had killed a man on the place."

Greene Johnson rose to object. How could such an accusation be part of this trial? He urged the judge to excuse the jury while the lawyers hashed out the question. Hutcheson agreed and directed the twelve from the room. Once they were gone, Howard declared that the state expected to prove that eleven men had met their deaths on and around the Williams farm in such quick and continual fashion that they manifested an intent, on the part of their killer, to eliminate all members of a class of people—namely, the men Williams held in peonage. Brown's testimony helped establish that. Johnson argued back that the only effect of allowing testimony about an alleged killing so far in the past would be to prejudice the jury and divert the case down umpteen side alleys that had little or nothing to do with Lindsey Peterson.

The judge divided the question, ruling that Brown could continue provided he restricted himself to matters connecting Williams to the Peterson killing and establishing motive. What the agent might have "heard" about past goings-on at the plantation, however, would be barred. With the jury still out of the room, Brown testified that LeRoy Williams denied killing a Negro, and that the agents saw he had a pistol in his pocket as he said it. He told LeRoy that carrying that pistol looked bad, Brown said.

Judge Hutcheson summoned the jury back in. Brown described speaking alone to farmhands in the field—Charlie Chisholm, Fletcher Smith, Clyde Freeman. "I returned then back to where Mr. Williams and Mr. Wismer were—they were all standing there—and we went back to the car and Mr. Williams carried us back to his place, and we told him good-bye there. And Mr. Wismer and I got in the car we went out in, and went on to some other work."

But before they left, Brown said, Williams admitted that it was possible he had violated the peonage laws, albeit unintentionally. "He stated that he had worked some stockade Negroes on his place, and while he had worked them he instructed them that they must not leave his place until they had paid him back what he had paid out for them." Those men had come from the Atlanta and Macon jails, Brown quoted Williams as saying. "I don't recollect that he stated the number that he had gotten, but it was several," and Hulon had paid the fines of some, too.

"I told Mr. John S. Williams that it had been reported to us that he was not letting them leave his place," he said. "And I told him our information was that Clyde Manning . . . kept them locked up on John S. Williams's place, and that on Hulon Williams's place, Claude Freeman was the man who kept them locked up.

"He denied that—said they didn't keep them locked up, neither his place nor Hulon Williams's place. They didn't keep them locked up on any place."

———

Greene Johnson began his cross-examination by honing in on Manning's denial to the agents that Gus Chapman had run away from the farm and that he, Manning, had played a role in his capture. When Williams told a different story, he asked, hadn't Brown pointed a finger in Manning's face, and called him a lying scoundrel? No, Brown replied, "but I told him he had lied about it. I told him that in the presence of Mr. Williams."

The point now established that Clyde Manning was a liar, and that a federal agent said so, Johnson launched a sly attack on the idea that Williams had anything to fear from the peonage investigation, while skewering Brown himself: Wasn't it true that the agent had spoken with Doyle Campbell about what he'd found at the plantation? Brown replied that he spoke with Campbell "before and after my investigation at the Williams farm and others."

When had he spoken to him after his visit to the plantation?

Brown: "On Saturday morning I talked to Mr. Doyle Campbell, after I had been to Mr. Williams's place on Friday."

And didn't he tell Mr. Campbell that he found nothing to suggest there was a stockade, or a place to lock up the hands, on the farm?

Brown: "I don't remember making such statement. I don't think I made it, for there *was* one there, to the best of my knowledge."

Didn't he tell Mr. Campbell that he had found nothing objectionable?

Brown: "I did not tell him, in that conversation then and there, that I found nothing objectionable on the place."

Didn't he tell Mr. Campbell that the only thing that bothered him about the visit was seeing a man with a gun in his pocket?

Brown: "I told him, 'One of the boys carrying a pistol looks bad.' I did not tell him that was the only objectionable feature I found on that place. I did not make that statement."

Did he not tell Mr. Campbell that the hands on the Williams farm looked better fed and better clothed, and generally better cared for, than other Negroes the witness had investigated in Jasper County and elsewhere in Georgia?

Brown: "I told him in that conversation that the Negroes on [Williams's] place looked better fed, and better cared for, and better clothed than some I had investigated *that day*."

Who was he comparing them to, then? What other Negroes had he seen that day?

Brown: "I stated they looked better cared for than the Negroes on Mr. Harvey K. Persons's place." As in the nephew of Jasper County Sheriff William F. Persons. The U.S. District Court in Atlanta had started the Persons trial two days before, on that peonage-adjacent charge of kidnapping a man into slavery. "I didn't make the general statement," Brown insisted. "I don't recollect it. I don't think I made it."

The defense lawyer opened a new line of questions designed to reinforce the notion that Williams had no reason to fear the federal investigators, and thus no motive to kill. Johnson asked Brown if he told the planter the agents were not going to make a case against him.

"At the time of this investigation, I did not tell Mr. Williams that we were not going to make any case against him," the agent answered. "I don't make the cases. I made my report to the attorney general of the United States and the district attorney at Atlanta. The case was still under investigation and not closed."

But the agents did not swear out warrants against the planter, Johnson noted.

"We don't swear out warrants unless we think the defendant is liable to escape," Brown replied. "That is the principal reason, when we swear them out."

Johnson asked whether it wasn't a fact that Brown did not swear out a warrant because he lacked the evidence to do so. No, Brown said—he had found enough evidence at the farm. But again, the case was still under investigation. He hadn't sworn out a warrant against Harvey K. Persons, either, yet Persons had been indicted in mid-March.

———

Next to take the stand was Special Agent Wismer. As he had with Brown, William Howard shepherded the witness through a step-by-step account of his time at the Williams plantation. Wismer related his initial conversation with Williams, their departure for the river tracts, Brown's inspection of the cottage down in the valley, and their joint visit to the red house. "The red building we looked at, the size of it would only be an estimate on my part," he told the special prosecutor. "I didn't look at it extremely close with that idea, in view of being able to give the dimensions. I presume it was twelve feet wide and perhaps sixteen to twenty feet long." Obviously, one or both of the federal agents had no talent for estimating size—Brown's red house was three times as big as Wismer's. Otherwise, however, Wismer corroborated his partner's account, but in quite a bit less detail—because, as he pointed out on the stand, "I don't think I talked to any niggers at the upper plantation. I think Mr. Brown talked with them."

Bear in mind, this was a federal agent again talking this way, this time in open court.

Greene Johnson's cross-examination focused first on the agent's interview of Clyde Manning before Williams's arrival. The lawyer wanted to know whether Wismer had told Manning that he was as guilty of peonage as Williams was. Wismer replied that he didn't think so. Pressed further, he said no, he had "stated nothing to that effect."

Next, Johnson floated the suggestion—first made publicly by Williams's oldest son, Gus—that the agents had been fomenting discord between the farmhands and the Williams family: Did Wismer ask Manning how long his workdays were?

No, Wismer said. "I was not concerned with that."

Didn't the agent ask Manning whether he worked more than eight hours a day? And tell him he was a fool if he did so? And didn't he tell him he should be making forty dollars per month?

No, Wismer insisted, "I certainly did not tell him he was a fool if he worked more than eight hours, and I did not tell him he ought to have forty dollars a month, nor nothing like that. And I did not state to him he was as guilty of peonage as Mr. Williams."

Johnson continued to press Wismer about the exchange. "I told Clyde Manning that I had information that a nigger named Gus Chapman had run off and that Mr. Williams and he and another nigger had gone after him and brought him back," the agent said. "I told Clyde Manning that. I don't recollect whether Mr. Brown was present when I told him that or not. Clyde Manning denied it, said he had not done so, and said nothing of that character had happened."

What transpired, the lawyer asked, when the government men questioned Mr. Williams about Chapman?

"He told us that it was true—that Chapman had run off, that he had got away," the agent testified. "And he and Clyde Manning and another nigger went and got him back." Chapman ran, Williams told them, because "he had assaulted some Negro woman on the place. He said something of that kind—I don't recollect just what his statement was."

At that point, Johnson asked, didn't he turn to Clyde Manning and say, "You scoundrel, what did you lie to us a minute ago about that for?"

"I did not," Wismer replied. "But I told him he had lied to us about that episode. Mr. Brown, in the presence of Mr. Williams, turned to Manning and told him, 'You lied to us about that.'"

Having succeeded in prompting a second government agent to brand Manning a liar, Johnson segued to Wismer's back-and-forth with Williams about the nature of peonage: Did the agents tell the planter that if he paid to get a Negro out of jail, then put him to work, he was guilty of the crime?

Not exactly, the agent testified. "We explained to him that peonage was involuntary servitude for the purpose of working out a debt, and there was some talk about what particular act might constitute peonage. . . . If he paid a nigger out of the stockade, paid his fine, and kept him working on his plantation, we possibly told him he would be guilty of peonage, since he worked the nigger against his will. It was the working against his will."

Did Mr. Williams remark that if that was peonage, a great majority of farmers would be guilty of it?

He could say neither that the planter had said that, nor that he had not, Wismer answered. "We had a good deal of conversation with Mr. Williams along that line."

Johnson's next several questions put Wismer on record about why he hadn't arrested or charged Williams immediately. He started with: Did he tell the farmer they found nothing objectionable about his operation? No, Wismer replied.

Did he make a case against Williams, or swear out a warrant?

"I don't make cases," Wismer said, echoing his partner. "That is not up to me, nor up to me to get out warrants. I have not taken out warrants. We don't swear out warrants nor make cases until we take them before the grand jury."

Johnson persisted: Was he saying he never told Mr. Williams he found nothing objectionable on his place?

"I did not," Wismer said. "I told him that the boy carrying a pistol was objectionable. I told him the worst I saw, not what I heard, was the boy carrying a pistol." He meant LeRoy Williams, of course, though reporters covering the trial were confused by his use of the term "boy"—a denigrating southern term for all male African Americans, regardless of age. A good many newspapers thus reported erroneously that the agents had seen one of the Black farmhands carrying a gun.

How about when he spoke with Doyle Campbell after their visit, Johnson asked—did he tell the solicitor general that he found nothing objectionable at the farm?

Wismer said he did not.

With little variation, Johnson continued to grill Wismer as he had Brown. Didn't he tell Campbell that the plantation's Black workers were better fed and clothed than on most places in Georgia? Didn't he tell

Campbell that he did not plan to pursue charges against Williams? Didn't he tell others he had found nothing troubling on or about the Williams place? Wismer denied all of it. But by the time he finished, Johnson had managed to dull the impact of the agents' testimony for the state. They had sworn they found evidence of peonage on the Williams farm, and their description of the red house left little to the imagination. But by repeatedly asking the same questions of both men, the defense attorney had raised doubts as to whether that evidence was sufficient to warrant prosecution—and, by implication, enough to motivate Williams to kill.

Looking to minimize the damage, William Howard rose for redirect examination. Did Wismer typically swear out warrants in peonage cases?

"I have never sworn out a warrant in a peonage case, and that is not my duty," the agent told him. "It is my business to report the investigation I make. We make a report to the chief in Washington, one report for our own office, the district attorney in whose jurisdiction" they worked, and others "who, in our opinion, ought to have one.

"We do that as part of our duty in the matter. If it is carried further and there is any indictment after our investigation and report—if it is an indictment—that is not our act, but the act of other officers of the Department of Justice. That is the business of the district attorney."

Wismer was excused. Clyde Manning was called to the stand.

19

THE *ATLANTA CONSTITUTION* PUBLISHED A PHOTOGRAPH taken from the gallery that Wednesday as Clyde Manning testified, and it offers startling insight into just how close were the quarters in the Covington courtroom. Judge Hutcheson is seated at front center, between two pairs of narrow windows that stretch very nearly from the floor to the high ceiling. The dais from which he presides is elevated no more than a foot or two. Standing spectators press in from his right; the space in front of the bench is filled with seated men.

Manning occupies a wooden armchair, perhaps a dozen feet to the judge's left, his back to a slender strip of wall between two of the windows. The space before him is packed with court reporters and members of the press, some of whom look close enough for him to touch. Behind this gaggle are the tables occupied by the lawyers. To Manning's left, no more than ten feet away, stands the jury box, its back to a side wall, its members facing witness and judge. In an era that relied on unamplified testimony, the jurors had to be close.

Every other square foot of the room is occupied by onlookers. Every seat is filled, every aisle stuffed. The windows are raised, but the seep of fresh air they offered would have done little to combat the room's rising temperature and humidity. From the midst of this sweaty crush, William Howard rose to question the state's star witness. The former congressman was a bulky man with a squarish head, a thin mustache, and a resting expression suggesting he'd caught a whiff of something foul. He dangled his eyeglasses from a black silk cord as he walked Manning through his life story: The farmhand was three days from turning twenty-seven years old. He did not know where he was born, but when he "was large enough to remember," he was living on the Jasper County farm of Frank Persons, brother to the sheriff. He had lived on John S. Williams's farm since he was fourteen, or nearly half his life. "I was living with Mr. Williams, working for him for wages, last year and this year," Manning told Howard. "My wife worked for him. She was cooking for him."

Howard took his time getting his witness comfortable on the stand, gently teasing out details of daily life on the farm. He had him name the Black workers there. Williams "had a fellow named John Brown," Manning said. "One named Johnnie Williams. One named Rufus Manning, and Jule Manning, and Gladdis [Manning], and John Freeman." The Mannings he named were his brothers, he explained, with the exception of his uncle Rufus. "My brothers and me come there together. And Rufus Manning, he come the next year after we moved there. Then John Freeman"—Clyde and Claude Freeman's father—"he came the same year Rufus Manning did."

Howard had him list the Williams children, including the three sons who worked the river tracts. He then asked about other farmhands living up beside the lake. Besides Clyde and Claude Freeman, they were peons: Johnnie Green, who lived with Mr. Hulon and "came from the Macon stockade, so they said," and Will Preston, also from Macon, and Charlie Chisholm, who was bailed out of the Monticello jail. "He has been with them something like three or four years," Manning said of Chisholm. "May have been longer, I don't know.

"Then there was Lindsey Peterson. He lived with Mr. Hulon and Mr. LeRoy Williams and came from the Macon stockade." He recited the names of others bailed out in Macon—Frank Dozier, Fletcher Smith, John Brown, and Johnnie Williams.

Howard asked about a peon named Harry Price. "I didn't know a fellow named Price," Manning told him. "I know a fellow called Foots." He came from the Macon lockup. He also knew Jim Strickland, who came from the Atlanta stockade. Both had stayed with Mr. Marvin. Another fellow who went by Preacher: "I don't know whether he was a preacher,"

Manning said. "I never did hear him preach." He was gone before the killing started. He named others pulled from the Atlanta Tower—Big John and Little Bit, who lived with Mr. Marvin; Artis Freeman, who stayed with Mr. Hulon. He finished the roster with Iron Jaw, "a nigger man by the name of Blackstrap," and a "boy" named Willie Givens.

Howard, leaning on the prosecution team's leather-topped table, now lowered his voice. "Clyde," he asked, "do you know whether Lindsey Peterson is living or dead?"

"Yes," Manning answered. "He's dead."

What about Will Preston?

"Dead."

Harry Price, called Foots?

"Dead."

Charlie Chisholm?

"He is dead."

So it went, Howard calling the names of all eleven men pulled from the ground or the rivers in recent weeks, and Manning responding that each was dead.

Tell the jury when Lindsey Peterson died, the prosecutor instructed.

"It was one Saturday night," Manning recounted. He could not pinpoint the date, but it was "the first of last month or the month before that, the last of February or the first of March, that he died." Will Preston died with him, and Harry Price, too. "These three men died the same night."

Howard asked Manning whether he recalled meeting Special Agent Brown. Manning pointed him out and explained the agent "came to Mr. John S. Williams's place and had a talk with me." Manning did not recall Wismer's name, but recognized him in the courtroom and pointed him out, as well. The three men died "after Mr. Brown and that gentleman had the talk with me and Mr. John S. Williams," he said. "It was in the next week, Saturday night of the next week that they died."

Tell the jury how they died, each one of them, Howard said.

"Lindsey Peterson, he died by a chain around his neck and a weight to it. Him and Will Preston, they were tied together, a chain was put around their necks, and they were put in Yellow River."

What place?

"They was put in the river along about the middle of the bridge. The bridge is named Allen's Bridge, across Yellow River."

Had Manning been to that bridge before?

Yes, the witness replied. "Not very many times, but I know where it is. I had crossed it in going over to Mr. Johnny's son's house, over to Dr. Williams's house. We crossed that bridge going to Dr. Williams's house."

Howard directed him to tell the jury all he knew about how this man Peterson was thrown into the river that night.

"There was a chain—it was a trace chain—around their necks, the necks of Will Preston and Lindsey Peterson," Manning said. "They were chained together, and Harry Price, he had a chain around his neck, too, and he was begging, begging not to kill him, talking and begging of Mr. Johnny not to kill him."

What happened when they got to the river?

"Mr. Williams told Lindsey Peterson and Will Preston to get out and then he told me and Charlie Chisholm to throw them over."

Howard had Manning back up and describe the crime in greater detail. "The chain was put around their necks between what they call Polk's store and the bridge," he said, meaning the Waters Bridge over the Alcovy. The tiny Polk's, a local landmark and gathering spot, stood on the roadside just past the highway's fork at Stewart, in Newton County. After the men were tied, Williams drove on to the fork, turned south toward Jackson, "and at Yellow River he stopped the car and told Lindsey Peterson and Will Preston to get out. When they got out of the car, they had this trace chain around their necks and the weights were tied to it. It was a weight of rocks in a sack."

Did he see the rocks?

No, Manning said, "but I saw the sack, and they were rocks in the sack." He lifted the sack, and "it weighed one hundred pounds, it looked like to me."

Howard asked for further details about what happened on the bridge.

The doomed men struggled, the witness replied. They "were scuf-fling and trying to keep back, to keep from going over." He and Chisholm dragged the pair to the railing "and throwed them over, and then we got in the car and left there." Manning sat stock-still in the chair, hands folded in his lap, speaking loudly enough for everyone in the otherwise silent room to hear, but without passion or inflection. His calm was both impressive and unsettling. The bindings, he continued, were such that the men could offer little resistance: "Each man had his hands tied together with wire, and then the hands of both men were tied together with wire. And the necks of the two men were tied together with a trace chain, and the bag of rocks, it was fastened to the trace chain, sort of between the two. That bag of rocks was tied right up to the trace chain. . . . And that sack was above their feet, and up above the floor of the bridge."

Had he seen the two men after he threw them over the side?

"After we throwed them over, I never saw or heard anything more of them until they come to the top, not until after they found them in the river," Manning said. "After we threw them over, that was the last I saw of them that night."

Howard now asked for a key detail: How had he managed to get the men to the banister with a hundred-pound sack of rocks dangling from their necks?

"Mr. Johnny, he handled the sack of rocks, after it was tied to the chain," Manning said. "He helped take the men out of the car and carry the men to the banister. He carried the sack of rocks that was already on the men." Before they reached the bridge, the sack "was laying in their laps in the car," but on the way to the banister, "Mr. Johnny Williams was car-rying the rocks. He held the sack of rocks up."

Who drove the car?

"Mr. Williams drove that car."

What kind of car was it?

"It was a seven-passenger Chandler," came the answer.

Whose car was it?

"It was his car," Manning said. "It come from his house."

Where was the third man, Harry Price, while he and Chisholm were pushing Preston and Peterson into the river?

"The other man was in the car."

After they threw the two into the Yellow River, where did they go with him?

"We took him to the South River."

Greene Johnson jumped to his feet. "I object, and we might as well settle this right now," he said. "I'll ask that the jury retire." The judge concurred, and the proceedings paused as the jurors left their seats. When the door closed behind them, the judge told Johnson to proceed.

"The indictment on which we are trying Williams charges him with killing Lindsey Peterson," the lawyer argued. "The state is trying to get evidence before the jury on other killings. We object to testimony concerning these other murders on the ground that it is irrelevant and prejudicial to the defendant."

"It makes no difference how Harry Price was killed," Johnson insisted. "His death is entirely different and separate from the one for which Williams is being tried. Price is alleged to have been killed the same night, but at a different place and time." It was "another alleged crime for which there is no indictment at this trial."

Johnson ran through several past cases in which evidence of crimes beyond the focus of a trial had been admitted, only to be struck down or questioned on appeal. The Leo Frank case was one: the court had allowed testimony about Frank's conduct with women besides Mary Phagan to suggest he was a sexual deviant. The state Supreme Court had split on whether that was allowable, Johnson reminded the judge.

When William Howard's turn came to speak, he embarked on his own tour of case law establishing the opposite: that closely bound components of a single, extended crime were relevant and admissible to show motive, context, and intent. The evidence was necessary to a full understanding of Lindsey Peterson's death and Williams's plot to "kill Negroes by the wholesale in order to cover up shady practices on his farm."

Lucy Williams wept as the prosecutor spoke. Her husband yawned. Clyde Manning nodded off in the witness chair. "The motion is overruled," Judge Hutcheson declared. "Let the jury be brought back." As soon as the panel was seated, the judge recessed court for lunch.

Hutcheson's decision to allow the state to describe Harry Price's death to the jury was critical, for it opened the way for the prosecutors to describe not only the occurrence on Mann's Bridge, but the full, unthinkable horror of what had occurred in Jasper and Newton Counties. As grim as the morning testimony had been, it was soon to get worse.

The jury returned to the courtroom at 1:40 p.m. Clyde Manning resumed his place on the stand. Howard returned to his questions: "After you threw Willie Preston and Lindsey Peterson into the Yellow River, where did you go with Harry Price?"

"We got in the car and went on to South River," Manning said, "and carried Harry Price, nicknamed Foots, and put him into South River."

How long was that journey?

"That is about a mile, or maybe more, from the Yellow River bridge," the witness said. "Not so very far. There was a bridge there. That was a pretty good-sized stream, too—it is a little bit larger than Yellow River."

Who drove the car?

"Mr. Johnny Williams drove the car from Yellow River bridge to South River bridge. In the car then was me and Harry Price, Charlie Chisholm and Mr. Johnny Williams."

Howard asked him to tell the jury what happened then.

"When we got to South River he told us, 'All right, boys, get out.' We got out and Harry Price, he got out, and I taken the weight that he had to him. And he says, 'Don't throw me over. I will get over.'"

Harry Price had a weight attached to him, as well?

"The weight was around his neck," Manning said. "It was put on at the same place as the other boys', between Polk's store and Waters Bridge—a sack with rocks in it. It was put on him when the other sack was put on the other boys." He repeated Foots's last request: "Don't throw me over." Then he "crawled up on the banister, set up on the banister. He set there just a little while, and he says, 'Don't throw me.' He says, 'Lord, have mercy,' and went right on over."

How was the weight attached to him?

"That weight was fastened around his neck by a chain. It had a ring in it, and the chain was run through the ring and fastened with a horseshoe, and the sack of rocks fastened to the chain."

And where was the defendant while Harry Price was going over the side?

"Mr. John S. Williams was right there with us when he went off the bridge into the river, right there by us."

Howard had his witness describe the scene on Mann's Bridge once more, to drive home that Harry Price, having watched two fellow peons murdered on Allen's Bridge, was so resigned to his own fate, so stripped of hope, that he sought some little control over his final moments. "Me and Charlie Chisholm and Foots got out, and when he got out I caught hold of the sack of rocks. And Foots says, 'Don't you all throw me over. I will get over.' Harry Price says that. And as he jumped off, I turned the rocks loose.

"And then we got in the car, me and Charlie Chisholm and Mr. Johnny, and went up the road on the other side of the bridge, and he turned around and we come back home, went straight back home. I reckon it was somewhere about eleven o'clock when we got back home."

Howard asked whether he saw Price after that.

No, Manning said. Foots had been found, but he had not seen his body. "I seen his shoes. I knowed his shoes," he said. "I don't know what condition he was in when we drove away from the bridge, whether he sunk down in the water. As soon as he jumped off, I didn't look to see whether he sunk in the water or not, and I never did see him again. I seen his shoes."

In retrospect, the order in which William Howard unspooled this narrative was close to the "inverted pyramid" storytelling style of old-school newspaper journalism: He started with the crime itself, related in broad strokes, then backfilled its details, then built its context. The result was a story not told in reverse, exactly, but not far from it. With the events on the bridges covered, Howard moved on to those that immediately preceded them. "We had been at work up on the river," Manning told him, "all of us, all the whole crowd. All the boys were just at work: me, and Foots—Harry Price, his name was—Lindsey Peterson and Will Preston and Charlie Chisholm, Gladdis Manning, Cliff Freeman. All of us had been at Mr. Hulon's place, up on the river."

John S. Williams "told us to quit before night and to carry the hogs down home, take them down to Mr. Johnny's house, where I lived. He told them to take the hogs down there"—the "them" referring to Peterson, Preston, and Price—"and we did the plowing and went on home. It was about five miles from where we quit plowing down to Mr. Johnny's home.

"Mr. Johnny told us to go on to supper and us went and ate supper," he testified. "He told me then, 'After you all eat supper go on down to your house. I will come down there.' After we got through eating supper he says, 'I am coming down there. We have to do away with them boys.'

"Me and Charlie Chisholm, Harry Price and Will Preston and Lindsey Peterson, we all ate supper there at Mr. Johnny's stove room with my wife—my wife cooked the supper. Then we went down to my house and they stayed down there," as ordered. "We were down there at my house, talking and going on, and so about eight or nine o'clock, Mr. Johnny come down and knocked on the door and I says who was it. And he says, 'Open the door.' So I opened the door and he told them boys he would carry them to the train." He had promised to take two other peons to the station the next morning, Williams explained, "and he would not have so much time" to take them, as well. "And he told them to come on and he would take them to the train that night.

"The car was setting under the shelter and we went up and got in the car. Harry Price got in the front seat with Mr. Johnny, and then me and Will Preston and Lindsey Peterson and Charlie Chisholm got in the back seat, and we left then, going to the river."

An attentive listener would have realized that the specifics of the three murders were decided as the men entered the car: Peterson and Preston were killed as a pair simply because they were both in the back seat; Price was killed separately because he chose to ride shotgun. The profound cruelty in the scenario was more obvious. Convinced they were about to be freed, the victims would have been filled with relief and joy. On the road minutes later, when Williams pulled the car to the shoulder, the terrible reality of their situation took shape. In the remote darkness of Allen's Bridge, the captive men grasped that not only were they about to die, but that Mr. Johnny planned to drown them. It was a needlessly complex, drawn-out, and sadistic style of killing, seemingly engineered to afford the victims ample time to ponder their fate, and thereby deepen their suffering.

Howard directed Manning further back in time, to the moment Williams first shared his plans for the slaughter. Manning offered up what was, by now, a familiar tale. After the government men came to the plantation, Williams "come to me one day and told me, he says, 'Clyde, it won't do for these boys to go up yonder and swear against us. They will ruin us.' He says, 'We will have to do away with them.'

"I says, 'Mr. Johnny, that is so bad, I don't want to do it.' And he says, 'You must do it.' He says, 'If you don't want to do it, it is all right—it is your neck or theirs. If you think more of their necks than you do of your own neck, it is yours.' That was after the visit of Mr. Brown and . . . before anybody was killed."

Howard had been moving the narrative backward in time. Now he changed direction, asking Manning to explain how the first man died.

Johnnie Williams had been among the peons who had lived in the other side of his cottage, Manning said. He had been on the plantation for thirteen months or so when the agents showed up. "I didn't hear the talk between Johnnie Williams and Mr. Brown," he testified. "After Mr. Brown left, Mr. John S. Williams asked us what [the agents] asked us and we told him they asked us about a boy named Blackstrap." Williams wanted to know what they'd said. They had told the government men "we didn't know anyone named Blackstrap," they replied. Williams "didn't seem to be satisfied with Johnnie and what we told him. And he said, 'If you ain't told it all—if you all told anything—I will find it out on you.'"

Howard asked who Blackstrap was.

"Blackstrap was a boy that Mr. Marvin got last year," Manning told him. "He was not there very long before he was killed. He was killed there at Mr. Johnny's house, under a little shelter there in the yard by his house, there in his yard."

Howard directed Manning to resume the story of Johnnie Williams's demise.

"Johnnie Williams was killed about dinner time in the pasture near Mr. Williams' house," he said. "I was there and I saw it. He told Johnnie Williams to drive the cows down in the pasture, and he told me to get the axe—he had some poles down there he wanted me to cut up." Williams had told him a day in advance of his plan. When the moment arrived, the peon realized he was about to be attacked and "kept backing around," Manning said. "I didn't want to hit him—he was begging and going on, and I didn't want to hit him—and [Mr. Johnny] asked me, didn't I mean to do what he said? He said if I didn't, to give him the axe, he meant what he said. And I was afraid to give [Mr. Johnny] the axe and so I hit [Johnnie Williams] with the axe, hit him one lick on the back of the head—sort of side of the head with the back of the axe—and then we dug a hole there." This happened "about the middle of the week" following the federal agents' visit to the plantation, he said, and a few days before the "incoming Saturday night" when Peterson, Preston, and Price met their ends. The courtroom, filled to suffocation, witnessed this testimony without a sound.

Tell the jury about John "Red" Brown and Little Bit, Howard instructed.

Mr. Johnny asked Red if he wanted to go home and Red said he did, Manning told him. And Mr. Johnny said he would run him "'over to Jackson and you can go home, or go anywhere you want to go.'" That night, both Red and Little Bit got into Williams's car, and he "taken them on to the river, mighty near to the river, between the crossroads and the river."

Hardy's Crossroad, to be exact. It's about a mile east of the Waters Bridge. Along that empty mile, Williams stopped the car.

"They were begging," Manning testified, "and [Williams] told Little Bit he was not going to hurt either of them—he just wanted to scare Red. He was just going to scare Red and he had Little Bit to help Mr. Johnny to tie the weight to him. And when he had the weight tied to him he tied Little Bit to him, too—they were both tied together—and he taken them on the Waters Bridge, to Waters Bridge on the Alcovy River." The water there was deep, Manning testified, and the men were weighted with "a big old round, iron weight, a big old thing off a press. I don't know the name of it, but it was an iron thing off a press."

Howard asked whether Manning was in the car.

"I was with Mr. Johnny Williams then," he said. He had taken a wagon up to the river tracts to work that day and "worked up there then, and then I left with him that night. When I went up there I knowed he was coming up there in the car." Charlie Chisholm made the journey, too.

What became of Red and Little Bit?

"I know they were drowned. I saw them when they were put in, and it was deep enough to drown a man, and I never seen any more of them after they were thrown in."

With Greene Johnson objecting, to no avail, Howard asked Manning to describe the next murder. "Big John, he was killed," Manning told him. "That was a fellow from the Atlanta stockade. I never knew any name but Big John." Investigators would determine that Big John's name was John Will Gaither, though they knew no more than Manning when he testified. "He lived with Mr. Marvin Williams. I know he was killed with an axe, up on the Campbell place—at Mr. Hulon's, up on the river."

Howard: The Campbell place?

"That was a place he bought from Mr. Doyle Campbell," Manning explained. "He was killed up on the Campbell place before Lindsey Peterson and the others were thrown in the river. That was the next week after Mr. Brown, the government agent, was there, the next week following."

Manning described how Mr. Johnny had instructed him and Charlie

Chisholm to dig a hole next to the newly built cottage. "Me and Charlie Chisholm got Big John and went over there and dug the hole," which was "round like a well" and "big enough for a well," though Mr. Johnny "was not aiming to dig a well there." At some point, Williams himself appeared. "Mr. Johnny told Big John to get down in there and dig. Charlie crawled out of the hole and Big John got in. I was already out of the hole. There couldn't but one of us dig at a time. That left Big John in the hole by himself and Charlie, he taken the axe and hit him right along there"—he paused to point to his own head—"and he fell over, right doubled over. And we just covered him up right there."

Lost on no one in the courtroom: John Will "Big John" Gaither was made to dig his own grave. Howard asked whether Manning had seen Big John again.

"I saw his body after that," Manning said. "I saw it there in the hole."

What had the killers done with the tools they had been digging with?

"Set them in the stove room, right in the house where we dug the hole. In the stove room in the house by the hole—the hole was dug right at the house. It was as close to the door of the house as from here to that door there, yonder." He pointed to a door in the courtroom's side wall, next to the jury box.

Howard asked when this killing occurred.

"It was before them were drowned in Yellow River. That was all that was killed before Lindsey Peterson, and Preston and Price was drowned in the river, to my knowledge, before those three were drowned."

It was hard to keep track. At this point, Manning had described seven of the eleven homicides, which had taken place in—what, three days? Four? Howard asked what happened next.

"Johnnie Green was killed," on the morning after the murders of Preston, Peterson, and Price. "Mr. Johnny Williams told Johnnie Green on Saturday before, that he would have to go to Jackson, and to come down to the house that Sunday morning and he would carry him to the train so he could go home." Johnnie Green had followed Mr. Johnny's instructions, had shown up outside the house that morning, "and Mr. Johnny told Johnnie Green to go down in the pasture and fix up the pasture wire. And Johnnie went down there, and Mr. Johnny went down with him.

"When we got down to the pasture, he told Johnnie he heard he was going off to try to have his boys' necks broke, and he said he was going to stick to his boys. And he told me to hit him. And when he said that, I hit him, and then he told me to hit him again. When he told me to hit him again, I hit him again with the axe.

"Then we covered him up in some pine straw and just left him there until that Sunday night. We didn't bury him then, that Sunday, but left him there 'til that Sunday night."

Howard asked Manning to describe what happened next.

"Mr. Johnny told us to take Willie Givens, that same Sunday, down in the pasture and kill him, and to cover him up. We killed Givens after we killed Green—the same day, but later in the day." He outlined the trap they'd laid for Givens with their supposed trip to the store, and how, at the pasture's edge, "I knocked him in the head."

What did they do with his body?

"We left him lay there and covered him up with pine straw, and left him there until that Sunday night. And that Sunday night we went back down there and dug two holes, and put Willie Givens in one and Johnnie Green in one, and covered them up and taken some pine straw and scattered it over that place where they were put. Them two were killed right close together, and buried right close together."

Howard asked whether John S. Williams was present when Givens died.

"Mr. Johnny Williams was with us when we killed Givens, and with us when we killed Green," Manning said, "and was with us when we buried them. And he helped to bury them."

Did the witness see those men again?

"I saw those bodies afterwards," Manning said. "They were where me and Mr. Williams and Chisholm had buried them, and they were the same people."

Howard's questions kept coming, calm and steady: Who next?

"Charlie Chisholm, he was killed, too."

The same man who had participated in many of the killings?

Yes, Manning replied. He named the nine victims so far. "He had helped us kill all of them. Charlie Chisholm had helped to drown Peterson, Preston, and Price, besides these others."

Howard asked how he, too, came to die.

Mr. Johnny "told Charlie Chisholm that Saturday evening he was going to send him off," Manning said. "And Saturday night he taken me and Charlie in the car. Mr. Johnny Williams taken us with him, and when we got mighty near to the Alcovy River, he told Charlie he heard some of his smart talk.

"And Charlie told him he hadn't said nothing. And [Mr. Johnny] told him, 'Hush, I don't want to hear a word from you.' And he told me to tie him, and I tied a weight to him, tied to his head, and a weight to his feet. And when we got to the river, we put him over the banister near the middle ways of the river and turned him loose." The water was deep enough to drown him, Manning said, "and it did drown him."

Howard sought clarification on which Saturday night this was.

"Peterson and Preston and Price was drowned like this Saturday night, and then like the next Saturday night coming, Charlie was drowned," Manning said. "Mr. Johnny and me pushed him over in the river."

At long last, Howard came to the final victim.

"After Charlie Chisholm was killed, then Fletcher Smith was killed," Manning told him. "The next week after Charlie was killed, he was killed up in the field of the Campbell place, up on Mr. Hulon Williams's place."

Howard asked how Fletcher Smith died.

"He was shot with a shotgun."

Describe for the jury how that came about, Howard said.

Mr. Johnny had been working with five farmhands up on the Campbell place, Manning said, and he sent two of them away to gather fodder, and a third to tend to the mules. "That left me and Mr. Johnny and Fletcher. He told me to go down to the branch and get a spade and mattock and bring them up there, and he had a shotgun in his hand. He went across the field and I went down to the branch."

The "branch" was a narrow stream that snaked across the Campbell place and emptied into the reservoir. "When I left there to go down to get the spade and mattock, Fletcher was over behind the hill, and Mr. Johnny was on this side of the hill," he said. "Mr. Williams went across over the hill from where we were to where Fletcher was, and that put him out of my sight." Manning was headed back when "I heard the shot, and when I got there, Fletcher was dead and Mr. Williams was standing there, about as far from Fletcher as to the side of the wall, there—ten or fifteen feet, I reckon. Just about that distance."

And the body?

"When I got back there and Fletcher was dead and Mr. Johnny was standing there with the shotgun, all he said was, 'Let us dig it right here, dig the hole right here.' That was right by the body and we dug the hole right there, a long hole like a grave, and Mr. Johnny, he dug with the mattock and I shoveled it out.

"When we got it deep enough, then we put Fletcher in and covered him up. After we got him covered up, we plowed over him again. And he says, 'Clyde, I don't want to hear nothing from this. There is nobody knows about this but just me and you.' He says, 'If I ever hear it come out, I will know where it come from.' I says, 'Mr. Johnny, I ain't going to say nothing about it to nobody.'

"That was the last one killed, to my knowing."

GREENE JOHNSON CUT A VERY DIFFERENT FIGURE from William Howard. The former congressman looked every bit an aging statesman—thick-chested and craggy, with stern eyes assessing the world (and finding much to question, if not dislike) from beneath a cornice of silver eyebrow. The defense attorney, in contrast, was a wisp of a fellow, bony and narrow-shouldered and jug-eared. He posed little visible threat and could be easy to underestimate.

Johnson's cross-examination of Clyde Manning began quietly: He asked the farmhand to recount his arrival at the plantation in his teens and his life since—how he'd been married to Rena for about eight years, and how he'd worked "on the halves" with Mr. Johnny early in his marriage, meaning that he sharecropped, splitting the cotton he raised and the money it earned with Williams in exchange for his food, housing, and farming supplies. Manning described how, for the last two years, he had "made a trade with him" to instead work for straight wages of twenty dollars a month.

Johnson eventually eased into the meat of his inquiry, with the out-of-town trip the three Williams sons had taken, supposedly to Texas. When was it that they left?

He could not fix the date exactly, Manning said, "but it was after these here men come down there, after the Revenue men come down there, the United States protectors." This was the first time the jury had heard him use that job title. "It was not very long afterwards that they left—it was a week after they come down there, I think, about a week."

Johnson asked whether John S. Williams kept a car at the plantation.

"Mr. Williams had an automobile there, one."

Did Manning drive it?

"I could drive the Ford," he replied, "but I couldn't drive the Chandler. I never did try to drive it but one time. Mr. Johnny would not let me. I never did try to drive it but one time, and then I run against the mailbox." The remark earned a chuckle from the room, including Williams. Judge Hutcheson ordered silence.

Did Charlie Chisholm drive the Chandler?

No, Manning said. "If he could, I didn't know it."

Johnson noted that Manning had mentioned a Ford.

"That was Mr. Hulon's Ford," the farmhand said, "and that was not over at Mr. Johnny's place."

Johnson moved on to the visit by the federal agents, and asked about their interview with him behind the barn.

"Mr. Brown talked to me behind the gear house, not behind the barn," Manning said. "He carried me behind the gear house, that gentleman there—I know him as Mr. Brown—and he talked to me back there. I saw him for the first time then, and he told me he was a United States protector."

The lawyer asked whether Special Agent Brown had told Manning he was there to protect him.

"He didn't tell me he was there to protect me; he said he was a United States protector," Manning replied.

There were two of them there, Johnson said. Did the other man call himself a United States protector?

"I knowed if that one was, this one was, too."

Johnson asked whether Brown had accused Manning himself of keeping the peons from leaving the plantation.

"He told me he understood that I was Mr. Williams's boss," Manning said. "He asked me was I boss over them niggers for Mr. Williams and I told him, 'No, sir.'"

Johnson asked whether Brown had told him he was guilty of peonage, too.

"He told me if Mr. Williams was guilty of peonage, and I was doing this and keeping it a secret and I was helping him, I was just as guilty as the one having it done."

What else did Mr. Brown say, after that?

"He asked me then did I know a nigger named Gus Chapman, and he asked me if I had gone off and got Gus and brought him back to the Williams farm. And he told me he had information I had done that, together with Mr. Williams, and I denied it to him and told him I hadn't done anything of the kind.

"Pretty soon after that Mr. Williams came and they went and talked to Mr. Johnny, and I didn't say nothing," he said. "I didn't do any talking after Mr. Johnny come. I didn't take part in their talking."

Johnson asked about the agents' interview with Williams.

"They asked Mr. Johnny about this same Gus Chapman, and Mr. Williams told him he had gone after him and brought him back . . . that we caught him and brung him back. He didn't say *I* did; he said, 'The boys went and got him and brought him back.'

"Then, this gentleman here"—he indicated Brown—"turned to me and told me I had told him a lie behind that gear house. And I *had* told one. And I had told him one. I had lied to him about everything he asked me."

Greene Johnson was again showing the jurors that Clyde Manning was not afraid to lie to federal lawmen—or, by implication, to anyone else. He wandered off the subject of the agents' visit for a short while, then swung back to revisit a topic intended to stir up the farmers on the jury.

Johnson: Did these gentlemen ask you what you were getting as wages?

Manning: Yes. "And I told them."

Johnson: Did the gentlemen ask you how many hours you and the other hands worked?

Manning: "They did not ask me how many hours, or nothing like that."

Johnson: Didn't they tell you that you ought not to work but eight hours a day?

Manning: "I never heard anything about that. They didn't say anything to me about eight hours."

Johnson: Didn't you tell Mr. Williams that they had said that?

Manning: "I never heard nothing about eight hours and I never told Mr. Williams nothing about eight hours. I never heard nothing about eight hours until I heard Mr. Johnny talking, and that was a day or two before these men come down there and got me"—i.e., when he was taken into custody. "That was when I heard him tell some white people that."

Johnson retreated from that line of inquiry for another he'd broached earlier, hoping to show the jury that Manning and other prosecution witnesses were inconsistent in their testimony about times, distances, measurements—details likely to trip up the unschooled farmworkers. How far would he say it was, he asked Manning, from Mr. Williams's house to the bridge where Peterson was thrown in the river?

Manning replied that he did not know. "It may be ten miles or more. I know it is a long ways."

Fourteen miles?

"I don't know whether it is fourteen miles, but it is a long ways."

Did he know where Mr. Williams was earlier on the Saturday night he supposedly took this trip to the Yellow River?

"I don't know," Manning said, "but he left there and said he was going to Jackson, said he was going to carry Artis Freeman to the railroad."

Did he take Artis Freeman?

"He did carry Artis Freeman away."

Where did he take him?

"I reckon to the railroad."

Drawing on a narrative floated days before by Gus Williams, Johnson asked when, in relation to the agents' visit, Mr. Johnny had gathered the men and told them they were free to leave.

"He didn't call us all up and tell us we could leave," Manning answered.

He didn't tell them they could go on home?

"I never heard him tell them that," Manning said. "He never told me he was going to turn them loose."

He took Artis Freeman over to the railroad and let him go home, though. Why?

The Williams family of Jasper County, Georgia, in 1909. Behind John S. Williams and his wife, Lucy, stand, from left, sons Marvin, LeRoy, Hulon, and William Augustus, or "Gus"; daughter Mary stands at right; and in front are James Luke, Ivah Sue, and infant Lucy Claire. The Williamses would have four more children in the following decade.
John Edward Williams

The farmhouse at the John S. Williams home place, where the planter lorded over a vast spread of cotton and corn—and, in late February 1921, launched the massacre of his workforce.
Atlanta Constitution/*Kevin Swift edit*

At fifty-four, John S. Williams was seen as an upstanding
citizen, successful farmer, and loving family man. Then federal
agents looked into his exploitation of Black laborers he'd
"bought" from area jails, and he responded in extreme fashion.
Chicago Whip/*Kevin Swift edit*

Clyde Manning: trusted field boss on the plantation,
reluctant participant in Williams's criminality, and
the linchpin of the state's case against the planter.
Chicago Whip/*Kevin Swift edit*

What's left of Allen's Bridge over the Yellow River. The box-truss span that rested on these piers was the scene of two killings on February 26, 1921; the water below yielded the first bodies recovered in the "Murder Farm" affair, and one of those victims became the focus of Newton County's prosecution.
Earl Swift

The remains of Mann's Bridge over the South River, where
Harry "Foots" Price died shortly after watching two of his
fellow peons murdered.
Earl Swift

U.S. Attorney Hooper Alexander, who in January 1921 declared war on peonage in his Atlanta-based district. Federal agents called on John S. Williams a few weeks later.
Atlanta History Center

Sheriff Bonham L. Johnson, who led Newton County's investigation at the bridges—and who, with federal agents, coaxed a confession that broke the case open.
Newton County Sheriff's Office

Special Agent Adelbert J. Wismer of the Bureau of Investigation, whose visit to the Williams spread unwittingly provoked the death of eleven men. His later efforts to enlist the help of Governor Hugh Dorsey in prosecuting the killers proved central to the case.
Michael Anne Johnson

THE Chicago Defender

WORLD'S ☆☆☆ **GREATEST** ☆☆☆ **WEEKLY**

PRICE **10** CENTS

2D CITY AND FINAL MAIL EDITION

XVI NO. 14 SATURDAY CHICAGO, APRIL 2, 1921 PRICE TEN CE

ILLS II; BURIES 6 ALIVE

CHIORSTER WAS FRIENDLY WITH HIS WIFE

ver Love of Woman in the Untimely ath of Singer

en warned to cease at-
tions, Lavinia, Holmes, 2319
ret, by her husband, Al-
was ariciously cut by No-
1 on the night of March
Sunday morning at the
tal as a result of blood
a Choirmaster
ho has been in this coun-
4 years, came here from
Islands, at the age
led as a Hawaiian
ant, for her husband, —

SOME DAD, AND HE'S BACKED BY A GOOD RECORD

Virginian, Father of Thirty Children, Still Vigorous and Walks Miles Each Day

Suffolk, Va., April 1.—In Nanse-
mond county, Virginia, lives a father
of twenty-five children, all living.
There were thirty of them, but five
have died. This is Jason Boone, a
well-known citizen, who resides in
the new Hoosier road, about four
miles from this city, and who, though
81 years old, is still vigorous and
walks this town every Saturday.

Married Only Twice

Boone was a tree man and was
twice married. There were seventeen
children by the first marriage, and by
the second wife, who is still living,
there were thirteen children. Fourteen of the first set and eleven of the
second are yet living. About eight
years ago Boone's second wife left
him, going off with the Church of
God and Saints of Christ.

RIVER OF DEATH, SLAUGHTER HOUSE AND TWO VICTIMS

Scenes of Georgia murder farm where eleven met death at the hands of John Williams (white), a Southern plantation owner of the "slaughter house." Price in committing murder Williams buried his victims in this cabin, either kill them while imprisoned, or take them to Alcovy River to be drowned. Arrow indicates spot where two bodies washed together were dragged from the river. Federal agents are still fishing for more. Upper photo is that of Clyde Chisholm, lower one of Williams.

River and Grav Give Up Dead Bodies

U. S. PROBE ORDERE

Monticello, Ga., April 1.—The Belgian Congo has bee
done. John Williams, a white farmer, prominent in J
county, is known as the "Leopold of the
brutal murders to his credit and had planned others, but a
gruesome career. Manning, fearing he would be drown
the Alcovy River, escaped from the Williams plantation
told his story to federal authorities. An investigation wa
unediately ordered by U. S. District Attorney Alexander
agents were sent t
Williams farm to verify the story.

COLLECT EVIDENCE

Mute and revolting evidence was found when an inves
tion, led by Manning, was conducted on Williams' planta
Six bodies of men were dug from shallow graves back o
job because he had been threatened with death. Five
white man's house, where he had buried them under cov
night. Manning confessed that he helped "his boss" to d
job because he had been threatened with death. Five
decomposed bodies were found in the murky depths of
Alcovy River, some were chained and others were buri
with heavy reeds. Manning wept bitterly as he led the fe
ing party over the Williams farm. He repeatedly asserted
innocence by declaring that the white man forced him to
commit the brutal murders. Feeling became so intense ag
Manning, that federal agents secured permission of Gove
Dorsey to work under protection of an armed posse.

BEGGED FOR LIFE

Sensational developments have come, one after anoth
since the finding of the two bodies in Yellow River
together. Manning declared he helped his boss, Willie
hurl the bodies from a bridge. He declared the two men o
and begged to be shot, but Williams poured acid in t
ning asserted that Williams laughed about the incident w
riding to his plantation. He warned Manning to keep
"mouth shut" or he would suffer the same manner of de
From place to place the investigators followed Manning
ging at his direction and uncovering their gruesome f
With the recovery of eleven bodies the quest ended and M
ning, handcuffed, was returned to jail under heavy guard.

MURDER FARM INSPECTED

it is claimed. Several men have been employed on the
lliams plantation, and later mysteriously disappeared.
man seemed to have a killing at times," Manning said in
describing Williams. "He would tell me to get a shovel
follow him. Den he would order some other men to go sh
he would tell us to dig a deep hole." While we was diggin
hole he would tell us to step out and leave the other
Den he would take a axe and knock the men in the head t
was digging in the hole. Den he would holler loud, but we
throw dirt on dem, and bury dem right in the hole. Dey w
whimper, but we would keep on throwing dirt, and soon
covered up."

Slays With Axe

Manning pointed to a hole and
said: "Ma. Charlie Chisholm and
big John were digging here with Mr.
Johnny Williams standing over us.
He told us to dig a well and to have
it round. We were digging back
when Mr. Johnny told me and Charlie to get out of the big hole. As we
got out he took an African of the
big hole he struck Charlie in the
head and knocked him to the bottom.
Charlie was dead then. John and I
were then ordered to take John's
body and bury it in the well. At the
time of the shooting, who is blind in both
eyes."

DOCTOR'S RECORD TEARS DOWN COLOR BARRIERS

That our physicians have gained
advance recognition in the professional field in
Chicago is evi-
denced by the
appointment of
Dr. Walter H.
Grant, 3218 Lake
Park avenue, to
the largest
hospital repu-
tation to be the
largest institu-
tion of its kind
in America. Dr.
The medical stu-
dents took the
examination for

Dr. W. S. Grant

Dr. Grant is a graduate of Fisk
University, where he finished with
high honors, and for three years was
a patient of the Cook county
hospital.

SEE FIRST DARK FACE IN COUNTY IN MANY YEARS

Excitement and Curiosity Prevail When Stranger Gets
Off at Station by Mistake

Comanche, Texas, April 1.—No better indictment of the "manner of our
people in west Texas and the excitement one of them creates when
he appears in that part of the state

KILLS YOUNG GIRL TO SAVE HER FROM EVIL

Father's Bullet Halts Career
of Girl on Downward
Path; May Be Insane

New York, April 1.—In an effort to
wring a confession from Eddie Williams and Fred Maxwell, held in connection with the murder of George
Manor

CLAUDE M'KAY, AFRICAN POET, MADE CO-EDITOR

New York, April 1.—For the first
time in history, ability and literary
worth among out-
people have been
recognized by a
white magazine.
The Liberator,
published at 138
West 13th street,
is come to this
notice this week,
added to the edi-
torial staff
Claude McKay,
the African poet,

Claude McKay

One of many postcards depicting the Frank lynching. The victim's portrait appears in the inset at left; the National Pencil Company, where Frank worked with Mary Phagan, is pictured at right.
Georgia Archives

Hugh Dorsey delivers an argument during the 1912 Daisy Opie Grace trial—a defeat that set the stage for his zealous prosecution of Leo Frank the following year.
Atlanta Constitution/*Kevin Swift edit*

Thomas E. Watson, a political kingmaker and rampant bigot who promoted Dorsey's run for governor, then morphed into his harsh critic and political rival.
Watson-Brown Foundation, via University of North Carolina

Dorsey as Georgia's newly elected
chief executive. His two terms in office
culminated with his intercession in the
Williams case, followed by a bold and
controversial stand on race relations.
Atlanta History Center

Rev. Cary B. Wilmer,
an influential Atlanta
clergyman who opposed
Hugh Dorsey in the
Frank case, then allied
with the governor in
seeking justice for the
Murder Farm's victims.
Atlanta History Center

James Weldon Johnson, a success in myriad fields before becoming the first Black secretary of the NAACP. When the first bodies were fished from the Yellow River a few weeks later, he led the Association's response, along with its continuing campaigns against peonage and lynching.
Indiana University

Fair hair, pale skin, and blue eyes enabled the NAACP's Walter F. White to surreptitiously mingle with lynchers and other perpetrators of racial violence. When he wasn't passing for white, the Association's future secretary was a tireless critic of southern peonage.
Scarlet and Black Digital Archive, Rutgers University

The Newton County Courthouse in Covington, scene of the Williams and Manning trials in 1921 and 1922. The large courtroom was on the second floor, beneath the side-facing gable at the building's rear.
Earl Swift

The Fulton County Jail, better known as the Tower: home for months to Williams, Manning, and many of the plantation's Black workers.
Atlanta Constitution *Photo Archive, Georgia State University*

The interior of Judge John B. Hutcheson's courtroom on the trial's second day. As a crush of spectators listens, Clyde Manning—identified with an arrow—describes the murder of his coworkers to the jurors, seated with their backs to the wall at far right.
Atlanta Constitution/*Kevin Swift edit*

The governor drafted attorney and former congressman William M. Howard to assist the state's prosecutors. His questioning of witnesses and closing argument offered some of the trial's most dramatic moments. *State Bar of Georgia*

The leaders of the prosecution and defense teams: at left, Solicitor General Alonzo "Lonnie" Brand, who organized the state's case; and at right, Monticello attorney Greene F. Johnson, who relied on the jury's presumed racism in crafting his defense. Atlanta Journal/*Kevin Swift photo illustration*

Superior Court Judge John B.
Hutcheson pictured late in his career,
when he was a justice of the Georgia
Supreme Court. His decision to allow
testimony detailing the totality of
Williams's killing rampage was pivotal
to the trial's outcome.
Atlanta History Center

Williams in a family photo bearing
a handwritten date of 1921. It's
unclear whether he was in custody
when it was taken.
John Edward Williams

The Newton County jury that decided Williams's fate. The panel
included seven farmers, which caused some northern newspapers
to worry that the accused killer would walk.
Chicago Whip/*Kevin Swift edit*

EXTRA

THE AMERICUS TIMES-RECORDER

PUBLISHED IN THE HEART OF DIXIE

EXTRA

FORTY-THIRD YEAR.—NO. 84   AMERICUS, GA, SATURDAY APRIL 9, 1921.   PRICE FIVE CENTS.

WILLIAMS FOUND GUILTY

Jury Recommends Punishment Be Life Imprisonment

EUROPE'S CHIEFTAINS DON'T LOOK WORRIED, NOW DO THEY?

Five European premiers and military commanders have happy moments, this photograph would indicate It was snapped at Chequers, Lloyd George's country home, in England, as he was telling Marshal Foch and Premier Briand (right) of France a funny story. The photographer couldn't hear the story.

Wealthy Defendant Visibly Effected By Verdict Rendered

Mistrial Had Been Expected in Famous Case. Though Reports Said Jury Stood 10 to 2 For Conviction From First Ballot

COVINGTON, April 9.—The jury in the case of John S. Williams, wealthy Jasper county planter charged with the murder of Lindsey Peterson, a negro farm hand on his plantation, returned a verdict of guilty this morning, recommending Williams to the mercy of the court. The verdict means that Williams will be sentenced to serve a life sentence on the Georgia chain gang.

The case was given to the jury for consideration at 3:15 o'clock yesterday afternoon, and their verdict was returned early this morning.

Surprise was expressed when the verdict was read as it had been generally believed a mistrial would result. Last night, after it had been reported the jury stood 10 to 2 for conviction from the first ballot, the court delivered an additional charge upon certain points at the request of the jury.

Following the delivery of these instructions, the jury again began deliberating and at a late hour Judge Hutcheson left the court room, leaving word that he would return in the event a verdict was returned. The jurors shortly afterward sent word they were preparing to retire for the night, having been unable to agree upon a verdict.

Greene F. Johnson, leading counsel for Williams, announced following the verdict, that an appeal would be taken, but no bill of exceptions has yet been filed.

Although visibly affected by the verdict, Williams made no comment upon the outcome of the case.

Dr. Gus Williams, who has been with his father since the beginning of the famous trial, was in court when the verdict was returned, but none of his other sons, who were referred to frequently in arguments before the jury by counsel for both state and defense were present. It is believed all of them have left for parts unknown.

So far as is known here the Williams case is the only case in the history of Georgia criminal jurisprudence in which a reputable white man was convicted of murder upon the practically unsupported testimony of a negro accomplice.

There are ten other indictments pending against Williams, all of which charge murder, the alleged victims having been negro farm hands employed on his farm in each instance. A number of these negroes, the state alleges, were killed in Jasper county, but the murder of Peterson for which Williams has just been convicted, was committed in this county. Peterson and another negro having been chained together and thrown into Yellow river

$390,852 TECH QUOTA ACCEPTED BY SAVANNAH

Georgia's Second City Lines Up $5,000,000 Campaign

W. S. KIRKPATRICK,
Special Correspondent.

OPEN MIND ON PHILIPPINES

BY LINTON WELLS

CHARTER NIGHT GAY OCCASION AMONG LIONS

City's Newest Civic Club Proves Admirable Host

COTTON

AMERICUS SPOT COTTON

NEW YORK FUTURES

Royal Cafe Reduces All Food Prices 25 Pct

Minneapolis Flour Prices Drop 50c Bbl. in Week

Reading Shop Workers Refuse Wage Reduction

WEATHER.

AMERICUS TEMPERATURES

PLANTER FLAYED BY ATTORNEY IN SPEECH TO JURY

Verdict In Celebrated Trial May Be Reached Tonight

WILL REPORT UPON NEEDS OF FILIPINOS

Some of the plantation's workers, photographed when they were called to testify before the Jasper County grand jury in April 1921. Standing, left to right, are Clyde Freeman, John Freeman, Jule Manning, and Claude Freeman; seated are Emma Freeman, Clyde Manning, and Gus Chapman.
Atlanta Constitution/*Kevin Swift edit*

The surviving children of John S. Williams pose at a 1958 family reunion. Back row, left to right: Gus, Hulon, James Luke, and Robert. Front row: Edward, Ivah Sue, Julian S., LeRoy, Mary, and Curtis. Marvin and Lucy Claire were dead at this point.
John Edward Williams

"I don't know," Manning said. "He asked Artis if he wanted to go home, and he told him, 'Yes, sir.' And he took him to Jackson—that is where he said he was going—and he come back with the automobile."

What day was this?

"That was the day we took the trip to Yellow River."

Mr. Williams was at home that night, correct?

"He was at home that night and he ate supper that night, Mr. Johnny did. And I ate supper and Peterson and Preston and Foots were there then."

Was it after he got back from the train that he told Peterson and Preston they could leave?

No, came the reply. "I never heard him tell Peterson [that] as far as he was concerned they could go, he was ready to turn them loose. I never heard him tell them that. The only thing I heard he told them three boys—Harry Price, Lindsey Peterson, and Will Preston—[was] to quit before night and drive the hogs down to his house and he would take them to the train the next morning, Sunday morning."

But he did not take them on Sunday morning, did he?

"Mr. Johnny come to my house that Saturday night and said he had to take them other boys Sunday morning and he wouldn't have time to take them, and he would take them that night.

"Then, that night . . . they were down to my house, and he come down there, like I told you, and knocked on the door, and told them he would take them Saturday night—he would not have time Sunday morning, that he would have more time to take them that Saturday night, and that he was going to take Johnnie Green on Sunday morning."

Manning had said, had he not, that Mr. Williams gave Peterson and Preston some money?

He had not, Manning said. "I didn't say he gave both of them boys money. I could not swear he give them any money. I didn't see it. They were down at my house. That is what my statement is."

And was it his claim, Johnson asked, that he and Mr. Williams got in the car with all these men and drove them to the river?

"I claim that me and Mr. Williams and Charlie Chisholm and Harry

Price and Will Preston and Lindsey Peterson got in the car together that night. That is my claim. And Mr. Johnny. We all got in the car together."

What time was this?

"It was about eight or nine o'clock at night; it was getting sort of late in the night when we left."

Johnson asked how sure he was of the time.

"I ain't certain about the time," Manning said, "but I think it was getting late in the night. I didn't have a watch or nothing, and I didn't look at no clock. Eight or nine o'clock is getting tolerably late."

And you went to a party that night, after you left Mr. Williams?

No, Manning said, that was just a story he'd told his wife to explain his time away. "I hadn't been to a party. My wife asked me where I had been, and I told her I had been to a frolic. I never went to the party after I got back."

What route did you take in the car with Mr. Williams and the other men?

"We took the road that night that leads up to Waters Bridge and Mr. Polk's store." A public road, he said, that was home to "lots of folks."

Was it his claim, Johnson wanted to know, that they stopped along that public road, a busy public road, to tie up these men?

Yes, Manning said, it was. "I claim that somewhere along the road—that public road going from Mr. Williams's home to Yellow River bridge—we tied them niggers." They stopped on a wooded stretch, he added. "We tied them there in the car. The car was stopped and the engine, too."

How long did it take?

"It taken us about a half an hour to tie them."

Who tied them?

"Me and Charlie Chisholm did the tying. We tied them with a trace chain and wire and me and Charlie Chisholm tied the rocks to them."

Johnson floated an alternative scenario. Was it not true, he asked, that he and Charlie Chisholm did all of this by themselves, and that Mr. Williams was not present?

It was not true, Manning replied. "Mr. Williams was right there."

Did they pass a lot of other cars on the way?

"We didn't pass anybody in the road," Manning answered.

Did they see anyone else on the road?

No, Manning said, repeating that they didn't pass anyone, either.

Williams's lawyer was circling one of the most reckless elements of the crime, as the state had presented it: the contention that Williams had stopped his car on the main road between Monticello and Covington, on a mild Saturday night, and sat behind the wheel for half an hour while his victims were bound and weighted in the seats around him. Granted, he may have felt perfectly within his rights to kill "his" Negroes, and immune from any consequences for his actions. But he placed himself at enormous risk of discovery, for he regularly drove the stretch of highway between the Waters Bridge and Polk's store, and his Chandler—not a rare car, but not a Model T Ford, either—was sure to be known to his neighbors over that way. It was a touring car, too, meaning that it was not enclosed in the style of a modern sedan; the Chandler was essentially a four-door convertible without windows. Its sides were open to the weather and its interior to the view of passersby, further increasing the risk of discovery.

The lawyer asked whether they'd seen anyone at the Yellow River.

"We got on that bridge and we didn't see anybody," Manning said.

So, the witness was claiming to have seen no one in two dozen or more miles of driving, on some of the busiest roads in Jasper and Newton Counties?

"I never seen anybody," Manning said, "from the time we started until the time we got back."

His incredulity about the drive now lodged in the jurors' minds, Johnson asked Manning to again describe what happened at Allen's Bridge. Manning repeated his account, concluding: "Me and Charlie Chisholm pushed the niggers over into the river, me and him together, and Mr. Williams helped us. He took the sack of rock from me, and me and Charlie throwed them in."

Who actually threw the men off the bridge?

"We did the actual throwing. We put them over the banisters, and he put the rocks over."

———

Johnson had two goals in this lengthy cross-examination. First, to poke holes in the state's case, or at least muddy the prosecution's version of events. And second, to introduce the idea that Manning himself had a motive to kill his fellow farmhands; the suggestion of an alternative impetus for the crime might be enough to earn a mistrial, if not an outright acquittal. So now Johnson returned Manning to mid-February, and the day the "United States protectors" came calling. He asked how long they were gone before Williams announced they had to get rid of the farmhands.

"It was in the next week after they left," Manning said.

Where did he make this declaration?

"Mr. Johnny was at his house when he told me that."

At what time of the day?

"I don't know what time, but it was in the evening."

Johnson suggested that Manning had reason to get rid of the men, himself.

Not so, the witness replied. "There was nothing they could hurt me on."

But he had just testified that these United States protectors said he was just as guilty of peonage as Mr. Williams.

Manning acknowledged as much, but emphasized the hopelessness of his situation. "I had to do what Mr. Johnny told me," he said. "I was afraid not to do it. I know I had to do what he told me."

Johnson: Who told you to say you were afraid?

Manning: "Nobody told me to say I was afraid."

Johnson: Somebody must have told you to say that.

"Nobody told me to say that," Manning said. He would not be in trouble now, he added, if he had not been too fearful of Mr. Johnny to refuse him. "Nobody but my own self and knowledge told me to say I was afraid."

Johnson: You're saying that no one told you it was a good idea to say that?

Manning: "Nobody told me to say I was afraid. No one but my own self."

So, Johnson asked, was it his statement that this was all Mr. Williams's idea?

Yes, Manning said. "Mr. Johnny told me we would have to get rid of these niggers. That was several days after these gentlemen left. That is my statement about it."

Was it not true, however, that Manning was interested in getting rid of those men himself?

No, Manning said. "I didn't want to. They were not bothering me."

You were Mr. Williams's farm boss, Johnson said. Those farmhands could have told on you as well as on him.

That might be, Manning said, "but if they told the truth, they could have told what I done I was made to do."

A hard argument to make, Johnson suggested, when he had been boss all this time.

"When I hired to him I didn't hire to boss," Manning said. "I stayed with him thirteen years, but I didn't boss for him thirteen years." In fact, he had not taken the role until "after the Armistice was signed and his boys come home and he got some of these stockade boys. He told me he was looking to me to see after them."

Didn't he have his sons to do that?

"They had to see after their own farms. Mr. Johnny told me he was looking to me to see after them boys on his place."

Was he forced into the job?

"Nobody was compelling me to boss," Manning said. "He told me he was looking to me to look after them, and I told him, 'Yes, sir.' I didn't want to say no, and I just proceeded to boss because I was afraid to say no."

Johnson asked whether he always did as Williams said, even when he didn't want to.

"Whatever he told me to do," he affirmed. "If it was against my will, I would go on and do it. I had been there thirteen years. I was there long enough to find out you had to go ahead and do what he said."

But for all his fear, Johnson observed, Manning had not tried to run, even during and after the killings.

"I stayed there with him two or three weeks after the first killing happened," Manning agreed. "I didn't try to leave. I was afraid to try to leave, and I didn't try to leave." He had attempted to leave once, he said, long before the killings. He had "made a trade" with a neighboring farmer to go work on his place. But Williams had "jumped onto me about it and I never did try to leave any more." For a man who owed his existence to appeasing white authority figures, Manning was astonishingly steadfast in the face of Johnson's interrogation. "Mr. Williams told me we had to get rid of these boys," he said. "That is my statement about it."

Undeterred, Johnson now tried injecting another shot of doubt into the prosecution's narrative by insinuating that its star witness was on the stand because he had more to fear from federal investigators than he did from Williams. To that end, he had Manning describe his arrest and transfer to Covington for his initial questioning.

"They talked to me and asked me did I know Blackstrap, and asked me about those niggers disappearing," Manning testified. "And I told them, at first, I didn't know nothing about it. And they asked me about being there on that bridge and I told them I didn't know nothing about it and I denied the whole of it to them.

"They took me to the jail and done nothing to me, only locked me up. Then, that night, they sent down and got me and brought me up to the courthouse. They didn't tell me nothing on the way."

Johnson asked if the lawmen threatened to "pop" his neck if he didn't help them get Mr. Williams.

"None of them told me that," Manning said. "Nobody ever told me nothing like that."

Didn't they keep him up and talk to him until after four o'clock in the morning?

They did not, Manning said. "They wasn't talking to me all the time—they had two more boys they were questioning. They talked to us, me and these other two boys, at the sheriff's office and the sheriff was there. I was around the sheriff's office."

Didn't they hang him from the ceiling in the jail before they brought him up for questioning?

"These gentlemen never done nothing like that," he answered.

Didn't they carry him to the river wrapped in a blanket?

"They carried me to the river to identify them bodies, but I was not wrapped up in a blanket then."

Apparently trusting the jury would assume he had some basis for his innuendo, Johnson once again asked Manning to tell the twelve about when his interrogators put a rope around his neck. "They never put a rope around my neck," Manning insisted. "I have never had a rope around my neck, no more than when I was a little child, just playing." Johnson asked if the lawmen had threatened to do it. No, Manning replied.

Did they curse at him?

"Some," Manning allowed, but not "like they were mad at me at all. They didn't cuss like they were mad. They were just cussing."

Did their cursing him scare him into telling them stories?

"That wouldn't scare me," he told the defense attorney. "If they said something about going to kill me, or something like that, it would scare me. It don't take so much to scare me if they threaten to kill me, but just cussing don't scare me."

Johnson asked what had finally prompted him to speak to the agents. The safety of the jail, he answered—once he was behind bars and protected from Williams, he was emboldened to defy the planter's orders to keep his mouth shut.

What did they do to him in jail to make him speak?

"Nothing at all," Manning said. "They didn't do nothing but carry me down to the jail, and they had this Frank"—Frank Dozier, the teenage peon who had escaped the previous year—"and they pulled his clothes off to show them where he was whipped at. They didn't do nothing to me, only just put in there and lock me up."

For the third time, Johnson asked if the lawmen had terrified him into cooperating by hanging him at the jail.

Manning did not budge. "They never hung me at all."

Didn't they tell him that if he testified in this case against Mr. Williams, and put it on Mr. Williams, he would get off lighter?

No, Manning answered. "Nobody ever told me to say nothing about that."

Did he expect to get off lighter?

"I just expect to tell the truth, and take it just as it comes."

Did he expect to fight the case when he went to trial?

"I have a lawyer here," Manning replied. "I don't expect to fight the case. I expect *him* to fight it." Johnson's efforts to fluster him were failing. He was neither defensive nor combative. He had the same steady, utterly calm manner he'd displayed all day.

Who else, Johnson wanted to know, had come to see Manning in his cell at the Fulton Tower?

"There ain't been nobody else down there to see me at the Tower but them—these here two men and my lawyer," Manning said, indicating the federal agents. "Only them three, and then some newspaper men come down there to take my picture."

They told him the best thing he could do was to blame Williams, didn't they?

No, Manning said. "None of them told me nothing like that."

Wasn't that his real motive for testifying?

"I ain't putting no more on Mr. Williams than his part, and I ain't telling any more on myself than my part." If there was a takeaway line from Manning's testimony, that was it.

Johnson pointed to Lonnie Brand, who was sitting with Howard and the rest of the prosecution team. Had anyone told him that Mr. Brand here believed that if he—Manning—had participated in fear of his life or limb, he would not be guilty?

"I ain't heard nothing about it," the witness said. "I ain't heard nothing about that."

His lawyer had not told him that?

"My lawyer ain't told me that."

Did his lawyer tell him that he—the lawyer—had been talking to Mr. Brand and these other gentlemen for the prosecution?

"He ain't told me nothing about it. He just talked to me about the case, and I told him about the case, just how it was. He ain't told me nothing about talking to Mr. Brand."

His lawyer had never told him that he'd spoken with Mr. Brand and that it was understood that Manning would get off lighter?

"He didn't tell me that."

Did his lawyer mention going to a conference with these gentlemen of the prosecution at the Piedmont Hotel, where this had been agreed to?

"He ain't spoke to me about any hotel," Manning said. "He never told me anything about that."

Johnson was just about out of questions, and Manning had not wavered. Later, William Howard would declare that he had "never in my life seen a more remarkable witness." Greene Johnson would admit that Manning was "beyond a doubt one of the best witnesses I ever had to cross-examine." John S. Williams would allow: "They drilled him well." In spite of the witness's performance, however, Johnson had found ways to remind the jury that Manning's lawyers had met with prosecutors in Atlanta—string-pulling, backroom-dealing, thinks-it's-so-much-smarter-than-us-country-folk Atlanta—thereby planting the impression that a dirty big-city fix was in to railroad his client. The defense attorney wrapped up his cross-examination by asking the witness about the state of Lindsey Peterson's body when last he saw him.

"He was in a swelled-up condition," Manning said. "His face was swelled. His body was swelled."

How was it, then, that Manning had been able to identify him?

"I recognized him as his body," the farmhand testified. "I knowed it as him and I knowed him by other things—I knowed how he tied his shoes. I knowed him by the shoes, and the weight that were shown to me." The sack of rocks, he meant.

"And by his face," he said. "That is the way I recognized him."

<h1 style="text-align: center;">21</h1>

MIDAFTERNOON: AFTER NEARLY A HALF DAY of testimony and hostile cross-examination, Clyde Manning left the stand and the courtroom took a long, collective breath. Yet as wearying, repetitive, and sometimes maddening as Wednesday, April 6, already seemed, it was not yet concluded. Lonnie Brand prepared to call the state's next witness.

From this point on, he and his fellow prosecutors faced a challenging assignment. Though Manning was the only living witness to John S. Williams's alleged crimes, he was also his confessed accomplice—and Georgia law stipulated that an accomplice could not be the sole source of evidence in a conviction. Because the state's account of the murders could not be confirmed by anyone else, its lawyers would seek to fortify, corroborate, and contextualize Manning's narrative with information from other witnesses. They hoped that Greene Johnson and his team would be unable to shred the resulting quiltwork of circumstantial evidence.

Now taking the oath was Lessie May Benton, twenty-six, who lived up at Hulon's place and prepared meals for both the hands and Hulon's family. She had known and fed all of the dead men. She had seen most of them every day. William Howard opened his direct examination by asking when she last saw the three who died in the Yellow and South Rivers.

"The last time I seen Harry Price and Will Preston was Saturday at dinner," she told the jury, referring to the midday meal. "I can't recollect what month it was in. It was in this year."

Howard asked whether she recalled the federal agents' visit.

Yes, she said, she did "recollect about government officers coming to where I lived on Mr. Williams's place. Two came there." Benton could not recall the day or date, but said she last saw the three slain men "about two weeks" later. She saw Mr. Johnny that day, too: she had just cooked lunch and was carrying it out to the farmhands in the field when she encountered him "walking towards the house, toward his son's house. He was coming up and I was going down." Williams asked whether she had seen Artis Freeman. "I told him, 'No, sir,' [that] I hadn't seen him. That was all that passed between us. Artis wasn't there for dinner. They said he was going home."

Greene Johnson objected to her use of hearsay. Judge Hutcheson agreed it was inadmissible. Howard moved on, asking her to describe her dealings with Lindsey Peterson that same afternoon. "Peter, he come to the house—that is, Peterson—he come to the house where I was at work, come back to Mr. Hulon's house and got a pair of shoes. And I had patched him a pair of overalls, and Miss Catholine, Mr. Hulon's wife, gave him a white shirt. And then he got on his mule and went back to where they were at work at, and that is the last I saw of him." At first blush this testimony might seem trivial, but it established that Lindsey Peterson had been preparing to leave the plantation that Saturday. When Howard ended his questioning, Johnson chose not to cross-examine Benton. She stepped down.

Enter the state's next witness: Clyde Freeman, Manning's distant cousin and fellow informant, and the brother of Claude Freeman, the field boss of the peons who lived on the river tracts. Howard asked him, too, about the last he saw of the three men later drowned in the Yellow and the South.

"The last time was one Saturday evening they left from over there in the field to carry some hogs down to the house," Freeman answered. "That was, from the Campbell place—Mr. Hulon Williams was working the Campbell place. They quit the field about two hours by sun." He was using a now-obsolete term for two hours before sunset. "It was about five miles from where they got the hogs from to where Mr. John S. Williams lived. Mr. John S. Williams told them himself to carry the hogs down there." Freeman knew this, he testified, because he was there to hear

Williams give the order. "I know because he come over in the field. We had ate dinner where we were, and he came to the field where we were at work, them people were at work, and told them. They left the field about two hours by sun. He told them to bring them hogs down to his house."

And did the men take the hogs down there?

Freeman couldn't say for sure what happened once the men left with the animals—he did not see them again. What he did know, he said, was that Williams had promised them their freedom, because he had heard that, as well. "Mr. Williams told them to take the hogs down to his house that evening [and] he would let them go home," Freeman said. "He would take them to the train that night or soon Sunday morning. He told them to take the hogs down and he asked them if they wanted to go home, and they said yes, and he said he would take them to the train Saturday night or Sunday morning. That is all I know about it."

As for the vanished Artis Freeman, he knew Williams had "come for" him, the witness said. "He said he was going to take him to the train. He was in his car, his automobile. I didn't see Artis go off in the automobile with him. He taken the mules to the house and put them up. I never did see Artis with him; I don't know how he left there."

What kind of car was Williams driving?

"I don't know what car Mr. Williams had, what sort it was," Freeman answered.

This time, Greene Johnson did want to cross-examine the witness. His goal: to continue to troll for inconsistencies and to elicit testimony that Manning could drive. If Manning could drive, then Manning could have transported, murdered, and disposed of the three men without Williams. To that end, Johnson began by asking Freeman where he had been working that Saturday afternoon.

On the river tracts with Mr. Hulon Williams, he replied. He had been up there with Peterson, Preston, and Foots when John S. Williams visited the group by car. Mr. Johnny "told these boys he would let them go home if they wanted to go. They told him they wanted to go. Then Mr. Williams told them when they drove them hogs down there, to take them down that Saturday night and then that Saturday night or the next Sunday morning, he would let them go, I heard him say."

Johnson asked for clarification as to who on the plantation owned cars.

"Mr. Hulon had an automobile and Mr. Williams had one," Freeman said, then corrected himself: "He didn't have but one and Mr. Hulon had two—Mr. Hulon Williams had a Chandler and a Ford."

Had Freeman seen Clyde Manning drive the Chandlers?

No, he said. "I never seen him drive either one of them."

Did Freeman recall a time when Clyde Manning drove Mr. Williams's Chandler and tore it up?

"I don't remember that at all," Freeman said.

Did he ever see Manning drive the other car?

"I never seen him drive either one," he said. "I seen him drive the first Ford Mr. Johnny owned. He never drove it any further than out from under the shelter, and would wash it off."

Johnson changed course to build the impression that Freeman had been coached. The lawyer asked whom he'd spoken with in the Atlanta jail. No one, Freeman replied. Hadn't the federal agents been up there to see him? No, the witness said. They spoke to him in the Covington jail, just after he was taken into custody.

Didn't they take him to their offices in the post office building up there, to talk?

"I have not been outside the jail in Atlanta since they taken me there."

So, Johnson said, Freeman had not been talking about what he would say as a witness?

No. The only conversations he had about the case since arriving in Atlanta were in his cell, with fellow prisoners.

Thwarted for the moment, Johnson turned the witness back over to Howard, whose redirect examination focused on Freeman's identification of the bodies under Allen's Bridge. The prosecutor asked whether he had seen Peterson and Preston since that Saturday.

He had. "They were dead when I saw them. I don't know the name of the bridge where I seen them, but it was at a bridge somewhere in this county."

He couldn't name the bridge?

"I don't know what bridge it was," he repeated. "It was a bridge over the river; I don't know the name of the river."

Howard asked what he had seen at this bridge.

"I saw the bodies of two persons buried near the river bridge, Peter and Will Preston."

How long ago was that?

"I don't know, sir, hardly how long that was. But the last time I saw them was that Saturday afternoon, until I saw their dead bodies at the bridge—something about a week or two weeks, I don't know exactly. I think somewhere about two weeks from that time."

Howard asked whether he had seen Harry Price.

"I never saw him after that Saturday afternoon," Freeman answered, "and I never saw his body."

Howard was finished. Freeman was excused from the witness chair. Judge Hutcheson recessed court until nine the next morning. As John S. Williams said his goodbyes to his family, those onlookers pausing in their exit from the courtroom might have noticed just one of his adult sons shaking the farmer's hand. Hulon, LeRoy, and Marvin Williams had again failed to show up.

IT WOULD BE NATURAL TO ASSUME that, with Clyde Manning's testimony, the trial of John S. Williams reached such high drama that whatever followed would pale in comparison. But the proceeding's third day—Thursday, April 7, 1921—offered surprising and disturbing revelations of its own.

Williams, wearing an air of insouciance and a dark alpaca jacket, a sprig of cape jasmine in his lapel, navigated his way once again down the clogged aisle to his seat. His wife, daughters, and oldest son took their places around him. Hulon, LeRoy, and Marvin did not. With a rap of the judge's gavel, the day's business began promptly at nine o'clock.

Lonnie Brand called the state's next witness: Rena Manning, Clyde's wife. She was all nerves as she settled into the witness chair, and chewing gum like she meant it. William Howard walked her through the principal facts of her life: She was twenty-three and had lived at the Williams place since her marriage. She cooked for Mr. Johnny and his family—or had, at least, before she was brought to Atlanta for questioning. After that, she returned to the farm and lived briefly on the river tracts with Clyde's mother, India, before they were both snatched up by federal agents and placed in protective custody in the Tower.

Howard's initial questions trod familiar ground: Had she known Peterson, Preston, and Foots? Did she remember the last time she saw them? What were the circumstances? "I knowed them when I seen them," Rena Manning said. "They did not work or live with Mr. John Williams. They worked with Mr. Hulon Williams." The last time she saw them "was the time they drove some hogs down to Mr. Johnny's house. That was the last time I seen them, down to Mr. John Williams's house." She had not seen them driving the hogs, but she saw the hogs the next morning, penned near the house.

The doomed men "ate supper at Mr. John Williams's house that Saturday—Charlie Chisholm, Harry Price, Will Preston and Peter, and Clyde, my husband," she said. "I cooked supper at Mr. Williams's kitchen, and I got through washing dishes and we all went home, down to my house, where I stayed at, all them boys. And we made a fire and set down by the fire and was talking, and Mr. Johnny Williams come and knocked on the door, and Clyde opened the door. And he told Clyde he wanted them to go off a piece with him."

Howard asked how she knew who was at the door.

"I seen Mr. Williams at the door."

What happened then?

"Clyde got up and all them went on with him, all the boys that were in the house."

Remind the jury, Howard said, who those boys were.

"They were Lindsey Peterson, Will Preston, and Foots, and Clyde, and Charlie Chisholm. All got up."

What can you tell us about what happened after that?

"I didn't know where they were going," she said. "After they went out I heard the car start up and that is all I heard. It was a Chandler car. It sounded up towards Mr. Johnny's house. Mr. Johnny had a Chandler car. It come from the direction of his house.

"That was not very long after they left the house, the car started up—just about the time they could go up there, I heard it crank up."

Had she heard the car leave?

"I don't know whether it moved off or not. I heard the cranking up." It was late, perhaps midnight, when she next saw her husband.

Howard's following questions were memorable for their brevity and the power of the answers they elicited. Did he have Charlie Chisholm with him?

"Charlie Chisholm didn't come back with him."

What about the other men?

"Harry Price, Foots, not Will Preston, none of them come back with him."

Howard asked whether she saw the three afterward. No, she said. "And I don't know where they went, and don't know what became of them."

Howard returned to his seat. His witness had provided exactly what was needed: corroboration of the state's timeline for that Saturday night. She had reinforced the earlier testimony about John S. Williams's offer of freedom to the men up at the river tracts, and their activities at the home place after arriving with the hogs. Most importantly, she had placed Lindsey Peterson and the other doomed men in Williams's Chandler—and with Williams.

Greene Johnson rose for his cross-examination. His aim, once again, was to nitpick the witness's testimony and hint that she had been coached, thereby sowing just enough doubt in the minds of the jurors that they'd have reason to disregard her testimony as a fiction planted in her head by the prosecution. His first question for Rena Manning was how long she had been cooking for Williams. Since December 1919, she thought— "something over a year, mighty nigh two years."

He asked how long she and Clyde had been married. Like most of the prosecution's Black witnesses, she had only a rough command of math or calendar dates, having never been schooled in their use. Johnson surely knew this. "About nine years," she said. "I was fifteen years old when we was married and I am twenty-three now."

They were separated for a time, weren't they?

"We parted, and I stayed away from him about two years."

That was because Clyde beat her, wasn't it?

"Clyde never beat me up," she said. "That wasn't the reason I stayed away. We just quarreled and I went away from him."

Having created the impression that Manning might be a wife-beater, Greene continued with the now-expected questions about hogs, the names of the murdered men, cars, and, of course, dates and times.

When she said they drove the hogs down, Johnson asked, what day was that?

"That was Saturday."

Which Saturday?

"I don't know what Saturday it was. It has been a good while."

How long ago?

"I don't know, sir, how long it has been, but I know it has been a good while, something like a month."

Could it have been two months ago?

"I don't think it has been two months."

What month was it?

"I don't know what month it was in, whether March or February—whether it was January. I don't know what month it was, but I just know it was Saturday."

How did she know it was Saturday?

"I know it was Saturday." Untutored in the calendar though she might have been, Saturday nights stood apart on the plantation. Once work was wrapped up for the day, peons and farmhands typically had a few hours to themselves and could look forward to a relatively light workload come Sunday morning—a brief respite from their otherwise grueling existence.

Who told her to come up here on the witness stand and say it was Saturday?

"Nobody told me to say it," she testified. "I said it was Saturday myself. It was Saturday."

About what time was it when she finished cooking supper that night?

"About eight o'clock, I reckon."

Did they have a clock there at Mr. Williams's?

Yes, she said.

Did she have a clock at her house?

"I had a clock at my house, but I didn't have any time—the clock was not running at my house."

So she thought it was about eight o'clock?

Yes, she said. After eating and cleaning up, the group left the main house for the cottage she shared with Clyde. "All of us went home together, me and Preston and Charlie Chisholm and Foots, and then we made a fire and set down by the fire. We were just talking and having fun and carrying on in fun, talking and laughing." After about thirty minutes, she testified, Mr. Johnny knocked on the door.

Johnson asked how she knew it was Mr. Williams.

"I seen him," she said.

Who told you to say that?

"Nobody told me to say I seen him."

What did he want?

"He told Clyde he wanted him to go off with him, and Clyde and all of them got up and went off with him."

Did he say the others should come along?

"Clyde told these other niggers to come on. When he told them to come on, they all went off together. They all went out the door."

Where did they go from your house?

"I don't know which way they went. I didn't go to see. It was dark."

How can you be sure it was Mr. Williams at the door?

"The light was shining in the house and he was standing in the door and I could see him good."

And she did not know where these men went?

No, she said, but she heard the car start, after just about the time it would take the men to walk to the parked Chandler.

Johnson asked whether she knew the difference between a Ford and a Chandler.

"I have seen the Ford car, and I know a Ford when I see one," she told him. "And I have rode in them. And I seen the Chandler car and I have rode in it."

So she knew all about them?

No, the witness said, "but I know a Chandler from a Ford when I see them."

And what made her think, Johnson asked, that it was the Chandler she heard starting?

"The Ford makes a louder noise cranking than the Chandler. I know that was the Chandler car cranking up that night."

Again: Who told her to say it was?

"Nobody," she said. "I heard it. I could tell the Chandler, the way it exhausted. I know that was the Chandler and it was not a Ford, and I heard it. That is all I know about it."

Judge Hutcheson paused the morning's business to give at least a few of the onlookers crowding the aisle, the floor before the bench, and along the courtroom's walls a chance to find seats. Once the commotion subsided, Lonnie Brand called Sheriff Bonham L. Johnson to the stand. Howard asked him some general questions about the geography of the county's south end—about the Yellow and South Rivers, and their distance from the county line, and whether the Yellow was deep enough to drown a man. He tussled with Greene Johnson, again, over the admissibility of testimony regarding Harry Price's death. Then, several minutes into his examination, he turned to Manning's behavior and treatment in custody.

The sheriff was unequivocal. "While in my custody, he was not cursed or threatened or menaced, or any physical act done towards him, to compel him to say or do any particular thing with reference to the matter about which he was in my custody. The only thing that was said to him was that he had been lying.

"Nothing happened to Clyde Manning while in jail," he insisted. "No hanging up with a rope, or by the neck, or anything in any way to compel him to make any statement connected with this case. No such things were done, nothing of that kind at all. There was not anything done in my presence, in any manner, at any time, by any person, subjecting him to abuse or torturing him or threatening him for the purpose of compelling a statement, at any time."

That slammed the lid on Johnson's insinuations that lawmen had beaten Manning's confession out of him. For the moment, anyway. Howard moved on, asking the sheriff to describe the Easter weekend trip into Jasper County in search of bodies. The witness recalled that he'd found head wounds on two victims dug up on the plantation—"I could not tell whether the skulls were broken, but they had been hit in the head"—and a similar injury to Fletcher Smith, whom John S. Williams had entombed under a new crop of corn. In answer to another question from Howard, he recounted the horrific discoveries at the Waters Bridge.

Howard returned to his chair. Despite the sheriff's forthright testimony of only a few minutes before, Greene Johnson opened his cross-examination by returning to Manning's interrogation. "Mr. Chastain and Mr. Wismer were here. I was right there the whole time," Sheriff Johnson told him. "They told him that they wanted him to tell the truth, he had been lying long enough."

Lying about what?

"They had been talking to him about the Negroes. They told him in a very mild manner he had been lying about it and they wanted him to tell the truth about it, and after some time he came to his statement."

This was at four o'clock in the morning, wasn't it?

It wasn't as late as that, the sheriff said.

The defense attorney turned to the remains recovered at Allen's Bridge, apparently aiming to create doubt as to their identities. He asked the sheriff if he had seen the bodies there.

Sheriff Johnson: Yes.

Lawyer Johnson: Describe them for the jury.

Sheriff Johnson: "They looked to be pretty good-sized men. One was larger than the other."

Lawyer Johnson: When did you first see them?

Sheriff Johnson: "I saw them the same day they were found in the river. I think it was Sunday, March the thirteenth."

Lawyer Johnson: What was their state of preservation?

Sheriff Johnson: "I think I could have identified them if I had ever known them. They were in pretty good condition."

Lawyer Johnson: But you could not identify them?

Sheriff Johnson: "I, myself, could not identify them. I had never known them."

Lawyer Johnson: When was it that Manning saw them?

Sheriff Johnson: "My recollection is that Manning saw those bodies three weeks ago today. I took him down there myself. They had been buried ten days or two weeks then."

Lawyer Johnson: What was their condition at that point?

Sheriff Johnson: "The bodies were in a worse condition then than the first time I saw them, when they were buried, but I could have told very plainly they were the same bodies."

Lawyer Johnson: Do you think you still could have identified them?

Sheriff Johnson: "I think if I had known the men in life, I could have recognized them at the time they were disinterred. I don't think it would have been any difficulty. I think if I had known them in life, I would have known them then."

Lawyer Johnson: Isn't it true that they were in such poor condition that while one of the bodies was being disinterred, the feet came off?

Sheriff Johnson: "That is not true."

Lawyer Johnson: Hands?

Sheriff Johnson: "None of their hands came off."

Lawyer Johnson was finished. Howard stood for a brief redirect. The night Manning was brought to the courthouse for questioning—had the sheriff been present for the entire interview?

"I was with them all the time at the courthouse," Sheriff Johnson answered. "I was present all the time until he was turned over to the jail."

Howard returned to his seat.

The state had no further witnesses.

23

THE DEFENSE TEAM HAD A BRIEF RECESS, during which John S. Williams and his lawyers conferred outside the courtroom. When, at 11:15 a.m., Judge Hutcheson returned to the bench and gaveled the trial back into session, the audience sat shoulder to shoulder in expectant silence, the only sounds "the creaking of seats as men leaned forward and the whispers of the attorneys' last minute conference with their client," according to the *Constitution*.

The conventional wisdom, as expressed in the papers, was that the defense would call multiple witnesses. The three Williams sons were assumed to be among them, along with, perhaps, some of Williams's friends and neighbors. So Greene Johnson was departing from the expected script when he stood, looked to the jury, then to the judge, and said: "Your honor, the defendant will take the stand in his own behalf. I will request you to instruct him."

John S. Williams was about to take advantage of a peculiarity of Georgia law at that time: he had the right to make a statement to both judge and jury without swearing to tell the truth. Theoretically, such unsworn testimony would carry less weight than that enforced by the penalties of perjury. But the gambit was attractive because a witness making such a statement could not be cross-examined. It gave Williams a chance to tell his story without fear of contradiction or consequence.

He walked to the witness chair. The press was divided on the impression he made as he did so. Rowland Thomas of the *New York World* wrote that he crossed the floor with a vigorous stride. The *Constitution*'s Marion Kendrick thought that he "showed the first strain from the long trial as he mounted the stand," and that he was "noticeably nervous" once seated, "rubbing his cheek and playing with his mustache" with "trembling hands."

Whatever the case, now he spoke. "Well, gentlemen," he said, "if I live to next October I will be fifty-five years old. I have a wife and twelve children, who I am very proud of. I was born in Meriwether County, lived there 'til I was about twelve months old, and moved to Jasper. I have been there all my entire life with the exception of seventeen years I lived in Monroe County.

"I have never had any kind of crime charged against me in my life, and neither have my boys. I have always tried to teach them to be law-abiding citizens, which they have always proved to be. When our country was called to arms a few years ago, my boys were one of the first four boys to volunteer, and went to their country's aid and did their duty, and they were discharged with honorable discharges, made good records plumb through." This was a remark sure to resonate: hanging high over the bench was a banner paying tribute to Newton County's war dead.

"I have a plantation in Jasper County," he said, "not near so large as newspaper reporters say, and what I have, it is under mortgage. Niggers, boll weevil and low price of cotton just about cleaned me up. I have no idea if it was sold today I could pay my indebtedness."

In truth, remember, he had cashed out of the place days before. Williams spoke softly, so that those listening from the courtroom's rear could only catch the occasional word. The *World* reported that he used "a conversational tone such as he might have addressed to a group of other farmers around a stove in a country general store." He "did not appear to be pleading for his life, nor could one realize from his manner that his fate might hang on his adequate or inadequate powers of verbal expression."

"I am like most farmers that I know," Williams continued, "that at times I have bonded out and paid fines for niggers with actual agreement that they would stay there 'til their fines were paid, or 'til he was relieved from his bond—which in many instances I have rehired them after that, and paid them wages just like I would any other nigger I would hire going through the country, and which I thought I had a perfect right to do.

"About two months ago, some federal officers came to my house. I was not there at the time, but while they were there I drove up in my car, and there is one of the gentlemen." He pointed to Wismer. "He was sitting out in front of my house, in a car, talking to two niggers. I got out and went and introduced myself to him and he told me his business: he was around investigating some peonage charges through the country. I says if that is your business, everything there that I did he had free access to it, and I would do anything I could to help him, that he could go around and investigate everything. And in which I would help him, if he liked, and I would like to know the law of peonage.

"He says, 'If you pay a nigger's fine or go on his bond and you work him on your place,' he says, 'you are guilty of peonage.'

"I says, 'Well, if that is the case, me and most of the people who have done anything of the sort were guilty of peonage.' About that time, that gentleman there"—he pointed to Brown—"came and walked out from behind the house with Clyde Manning. Clyde looked like he was mighty near frightened to death.

"He walked up to me and says, 'Have you ever worked a nigger by the name of Gus Chapman?' I says, 'I have.' He says, 'Did he run away from you last July?' I says, 'He did.' He says, 'Did you take some nigger laborers and bring him back?' I says, 'I did.' He turned to Clyde Manning and says, 'You lying scoundrel, you. You ought to have your neck broke. You have just been telling me a bunch of lies. I believed it when you were telling it.'

"So he called out some names and wanted to investigate them. I says, 'They are up on the river, on the boys' place,' the niggers were up there. I says, 'Gentlemen, everything is open. I will go and show you everything that you want to see.' I says, 'I may be plumb guilty of peonage, but I am not going to tell a whole bunch of lies about it.' So we got in my car and went on up there."

Here, Williams embarked on a somewhat tongue-tied account of their visit to the river tracts. It aligned pretty closely with the agents' testimony, except that he made no mention of the red house. "After we come from there and come back home to my house, I says, 'Now, gentlemen, I would love to know what you think of the surroundings.' He says, 'It is quite different to what we expected it to be, from all reports.' He says, 'The worst things we seen was your son with his pistol.' He went on talking and says, 'I have a perfect right to arrest you, going around here with a pistol in your pocket.'"

Presumably, Williams was quoting Brown. "My son says, 'I have bought this pistol and I have a license to carry it, if it is on the outside,' which it was. He says, 'I didn't know that.' He says, 'I am not going to make any charges against you for that.'" He had described this scene out of sequence, as neither LeRoy nor his brothers accompanied the farmer and agents back to the home place. As the *Atlanta Journal* put it, he "was not connecting the events in the case but was rambling along, making such statements as entered his head from time to time, it appeared."

Williams: "I says, 'I would love to know what you think of the surroundings.' He says, 'They are much better than we expected.' He says, 'Technically, you may be guilty of peonage.' He says, 'We have looked at your hands. They are well dressed, and shows they are well-fed. All we talked with seem to be satisfied. I don't think you need to have any fear of any case before the federal grand jury.' And the grand jury made no case. None was presented before it. And they left then."

Until now, Williams had been speaking of events witnessed by other white men. Now he offered his version of what happened "a few minutes after they left," when "Clyde Manning come up to me and says, 'Mr. Johnny, I don't think you treated me right.'

"He says, 'You just made me out a liar right before them Revenue officers.' I says, 'How was that?' He says, 'I denied everything about Gus running away and us going to catch him and bringing him back,' and says, 'You up before me and made me out a liar,' and says, 'I believe they are going to get me.'

"He says, 'They told me I was just as guilty of peonage as you,' and he says, 'They asked me how many hours I worked.' He says, 'I told them all day. I worked all day.' He says, 'They says, "How much are you getting?"' He says, 'I told them twenty dollars a month.' And he says, 'They says, "You ignorant fool," says, "You ought to be getting forty dollars a month and work eight hours a day,"' and talked about taking me down to the jail."

His narrative was convoluted, but he appeared to be suggesting that the agents talked of arresting him—Williams—for underpaying his workers. "Mr. Brown had been talking to him and claimed to be his friend," Williams said. He added, as an aside: "He may be his friend now. I don't know." He had, in a few sentences, assigned the same motive to Manning that the state had pinned on Williams himself, while bolstering his attorney's characterization of the federal agents as out-of-town agitators looking to provoke trouble for local farmers.

"Then, in the morning, I called all my hands," the planter told the jury. "They were gathered around the wood pile up there. I called every one of them up. I says, 'Boys, all of you who want to leave, I want you to talk up.' I says, 'The federal officers have been up here and got everything stirred up.' I says, 'What they say about peonage and all, if you want to [step] right off you can do so, and you can give me any trouble you want to.' And I says, 'All of you who want to go, there is the road. You can just go right on off. You are at perfect liberty to go.'

"It went on 'til Saturday at noon." He was evidently referring to Saturday, February 26, eight days after the agents' visit—the day that Peterson, Preston, and Price met their deaths. "So Saturday, I says, 'Boys, I am going to Jackson today. All who want to go with me can go.' That Negro Artis Freeman says, 'Mr. Johnny, I would love to go. My folks live over there.' I says, 'Artis, you go put on some clothes. I am going to start right after dinner.' And after dinner we started and went on by J. L. Bunny's." Williams was likely speaking of a neighboring farmer, James Lee Burney, and the court reporter went with a phonetic spelling of his drawled pronunciation. "And he said he would like to go with us, so he did, and we went to Mr. A. A. Howell's stable. He deals in mules.

"We talked a little bit. When we come back out, this Artis was standing, leaning up against the car in front of the stable, and I walked up to him and give him two dollars. And he said he lived up there about Locust Grove or Luella, somewhere up in there." Those were communities off to the west in Henry County, and a haul from the Williams home place. "He says, 'Mr. Johnny, I want you to come to McDonough Wednesday. I want to come back with you.'" McDonough was a sizable town near Locust Grove.

"I promised the nigger I would, but after thinking about it, if I would carry him back, I didn't know what might happen with the nigger and I didn't go for him. And then I went on back home with Mr. Bunny, got back about dark, somewhere between sunset and dark, somewhere around there—I don't recollect exactly the time, but somewhere between sunset and dark."

Hearing this, it must have seemed a good bet to some in the courtroom that Bunny/Burney would be called to testify, and perhaps A. A. Howell, too. Artis Freeman might have been another solid witness, except that he had not been seen since. Williams did not speak to what had become of the peon; instead, he turned to the subject of the man he was on trial for killing and, once again, tried to implicate Manning and Chisholm, as well. "I attended to the stuff," Williams said, "and this nigger Lindsey Peterson, Will Preston and Foots come up driving some hogs and they turned them in the lot. And in a little bit Clyde Manning and Charlie Chisholm—I don't recollect whether any other niggers—come on in the wagon, in a few minutes.

"Well, Lindsey Peterson, Will Preston and Foots, the three I mentioned, says, 'Mr. Johnny,' says, 'We taken a notion we want to go and see our folks.' I says, 'That is perfectly all right.' But [the three] says, 'We want to come back.' I says, 'That is all right. If you want to go and come back, you can come back yourselves. That is perfectly all right with me.'"

"I give them five dollars apiece, and told them, I says, 'I will take you to the train in the morning, if you want to go.' They says, 'All right.'" Manning and Chisholm, he added, asked for a half dollar each. Williams said he gave it to them. The hands "went off together" a short time later. Three men with fifteen dollars between them, and the last people seen with them were Manning and Chisholm: with this, Williams was telling the jury that Manning had a second motive to murder—robbery—on top of the first he'd floated, about the field boss's supposed fear of being charged with peonage.

"My older boys left about the twenty-fourth or twenty-fifth of February," the planter continued. "This was the first of March, as well as I recollect, and my older daughter, she had married. My other little one next to her was going to school in Barnesville, and my little boy was staying with his sister-in-law, and there was none but my little bit of kids and my wife there at home.

"I went in there then, and stayed there all night. Never went out at all, never to the next morning. And the next morning, none of them come up but Clyde. I says to him, 'Tend to everything.' I says, 'Clyde, where is the other boys?'

"He says, 'They went on off last night.'

"I says, 'I intended to carry them to the railroad. I would have carried them to the train.'

"He says, 'No, they went off last night and ain't come back.'"

The balance of Williams's statement presented the speaker as an innocent bystander to the murders, and Clyde Manning as the real culprit. This version of events was incompatible with his contention that he'd allowed his peons to leave the property, but if that occurred to him, he didn't let on. He sat with legs crossed, eyes on the jury. Some of the twelve men in the box met his gaze. Some looked elsewhere. Several chewed tobacco.

"I heard down there in a few weeks that some niggers had been found in Middle River over there," he said, "and Eberhardt [Crawford] said he knew the niggers and knew they come from my place. So I heard.

"Like any other man, I went to see Eberhardt, and I says, 'Eberhardt,

I heard you said you knew these niggers and knew they come from my place,' and I says, 'If you did, I want to see them and see if they are my niggers—and if they are, I can identify them, too.'

"He says, 'Mr. Johnny, I didn't know them and I didn't make any such remark.' He says, 'You can ask the coroner.' I says, 'That is all right.' I says, 'If you said you knew them, and thought they were mine, I wanted to investigate, and see if they were niggers from my house.' So I went over to Mr. Polk's store. I told them what I heard Eberhardt said."

Among his listeners, Williams said, was a man who had been present at Allen's Bridge. According to the planter, this unnamed man "said he didn't think Eberhardt said that—and he knew he didn't say that before the [coroner's] jury. He says, 'I don't hardly think any man could have known them. I could not have identified them.' I says, 'If they were from my house, I would have identified them, and did everything I could to catch the one who did it.' I says, 'If they were put in the shallow water, they were put in there for a purpose. There is no question about that.'"

A few days later, he appeared before the grand jury, Williams said, and Lonnie Brand "asked me about going to Eberhardt and says, 'Where are those two men that went in your car with you to Eberhardt's?' I says, 'Not a soul with me. I just went by myself.'" Brand would have been referring to the second visit paid to Eberhardt Crawford's house that night in mid-March—the one that ended with the place full of bullet holes. "I never meant any harm," Williams said. "I thought Eberhardt would have been a friend to me, to have helped find out who they was." All he sought in speaking to the man was to "help in any way I could. I didn't want any trouble. I was not hunting for any trouble."

Now Williams turned to the charges against him. "If I had done this crime, gentlemen, I would have certainly known them," he pointed out. "And I had plenty of time—and I would have certainly have been plumb away from here, where they could never have put their hands on me, before any bills was got." But he "knew nothing about it. I don't know nothing about it. And I just simply don't mean to leave, and never expect to leave or anything, when I am falsely accused of anything." Lucy Williams, clad in black, sat fidgeting with a folded newspaper. "Her eyes never left her husband," the *Constitution* noted.

Williams took up the subject of his accuser, "this nigger, Clyde Manning." Officers had arrested the field boss and brought him to Covington, where they "insisted on him telling something on me and that he positively denied knowing anything. And they taken him to jail, so I was told, and threatened him, and threatened and cussed him, and finally after the whole afternoon and most of the night, how they got it out of him—or what they done to make him tell something on me—I don't know." The jailer perhaps could offer some insight on the question, he suggested.

"I was arrested here on Thursday and kept here 'til Friday, and was sent to Atlanta, and I have been there in jail ever since. I have had no time to get up anything for my defense. I didn't know 'til this trial what that nigger was going to testify, only what I could see from the [newspaper] talk. You know they have thrown hot air everywhere. Nothing that they could say, it looks like, they have failed to say. If I had been out, and had time, I could certainly have got up things to contradict Clyde in these many things he has said."

Williams laid into his longtime hand. "He is a very cruel nigger to the niggers. The whole Manning crowd is. I had to call him down time and time again, and his brother is the same way. His father worked there about twelve years ago. Clyde was a boy then, just beginning to plow. One Sunday morning [Clyde's father] was ambushed and shot all to pieces with a shotgun by someone in the bushes, and Clyde and some of them come over for me and we went over and we could never find any trace of who did it.

"His mother was there, and her children, and Clyde was the only one who was big enough to work. His mother, which they could have put on the stand, asked me to help her with these children, to raise them, and they were very hard-headed. I done my best to help them along." He enumerated the sins of Clyde Manning and his younger brother Gladdis— how Gladdis "went up to a nigger church and got shot up . . . by a little nigger up there at the church," for which Williams was still paying the medical bills; how their mother called on him "time and time again" for help controlling them; how they "would fight each other, and fight her, and fight her sister here"; how he had "tried to get them to go on and do right," but had been confounded by their wild and stubborn ways.

He had just a few points left to make. The first would be seized upon by the press and the prosecution. "As far as the case in Jasper and these other cases, they are separate and, I understand, are distinct cases," he said, "and whenever they are called for trial I shall explain them to the satisfaction of the jury. I don't think it is necessary in this trial to say anything in regard to them. But whenever they are called, I will certainly explain them."

His next point returned him to the character of Clyde Manning. "As far as the case now, in regard to his wife, he was cruel to his wife and whipped her and run her off" to a neighboring plantation, he said. "And he followed her . . . and his sister and brother were swifter niggers and knocked the pistol out of his hand, or he would have killed her.

"He was a bad nigger, and they kept him from killing her," he said. "Now, his wife is a pretty good nigger, so far as niggers are concerned."

Finally, Williams wrapped things up. "As far as the other cases are concerned, and whenever they come up, I expect to explain them fully," he again told the jury. "But as far as the case I am on trial for now, I am absolutely innocent. I don't know anything about that at all. I didn't think anything about the niggers being gone 'til they found some, and I heard what Eberhardt should have said. And me, like any other man would have done, or you would have done, I wanted to know if the niggers were from my place.

"In this case I am as innocent as any human being on Earth, I don't care who it is.

"That is about all I can say about this, I believe."

Williams stepped down. As he did, Greene Johnson stood and uttered a sentence that shocked the courtroom: "That's our case, your honor."

The defense team, it seemed, was trusting that the all-white jury would do what Georgia juries had been doing as a matter of course since Reconstruction: place its faith in the word of a white man, even if that white man wasn't giving his word. Lonnie Brand, rising, announced that the state, too, rested. And just like that, testimony in *Georgia v. John S. Williams* came to a halt, defying the expectation of court-watchers that the proceedings would drag on long enough, in the words of the *Atlanta Journal*, to "prove tedious."

The trial was not over, however. Now came the arguments, which, in an age that placed great stock in speechmaking, often produced a criminal proceeding's most memorable and persuasive moments. This would take some time, for each side would offer three arguments from different lawyers, and the judge had decided he would not limit the time they took.

Custom dictated that because the defense had relied on a single statement to the jury, it had the right to open and close. Both teams agreed that Charles Chester King would open for the defense, followed by state assistant attorney general Graham Wright, then defense lawyer William Hicks Key, then Lonnie Brand. William Howard would close for the state. The last word would go to Greene Johnson.

The judge gave them the lunch recess, seventy-five minutes long, to prepare.

FIRST UP: CHARLES CHESTER KING, forty-six years old and Greene Johnson's law partner. The great-grandson of Newton County pioneers, he was a 1900 graduate of Emory College, then located just outside Covington. He earned a Bachelor of Laws from the University of Georgia in 1908 and was admitted to the bar late that summer. He had practiced in Covington since.

King revisited the case law that, the defense believed, foreclosed the state's mention of any killings but those of Lindsey Peterson and Will Preston. It was dry stuff, delivered largely to the bench. King asked that Judge Hutcheson consider it when drawing up his charge to the jury. He also asked him to instruct the jury that the defendant had a valid alibi—that he was at home when Peterson died.

Those formalities complete, he walked to the jury box. The visit of Special Agents Wismer and Brown had not produced evidence of peonage on the plantation, he told the twelve. The state had failed to establish a motive for John S. Williams to kill anyone. But that visit did give a motive to the lying traitor Clyde Manning. "When Brown told Clyde Manning that he had lied to him about the Chapman affair, the Negro was frightened," King declared. "'You lying scoundrel, you lied to me and ought to be hung.' That's what Brown told him, and right here, if you are looking for motives, you can have one for Clyde Manning." The field boss subsequently "schemed to destroy the eleven Negro hands who might incriminate him by exaggerated stories of their condition of servitude." And after the fact, King said, Manning took this "motive he had in his own mind, and ascribed it to Williams." He was what white planters feared most: a "cunning Negro."

The courtroom, which had been close and sticky from the trial's start, grew so hot that paper fans were passed out. Lucy Williams had her husband fan her as they listened. "And what corroboration has the state to support this Negro's testimony?" King asked. "Out of seven witnesses introduced by the prosecution, only Rena Manning has served to corroborate her husband's testimony. And in this case, I say that the wife of an accomplice should not be credited."

Besides, both of the Mannings had "been well trained by somebody, gentlemen." Rena Manning had made "one statement alone which should demonstrate to you that she was lying. Locked in her home, she tells you, she heard the exhaust of an automobile as far as from here to the jail. You know as well as I do that it is impossible.

"We say, gentlemen of the jury, that in this case there is a lack of corroborative evidence to support Clyde Manning's story. If you were to take Clyde Manning's story out of this case you would have nothing in the world to connect Williams with this case. Where there is an accomplice in a case, the law says you must go further and get other evidence which is independent of the accomplice story to support it before you can convict. They have produced no such evidence."

This wasn't an inquiry into eleven deaths, King reminded the jurors. It concerned just one, for which the deceiving Clyde Manning was solely responsible. Manning was a proven, self-admitted liar. His account didn't deserve the jury's consideration. John S. Williams should be acquitted.

King sat down.

Graham Wright rose for the state. The youngest of the trial's lawyers, at twenty-nine, the assistant attorney general was from Rome, near the Alabama line northwest of Atlanta. He and the older and more experienced Richard A. Denny had been law partners there before Hugh Dorsey appointed Denny attorney general in the spring of 1920; Denny had brought Wright with him to the capital.

He opened, as had King, with case law citations, and, like the defense lawyer, he addressed most of his monologue to Hutcheson, emphasizing that he should instruct the jury that the legal burden for establishing an alibi rested with the defense. Turning to face the panel, he sketched out a brief history of the case and the evidence amassed by the state. "There never has been a more horrible, more heinous or more damnable crime than this committed in Georgia," he declared. And it wasn't Clyde Manning's word alone that pointed to John S. Williams as the guilty party: the circumstantial evidence drew so tight and inescapable a web around the planter "that no human mind can resist it."

Williams fanned himself as Wright scoffed at the defense's suggestion that Manning, not his boss, had murdered the men. For one thing, noted the prosecutor, the idea that Manning "could have killed these Negroes under the very eyes of John Williams, and buried them on his place without Williams knowing it, is absurd and an insult to the intelligence of any man.

"Manning's story is true and John S. Williams is guilty," Wright finished. "The state asks and expects a verdict of guilty in this case."

Came now William Hicks Key, lawyer of Monticello, to address the jury on Williams's behalf. Thirty-one years old and a member of the state legislature, Key opened with an impassioned plea for Williams's family, whom he called "innocent people" brought to grief by Clyde Manning, whose entire testimony had been made out of whole cloth. Turning from the jury, he demanded that Lonnie Brand explain what the state would do with its star witness. "Are you planning to turn him loose on Decatur Street in Atlanta?" he asked. "That's the kind of nigger Atlanta seems to want." Once again, this was an officer of the court speaking, not to mention a lawmaker. "Let me ask another question. What happened to Clyde Manning as he sat in jail with a rope around his neck?"

Brand objected, pointing out that no evidence had been introduced to show that any such thing had happened to Manning. "If your honor pleases," Key replied, "Mr. Williams stated to the jury that Mr. Hays, the jailer, told him that he had heard Manning had a rope around his neck." Howard countered that Williams's statement was unsworn, and that therefore the defense had no right to treat it as fact. Key shot back that he had "the right to draw inferences from Mr. Williams's statement." Howard rose from his chair. "We are perfectly willing for Mr. Key to draw inferences," he said, "but not facts."

Key pivoted to mocking the state and its case. Governor Dorsey had been moved "to employ able and eloquent counsel" to reinforce Brand, he said, because the evidence was not sufficient to get a conviction. The state wasn't relying on facts, but on fancy talk, on speeches. And most of all, it was relying on testimony from a liar and confessed murderer, who was now being coddled by the prosecution. Would those prosecutors even bring Manning to trial? Key turned to the opposing lawyers, shouting: "What is the state going to do with Manning, Mr. Howard?"

"My young friend," Howard replied with calm, "the laws of Georgia provide, and have provided for many years, what shall be done with Manning."

Key took his seat. Lonnie Brand launched his argument by going after him. "The gentleman preceding me frequently intimated to you that I would not prosecute Manning," he said. "As an official of this good old state of Georgia . . . I will prosecute Manning and do my best to convict him." He turned toward the defense attorneys and shook his finger at Key. "Is that plain?" he demanded. "Could it be made any plainer to you what course I shall follow?"

Key's "grandstanding," Brand said, was intended to obscure the abominable nature of the crime Williams had committed. He refreshed the jury's memory with a vivid synopsis of the deaths at the Yellow and South Rivers—the victims' terrifying ride into Newton County; the shocking brutality of the executions on Allen's Bridge; the self-evident aim of John S. Williams "to do away with these Negroes to save himself and his sons from [the] penitentiary."

That Peterson and the other ten dead men were Black did not lessen the grievous nature of the crimes against them, the prosecutor reminded the jurors. They had the same right to protection in the courts as white men. The state's most important witness was a Negro, too, but again, that did not matter, because he spoke the facts: "Never in my experience have I seen a more truthful witness," Brand declared. "At no time did Manning vary in his evidence, although Colonel Johnson tried for an hour to break down his story." Rena Manning had corroborated her husband's account, he said, and her testimony, too, "stood like a rock" under Johnson's fusillade of questions.

This was a case of a white man recruiting, as his accomplice, a man who was helpless to do other than what he was told. "Gentlemen, I've worked Negroes and many of you have seen Negroes worked," Brand said. "And you know, and I know, that after a man has worked a Negro for thirteen years he can make him do anything. He not only can make him kill a Negro but he can make him kill a white man."

If there was a moment in the trial that underlined the racism baked into every aspect of Georgia life in 1921, this might have been it—even the prosecutor knew how to "work" Negroes. Even he knew how it was done. Evidently, the remark did not seem all that dramatic to Brand, who pushed on without pause: Now, freed from the influence of his unrestrained master, he said, Manning had shared what had happened to his fellow farmhands in great detail. His "story sounded like the truth," Brand said. "It sounds like the truth because it *was* the truth."

He asked the jury to convict, then walked to his chair.

Judge Hutcheson declared the trial's long third day finished.

25

THRONGED AS IT WAS FOR MANNING'S TESTIMONY, the courtroom was even more densely packed on the trial's fourth morning. Covington high schoolers had been freed from class to hear the keynote arguments from William Howard and Greene Johnson. Women were present, too—women unrelated to John S. Williams, whose wife and daughters had been the only white women watching before now.

The room was already steamy by 9:20 a.m., when Howard began his summation. His mission: to knot all the strands of the state's case tight around the defendant, while bolstering those threads the defense had previously attacked and was expected to slash at again—Clyde Manning's veracity, the strength of the circumstantial corroboration, the motive.

"There are before you in the evidence eleven murders," he began. "They may be classified according to time, place, manner of killing and the character common to the persons murdered.

"First, Johnnie Williams, killed with an axe. Next, Big John, killed with an axe. Next are Johnnie Green and Willie Givens, killed with axes. Then Fletcher Smith, killed with a gun. Then we should take those killed by drowning. These are Lindsey Peterson, Willy Preston, in the Yellow River; Harry Price in South River; and John Brown, Charlie Chisholm, and Little Bit, drowned in the Alcovy River. Six drowned and five killed on the Williams farm or the farm of his son.

"The destructive malady from which all these people came to their death was located on the farm of John Williams, and the method by which they came to their death is connected with John Williams or someone on his places."

With the reference to a "malady," Howard signaled the device he would use to characterize the killing spree: A sinister plague had descended on the plantation and ravaged it. It arrived soon after the federal agents' visit, and claimed its first victim on or about the following Thursday. All "not immune to it" were destroyed over the subsequent twelve days. By March 8, five days before the discovery of the first bodies at Allen's Bridge, it had decimated the farm's population of peons. When doctors studied terrible diseases, they always sought the cause, Howard told the jury. "We must do the same."

The temperature in the courtroom ticked upward. Williams and his family fanned themselves as the special prosecutor described the origins of peonage outside the United States, through its appearance in the South and the nineteenth-century efforts to outlaw it, all the way to present-day Jasper County. The Department of Justice agents had filled Williams with fear, Howard said, but "even before this horrible series of killings began, federal agents were investigating murder on Williams's farm. One of the men killed was a Negro named Blackstrap, who was killed, according to testimony in this case, in the presence of Williams himself. When federal agents [brought up] these killings, Williams and his boys denied two of them and admitted they killed one in self-defense."

Howard held up a stenographic copy of Williams's unsworn statement from the day before and read an excerpt to the jury—the defendant's assertion that if he were guilty, he could have fled beyond the reach of the law. Was that Williams's thinking when he sent his three sons out of town? To put them far from the crimes, in case something went wrong with his destruction of the evidence? Whatever the case, the killings had started just after the three left Jasper, and did not stop until "every chain gang Negro on the place was destroyed."

Howard derided the defense team's bid to pin the slayings on Manning. "Where was the interest?" he demanded. "*Who* leased the prisoners? *Who* ran the farm? *Who* got the Negroes out of the stockades? Was

it Clyde Manning? No, it was not Clyde Manning. It was John Williams."
The United States' investigation into his operation had so unnerved the
planter that he was "willing to kill eleven men to save himself from federal
prosecution." He might be able to skate through a trial by his neighbors
on a state charge like murder, but the federal government was another
matter. The federal government was beyond his influence.

As for Manning, Howard noted, Williams had denounced his testimony as a lie. Maybe Clyde Manning was indeed a liar, but he had "told
the truth about this thing," the prosecutor said. "The men were found dead
down there on Williams's farm, weren't they? The men were found in the
river where he said they were thrown, weren't they? What if Clyde Manning did tell it—the men are dead, aren't they?

"The biggest liar in the world can tell the truth," he pointed out. "A
liar can say that the sun sets in the West, and it's the truth, even if a liar
does say it."

The temperature in the room continued to climb. Howard, sweating
in his suit and bowtie, and not particularly fit to begin with, pressed on.
"The defense talks about lack of corroboration of Manning's statement.
Do you men on the jury place any credence in the evidence given you
by these government agents, by Rena Manning, by Clyde Freeman, by
Sheriff Johnson, and these other Negroes?" he asked. "Has the defense
impeached them? Has it even *tried* to impeach them?

"Where was Williams's evidence? What became of the witnesses his
lawyers said they would introduce?" Howard turned up the volume. "Oh,
gentlemen, he can't get away from it," he bellowed. "It's murder, murder,
murder!"

The sweltering onlookers absorbed this moment without a sound.
Now more than an hour into his address, Howard turned quiet again. He
spoke of Williams's exalted position within his community and compared
it to the humble lives of his victims. "Do the laws of Georgia fit John S.
Williams? Can they be applied to him?" he asked. "If so, this jury's course
is plain. Surely, there can be no difference between Williams and any
other man in the eyes of the law.

"Miserable, foul, outrageous murders, all planned and executed by John S. Williams!" he thundered. "And when Williams takes the stand he only tells you of two of the killings and says he will explain the [others] later. Does that kind of procedure look like the tactics of an innocent man?" Howard pretended to channel Williams's thoughts: "'In the midst of these foul, outrageous murders, I content myself with saying I know nothing about the three in Newton County. As to the others in Jasper County, I will explain them in the proper time.'

"Could the man live who knew nothing of the Yellow River killing, yet can explain the pasture murders?" The moment called for a scowl, though Howard scowled as a general rule. "No, gentlemen. The man who can explain the pasture murders knows all about the Yellow River murders. That man is John Williams."

Observers noticed that Howard looked unwell.

"You can't bring back these eleven Negroes, who went to their fate as men without the rights of citizens because they had disobeyed the law and were ex-convicts," he said. "We can't compensate their families.

"But," he concluded, "we can see that justice is done and the majesty of the law upheld."

At that moment, as Howard turned from the jury box, he lurched backward and fell against the prosecution's table. He was struggling to arrest his fall when Graham Wright jumped from his chair, steadied the older man, and helped him from the courtroom. Judge Hutcheson announced a ten-minute recess.

Few spectators left their seats during the break, instead watching in silence as Greene Johnson readied himself for the defense's final act. A reporter for the *Atlanta Journal* sidled up to Williams and asked him whether he still expected an acquittal. "Absolutely," he replied.

Hutcheson pounded his gavel and it was Johnson's turn to stand before the jury. In contrast to Howard's impassioned monologue, he reprised a theme he had introduced during jury selection: that this was all a production cooked up by Atlanta know-it-alls. Referring to Brand as "the distinguished solicitor general," the defense attorney made a show of taking the jury into his confidence. "Just 'tween me and you, gentlemen of the jury—confidentially—I can't escape the conviction that Mr. Brand has not received a square deal," he said. "Just beginning his term of office and having worked up his first big case, he was about to reap the reward of his labor and had visions possibly of honors from it—of the governorship, even—when this 'Atlanta crowd' got busy and sent these distinguished men to take his place."

Was that a not-so-subtle dig at Hugh Dorsey, and *his* path to the governor's mansion? Johnson motioned to the prosecution table. Howard, he said, stood apart from the others there. Brand and Wright were public servants, doing their duty. But Howard was a hired gun, paid for by "private prosecutors." Those Atlanta men had also seen fit to hire another lawyer to advocate for "this splendid character—Clyde Manning.

"That's a great condition of affairs," Johnson sneered. "They pay their good money to prosecute Williams and shield the Negro." If he didn't shake his head in disgust, it was surely implied. "William M. Howard is the ablest lawyer in Georgia, and probably in the whole country. He has tried to stampede you into a verdict. If you allow yourselves to be stampeded, you may see the time to regret it.

"I suggest that the Atlanta crowd clean up their own town before they send [men] down here telling you what to do."

This was, after all, a local case, Johnson told the jury. A Newton County case. It was only a national affair because hypocritical Yankee newspapers wanted to distract their readers from their own race-based troubles. "But we are trying this case in middle Georgia, where men know the value of a white man's testimony against a Negro's," he said. "We are trying it under conditions as they are here and not by any Northern jury or any Northern metropolitan newspapers."

Johnson shifted his aim to the prosecution's dependence on evidence and testimony that he characterized as irrelevant. "Mr. Howard spent one hour and fifty-five minutes talking about the wholesale slaughter of

Negroes and the general complexion of the case and only five minutes discussing the specific indictment under which the defendant is on trial," he complained. "You are trying John Williams for killing Lindsey Peterson, not a long list of Negroes. Let's try these cases one at a time. That's fair. That's legal. That's just."

He had plenty to say about the federal agents, too. "These so-called government protectors put bad ideas in the heads of those Negroes," he said. "They put more meanness in their minds in ten minutes than can be gotten out in ten years." At this, laughter burst from the Black spectators in the courtroom's gallery. Judge Hutcheson gaveled them quiet, and warned that another such disturbance would see them ejected from the building.

Johnson paced in front of the jury box. "Manning, this human butcher, told you with remarkable composure that he lied to the federal agents about everything they asked him," he said. "Gentlemen, can you doom a white man on the testimony of that kind of Negro?" Williams gave him an appreciative nod. "If that Negro Manning's story were true, don't you know those other Negroes on the farm would have fled from that plantation like people from a plague, a stricken district?" the lawyer asked. "Manning's statement was an inveterate, unbelievable lie, and the state couldn't corroborate a word of it." It would be up to the jury to decide "whether you believe John Williams or this perjured Negro, who admitted on the stand that he had lied time and again."

It's worth noting that testimony had shown that Manning lied twice to the federal agents, once about his status as field boss and again about Gus Chapman's escape—and he had told the second lie at least partly to protect John S. Williams. In Johnson's telling, however, he lied with his every word. And he was worse than a simple liar, the lawyer said now—he was "a vicious Negro and a cunning Negro" who was the true murderer of his fellow farmhands. "He either killed these first Negroes to rob them of the money which they had just received, or from a monomaniacal mania to kill." The jury need look no further, he said, than the method by which Lindsey Peterson was dispatched. "Manning tells you that Williams took him and three other Negroes in his car and drove up a public road early in the evening on Saturday. That's unthinkable, impossible—a ridiculous lie—and you jurors know it. That's not a white man's conception of the way to destroy life. It's a Negro's idea. Manning was the brains of the plot, and it was conceived for the purpose of committing robbery or inspired by fear over what the federal agents had told him.

"Deeply seeped in this low, cunning Negro's brain was fear—fear of imprisonment, implanted by federal agents when they told him he was guilty of peonage," the lawyer said. "The Negro did not know the meaning of peonage, but he knew how to destroy evidence."

Johnson added one more point: "Remember, too, none of Manning's family were touched," he said. "Remember that." The line was theater, without substance, because no member of Manning's family was a peon: as long-term "free" residents of the farm, the Mannings were not targets of the killing.

Judge Hutcheson called a recess for lunch.

Williams dined in the sheriff's office with his family. When the recess neared its end, he strode back into the courtroom, which had somehow gained even more occupants; the air was dank with the heat and moisture of their bodies and breath. The defendant appeared newly serious as he sat down behind Greene Johnson. His wife, too, "wore a solemn expression," the *Atlanta Journal* noticed, "and the children seemed to realize their father's fate was hanging in the balance."

Williams clapped Johnson on the back. "It will be over now soon," he said, "and I believe we have whipped 'em." He thanked his lawyer for his "mighty fine work," and as Judge Hutcheson gaveled court back into session, reiterated his confidence that he would "come clear."

Hutcheson directed Johnson to proceed. The attorney stood, then complained that the room was simply too hot. The judge ordered men who had crowded onto the windowsills to find somewhere else to sit, in a bid to encourage fresh air into the space. Johnson approached the jury box and began to pace. "I have already pointed out the inherent improbability of this Negro Manning's story," he said. "Let's consider it further. The state says Williams is an arch criminal. But don't you know, if Williams killed eleven negroes to hide peonage, he would have made out the dozen and got Manning, too?"

That was but one of many aspects of the state's case that made no sense, the defense attorney argued. "It is unreasonable to believe that any man would kill eleven negroes when it had not even been established that he was guilty of peonage. No sensible man would commit such crimes. No one but a pluperfect fool would be guilty of such." Why Williams was on trial at all was a mystery, he said. Without Manning's testimony, "the state is helpless, and you know as well as I that the Negro's evidence has not been corroborated.

"According to the Negro's confession, he and Williams killed the Blacks, but so far no direct evidence has been presented by the state that the defendant participated in the crimes." No way could Manning's own testimony, by itself, justify Williams's conviction, he told the perspiring jurors. The fact that bodies were found where Manning said they would be found proved nothing, except that Manning knew where those bodies were buried. None of it meant that Williams was involved. Most of the circumstantial evidence was equally hollow. "Because Manning identified the bodies does not support the charges against the defendant," the attorney said. "It cannot be shown that Williams was connected with the murders because the Negroes drove the hogs to Williams' farm." The only testimony that tended to corroborate any part of Manning's story, Johnson said, was that of his wife, Rena—and her testimony was unbelievable. "She told you a remarkable tale of a wonderful feat of hearing," he said, smiling as he leaned on the jury box. In doing so, she had contributed "the most ridiculous piece of the state's case."

Johnson moved into his conclusion, the part that his listeners would likely best remember. In it, he "resorted to the wildest, most spectacular forms of oratory," as the *New York Call* described it, "and his appeal to the deep-rooted racial prejudices of the jurymen appeared throughout to be his trump card—indeed, almost his only card." Charles Stump, a correspondent for the Black-owned *Broad Ax* of Chicago, described the scene more colorfully, writing that Johnson "played race prejudice for all it was worth. He played that harp and played it loud," and that he "certainly did do the shimmey on the Negro question."

Johnson told the jury, for example, that scientists and travelers to Africa could attest that some native tribes of the continent were peaceable, while others were fierce and warlike. A few were even cannibals. "I am willing to venture," the defense attorney said, "that way back there, Clyde Manning's ancestors were cannibals." He declared that the conviction of a white man of John S. Williams's stature "on the testimony of a Negro like Manning" would be a "calamity that heaven would frown on." And he said this: "You must have confidence in Manning's testimony to believe him. That's the foundation of the law. Would you believe him on any other issue in life? Would you be afraid to meet him in the dark?"

"Ponder these questions. Manning admits to you that he has lied. He gets on the stand before you and tells that he lied to Brown about the Chapman case." The lawyer was drenched with sweat; it dripped from his nose as he paced. "Will you hang this white man on this Negro's testimony? What will become of the Negro? You know as well as I do that this Negro will not be sentenced to die on the gallows. You know that he will probably be set free.

"Suppose you consider this picture while we are on the subject. If you sentence Williams to hang, while his body lies moldering in the grave, Manning will be walking scot free. What if you were to meet the Negro on the road? Would you not look into his face and think what a tragic mistake you have made in hanging Williams on his evidence?" Mrs. Williams wept now, loudly enough to be heard around the room. One of her daughters cried beside her, her head resting on the defense table. Johnson nodded toward the girl. "Yes, suppose you walked on and met this child, whose life you had blighted," he said. "Would you not carry a burdened conscience to your grave? I ask: can you convict this man on that worthless Negro's testimony?" He stared down the jury. "I don't believe it.

"Remember, before you do anything today or tonight, that you will be called to the bar of a higher justice, and your only plea will be that of mercy.

"Remember this man's children and his waiting wife."

Johnson retreated from the jury box. Williams sat motionless, eyes on his lawyer, a tear rolling down his cheek. Judge Hutcheson excused the jurors. Johnson was mobbed at once, the press reported, by more than one hundred spectators offering congratulations.

Rowland Thomas of the *New York World* offered a tidy summation of the defense attorney's closing argument. "The Williams family's presence in court and the notion that twelve white men should be asked to hang another white man on the testimony of 'a worthless negro' were two of the chords he struck most strongly and returned to most often," Thomas wrote. "The case at its close was, therefore, as at its opening, brought to the single clear issue of credibility between a negro and a white man."

26

LATE IN THE AFTERNOON, Judge Hutcheson summoned the jury back and read them his charge—his detailed instructions on what its members were to consider, and what they were to ignore, in reaching a verdict. "The defendant enters upon the trial of this case with the presumption of innocence in his favor," he began, "and this presumption remains with him until and unless the state shall overcome and remove it by the introduction of testimony, in your presence and hearing, sufficient to convince your minds beyond a reasonable doubt of the guilt of the accused."

Much of what followed was boilerplate. He offered a definition of reasonable doubt. He reminded the jurors they were the sole judges of the testimony and its credibility. He told them they could give Williams's unsworn statement as much weight, or as little, as they saw fit. In most cases before the court, he noted, the testimony of a single witness was sufficient to establish a fact, but as this one concerned a felony, the jury "would not be authorized to convict upon the testimony of an accomplice alone, unless that accomplice's testimony is corroborated by other evidence in the case, either direct or circumstantial." It was up to the panel to decide if the state had provided the necessary corroboration, bearing in mind that it must "connect the defendant with the perpetration of the crime and tend to show his participation therein."

Hutcheson then veered from his typical instructions. Before the jurors decided whether Manning's testimony was sufficiently backed up, they first had to determine whether he was, in fact, an accomplice. The jury could "look to the evidence" to decide whether Manning was coerced to participate in the killing. "And if it appears to you that such witness was forced by coercion to take the part that he did—provided you believe that he did, in fact, take a part—and that such coercion was of such a nature as to excite in the mind of such witness a reasonable fear that his life . . . was in danger," *then he was not an accomplice,* "and the rules which I have given you with reference to the corroboration of an accomplice would not be applicable to his testimony."

The judge had laid before the twelve a central question underlying the whole terrible affair: Was Clyde Manning a perpetrator, or a victim himself? From his first interview with lawmen, through his grand jury appearance, his comments to reporters, and his testimony at trial, the field boss had emphasized that he acted out of the certainty that if he did not follow Williams's orders, he would die. He insisted he was no equal partner in the killings, but acted only out of fear for his own life.

If the jury agreed, it was bound by law not only to convict Williams, but—despite Lonnie Brand's promise that he would prosecute Manning and seek his conviction—to view the field boss as innocent. It was a complex, thorny question that was "exclusively . . . for you to determine," the judge told the panel, "and upon which the court intimates no opinion. . . .

"Take this case, gentlemen, and under the instruction as given you by the court, decide what the facts are and let your verdict speak the truth," Hutcheson said. "The laws of the state are made for all alike. All are amenable to the same law. All are triable alike in the courts of the state. Decide the case fearlessly and impartially between the state and the accused, as it is your duty to do, and let your verdict speak the truth."

The jury left the room. John S. Williams remained in his seat, "smiling and unconcerned" and chatting with well-wishers. Neither did the lawyers stray far, nor most of the audience, for experience suggested that the deliberations would not take long. Business as usual dictated that Williams would either be acquitted or that the jury would force a mistrial by failing or refusing to reach a verdict. Out-of-town newspapers predicted the latter with near certainty. The *New York Tribune* headlined its story about the close of testimony "Peonage Murder Case Goes to Jury; Mistrial Forecast." After all, when was the last time a white Georgian had been convicted of a capital crime on the word of a Black witness? The readiest example was the Frank decision—but in that case, the victim had been white, and the defendant seen as not quite so.

For an hour the courtroom stayed crowded, waiting for the jury's inevitable return, for the expected to happen. Yet after that hour the jury room remained locked, and those in the audience and up in the gallery began to drift away. Someone brought soft drinks to the Williams family. The children drank them while their father confidently held forth with friends gathered close. Later, the family held another indoor picnic. Williams "appeared as cool as any person in the house and did not seem to take the case seriously," the *Georgian* reported. "He waved his hand now and then at some friends in the crowd." He told one of his neighbors: "I'll be over to see you Sunday."

The jury broke for supper, only to return to its locked chambers. One by one, the lawyers quit the courthouse for their hotels. Outside, Dr. Gus Williams sat on the building's front steps, keeping vigil with reporters. "I wish you all could have known papa and the rest of us before all this happened," he told them. "Things might have looked different to you. We've always been a right happy family. And all the neighbors liked papa."

Seeing as how virtually everything the doctor had said to the press in recent days had stretched the truth—to put it charitably—he may have overstated the neighbors' feelings for his father. When a visiting reporter tried to get other Jasper farmers talking about Williams, they begged off out of fear of saying the wrong thing, the operative word being *fear*. The most candid of them said he understood that "things were sort of bad on Williams's place."

Gus Williams might have more accurately said that the neighbors respected his papa, for there was no denying that—or that, like him or not, the trial had shaken many of those who'd lived alongside him for decades. That very morning, an essay had appeared on the front page of the *Monticello News* that attested to how unmoored Williams's neighbors felt on the eve of the verdict. "I am [John S.] Williams' pastor," Rev. James J. Winburn wrote. "I am [John S.] Williams' friend. It has been my privilege to be entertained many times in his home. I have been permitted to baptize and receive into the church four of his children—I have prayed and shall continue to pray for him, but, let me say this with emphasis, I am not engaged in his defense. If he is guilty of the atrocious crimes with which he has been charged, then let justice be done—and the heart and soul of Jasper county speaks through my pen."

Winburn went on to enumerate the Williams family's contributions to the war effort before concluding: "Personally I have been slow to believe. I have been many times a guest in this home and have seen the almost adoring worship of wife and children as they gathered around. I have thought that I have seen the flow of a tender heart shine on this man's face. I have knelt and prayed with him for sons 'somewhere in France.' From where I sit I can see church and school made possible by his contribution.

"Personally I have been slow to believe, and for that I offer no excuse."

Late that night, hours after the last of the onlookers had wandered off and John S. Williams had been escorted to a cell in the Newton County Jail, the jury sent a messenger to rouse Judge Hutcheson with a request for further instructions. The judge sent for Lonnie Brand and Greene Johnson, then hurried to the courthouse.

Shortly after midnight, Williams, having hastily dressed at the jail, stood before the bench without a necktie, hair mussed. The lawyers stood as the jury entered. "We would like to be recharged, your honor," the foreman, a farmer named T. R. Starr, told Hutcheson.

"On what?" the judge asked.

He wasn't sure, Starr said: "It is a point of law, and we cannot place it exactly."

"You wish me to give you the entire charge?"

"That would be the only way I know," the foreman replied, "as I can't explain it exactly to you, just the point."

"You wish me to give you the recharge tonight, or do you wish to go to your hotel and have it in the morning?"

"We would like to have it tonight," came the answer.

Hutcheson reread his charge, then adjourned court until nine in the morning. The jury deliberated for a brief while longer, then broke for the night. Everyone else was left to wonder what the episode meant. Did it signal that the panel was deadlocked, auguring well for the defense? Or was the foreman simply taking care to stick with the letter of the law?

The answer came soon after the judge gaveled the trial's fifth day to order. Members of the panel straggled in, looking weary. Few onlookers were present. Compared to the previous morning, the room felt practically empty. Among the missing was special prosecutor William M. Howard, who had gone home to Augusta after his collapse. Also missing, for the fifth morning straight, were Hulon, LeRoy, and Marvin Williams.

"Have you reached a verdict, gentlemen?" Hutcheson asked.

"We have, sir," Starr answered. He handed a folded slip to Lonnie Brand, who opened it and read it aloud: "We, the jury, find the defendant, John S. Williams, guilty, and recommend mercy."

Williams met the news without expression. From his wife, sitting beside him, rose a terrible keening that stilled the room and was quickly taken up by his daughters. Brand and Greene Johnson huddled briefly with the judge to establish that by "mercy," the jury meant the lesser of two possible sentences arising from a guilty verdict—life in prison, rather than death by hanging. The judge turned to the defendant. "Stand up, Mr. Williams."

From Rowland Thomas of the *New York World*: "And the prisoner, clean-shaven, fresh-skinned, dressed as all through the trial in an unwrinkled suit of dark mohair and a newly laundered soft shirt, laid the newspaper he had been holding on the table just in front of the chair where he sat between wife and elder son.

"He arose, his great shoulders squared, his head thrown back, his eyes fixed on the judge with a gleam that bespoke defiance to the words he knew would make him a striped felon for the rest of his days."

"The jury has found you guilty, Mr. Williams, with recommendation for mercy," the judge told him. "Under the law this means a sentence of life imprisonment, and the verdict of the jury is the sentence of the court." He told the convict to sit down. As Williams did so, his wife buried her face in his shoulder, weeping loudly. His two daughters wailed; eleven-year-old Lucy Claire became so frantic that she was carried from the room, crying, "My God, Daddy, I can't stand it!"

Greene Johnson moved for a new trial, calling the verdict "contrary to the evidence, contrary to law and without evidence to support it." The judge scheduled a hearing on the motion for the month's end. A reporter asked Lonnie Brand for a comment. "I never gloat over the misfortunes of other folks," he said.

Williams kissed his family and was led from the room. Gus Williams half carried his mother down the aisle. Outside, scores of local farmers clotted the stairs, the sidewalk, and the square, discussing the verdict. Williams weaved through this multitude toward a car waiting at the curb to take him back to the Tower. One of the farmers, visibly anguished, clasped his hand as he passed.

"Goodbye, Johnny," the man said.

PART FOUR

American Congo

27

SO IT WAS THAT ON SATURDAY, APRIL 9, 1921, the unthinkable occurred. Less than four weeks after the bodies of Lindsey Peterson and Will Preston were discovered at Allen's Bridge, an all-white jury convicted the white man who killed them, principally on the testimony of a Black man. In Covington's courthouse square, the majority view, if not consensus, was that the jury had demonstrated "horse sense" with both its guilty verdict and its lenient sentencing recommendation.

Beyond the Newton County seat, the verdict was greeted with a mixture of satisfaction and relief. Few were more pleased, it seems safe to say, than the prosecution's architect, strategist, and whip. "The result of the trial is not only what I had hoped it would be for the sake of justice and the good name of our state," Hugh Dorsey told a reporter later in the day, "it was also what I had known it would be if the wish of every good citizen could receive effective expression.

"If anywhere men have been asking what Georgia means to do about such things, this superbly orderly trial, the verdict rendered this morning, and the grand jury probe which begins in Monticello next Monday, are an answer Georgia would ask to have considered." The governor praised Judge Hutcheson, Lonnie Brand, "and the officials and men of Newton County" while downplaying his own role as prosecution chess master. "I could lend only my influence to help them," he said. "I shall continue to lend it and do everything in my power to see that investigation and action wipe out every vestige of the blot which the Jasper County revelations put upon the state's reputation."

In the main, the rest of the world seemed equally impressed by the verdict. "A high and solemn message" had been delivered by the jury of "plain, upright citizens," the *Atlanta Journal* proclaimed, that message being "that the law shall be upheld, that wrongdoing shall be condemned, that righteous dealing must prevail, for even the lowliest and poorest in the land." The *New York Tribune* reckoned that Williams's fate offered "more hope of light in this darkest problem of the nation than any event in years." Charles Stump, the *Broad Ax* correspondent, decided the jury had "shown to the world that there is manhood in the white man, and he can rise above race prejudice and issue out justice."

The *New York World* saw the verdict as "a hopeful augury for the future of the negro." It tempered its enthusiasm, however, with the observation that "if the principals in the case had been reversed, if Peterson had killed Williams, Peterson would have been executed." Once they got past their initial surprise at the jury's decision, many commentators, southern and otherwise, came to share the *World's* worry that Williams got off easy. "In accordance with strict justice and the facts in the case, Williams should hang," James Weldon Johnson wrote in his *New York Age* column. "Indeed, to use an old expression, hanging is too good for him." The *Chattanooga Times* echoed that sentiment, declaring that the planter "richly deserved hanging." And Georgia's own *Columbus Enquirer-Sun* served up what might have been the most eloquent lament: "If we brush aside all subterfuge and hypocrisy and tell the plain truth about it, the verdict—as great a travesty of justice as it is—is not difficult to understand," the paper ventured. "And this plain truth is we have not yet reached that state of grace, or of justice, in Georgia where we 'hang a white man for killing a nigger,' as the expression is and has long been."

Dorsey, in New York on state business, acknowledged this rumbling unease two days after the trial's end. The jury's decision, he said, might not set well with many Georgians who "thought if the guilt of Williams were proved beyond a doubt that he should be sentenced to be hanged," but they could take heart that most of the jurors agreed. "It is my understanding that four men on the jury were determined on a mistrial, rather than agree to a verdict that would spell hanging," the governor divulged. One of the four was known as a hardhead who never budged from a position. The other eight jurors, all of whom favored executing Williams, realized after hours of debate that they would never achieve a unanimous vote for the noose. They "apparently thought—and *I* think—that the compromise verdict was to be preferred to a mistrial," Dorsey said, and switched their votes—and thus avoided disaster. A hung jury "would have been interpreted by the country as meaning that in Georgia, a white man cannot be convicted of any crime against a Negro."

Besides, those hoping to see Williams hang should find comfort in the state's continuing prosecutions against him. With additional charges pending in both Newton and Jasper, there was "still ample opportunity for the extreme penalty to be applied."

Dorsey made those remarks even as a grand jury met in Monticello to redeem the good name of Jasper County—or take a first step toward that daunting goal, at any rate. In the wake of Newton County's quick and efficient prosecution, the pressure was on not only to convict Williams for the eight killings on the plantation and at the Waters Bridge, but to bring the boom down on his sons Hulon, LeRoy, and Marvin, as well. In recent days, prosecutor Doyle Campbell had firmed up the details surrounding the three earlier slayings on the Williams place implicating the brothers. The first was that of a peon named John Singleton, dispatched with a blow from a heavy iron wrench in April 1918. The next was that of Iron Jaw, whom authorities would eventually identify as John Davis, shot in the summer of 1920. The third was that of Blackstrap—whose real name, authorities would come to believe, was Robert Nathaniel Williams—who was shot while being whipped later the same year.

"I want you gentlemen to ascertain the perpetrators of these gruesome crimes and to return indictments against all persons connected with them," Judge Park instructed the grand jury. "Do your full duty and leave no one unindicted, if the evidence before you points to his guilt."

He ended his charge with a touch of doomsday. "Lawlessness in this section has now reached the point that it will cause us to be shunned unless we check it," he warned. "We will soon reach the stage where no capital will come here and help us to develop our great natural resources. Unless the law takes hold and checks these cold-blooded murders and outrages, I firmly believe that God Almighty will soon take the situation in hand."

The first witness was Clyde Manning, transported to Monticello from the Tower early on the morning of April 11 along with two other Black workers from the farm. In addition to retelling his story of the eight recent deaths, Manning described Blackstrap's murder, noting that another witness, Gus Chapman, could corroborate his account.

Gus Chapman did just that, detailing how Mr. Hulon had commanded Charlie Chisholm to shoot Blackstrap even as he—Hulon—savagely whipped the peon. In a conversation with a reporter before he took the stand, and again before the jury, Chapman also offered the first public account of how he twice escaped from the plantation. "One night I asked Clyde Manning to turn me out of the guard house, and he did it," he said of his July 1920 getaway, which Manning had covered up with the story that Chapman had attacked his wife, Rena. "I left the place quick, but they caught me and took me back. They beat me and Mr. Johnny Williams and Mr. Marvin said they ought to kill me, but I begged so hard and promised everything so they let me off. They said they would kill me like I was a snake if I ever left again.

"The next time I left was about Thanksgiving," Chapman said. "Clyde turned me out of the guard house that time, too. This time I got away and returned to Atlanta. I knew if they caught me that time, I was a goner."

Manning was recalled before the jury to verify Chapman's tale of his escapes. "Yes, gentlemen," he reportedly testified, "I turned him out, because I didn't think it was exactly right to keep them boys fenced up like that every night." If Chapman's first bid for freedom put Manning at risk, his second was doubly dangerous. "Mr. Johnny was mighty mad," he said, "and told me I would have to do two men's work to make up for him."

The grand jury made short work of its assignment. Within hours, it returned a dozen indictments against members of the Williams family. Eight of the charges—covering the murder of the five peons killed on the plantation and the three drowned at the Waters Bridge—named both John S. Williams and Clyde Manning. Hulon was indicted for killing Robert Nathaniel "Blackstrap" Williams. LeRoy and Marvin were indicted jointly for the murder of John "Iron Jaw" Davis. Marvin was indicted separately for killing John Singleton.

At that point, no one had reported laying eyes on the three brothers in more than a week. Visits to the plantation turned up no sign of them. Greene Johnson, who represented the three, maintained that he had no idea where they were. Prosecutor Campbell reckoned "they are not within a thousand miles of here, and I think they are gone entirely." Rumors circulated in Jasper that they'd run off to Mexico.

Hugh Dorsey, who had been stymied by Judge Park's refusal to arrest the three, refrained from any public "I told you so." Instead, he arranged with Campbell to offer a reward for the trio once their indictments were in hand. Now, while still in New York, he wired instructions to his executive secretary to issue a bounty of five hundred dollars a head for the "apprehension and delivery" of the three Williamses to Sheriff Persons.

No sooner had word of the reward made the papers than the family's reputation took another devastating hit. Several former field hands on the Williams plantation—some of whom had been sought by officials since the first raid on the place, and all of them fearful—appeared at the Bureau of Investigation's offices in Atlanta. Murders on the farm did not start with Will Napier, they told the agents. Mr. Johnny had been killing his workers for a long time. Aleck Dyer, a Black peon, had run away twice before he was brained with an axe while working in a field in 1910 or thereabouts. And Nick and Mamie Walker, an aged couple who had lived on the farm for twenty years, were shot to death at about the same time because they'd grown too old to work much, and were thus considered a drain on the operation.

The witnesses reported that Williams's sadism was not restricted to peons: He or his sons had also murdered a three-day-old baby belonging to one of the family cooks. Mr. Johnny had confronted the mother with the words: "Do away with that baby. You've got to cook and have no time to mind children." The next morning, the baby had vanished.

The farmhands intimated that the plantation's reported death toll, which now stood at eighteen, might be higher still—that over the years, anyone judged guilty of any transgression by Mr. Johnny or his sons disappeared "mysteriously and overnight," and that those left behind were too terrified to so much as whisper about them.

The agents allowed newspaper reporters to listen to the workers' accounts, provided that their stories not name them. One older refugee from the plantation said he'd been there in 1910, having been bonded out of the Macon jail by Williams. "I tried mighty hard to get away several times, but there was very little chance, because they kept us under guard in a little house every night," he said. "In the daytime they put balls and chains on our legs before we went to the fields to work. Mr. Hulon and his brothers were boys in knee pants then, but they would ride over the farm and crack niggers over the backs with big whips if they caught any of 'em stopping to rest a minute."

In six years on the farm, this man said, he was paid exactly one dollar and subjected to constant terror. "If Mr. Johnny had told me to kill a nigger, I certainly would have done it," he told the newsmen. "I'd have known better not to do it."

28

IT WAS IN THE FLUSH OF VICTORY after the initial indictments that Hugh Dorsey, still encamped at Manhattan's Vanderbilt Hotel, heard from James Weldon Johnson, in the form of a telegram conveying the NAACP's "hearty commendation and sincere thanks for your splendid action in the Jasper County cases." Johnson also asked to meet with the governor while he was in New York. Dorsey answered two days later with his own telegram, all-business as usual: "Can see you at Vanderbilt Hotel at six o'clock today."

And so, two principals of our story met face to face—two accomplished men from very different backgrounds, both now at the height of their influence and, for the present, united in an effort that had captured the nation's attention. They convened in Dorsey's hotel suite. The record of their conversation is sketchy: Johnson's office diary entry for April 14 reads simply: "Talked with the Governor about peonage conditions in that state." Whatever was said, Johnson followed it up with a lot of public love for Dorsey. The day after their meeting, the NAACP issued a statement expressing its thanks to the Georgian for insisting that the law protect all. "His example is worthy of emulation," the Association declared, "and we do not hesitate to recommend it to the one who is soon to succeed to the place now held by Governor Dorsey."

The day after that, Johnson devoted his column in the *New York Age* to the trial, making a point to say that Dorsey should be "commended on the stand which he took." The column closed by prescribing what must happen next: "The thing needed to be impressed upon the public mind at present is the truth that these conditions are not confined to Jasper

County, Ga., but that there are similar conditions throughout the whole South, especially in all the cotton raising districts. It merely happened that in Jasper County more Negroes were killed at one time and in one place than in general.

"Colored Americans should take immediate advantage of the state of the public mind resulting from the Jasper County trials," he wrote, "and every colored man and woman who can possibly do so should at once send a telegram or a letter to the Attorney General at Washington demanding a wide and thorough investigation of peonage throughout the whole South. The Department of Justice at Washington should be flooded with telegrams and letters within the next few days making this demand.

"If the final outcome of what has happened in Jasper County in the last month is a general investigation leading to the abolishment of peonage in the South, we repeat that the Negro peons who lost their lives on Williams' plantation will not have died in vain."

That was an oft-voiced hope in the days after Williams's conviction, from law enforcement officials, politicians, and journalists across the country—that the lives of the eleven who died in the spring of 1921 would count for something more than pointless misery. It was coupled with confidence. Surely, peonage was destined to vanish from Georgia and the South. The Williams horror had illuminated a crime only dimly understood by the public, and now that it was exposed, debt servitude would be rooted out and crushed. As a tobacco-chewing Newton County farmer put it: "Before this Williams case peters out there'll be a hundred wealthy Georgia farmers in the penitentiary, I reckon, and the sooner the better."

And indeed, the Department of Justice seemed to be pressing its investigations into the practice with urgency. "I have sent white men to jail here for peonage," U.S. Attorney Hooper Alexander assured the public in Atlanta. "I shall investigate every complaint. I shall seek indictment in every case where I get evidence and I shall try my best to send every indicted man to the federal penitentiary, where he belongs."

That commitment translated into a heavy workload for the federal agents reporting to Alexander. "The bulk of our work now is on peonage complaints, and there are more of these than all other cases combined," the Bureau of Investigation's Vincent Hughes said. They were not easy cases. Plentiful though the complaints were, those that actually met the legal definition of peonage were challenging to find and difficult to prove. "We find ourselves handicapped in handling many of these complaints because the law is not broad enough," Hughes explained. "The technical crime of peonage is only committed when involuntary servitude exists on a basis of debts, and many Negroes are held in servitude through fear and other coercion, perhaps more so than for debt." In other words, the federal government had little trouble finding Black people held against their will. But in many cases, it lacked the tools to do something about it.

According to the Bureau, there was a surprising second reason Georgia's court dockets had not overflowed with peonage cases. Judging from the complaints his office received, Hughes said, the crime wasn't a statewide issue, but cropped up "in two or three sore spots," involving mostly "country Negroes." Hugh Dorsey said as much himself. Backtracking from his earlier remarks on the subject, he told reporters in New York that the practice could be found in just "three or four of the 156 counties" in Georgia.

This marked a sudden shift from the prevailing view in the first days after Williams's crimes came to light—that "peonage was widely practiced in the state," as the *Washington Star* put it, and "other horrors would be uncovered." Instead, as Georgians began to recover from their professed shock that a form of quasi slavery had endured for generations past the Civil War, the notion that peonage was a more limited scourge gained increasing and unjustified currency. "There is no peonage in Morgan county and very little in Georgia," as the editors of the newspaper serving Madison, a town east of Covington and northeast of Monticello, wrote. "Our people are easily swept off their feet and are given to jumping at conclusions."

This backpedaling was hogwash, and it's difficult to understand why Dorsey engaged in it. In terms of the specific style of peonage the Williamses had practiced, it might have been possible that the crime was restricted to isolated trouble spots. Doubtful, but maybe. But if one included the peonage laced throughout the sharecropping system, in which tenant farmers were kept prisoner as surely as peons bailed out of jail and forced to work off their sentences, it was nothing more than wishful thinking. Sharecropping was essential to Georgia's cotton production, and its abuses were endemic. Surely the governor knew that.

The NAACP sounded no such retreat. W. E. B. Du Bois devoted an editorial in *The Crisis* to the Williams case in which he took no quarter:

> Slavery still exists in the United States. In the courts of Carolina, Georgia, Alabama, Mississippi, Louisiana, Arkansas and Texas, human beings are daily sold into slavery to men like the murderer Williams of Jasper County, Georgia. Throughout the South—but especially in the Mississippi and Red River bottoms, from Memphis south; in middle and south Georgia and Alabama; and in the Brazos bottoms of Texas—Negroes are held today in as complete and awful and soul destroying slavery as they were in 1860. Their overseers ride with guns and whips; their women are prostitutes to white owners and drivers; their children are trained in ignorance, immorality and crime.
>
> Every Southerner knows this. The States know it. The Government knows it. Distinguished Southerners are getting wealthy on the system; the Southern White Church is sending missionaries to Africa on its proceeds; lovely young white ladies are being finished in exclusive schools on its dirty blood profits; and yet it goes on and on and on, and it will go on until one day its red upheaval will shake the civilized world.

Du Bois detected a "ray of hope" in the Williams verdict and "the fine spirit of press and people that stand behind it." But there was nothing in his comments, or any others from the Association, acknowledging that debt slavery was restricted to a handful of localities. On the contrary, James Weldon Johnson recognized that the Williams prosecution would be used by white supremacists as a rallying point. He was engaged, at the time, in his second war on D. W. Griffith's *The Birth of a Nation*, which was enjoying a revival six years after its debut. Johnson thought he knew why it had returned: "to offset the shocking revelations that have just come out of Georgia."

The entire country had been "stirred by the accounts of barbarous brutalities committed in connection with the Jasper County peonage cases," he wrote. "Now comes this picture to instill the idea that no matter how brutally the Negro in the South is treated, there are justifications for the treatment."

While Dorsey wrapped up his work in New York, he was dealing with evidence that, the trial victory notwithstanding, Georgia remained Georgia: Two Black people had been lynched in the state's far southwest. The news had reached him in dribs and drabs before he started his trip, some of it in a letter from an African American man who had fled the area and reported that "mobs were riding every night beating and killing negroes," and that one old woman was seized in her home and drowned in a nearby creek. Her family was too terror-stricken to recover her body.

The governor wrote the local sheriff to find out what was going on. The lawman replied that he had contended with some "very bad" trouble lately, but that it had since passed; he had called on three neighboring sheriffs to help quell the disturbance. It started, he wrote, when a local Black man killed a county constable "for no cause at all and the same negro the next day shot another man that was feeding some hogs on the river banks." He didn't mention what became of the suspect, but soon after, a mob formed and killed two others who were "trying to help the Murderous negro to escape."

One of these accessories was the old woman, whom the sheriff initially rescued from the mob and locked up for her own safety. He could "not keep her in jail for nothing," he explained, "so after the mob broke up I carried her home or at least I carried her to the man she was working for." Her boss advised her to flee. "So I told her if she did not want to stay down there to come back with me and I would protect her, but she said that she was going to stay there. She didn't think that they would bother her, so a week from that day the mob went down there and got her and put her in [the] creek and that is all I know about the woman getting killed."

The other lynching victim was apparently a man who owned several guns, and was told that if he didn't depart the area, his neighbors would seize his arsenal. He replied that they'd never take his guns. "So the mob"—numbering "something like four hundred men"—"got hold of what he said," the sheriff reported. "They went and got him and killed him the very same day." In the sheriff's telling, it was almost as if an unstoppable act of nature had claimed the victims, rather than people he knew.

Business as usual in the Peach State—and a style of business most certainly not restricted to a few trouble spots. As the governor reviewed the case, he pondered another public statement he was planning to make in a few days. In it, he would reverse his earlier waffling on peonage. And he would go further: historian John Dittmer would call Dorsey's words "probably the most candid and courageous attack on racial injustice issued by an American governor."

On the evening of Friday, April 22, Dorsey appeared before a group of prominent white citizens he had invited to the Piedmont Hotel, a slim booklet in hand. Titled *A Statement from Governor Hugh M. Dorsey as to the Negro in Georgia*, it was a clarion call to end the living nightmare endured by a huge share of his state's population. In it, Dorsey laid out 135 allegations of brutality toward Georgia's Black citizens—all of them, he said, committed within the previous two years, and all of them landing on his desk without solicitation. "In some counties the Negro is being driven out as though he were a wild beast," he read aloud from the document. "In others he is being held as a slave. In others, no Negroes remain.

"To me it seems that we stand indicted as a people before the world. If the conditions indicated by these charges should continue, both God and man would justly condemn Georgia more severely than man and God have condemned Belgium and Leopold for the Congo atrocities. But worse than that condemnation would be the destruction of our civilization by the continued toleration of such cruelties in Georgia."*

Dorsey followed with the 135 charges, divided into four categories. The first, "The Negro Lynched," offered five accounts of vigilante murder. One seemed to recount the death of Eugene Hamilton, the schoolteacher and preacher mobbed in Jasper County in October 1919—though, like all entries in the booklet, it mentioned no names and identified the county involved only by number. A second entry described the kidnapping of a Black man while he was being escorted to jail for allegedly shooting a white farmer. A mob drove him back to the scene of the crime, "where his bullet-riddled body was found hanging in a tree." Yet another detailed a Black murder suspect burned to death on a "'slow fire,' the torture being prolonged as much as possible," before a crowd of three thousand people.

The next category, "The Negro Held in Peonage," rolled out twenty cases, thirteen clearly describing events on the Williams plantation, and nine of the thirteen classified as "wholesale murder." As Timothy Pitts has observed in the *Georgia Historical Quarterly*, the public clamor over the Jasper County affair, and the attention Dorsey devoted to it in the booklet, leave little doubt that his impetus for writing *The Negro in Georgia* "was almost certainly the Williams case."

The third category, "The Negro Driven Out by Organized Lawlessness," included the Gwinnett County KKK case in which Dorsey had intervened in January, along with a host of others. Three Georgia counties, Dorsey wrote, had been emptied of their Black residents. Every last one.

---

* His reference to the Congo invoked Belgian king Leopold II's reign of terror during his private ownership of the central African state. He turned what later became a Belgian colony and is now the Democratic Republic of the Congo into a brutal forced-labor state for the production of rubber and other resources. Before the regime's orgy of kidnapping, murder, torture, and dismemberment ended in the midst of worldwide outrage, Leopold's policies—along with disease introduced by European colonists—had killed an estimated ten million Congolese.

Finally, "The Negro Subject to Individual Acts of Cruelty" listed fourteen examples of debasement and violence, first among them the account of "A Thrifty Negro" in "County 21":

Near a small town in this County a negro was born fifty-eight or sixty years ago. By work, he accumulated a little money with which, ten years ago, he bought a farm of 140 acres, where he lived with his wife and twelve children. Three of his daughters were educated. They were school teachers.

A three-room house was on the farm. The farm was well stocked, the negro owning in 1919 outright five mules, and having made payments on the purchase of a horse, a cow and thirty-five hogs.

During the war with Germany, this negro family bought approximately $1,000 worth of liberty bonds and thrift stamps. The negro headed an organization of negroes, who raised between $10,000 and $11,000 for liberty bonds. His work was highly praised by newspapers at the time.

A white man, who can neither read nor write, owns a farm adjoining the farm of the negro. When the articles praising the man for his war work appeared, the white man remarked: "——'s getting too damned prosperous and biggity for a nigger." Trouble began.

The white man had his land processioned. The negro had no representative present. The processioners ran the man's line twenty-five feet over the negro's line, across a terrace which had been there since the negro was a child working for the family, from whom he bought the land. The deed given to him covered the land to this terrace.

The white man crossed the terrace, drove stakes along the new line and warned the negro not to cross the line. The negro disregarded the warning and continued to plow up the terrace, as he had been doing since boyhood.

Blacks and whites from the country crowd the town Saturday afternoons. One Saturday, the fall of 1919, the negro with his three daughters and son came to town. The town marshall [sic] approached the negro in the street and said: "I have a warrant for you."

The negro answered: "Mr. ——, what have I done? Read your warrant."

The marshall replied with an oath that he would rather kill the negro than read the warrant.

Here the evidence varies. The negro had a stick in his hand. Some say that the marshall, who is large and powerful, grabbed the stick and struck the negro in the face with a pistol, knocking him down. Others state that the negro, raising his stick, backed away, when the marshall rushed in and struck him to the ground with his pistol. Several other white men rushed upon him and began to choke and beat him.

Two of his daughters started to him. A man kicked one girl in the stomach. The other reached her father and began to wipe the blood from his face. The three were quickly overpowered. The third daughter and the son were caught. All were locked in jail. The girl who was kicked was menstruating. The blow made her deathly sick. She lay in jail moaning and begging that something be done for her, and her father, who was bleeding badly from his wounds. The sheriff locked them in and left them without medical attention and ignorant of the charge against them.

Next morning the negro learned that his neighbor had sworn out a warrant against him for trespass. The sheriff refused to tell him what the charge was against his son and daughters. The negro employed a lawyer. Then he found that he and his daughters were charged with resisting an officer in the discharge of his duty, his son with carrying a pistol. Only one witness claimed to have seen the pistol. This was the white neighbor who said that he had seen the son put the pistol in the buggy, while the crowd was on his father. The buggy was searched. The pistol was not found.

Talk of lynching the negro and his family caused their removal to another county. A committee of citizens waited upon the judge of the [circuit], who informed them, it is charged, that he would put the negro in the chain gang, when the case should come up for trial.

The man, his daughters and son were tried in the Superior Court. The father was sentenced to serve twelve months in the chain gang and pay a fine of $250.00. The girls were fined $50.00 each. The son was fined $100.00. The negro paid the fines of his children.

The man's smaller children and his wife were in his home, while he was in jail. A mob led by the town marshal went to the house, kicked the door and demanded admittance, then shot up the house and went away. This was night.

Next morning, the woman with her children, fled from her home, never to return.

A friend went by night and removed the live stock belonging to the family, and sold it for them at a great sacrifice. Their crop was a total loss. They will be lynched, it is said, if any of them ever return to their home.

The account's last sentence was perhaps its most heartbreaking: "The education of his children and the success of his thrift seem to be the sole offense of the negro."

Dorsey followed this appalling litany with two pages headed "The Remedy." He called for publicity—"namely, the careful gathering and investigation by Georgians, and not by outsiders, of facts as to the treatment of the negro throughout the State and the publication of these facts to the people of Georgia." He urged the establishment of churches and

Sunday schools for both Black and white citizens so that "in their separate places of worship, the young and old of both races will learn from suitable teachers the gospel of justice, mercy and mutual forbearance for all." He pushed compulsory education for all Georgians, regardless of race, and the creation of biracial state committees on Black-white relations. As he had in the past, he called for a state constabulary—a police force under the governor's control, whose members he might dispatch "into any County of the State to quell disorder or to protect the life and property of any citizen." He took direct aim at peonage with a plea to the General Assembly to repeal the state code sections spelling out the prima facie contract law that enabled Georgia farmers to keep modern-day slaves.

Finally, Dorsey suggested steps to breach the conspiracy of silence surrounding most lynchings. He wanted fines imposed on counties in which mob violence occurred, every lynching investigated by a state panel, and the governor empowered to yank any county official found to have failed to safeguard justice. He also wanted to give the governor discretion to authorize grand juries and trial juries drawn from the state at large— rather than a lynching's immediate vicinity—and to decide where such cases would be heard.

When he finished reading, those gathered resolved to "endorse the statement made by the Governor and give our unqualified approval to the remedy suggested by him," and to accept appointments as members of a new State Committee on Race Relations. Among those signing were the Reverends Wilmer and Jones; Clyde Manning's lawyer, E. Marvin Underwood; and W. Woods White, who had hired Underwood for the job.

Wilmer saw particular merit in publicizing the pains and perils of Black life in Georgia, as suggested in the first of Dorsey's remedies. "We will have the great moral strength of self-indictment behind us," he said, "and we need not fear the criticism of other sections of the country. If these sections desire to criticize us they may, but in the meantime we will be working to rectify our conditions."

———

It is difficult to overstate the risk that Hugh Dorsey took that Friday. His booklet marked an astounding departure from anything uttered by a southern politician since Reconstruction, and that's putting it conservatively. Dorsey had just exposed to sunlight a plague that had infected white Georgians for generations, for centuries. In doing so, he was wagering that the attempted cure wouldn't backfire and strengthen, rather than eradicate, the disease. And that was no sure bet. Just six years had passed since the anti-Semitic mayhem sparked by Governor John Slaton's commutation of Leo Frank's sentence. It had been seven short months since Tom Watson's primary victory in the Senate race, a depressing signal that his retrograde beliefs maintained a hold on much of Georgia.

Dorsey must have thought he had a unique moment in which to act. He was solidly popular. He had won strong support from white Georgians for his public role in the Williams case and the fight against peonage, and had seen the murders ignite widespread acknowledgment that the state's Black citizens had been denied a "square deal" and subjected to systemic oppression. And he had little to lose, politically. Denied election to the Senate, barred from another consecutive term as governor, he was fast approaching the end of his electoral life.

Beyond that, the governor was a practical man who loved his state, and likely feared the predictable economic cost of its savage treatment of African Americans. Droves of Georgia's Blacks continued to flee northward, posing an immediate threat to the livelihoods of Georgian whites. Dorsey had pointed out the cost of this exodus on several recent occasions. Early in the Newton County investigation, he had warned that the payback for mistreating the Black workforce would likely make itself obvious to the rich and powerful after it was too late to rectify. And just before John Williams's trial, the governor had worried aloud to reporters about the ultimate cost of peonage and other abuses. "After some communities in Georgia have driven away their farm labor and driven away their farm loans," he said, "they will have an opportunity to sit down and think over calmly whether it pays to deal justly with the Negro."

Alongside the loss of Black workers, Dorsey must have recognized that continuing to conduct business as usual might mean an end to business altogether—that, as Judge Park had foreseen in his charge to the Jasper County grand jury, Georgia's race woes would discourage industrial investment in the state, leaving it backward, impoverished, and an increasingly irrelevant player in modern American life.

His personal interests were at stake, as well. Whether he believed in Leo Frank's guilt or did not, he had to know that his contribution to the man's terrible end had made him a villain all over the world. His late-term heroics, first in the Williams case and now with the booklet, held the possibility of moderating history's verdict on him.

Last, but certainly not least, Dorsey might have consciously sought spiritual redemption for what he'd done to Leo Frank. We have no evidence that this was the case. We have no evidence it was not. The fact is, we know nothing of Dorsey's private calculus at all, because we have little record of his thinking, on this or anything else. He left no archive of personal papers behind. He wrote no memoir, kept no journal, and saved no telling correspondence that has surfaced in the century since his governorship. Whether by design or by accident, he bequeathed practically nothing of himself to history.

But there was, and remains, this one thing: Regardless of why he chose to release *The Negro in Georgia*, the fact is that he did it, and he did so knowing the risks. He had seen public opinion swing like a wrecking ball to smash John Slaton's reputation. He had watched the Ku Klux Klan reemerge, and his state's continuing, stubborn reliance on racial violence. Dorsey knew that entitled Georgians regarded white supremacy as an article of faith, and that unveiling his booklet would challenge that.

And he did it, anyway.

29

IN NEW YORK, THE NAACP'S NATIONAL STAFF heard about the *Statement* within hours. "We are greatly interested in the meeting of the Inter-racial Committee at Atlanta yesterday," Walter White wrote the governor, "and we wish to express our appreciation for your action in urging a wide spread publicity campaign to acquaint Georgians with the situation and to bring about the better relations between the races."

White immediately became a one-man publicity mill, using *The Negro in Georgia* as a springboard to decry the similarly dire state of affairs outside Georgia's borders. "While the conditions revealed by Governor Dorsey are horrible almost beyond belief, they are not unusual in the South nor are they confined to that state alone," he wrote. "If American citizens knew of the terrible conditions in the South where Negroes are treated worse than during the days of slavery, if white people who live outside of the South knew how many crimes were covered by the old story of Negroes committing 'the usual crime,' there would be an upheaval comparable only to the days immediately preceding the Civil War.

"Governor Dorsey deserves the highest commendation for his brave stand. It takes a brave man to do what he has done, even though he be a white man and governor of the state."

At first, the speech and booklet also earned high marks from press and public. "His presentation of the matter," the *Constitution* wrote two days after the Piedmont Hotel meeting, "and the interest he has taken in improving the situation, which was brought to a climax by the John S. Williams case, has attracted much favorable comment."

"Governor Dorsey has been very active in bringing to the attention of the people the lawless condition in the state and he deserves much praise for his splendid work along this line," the *Macon News* editorialized, adding: "We venture the prediction that lynchings are going to be less frequent than ever before."

Out-of-state reaction was even more enthusiastic. The *New York Globe* found that while Dorsey's words documented "an appalling condition," they also offered "greater hope for the solution of the Negro problem than any statement or action since the civil war."

"Georgia is most fortunate in an Executive who is not willing to wait for pressure from the outside," the *New York World* decided, "for if peonage and negro oppression are to be wiped out the work must be done from within. Even more encouraging than Gov. Dorsey's programme is the evident readiness of the people of the State to follow his leadership in a thorough community house-cleaning."

The *New York Times* also commended Dorsey's stand, predicting that *The Negro in Georgia* would earn "general approval all over the country." But the paper, and a good many other observers, were mystified by the governor's omission of names and specific places, which Dorsey had explained in the booklet's introduction: "I do not desire to give harmful publicity to those counties, when I am convinced that, even in the counties where these outrages are said to have occurred, the better element regret them."

The *Times* pointed out that the document "would have been more impressive, and perhaps more useful as the basis of prosecution" if it had included such details, and that the governor's stated reason for leaving them out "seems, as observed from a distance, to be a poor one: for while the guilty are not designated, the innocent remain the objects of an unjust suspicion."

Still, for a full two weeks, Dorsey must have been pleased with the booklet's reception, and no response was more satisfying than James Weldon Johnson's editorial in the *New York Age* of May 7, by which time copies had been distributed by the thousands throughout Georgia and beyond. Johnson was stunned by the *Statement*, calling it "one of the strongest indictments of the South for injustice, cruelty and brutality against the Negro ever yet made" and a document that "should be in the hands of every American citizen."

"It took undoubted courage and something more than courage for the Governor to do what he has done," Johnson wrote. "We know that for many years a small minority of high-minded southern white people have discussed the wrongs done to the Negro in the South and have deplored them, but they have done so behind closed doors. In this case we have Governor Dorsey and a few men like him proclaiming not only to Georgians but to the country at large the unspeakable conditions existing in their state. This is the sort of action that we have longed for on the part of 'the better element.'"

Johnson then called attention to the booklet's passage on "A Thrifty Negro" and its devastating last line, which he labeled "a most significant admission." Blacks had long been "led into the belief that all the Negro needed to do to secure himself was to get a piece of land, build his own house on it, be thrifty and lead a law-abiding life," he wrote. "It is absolutely folly to believe that the Negro or anyone else can protect his material and property rights unless he has all the other common rights of citizenship. If the Negro in this country does not get the full rights of American citizenship whatever else he does get will not matter."

Johnson concluded: "This is a terrible arraignment of the people of his state, but it is true and true not only of Georgia but of nearly every other southern state. We hope that the words of Governor Dorsey will drive this truth deep into the conscience not only of the South but of the whole nation."

As if on cue, news broke that federal officials were investigating a second murder farm in South Georgia, at which three Black workers were said to have been killed. At the same time, state and federal officials learned that night riders had been terrorizing Black people in Taliaferro County, east of Jasper, and that more were under attack in Baker County, in the state's far southwest. Within a day, federal agents in Savannah had made another peonage arrest there.

These revelations prompted "one of the highest officials of the state"—exactly who was not specified—to suggest to the papers that the time had come for Georgia to admit it needed help addressing its race issues, and to request the federal government to "take charge of the situation and remain in control until these violations are checked." In response, the Bureau of Investigation's Vincent Hughes said he had been assured by his bosses in Washington that they were poised to dispatch fifty agents to the state if he indicated the need for them. Dorsey distanced himself from any notion that he favored federal intervention, but announced that he would call on every solicitor general to prioritize cases of mob violence or cruelty to their Black constituents. "The situation in Georgia is unbelievable," he said by way of explanation, "and I cannot understand it."

James Weldon Johnson viewed this prospect of calling in the feds as "almost revolutionary," in that it defied the South's long-standing worship of states' rights. He also lauded Dorsey's pledge to call on every solicitor general. "This writer had a conference with Governor Dorsey when the latter was in New York several days ago," he wrote in the *Age*. "The Governor expressed these same sentiments and we believe that he is sincerely desirous of bringing about better conditions, if not particularly for the good of the Negro, at least for the good name of the state over which he presides."

Down in central Georgia, meanwhile, the Williams family continued its journey through the legal wringer. On April 30, Greene Johnson appeared before Judge Hutcheson to present his petition for a new trial in Newton County. He had not received an official copy of the judge's charge to the jury, however, and without it, was hamstrung in building his argument. The judge apologized for the court's delay in preparing transcripts and continued the hearing for a week.

The session would have been a forgettable footnote to the case, except that Greene Johnson spoke to reporters outside the courtroom—and predicted that Newton County would never try Williams for the murders of Will Preston and Harry "Foots" Price. His reasoning: They were killed at the same time, and during the commission of the same crime, as Lindsey Peterson, and Williams had already been tried for that offense. In his view, any prosecution for their deaths would, therefore, amount to double jeopardy. "It was one act inspired by one volition," the lawyer said, "and under the law, Williams cannot be tried again for the alleged crime."

Although the eight indictments against Williams in Jasper County posed no such conflict, Johnson ventured that those cases would never see trial, either. "I am of the opinion that it would be useless expense," he said. "It probably will be the view of the county officials that the final outcome of the case that has already been tried will be the permanent judgment and sentence in the case." The defense would be ready, either way.

His comments betrayed calculations that Johnson left unspoken. One: that the defense attorney wasn't optimistic about his chances for a new trial or a successful appeal in the Peterson case. Why else would he wave off the Jasper cases as redundant? He must have expected the Newton County sentence to stand. And, two: that the state was not bent on pursuing other opportunities to hang Williams, despite the governor's assurances to the contrary—that the life sentence the farmer received in Newton would be seen as sentence enough.

Court officials declined to confirm Johnson's forecasts, but the press did learn that Jasper County would not take Williams to trial on its eight indictments until after the Newton verdict wound its way through the appeals process. Discarded, apparently, was Hugh Dorsey's strategy of subjecting Williams to back-to-back trials even while his appeals took place. "The state will prefer to safeguard its rear before taking up a new attack on the front," the *Constitution* explained.

While that might have heartened Williams, he had little else to cheer about. A federal grand jury convened on May 2 in Macon, the seat of the Southern District of Georgia. Over three days, Clyde Manning and nine other farmhands, along with federal agents Brown and Wismer, testified about conditions and practices on the plantation. The grand jury returned indictments charging the family with both conspiracy to commit peonage and peonage itself. The conspiracy charge contained two counts. In the first, the jurors linked the Williamses to five overt criminal acts, ranging from bailing men out of jail and forcing them to work against their will to murder. The second count charged them with four overt acts, among them keeping dogs trained to hunt down escapees. The peonage indictment, containing eight counts, accused the four Williamses of holding men prisoner in violation of the federal peonage statute. In sum, the indictment charged, the family conspired to keep fourteen men in debt slavery.

With those indictments in hand, federal agents now joined the state's search for the three sons. Friends insisted they were still in Jasper County and had every intention of turning themselves in, but that they were lying low to avoid having to await trial in jail. That claim didn't make believers of many, but hope remained high that they would be caught. Once that happened, Jasper County would have first crack at them, then hand them off to the federal courts. At the same time, officials made it known that their father would not be tried on federal charges if his life sentence remained in place.

This drew closer to a sure thing on May 7, when Greene Johnson again appeared before Judge Hutcheson to present his petition for a new trial. The judge promptly ruled against him. Dr. Gus Williams delivered the bad news to his father at the Tower. Williams showed little emotion, jailers said. Instead, he complained about the food behind bars, and beseeched Gus to have friends and family catch fish and deliver them to the Tower as soon as possible.

Greene Johnson announced he would appeal the conviction to the state Supreme Court. His filing would be in the justices' hands by early June, he said, but he expected no decision before late fall.

30

SOON ENOUGH CAME THE BLOWBACK to *The Negro in Georgia*. On May 10, Superior Court Judge William E. H. Searcy Jr., of Griffin, forty miles south of Atlanta, wrote to Dorsey that his *Statement* contained errors in its account of "A Thrifty Negro," a case Searcy knew well enough to "identify the negroes as Ed White and his family, the county as Upson county, the little town as The Rock and the judge as myself." The governor's charges were not only "gratuitous, unwarranted, and untrue," Searcy claimed, but a "wholesale indictment of Georgia and Georgians."

Supplied to newspapers as or before it reached Dorsey, Searcy's letter ticked off a long list of the account's details as untrue, starting with its assertion that the judge had promised to put the thrifty Negro in the chain gang before hearing the case. "If you are the author of this charge you have deliberately slandered me," he wrote. "If you are only repeating the charge without investigation to discover if true or not, then you are recklessly indifferent to the character and reputation of the judiciary. In either event your conduct is inexcusable and unworthy. He who knowingly or negligently repeats a slander is as vicious as he who invented it."

In reality, Searcy declared, the thrifty Negro's white neighbor was "a high toned gentleman, than whom there is no more loyal and honorable [a] citizen." The sheriff was "as faithful and efficient [a] sheriff as any county ever had." And as for the hero of the story, he had dismissed his own objections to the land survey in court. Moreover, he "had a dispute with another white neighbor adjoining him on another side, a widow, and not only trespassed on her land and cut her timber, but traveled to and from the woods with a Winchester rifle across his lap." Another thing:

once the Whites were arrested, it wasn't the family's vulnerability to lynching that caused their removal to another county, but a request from Dorsey himself.

"If the other cases in your statement as to the negro in Georgia contain no more of fact and truth than these now under consideration," wrote Searcy, "a great and unjustifiable wrong has been done by you to the State and its people. Certainly the mis-statement as to these cases is an outrageous wrong against the people of Upson county, its public officers and the Superior Court and its judge."

In closing, Searcy suggested that Upson County officials could set the governor straight on the facts, as could "any white citizen" of The Rock. "You perceive I limit the witness to the white people," he added, "as I do not care to enter the field against you in procuring negro witnesses, which seems to be your forte. I leave this field to you without a rival, as far as I am concerned." Today, such a revealing sign-off—and his obvious contempt for one race of witness versus another—would brand the judge unfit for public office. But it played well at the time in Georgia.

Asked about the letter, Dorsey called Searcy "one of the best judges and most honorable men in the state," and said he was "inclined to accept" the judge's version of the story over his own. "I wish to add, however, that I sent a special investigator to Upson County," he said, "and the charges contained in my pamphlet are based upon his report.

"I do not personally vouch for the accuracy of all the charges in my pamphlet, but in this particular case, my special investigator furnished me the names of five citizens of the community who gave the information on which his report was based." It seems common sense that in assembling such an incendiary document, Dorsey would have taken every possible precaution to make it factually bulletproof. His admission that he had failed to do so only encouraged statewide demands that he reveal the identities of his investigators and sources. When he refused, he found himself besieged.

Dorsey had made a fatal miscalculation: he attacked the system while striving to avoid implicating its players. Those individuals had a lot of skin in the game, however, and his reliance on anonymity—followed by his weirdly eager deference to Searcy—emboldened his detractors and sabotaged the overall impact of his appeal. A Superior Court judge and solicitor general in eastern Georgia now found fault with another of the *Statement*'s cases. Dorsey's successor, Governor-elect Thomas Hardwick, branded the booklet "infamous slander" and promised to denounce it in his inaugural address. Searcy doubled down on his criticism, writing to Dorsey that "the conduct of your investigator and you as Governor of the State beggars my contempt." Sam L. Olive, president of the Georgia Senate, announced his belief that Dorsey should remedy his "awful mistake" at once.

In Macon, an outfit called the Guardians of Liberty called for a mass meeting of citizens to discuss the governor's removal from office. "Unless Mr. Dorsey is impeached every Georgian will be particeps criminis in his crime of blackening the character of the fairest mother man ever had— Georgia," the group declared. "No living man will stand by while a villain insults his mother. Georgia—our mother—is being defiled before the world. And by the help of the eternal God he shall answer for it."

As the Black-owned *Chicago Defender* observed: "The counterattack on the governor of Georgia has begun."

HUGH DORSEY DID NOT GO DOWN WITHOUT A FIGHT. In a May 13 letter to Judge Searcy, he reiterated that he had based his account of the "Thrifty Negro" on a written report by a white investigator he had dispatched to Upson County. "This report is now before me," he told the judge. "The name of the man who kicked the negro girl in the stomach; the names of seven leading citizens who testify as to the good character and reputation of the negro and who unite in expressing the opinion that the case against him was one of persecution; the names of four leading citizens in your circuit who stated that a committee had waited upon you and that you informed them that White would be put in the chain gang—the names and statements of these citizens are embodied in the report." The document also included "a detailed account of the shooting up of the negro's home, when only his wife and small children were in it."

Dorsey quoted his investigator directly: "'I was told by several good people that the trial of White was a fake and a travesty of justice. That a certain class of people in Upson county had it in for any negro that was the least prosperous and White especially; that they were determined to put him in the chain gang; that if it took ten witnesses to convict him they would get him; if it took 100 they would put up 100, and if took 1,000 they would put up 1,000.'

"The report covers twelve typewritten pages," the governor wrote. "I quote only enough of it to show to you the type of matter that was before me when I included this case in the number cited by me in my statement. You will, I believe, agree with me that these facts justify the use which I made of the information.

"It is not my desire to injure the reputation of any county, town or official, but I do wish to awake the people of Georgia to what I regard as a peril overshadowing all others threatening our state. This peril, I believe to be due to a failure upon the part of the majority of our people to appreciate what is taking place and the staggering sum total of charges made against us as a people in connection with our treatment of the negro."

One more point: yes, Dorsey acknowledged, he had asked that Ed White be moved to a safer jail, because he'd surmised that the prisoner was in danger of being lynched as long as he stayed in Upson County.

To the judge and solicitor general who had faulted the second case in *The Negro in Georgia*, the governor wrote a stinging response. The incident involved a nighttime attack on an African American who, the court officers charged, had it coming—he'd uttered an oath "which no southern white man accepts." Moreover, the victim had not been set upon by a mob, as suggested in the booklet, but by a handful of men who cornered him hours after he delivered his oath.

"I am sure that you will agree with me," Dorsey wrote, "that the true spirit of the Anglo-Saxon, to which you refer with a pride in which I share, calls for the resentment of such an insult at the time when given, and never justifies waiting for the cover of the night to go in a mob, however small, to beat the giver of the insult." The "members of the miniature mob" were no defenders of right; they were criminals, and their offense was "typical of the causes underlying the 415 cases of lynching which have disgraced our state." He expected the complainers to do their jobs and uphold the law.

This response only further incensed his critics. They were legion now, and they included the same newspapers that had supported Dorsey just weeks before. The *Macon Telegraph* was typical: It stood "firmly behind Governor Dorsey in his determination to make Georgia a law-abiding state," while at the same time complaining that he had "adopted an unfortunate method of going about the business." The *Telegraph* went on to second-guess its own support of Dorsey's attacks on peonage, suggesting that, on reflection, the whole controversy had been overblown. "There is no slavery in Georgia of any kind whatever," the paper told its readers, "unless the white man is the slave."

This radical shift was replicated dozens of times throughout the state. The Madison *Madisonian* laid talk of peonage to "the undue activity of daily newspapers, Atlanta preachers and federal agents." The *Americus Times-Recorder* called the booklet "a most deplorable act of a well-meaning governor, a piece of business which will do irreparable harm." The *Griffin Daily News*, the newspaper in Judge Searcy's hometown, decided that Dorsey's "Negro booklet" was a cynical ploy to earn the governor a federal judgeship. That claim did not survive even casual scrutiny—the Republican Harding administration was not about to appoint a lifelong and active southern Democrat to the federal bench—but that didn't stop several other papers from taking up the charge. Dorsey settled the question by promising that he was not a candidate for public office and would refuse any appointment that came his way.

One critic, Baptist preacher and KKK chaplain Caleb A. Ridley of Atlanta, issued his own booklet with a mouthful of a title—*The Negro in Georgia: Another "Pamphlet" Called Forth by Governor Hugh M. Dorsey's Slanderous Document, Scattered Broadcast over the Country, and in Which He Purported to Set Forth the Brutal Treatment Accorded the Negro by White Citizens of Georgia—The "American Belgian Congo."* Claiming that the "sentiments herein expressed are endorsed by 95 percent of all the white citizens of the state," Ridley teed off on Dorsey as a "sore-head" and "a political accident" who had been "swept into the governor's chair on a tidal wave of race hatred and is now the flotsam and jetsam of that receding wave." The governor, he said, was "willing to slander two million white people in order to court favor with Northern organizations and get his picture in the *Literary Digest*."

That was prelude to Ridley's central thesis, which consisted of the usual myths and old-fashioned (to borrow his term) race hatred:

Nowhere in his pamphlet does he refer to the white men murdered by the criminal negroes; nowhere does he tell you of the white women ravished and butchered by black brutes of uncontrollable passion; nowhere does he inform you that John Williams, of Jasper County, was convicted on the testimony of a criminal negro, and sentenced to life imprisonment for murder the negro says he himself committed; nowhere does he tell you of the boastful spirit created in negro breasts by his propaganda, and nowhere does he remind you of the inevitable results of this political bootlicking and willingness to slander his entire state because, here and there, [someone] has committed a crime.

No, he does not suggest the results, but every red-blooded American citizen now living on Georgia soil knows what the end will be if such campaigns of slander do not cease.

Ridley smelled a sinister influence behind Dorsey's "racial propaganda," and figured it had to be the NAACP, "with headquarters in New York City, officered and financed and influenced in large part by men who are neither negro nor white." That was the reverend's code for Jewish.

The NAACP's officers were no doubt delighted that Ridley had credited them with such a role, but they recognized that their brother in arms was in trouble. "The wolves of Georgia have at last turned upon Governor Dorsey," James Weldon Johnson wrote in the *Age*. "It seems that at first they were so dumbfounded by his revelations that they could not utter any cry, but they have found their voices and their howls are arising from every part of Georgia.

"This outcry is not based on the ground that the statements made by Governor Dorsey were untrue but upon the ground that he has defamed the state of Georgia. Of course, no attempt is made to explain how it is possible for the Governor to defame the state by stating facts.

"But on the Negro question the popular mob of the South is never rational," Johnson wrote. Dorsey had support among "a few high-minded and sincere white citizens, but unless their number is greatly and immediately increased, there is little doubt but what Governor Dorsey will suffer political martyrdom at least." Johnson hoped that Dorsey found the support he'd need "to beat back these howling wolves," but feared he would prove "too civilized a man to be able to live in Georgia."

In *The Crisis*, W. E. B. Du Bois noted that the Association's journal was often castigated for supposedly overstating the abuses suffered by the nation's Blacks. "But once in a while, thank God, the sickening shame becomes too much even for the shame-haunted digestions of white bourbons," he wrote. "The shrill cry of Governor Dorsey's revelations corroborates every word *The Crisis* ever wrote, every leaflet the NAACP ever printed: insult, intimidation, stealing, maltreating men and women, illegal arrest and imprisonment, outrageous public officials, almost unbelievable personal cruelty, lynching, torture, murder and deliberate slavery.

"Georgia stands naked and ashamed because one man dared tell the truth."

In late May, *The Nation*, a magazine owned by NAACP cofounder and board member Oswald Garrison Villard, found it "entirely in the cards" that the governor would "get into trouble with his fellow-Georgians by telling the truth about the ghastly conditions in his State.

"Governor Dorsey's offense was that he was both honest and brave, and that his was the first constructive program offered by a Georgia public official to make his State something other than the plague spot of our American civilization." It was now obvious, the magazine opined, "that the dastards who commit these unspeakable crimes are not the ones of whom Georgia wishes to purge herself. The real criminal is the man who faces the truth and thereby casts aspersions on 'the fair name of the sovereign State of Georgia.'"

Dorsey had other allies, but most of them were equally distant. The *New York Times* seemed especially eager to take up his defense, though it remained mystified as to why he hadn't named names. Acknowledging that he had been "less stern some years ago" about lawlessness in his state—that is, after Leo Frank's lynching—the paper commiserated on May 17 that "he now knows by personal experience what it is to be the object of violent denunciation" without evidence. His critics had "forgotten, apparently, the testimony recently given in their own courts—the testimony that resulted in the conviction by a Georgia jury of WILLIAMS of 'murder farm' fame—or the official admissions that came from several parts of the State to the effect that peonage in forms almost or quite as bad existed in several other places and should be both stopped and punished at once.

"What the present foes of Governor Dorsey want, apparently, is the scalp of anybody who reveals, or even hints, that there are bad folk in Georgia, as elsewhere," the *Times* concluded. "Hidden sins grieve them, no doubt, but the disclosure of sin fills them with rage."

Three days later, the paper published another editorial, this one arguing that neither Georgia's reputation nor character had "suffered from the disclosures which so enraged some of its distinguished but misguided residents. On the contrary, both have profited, or will, as soon as the Georgia negroes are treated exactly as Georgia's critics admit that negroes ought to be treated and as they say the Georgia negroes are treated."

Closer to home, an Atlanta convention of Baptist and Methodist ministers resolved to support Dorsey's efforts to publicize and stamp out peonage, and gave its "hearty indorsement" to his booklet. "If the fair name of Georgia is in the hands of such men as Caleb Ridley," one of the ministers added, "then God help Georgia."

U.S. Attorney Hooper Alexander, never before an ally of Dorsey's, also backed him up, declaring that he could produce witnesses to testify in many cases beyond those cited in the pamphlet. "It is not true that an appeal to the people of Georgia to put a stop to these evils is a reflection on the state and her people," he said. "It is the honorable and proper course to take—and if it is not, then, in the name of justice, what is?"

But those voices were all but lost in a cacophony of anger and insult.

The ground had shifted. The hero of April was the whipping boy of May.

His critics were eager to point out that the year before, while he ran for the Senate, Dorsey had helped launch a publicity campaign to broadcast Georgia's charms far and wide. A bid to attract outside investors, industry, and workers, the "Advertise Georgia" enterprise was welcomed throughout the state and bankrolled with $300,000 raised by private subscription. "We have had enough of bad advertising," the governor told a crowd in Athens that September. "It is time the United States be told the truth about Georgia."

Now Dorsey had his publicity, and America had been told the truth. Neither was what he, or anyone else, had anticipated.

"The discussions over peonage and the race question will have the effect of tearing Georgia to shreds," the *Jackson Progress-Argus* fretted. "Class will be arrayed against class. Mass will be pitted against mass. Not a single good thing can come from the whole sorry, sordid mess." It was "the most unfortunate, most regrettable, most damaging thing that has happened to Georgia since the War Between the States," according to the paper. "Georgia has been stabbed to the core."

As May closed, newly seated senator Tom Watson opened another broadside at his onetime ally. Dorsey, he pointed out, had been a prosecutor for years, but had never leveled peonage charges at anyone. (Never mind that, as a federal offense, peonage lay beyond a local prosecutor's purview.) He'd been governor for four years, and "not once during that long period did he assail his state." It was only as Dorsey's term approached its end, and after he'd run for the Senate "opposing the man . . . who had done most to make Mr. Dorsey the chief magistrate of Georgia," that he'd turned on his own people: "The wicked Georgians . . . would not send him to the senate; hence the sore head, and the morbid mind and vengeful spirit of the repudiated Dorsey."

The Negro in Georgia had overstated the prevalence of peonage, in Watson's view. "Let any honest investigator examine those official records," he wrote, "and then ask himself the question—How could the negroes of Georgia have become the owners of so many farms, so many houses, so much livestock and other property had they been generally the peons of such individuals as Williams, of Jasper county?"

As flawed as that thinking was (Dorsey had never supposed that Black people were "generally" peons), it seemed genius next to what followed:

> As to lynchings for the rapes of white girls and women, the blacks have the remedy in their own hands and that remedy reads: "Let the white women alone."
>
> Since the Civil War, the south has had a tremendous struggle to maintain her social standards and the purity of the blood of the whites. We will not tolerate social equality, mixed marriages and cur-dog mongrelization of our Anglo-Saxon race.
>
> The life of one negro, of a hundred, of a thousand, or a million, will count for nothing with us, in comparison with saving our homes and our civilization. . . . Stop the hideous rapes committed on little white girls, on aged white women, on white maids and matrons. Stop these! Then the lynchings will stop of themselves.

In the face of the continuing onslaught, members of the newly founded Committee on Race Relations met, without Dorsey, to explain their role in the *Statement*'s release and take some of the heat off the governor. Dorsey had written the booklet in its entirety before he appeared before the group, but its members now insisted that they, not he, bore responsibility for its contents and had decided to publish it. Furthermore, the committee stood behind its findings. "These 135 cases added to the 415 lynchings of negroes which have occurred in Georgia in the past thirty-five years shock the conscience of all Georgia," the committee argued. "They demand a remedy. He who would oppose an intelligent effort to correct such conditions should be, and will be, recognized either as an enemy to the common good, or a man lost to reason." With those remarks, the committee laid down a stouter defense of *The Negro in Georgia* than Dorsey had offered himself. That was the point: his message was being subsumed by the maelstrom it provoked, and the group's act of self-sacrifice was a desperate attempt to salvage the situation.

That said, even this farsighted and liberal sampling of Georgia society was unwilling to push too hard. While decrying racist atrocities, the group emphasized that it was opposed to social equality between the races—the notion that whites and Blacks should rub elbows in restaurants, hotels, swimming pools, social clubs. The idea that the races might intermarry.

Members believed in a square deal for Black Georgians.

But only so much of one.

PART FIVE

"Give Me Justice"

32

BY THE TIME NEWTON COUNTY brought Clyde Manning to trial, in late May 1921, white Georgia's curiosity about the atrocities on the Williams plantation had been satisfied. Two months of intense press coverage had mined the story for most of its gore and horror—what could possibly be left to discover? Besides, prosecuting a Black man for murdering another promised far less drama than trying a white defendant for the crime. So Manning's trial drew little interest from the press and attracted a mostly Black audience to the Covington courthouse, and to the limited seating in the gallery; the floor level of Judge Hutcheson's courtroom, reserved exclusively for white observers, had plenty of empty seats.

That Georgia was politically bound, rightly or wrongly, to try Manning for Lindsey Peterson's death was never in doubt. But at the trial's start, one question hung in the air: What with the state's reliance on Manning to put Williams behind bars, its insistence that he had no motive to kill his fellow peons beyond fear for his own life, and its argument throughout the Williams trial that Manning was more a victim than an accomplice, just how hard would Lonnie Brand push for a conviction?

Brand kept everyone wondering until near the end of the two-day trial, opting to use the state's witnesses to build a straightforward timeline of the killing frenzy. For this he called first to the stand Carl Wheeler, the young Newton County farmer who had pulled Lindsey Peterson and Will Preston from the Yellow River on March 13. Next came Dr. C. T. Hardeman, the occasional Newton County coroner, who told of inspecting the bodies and concluding that the men were thrown alive from Allen's Bridge.

Others fleshed out details of the case. Sheriff Johnson described being summoned to the riverbank, the discovery of Harry Price's remains a few days later, and Clyde Manning's confession. Special Agent Wismer related his visit to the plantation and Williams's claim that the only man killed on the property was a farmhand named Will Napier, who had allegedly come at one of his sons with a knife. When it came time to tie Manning to the murders, Brand simply read aloud a brief of the field boss's testimony at the Williams trial.

E. Marvin Underwood, Manning's attorney, objected repeatedly to the state's references to killings besides that of Lindsey Peterson. As he had at the Williams trial, William Howard argued they were essential to establishing motive. "So long as one of these Negroes lived, the defendant knew that testimony could be offered against him," the prosecutor argued. "This was the reason Manning acquiesced to taking part in the murders. It was the scheme and the motive of both Williams and the Negro—the one a part of another." This was a stretch, at best, in that the state had expended a great deal of energy at the previous trial making the point that Manning did not "scheme" with Williams about anything. But, as he had before, Judge Hutcheson overruled the objections.

On cross-examination, both Johnson and Wismer sounded more like witnesses for the defense than the state. Manning "stated he participated in the manner of the deaths that I have described, in each one of those cases, because he said he was afraid not to do it," the sheriff told Manning's attorney. "He was afraid Mr. Williams would kill him.

"He voluntarily made the confessions and admissions, but always stating that he did it at the command of Mr. John S. Williams, and because he was afraid not to do it."

Wismer testified that he had been present throughout Manning's interviews with lawmen. The defendant's admissions were "always coupled . . . with the statement that he acted for fear of death at the hands of Mr. Williams.

"I have never heard him make any statement with reference to admissions that was not coupled with that assertion," the agent said. "Clyde

Manning said that every one of the killings was done at the command of Mr. Williams, and through fear that if he didn't do that, that he would be killed."

Some of the farm's other Black workers spoke of their own fear and abuse when called to the stand. Clyde Freeman testified that he did not say anything to the visiting federal agents because he was too "afraid to tell them anything. . . . I was afraid of Mr. Hulon and Mr. Johnny and all of them. I was afraid of Mr. Williams and of his boys. I was afraid of Mr. Marvin and Mr. LeRoy Williams. I was afraid to tell anything at all, and that was the reason I didn't tell, was because I was afraid." When Underwood asked what he would have done if Williams had told him to kill someone, Freeman replied: "I would have tried. I would have been too scared not to."

Frank Dozier, the teenage peon who broke his leg falling off a mule and later escaped from the plantation, showed scars on his head left by beatings from Marvin Williams. "I couldn't tell you how many I got," he testified. "He would whip me for just most anything, mostly about just anything I would do. He whipped me once because I could not pick up a log. It was too heavy—I couldn't lift it—and he whipped me then."

James Strickland, who, along with Gus Chapman, had first reported the conditions at the farm to the feds, told the jury that the Williamses shot across the fields at him to hurry him along. Once, a bullet knocked his hat off. Emma Freeman, Clyde Freeman's wife, told the court she had seen "men on the place whipped," a "heap of them whipped," and that John S. Williams had once struck and badly injured her fellow servant Lula Benton. "I seen her after she was hit," she testified. "She was just as bloody as she could be. She was hit up there in the head."

Last came Claude Freeman, twenty-one, Clyde's younger brother and Hulon Williams's field boss. "Those niggers there were afraid," he told Underwood. "I could tell from their manner and physical appearance and what they did [that] they were afraid." Hulon "would threaten to shoot them or kill them or whip them. I have heard him tell them lots of times he would do such things." When a farmhand disappeared or was killed by the Williamses, the survivors knew better than to discuss it. "Niggers on the place didn't talk about them things," Claude Freeman explained. "We wouldn't talk about it. We wouldn't get in a crowd and talk. We never done that around there. We were all scared to say anything about it. I know I was scared."

In sum, by the time witness testimony closed, the jury had ample evidence that Clyde Manning had been right to fear Williams, and to believe that Williams would kill him in a minute if he did not do as he was told.

Terror greased every aspect of the Williams operation.

Reading over the testimony today, one strategy comes to the fore: much of it centered on killings that had occurred before the federal agents' visit—murders in which Clyde Manning took no part. As most of this evidence was offered by defense witnesses, Underwood evidently intended to show that the Williamses had violent contempt for Black lives with or without a federal investigation hanging over their heads, and thus to underline the pain, dread, and peril under which Manning and the other hands had worked and lived.

The first described was the shooting of Will Napier. The hands were slaughtering hogs on the Campbell place one winter's day in 1919 when they heard a shot. A short while later, Hulon Williams called to Clyde Manning and the Freeman brothers from behind his house "and told us to come down there," Claude Freeman recalled. "When we got there, Will Napier was lying right behind the buggy house, and he was shot."

"We found him about twenty steps back from the kitchen, back behind a little buggy house," Clyde Freeman testified. "We asked him how he felt, and he said he felt all right. He didn't say who shot him. He didn't say anything else to us, never anything about how he got shot."

Claude Freeman: "There was just Will Napier and Will Napier's wife. She was there, where we were. And Mr. [John S.] Williams was there, too. He was standing there when we got there.

"We picked up that body, Will Napier's body, and carried it in the house and put it on the bed. He was alive then."

Clyde Freeman: "Then they had two doctors—two—come, and that evening they operated on him, and he died that night. He was killed by being shot. He had been shot with a pistol."

Claude Freeman: "Mr. Hulon Williams said he had shot him."

The testimony argued that John S. Williams had lied when he told agents that Napier had advanced on his son with a knife. Would the Williams clan, given its murderous history, have summoned doctors to save the dying man if he had threatened one of them? It seemed far more probable that Will Napier was the family's nineteenth known murder victim.

Neither Freeman brother mentioned it, but Napier's wife was Clyde Manning's sister Grace. Hulon made her a widow at eighteen.

The witnesses detailed the killing of John "Iron Jaw" Davis, as well. James Strickland testified that the peon "run away and they caught him and brought him back and whipped him—Captain Marvin Williams and Captain LeRoy and Captain Hulon and Clyde Manning and Jule Manning"—Clyde Manning's younger brother Julius—"all whipped him.

"After that we were up in the hog pasture and Clyde Freeman went over to the Campbell place to get some wire, on Saturday morning, where he was going to build a hog pasture. And he had me cutting posts to put in some post holes, where he was going to put up the wire." Iron Jaw went off to help fetch that wire; he was rolling it back to the pasture, Clyde Freeman said, when "Mr. LeRoy told Charlie [Chisholm] he was not having it done right, and he got a stick and hit Iron Jaw and told him he would kill him."

Strickland recounted the same story that he had told the federal agents more than four months before: Iron Jaw begged LeRoy to stop. When the blows kept coming, he said he'd rather be killed and get it over with. "And [LeRoy] shot him in the arm, and then he asked [Iron Jaw] did he want him to shoot him and kill him, and he nodded his head."

Clyde Freeman: "Iron Jaw didn't say anything when he shot him. Only, when the last bullet hit him, he says, 'Now, then.'

"Then they took Iron Jaw down to the river, down to the pond, and throwed him out there in the pond. The only preparation they made to put the body in the pond, they just put a little rock to him, tied some rock to him, and then Charlie paddled the boat and Mr. Marvin Williams and Foots was in it and they took him out in the pond."

Frank Dozier: "Mr. LeRoy come to us and said he didn't want to hear anything about that. He didn't want to hear anything from any nigger about it, or he would kill us next."

About the death of Robert Nathaniel "Blackstrap" Williams, Gus Chapman testified that he "heard Mr. Hulon tell Charlie Chisholm to shoot him, to kill him, and Charlie shot him.

"Blackstrap didn't say nothing after they shot him. He had been whipped pretty bad up to that time. They were sure beating him, and he was begging them and said he was not going to run away any more. 'Please, don't whip me anymore,' he says."

Emma Freeman described the epilogue to Blackstrap's death. Several days after, she "went down to the river and seen him laying down in the river, where he had come up to the top of the water, and I recognized him." The peon's body, sunk in the pond, had untangled itself from the bottom and was floating on the surface for all to see. The same thing happened after John Singleton's murder, she testified. She had not seen Singleton killed, but she did see his body the week after: "The buzzards were flying around there so thick, the buzzards flying over the pond," she told the jury. "And that attracted the attention to this body, and they found it was the body of John Singleton, and had done come up. It had done riz in the pond."

Claude Freeman: "That was about eight or ten days after it was done. We were down there and the buzzards were flying around so thick, and Mr. Marvin was over there with us, and he sent [a worker] to the house to get some ropes and some wire and we . . . got the boat, and me and him got a big rock and put in the boat, and we dragged his body out in the water where it was deep, and we tied the rope to the rock and then tied it to his body, so the body would go down, and sunk it." The message this testimony left with the jury: the farm's workers were so terrorized by the Williamses that they were compelled to help dispose of their slain friends and colleagues, lest the same thing happen to them.

"And I saw the body go down," Claude Freeman said.

The highlight of the trial's second day was Clyde Manning himself. Like his former boss, he made an unsworn statement to the jury—a long, meandering discourse that he began by recounting his early boyhood on the Persons plantation and his family's move to the Williams place. He described the one occasion on which he'd tried to leave since, when he "made a trade" to go work for a neighboring farmer, prompting Mr. Johnny to attack him with an oversize pipe wrench and break his arm. "I never tried to leave any more after that," Manning told the jury. "I didn't want to have any trouble with him. I didn't want him to jump on me anymore. I didn't want him to be mad with me because I knowed what he would do."

Here, by way of illustrating the Williams family's capacity for violence, he abruptly shifted to the first murder of which he had direct knowledge: "Me and Johnny Singleton, Mr. Marvin, and Charlie Chisholm was plowing in the field," he said. "Mr. Marvin was plowing way up across the field from us, with Johnny Singleton. Me and Charlie was plowing down below John Singleton and Mr. Marvin, and along about night, just about time for us to quit—we quit just at dark—he come down across the field and told me and Charlie Chisholm to go up there with him, he done killed John Singleton.

"He wanted us to help him get him away from there, so when me and Charlie Chisholm got up there, John Singleton was dead. He had been dead long enough to be getting stiff, and [Marvin] told us to take him. And me and Charlie put him across a mule and carried him down to the river, to the pond, and he told us to take a trace chain off one of the mules and put it around his neck, and we took the trace chain and done that, and then got a long rock like he told us, and tied it to him. And me and Mr. Marvin and Charlie Chisholm carried John Singleton out in the river in the boat, out in the pond, carried him out there in the boat, and turned him out of the boat, and throwed the rock off."

"Then, Mr. Johnny, he come up there the next day and he said he didn't want to hear nothing about that at all, because if he heard any report come out on his son he was going to kill somebody—he knowed where it come from. We didn't say nothing about that, none of us. If it was told anywhere, I know I didn't tell it. I knowed Mr. Johnny and I knowed what he would do. I had been with him long enough to know he would kill us."

Manning provided some background on how he had come to know Williams so well: "I come there a little boy, and was raised up under Mr. Johnny, raised me right there like his children was, and I had him to mind," he said. "Even [as] a boy there he would jump on me, and he would beat me worse than he did his children. It made no difference what I done, and if my folks told me to do anything—if my poor mother told me anything to do, I had to go along and mind him. I had to do just as he said. If [my folks] said anything for me to do, I had to let them alone and do just what he said to do."

Now Manning did something that jolted the room, that he had never done in all the months of his incarceration, the long hours of questioning by the sheriff and federal agents, his tense and wearying days in court. The mask he had worn throughout—the flat, clinical manner that had both impressed and disquieted his listeners—all of that armor crumbled. Clyde Manning broke down and wept, and for a while he couldn't stop.

"Gentlemen of the jury," he said, struggling, "I am just connected here with what somebody else has done. I didn't want to do it; I had it to do. If it had been left with me, I would not have been into this. There would not have been nothing to it. I asked Mr. Johnny to let me out of this. I told him I didn't want to do it, and he told me it was all right—says, 'It is all right me with me, if you don't want to do it.' He said, 'It means your neck or theirs.' He says, 'If you think more of their neck than you do of yours, it just means yours.'"

Manning burst into tears once more. "I seen by that I had to go on and do it just to save my own self," he managed. Then, regrouping, he returned to murders he'd witnessed, beginning with Hulon Williams's commanding Charlie Chisholm to kill Blackstrap: "Charlie shot him. Charlie shot him in the head. Then the boy Blackstrap raised up off the barrel and set up on his knees a few minutes, and made one or two curious moans, and fell over."

Will Napier died, Manning said, because he'd tried to run. He wanted to return to his home near Macon, and his escape attempt angered Hulon Williams. After Hulon shot Napier, Manning watched three doctors—among them the oldest Williams son, Gus, and C. T. Hardeman, the sometime-coroner in Newton County—operate on the wounded man. "Dr. Hardeman, he treated him with ether to put him to sleep, and Dr. Payne and Dr. Williams operated on him. He was shot right through here"—he pointed to just above the small of his own back—"and it come out right here"—he pointed to his belly—"and they cut him open here and they sewed up his entrails. And I stood right there, looking at them sewing his entrails and sewing him up, and he died before they got through sewing him up."

Manning next walked the jury through the murders of Lindsey Peterson, Will Preston, and Harry Price, beginning with Mr. Johnny's offer that Saturday afternoon to drive Artis Freeman to Butts County. "Whether Artis got to Jackson, I don't know," he said. "I know he put on clothes to go to Jackson. I heard some of them say he left Mr. Hulon's with Mr. Johnny, but how far he got, I don't know." Unsaid but understood by his listeners was that Artis Freeman was either the Murder Farm's twentieth victim, or the luckiest man to ever breathe in Jasper County.

Of the terrible ride with the three doomed men to the Yellow and South Rivers, Manning's account stayed true to the narrative he had related since his arrest. Before pulling over, Williams confronted the young men. "'I heard you boys was all going off to try to have my boys' necks broke,' and they all says, 'No,' and begun begging," Manning told the jury. "And Harry Price . . . said, 'I ain't going nowhere. Keep me. I want to stay with you.' And he went on begging, and Mr. Johnny just says, 'Tie them.' And me and Charlie Chisholm tied them.

"I didn't want to hurt them," he said. "Gentlemen, I done it. But I says, honest before my living God, I didn't do it because I wanted to do it, and I done it against my will—and done it because I had it to do and done it just on account I was afraid I would be killed. I knowed Mr. Johnny would do it."

As for why he didn't flee, Manning largely repeated what he had said at the first trial. He feared the bloodhound, and rarely slept through a night without Williams waking him to "ask me, 'Wasn't the cows out down there in the wheat?' And I would get up and go around to see. . . . And he called me sometimes up to the house, and wanted me to go around and see what was the matter with the mules, some was kicking around, and wanted me to see if they wasn't hung some way."

"I just knowed he had been calling me that way of night to see if I was around anywhere, so if I had been gone he could put the dog on my track." Even with a two-hour head start, he would not have been able to outrun that dog, he said. "So I had to stay. I didn't stay with Mr. Johnny because I wanted to stay with him. I stayed there because I *had* to stay with him, because I could not get away and make myself safe. If it had been left with me, I would have gone off. But I seen what he done to them other boys, and I knowed it was not safe for me to get away. I didn't want him to kill me, and I knowed he would. And I knows there had been other boys killed on account of running away." Manning elaborated for a while about his decision to stay and about Williams's cruelty to the farm's other Black workers, then returned to his central argument: He was only on trial because of what Williams had done and forced him to do. "I never have been in a minute's trouble before in my life. I didn't know nothing about law before," he said. "I never even have been in a courthouse as a witness. I never had nothing sworn out against me.

"I am just messed up in this here, and been laying in jail two level months and seven days yesterday, just because what somebody else done. I am just sitting up here before you men just on account of what somebody else done and got me to do, and made me do it."

He was so frightened after the Peterson and Preston murders, Manning testified, that he "never even told my wife. I knowed if I said anything to her, she might tell some of her people, and some of her people might tell it to someone or say something, and it might keep working around 'til it got right back to Mr. Johnny, and then I knowed I would have been killed. Mr. Johnny killed Charlie Chisholm, and I knowed if it got out he would have killed me just like he did them. I knowed what would become of me. I knowed he did not have any more care for me than he did for Charlie Chisholm. Mr. Johnny would have killed me just as quick as he did Charlie Chisholm."

Manning fell silent. When it became clear he had finished, his lawyer addressed Judge Hutcheson. "In view of the fact this defendant is illiterate and cannot read nor write, and the facts in this case are so numerous," Underwood said, "I would like, with your honor's permission, to call his attention to some facts."

"You can remind him, if you desire," the judge replied, "but you cannot go into details."

"That is all I wish to do," Underwood told him. He turned to Manning. "You have not said anything about John Long." Meaning John "Iron Jaw" Davis.

Manning replied that he had little firsthand knowledge of that killing. When he learned of it, he said, Iron Jaw "had been killed about a week," and he knew better than to ask questions. "Whenever anything like that happened, if there was two standing around looked like [telling] secrets, they"—the Williamses—"thought you were plotting something, and if you had any secrets to talk, you had to talk to them. You could not talk, two of your color. You couldn't talk to yourselves. If you have any secrets to talk about, you have to tell it to them."

Underwood: "You have not stated anything about Negroes running away, different ones, or any Negroes being shot. Do you know anything along that line?"

Manning did not. He listed some of the peons who had escaped, but "they were up on the river place, and I was down at Mr. Johnny's." He'd heard that Hulon Williams once armed a peon with a revolver and gave him orders to shoot another farmhand. The peon had tried, only to find the gun was unloaded. "If they told any of them to do anything," he insisted, "they knowed they got to do it."

And with that, the defense rested. Brand stood, announced that the prosecution had no rebuttal to offer, and rested himself. The two sides prepared for closing arguments.

33

WILLIAM HOWARD OFFERED the first of the prosecution's summations. Anyone in the courtroom who had attended John S. Williams's trial would have been shocked by his remarks, because while he had earlier praised Manning's testimony and mocked the notion that the field boss had a motive to kill, he now completely reversed course. "The defense has said that the state could not show a motive for Manning's crime, except fear for his own skin," he told the jury. "Manning's motive was identical with that of Williams, the owner of the place. Williams and Manning both had been practicing peonage, both feared federal investigation, and they plotted and acted together to get rid of the human evidence before the federal authorities should take a hand in the case.

"There will be one question for you to decide," he told the jury. "That is, was Manning *legally* responsible for these killings?" That he killed Lindsey Peterson was beyond a doubt—his own testimony at the Williams trial and his many statements to police, prosecutors, and federal investigators established that. Now, Howard said, the jury must "distinguish between moral responsibility and legal responsibility. If a drunken man kills another he is not morally responsible, but he is certainly legally responsible." By the same token, if Manning committed murder out of fear for his own life, then he was not morally responsible. But the question of his legal responsibility remained. "The law says a man is coerced when, through fear, the will of another is forced upon him," the lawyer concluded. "That will be your question."

Howard took his seat. He had not delivered his trademark long, fiery oration—the kind that had so captivated observers at the Williams trial before he collapsed in the heat—and he had not spoken for nearly so long. But then again, in the Georgia of the day, prosecuting a Black man, even Clyde Manning, was a largely pro forma undertaking.

Rising for the defense was fifty-four-year-old Albert Delaware Meador, until recently Newton County's "ordinary," or judge of the probate court, with jurisdiction over wills and estates. Judge Meador, as everyone in and out of the courthouse continued to address him, began by pointing out to the jury that the prosecution's witnesses had done a fine job of helping the defense. "Is there any evidence in this case to show that Manning committed these crimes on his own free will and volition?" he then asked. "The state has failed to make out its case.

"It may maintain that the defendant should have escaped, but I tell you that fourteen years on the plantation under Williams's influence were enough to keep him there. He acted under threats and menaces of Williams and cannot be held responsible for the murders."

Meador closed with a plea to the all-white jury: "I ask of you, and I believe, that when you go to your room you will not let the fact that the defendant is a Black man influence you in making your verdict."

At this trial, the prosecution would make the first and last of the closing arguments, so Meador was followed by E. Marvin Underwood, delivering the keynote for the defense. Bespectacled, polished, and sober, Underwood reminded the court that Manning had spelled out the facts of the case himself, and had done it so many times with so little variance that he had to be telling the truth. And central to that narrative was that Manning had acted without malice toward Lindsey Peterson or any other victim. "Was there a fear of Williams on the farm sufficient to cause the Negroes to do anything he ordered, even to the killing of human beings?" Underwood asked. The attorney answered his own question. Yes. There was. "The best evidence of this is the actual killings. In every instance it has been shown that Williams' orders were obeyed. Evidence submitted by the state has proved this."

The state had asserted that an unwilling participant would have attempted escape, Underwood said. But in this case, attempted escape was a well-established cause of death. The defense attorney described in graphic detail how trained hounds were used to run down Black fugitives. He referred to testimony from the Black witnesses on how they had been hunted down, shot at, and beaten. He recounted the bids for freedom that ended in death for various peons at the Williams farm. And he told of John S. Williams's almost complete dominance of Manning's thoughts and deeds over the fourteen years of his servitude.

"The state has advanced, as its weak motive, that Manning was afraid of federal authorities," Underwood said. "In Manning's statement in the previous trial, which the state has introduced, he [testified] that he was not afraid of the officers because he knew they could get him only for doing something someone had compelled him to do." Clearly, Manning had no motive "to carry out such a scheme." Then, catering to the presumed bigotry of the jury, the lawyer continued: "How could a Negro plan such a series of crimes? He was only a tool in the hand of a greater, driving force, and under the law is not guilty of murder."

Lonnie Brand, playing the lead role denied him at Williams's trial, now approached the jury box to finish for the prosecution. On appearances alone, he still seemed miscast for the job—soft, overheated, awkward. That impression evaporated when he opened his mouth. All of Manning's years in the thrall of John S. Williams had left him a "mean nigger" who strove for a place in the good graces of his even meaner boss, Brand told the jury. "Williams was a king. A monarch of all whom he surveyed, and his sons were worshippers at his throne," he said. Manning was equally in his thrall. "Clyde needed no threats to make him do anything. There was no fear of losing his life. He committed the crimes to please his boss, and he is just as guilty as Mr. Williams and should be meted the same punishment."

Brand scoffed at Manning's explanation for why he didn't flee the plantation: "He made no effort, he tells you, because bloodhounds were on the place and Mr. Williams called him at all times of night. But I tell you that if this Negro had gotten a half-mile ahead of the hounds, no race horse in Georgia could have caught him.

"Did he want to escape? No. He wanted to stay and bask in the fiend-ish crimes of his master. There has been no evidence of real danger to Clyde introduced in this case." Like virtually every other officer of the court, the prosecutor referred to Manning by first name, as one might a child. "He's made a clean breast of everything," Brand allowed. "He has told the truth and should be commended. But this does not mean that he should escape punishment for his crimes. And to you, who hold the scales of justice, I leave the fate of this Negro in your hands."

Judge Hutcheson's charge to the jury was, once again, mostly legal boiler-plate. But well into his remarks he veered from the standard to the spe-cifics of Clyde Manning's predicament. "Gentlemen, the defendant has admitted he did certain things in conjunction with the co-defendant in the bill of indictment, John S. Williams," the judge said, "but he says he acted under threats and menaces and under coercion. And in determin-ing this question you can look to all the facts and circumstances of the case." If the jurors decided such coercion existed, and that Manning "did those things by reason of threats or menaces . . . then he would not be guilty of any crime, and it would be your duty to acquit him."

At that, the panel left the courtroom. It had much to consider: namely, whether or not it was possible for Manning to have felt a fear "so strongly gripping . . . as to hold him spellbound while participating in no less than eleven murders of the foulest form," as the *Macon Telegraph* put it. The ju-rors would have to balance that against the fact that however sympathetic a character Clyde Manning might be—as a man steeped from childhood in violence and abuse, who had spent his every waking moment in fear, and whose long exposure to the trauma of life on the plantation had ren-dered him an emotional zombie—he was not wholly innocent. He had advance knowledge of all eleven of the killings. He knew, when John S. Williams offered freedom to Lindsey Peterson, Will Preston, and Harry Price that Saturday afternoon, that the boss planned to kill them by day's end; yet he continued to work alongside them without a word. He sat in his cottage with them after supper, laughing and carrying on, before Williams appeared at the door; he said nothing to alert them that if they climbed into the Chandler, all would be lost. Likewise, he failed to warn the others Williams killed in February and March 1921. These men were his friends or, at the very least, shared his membership in a nightmarish fraternity. Had he not owed them more than he gave?

Granted, it's easy to judge, a century later. He was in a no-win situation, with just two options—do as Williams said, or die. But his role did not end with simply failing to warn his fellow farmhands; Manning had done much of the actual killing. Legal precedent suggested that while he might be permitted to kill in order to save himself, he could not kill an innocent third party to do so. That concept lay at the heart of several American court cases over the previous twenty-five years that had ended in the conviction of people offering defenses not much different from Manning's. And it went back a lot further than that: as Sir William Blackstone wrote in his *Commentaries on the Laws of England*—an eighteenth-century, four-volume study of legal principles that had enormous, early influence on American law—a person in Manning's position "ought rather to die himself, than escape by the murder of an innocent."

Blackstone did offer him one avenue of escape: "In such a case he is permitted to kill the assailant," he wrote, "for there the law of nature, and self-defense its primary canon, have made him his own protector." And indeed, Manning and Charlie Chisholm could have joined forces with Peterson, Preston, and Price to kill John S. Williams on the ride to the bridges.

True, that would have merely delayed their deaths, for they'd almost certainly have been made to pay for the deed by lynch mob or hangman. It was probably beyond comprehension to Clyde Manning, anyway. Judging from their behavior in their final minutes, it was just as foreign an idea to the doomed peons.

As Manning said of the victims: "They didn't a one of them fight; all they did was beg him not to do it."

———

The jury took just forty minutes to reach its decision. Manning was smoking a cigarette at the defense table when the twelve reentered the courtroom. He tossed it away as court was called back into session. "Have you gentlemen reached a verdict?" Judge Hutcheson asked. The foreman nodded, and the judge asked Lonnie Brand to receive it. The solicitor read the decision aloud. Reporters watched Manning's head drop to his knees as Brand reached the word "guilty," then lift again, his face bright with relief, at the jury's recommendation of life in prison.

"Stand up, Clyde," the judge told him.

Manning stood. "Clyde, the jury has found you guilty with a recommendation for mercy," Hutcheson said, "and the sentence of the court is that you spend the rest of your life in the penitentiary. Have a seat." That evening, Manning was returned to the Tower. Underwood filed a motion for a new trial.

To the editorial writers at the *Constitution*, the verdict felt right. "Any human being who has committed eleven murders, regardless of the circumstances under which the murders were committed, is unsafe to be at large," the paper reasoned. "To him human life is essentially too cheap; he is too inured to human butchery, to be a safe member of society."

34

THAT SAME DAY, THE NAACP'S ATTENTION was pulled from the case when word came that a race massacre in Tulsa, Oklahoma, had killed an untold number of Black citizens, plundered their homes, and put their business district—nicknamed "Black Wall Street"—to the torch. The Association dispatched Walter White to the scene, where, as usual, he was able to blend in with those responsible. He found that a white mob of "around five thousand," armed with gasoline bombs, machine guns, and even airplanes, had killed indiscriminately and erased forty-four blocks of the city.

"Special deputy sheriffs were being sworn in to guard the town from a rumored counter attack by the Negroes," he wrote. "It occurred to me that I could get myself sworn in as one of these deputies. It was even easier to do this than I had expected. That evening in the City Hall I had to answer only three questions—name, age, and address. I might have been a thug, a murderer, an escaped convict, a member of the mob itself which had laid waste a large area of the city—none of these mattered: my skin was apparently white, and that was enough.

"After we—some fifty or sixty of us—had been sworn in, solemnly declaring we would do our utmost to uphold the laws and constitutions of the United States and the State of Oklahoma, a villainous-looking man next [to] me turned and remarked casually, even with a note of happiness in his voice: 'Now you can go out and shoot any nigger you see and the law'll be behind you.'"

While being deputized, White experienced one of his now-trademark close calls. An army captain appeared to recognize him and, with four menacing associates, pressed in close to inform him that they belonged to an organization that "doesn't love niggers" and were keeping their eyes peeled for officers of the "damned nigger advancement association." White kept his cool and the moment passed. But his report so unnerved the NAACP's directors that they decided that "except in cases of extraordinary and unusual circumstances," the Association's assistant secretary was to tackle no further undercover investigations without their approval in advance.

Even as James Weldon Johnson the activist devoted his energies to Tulsa, Johnson the journalist kept an eye on the goings-on in Georgia. His attention was drawn, in particular, to Caleb Ridley, the preacher who circulated his own pamphlet in the wake of Hugh Dorsey's *The Negro in Georgia*. Ridley was the putative head of the Dixie Defense Committee, a front for the KKK (recall that Ridley served as the Klan's chaplain), and he and the group were waging a war on what he called "vicious propaganda" against the South and "slander and libel" aimed at its sacred traditions. The source of this river of ill will, in Ridley's view? The NAACP.

Johnson wasn't about to let such foolishness stand. "We suppose the Dixie Defense Committee is being organized specifically for the defense of the State of Georgia," he wrote in the *Age*. "Georgia does need to be defended, but it does not need to be defended against the National Association for the Advancement of Colored People, or any other organization fighting for the common, legal and citizenship rights of the Negro.

"What Georgia needs to be defended against are her brutal and bloody practices of peonage and lynching. If the Defense Committee will undertake to help [prosecute] the men who are fattening on the toil of ignorant Negroes whom they hold in the worst sort of slavery and the degenerate brutes who burn human beings at the stake, they will find there will be no need to defend their state against what they term 'slander and hurtful propaganda.'"

Meanwhile, in Atlanta, Hugh Dorsey weathered his final stormy days as governor amid continuing howls for his head. Former governor and senator Hoke Smith piled on in a speech in Washington, D.C. "You know and should let it be known," he said, "that with rare exception the white people of Georgia are law abiding citizens and treat Negroes just as kindly, and that the wholesale tirade upon the subject of peonage which has recently found its way into the press of the country is unwarranted and unjustifiable.

"Unfortunately in all the states there occur now and then crimes which shock the public sense, but this gives warrant to no one to indulge in general condemnation of that state." Besides, peonage had its place, Smith suggested: it enabled "the farmer to secure a needed laborer and the convicted criminal to escape the disgrace of working on the chain gang." While governor, he maintained, he had not heard a single complaint about it.

On Dorsey's penultimate night in office, Caleb Ridley spoke before a self-styled "mass meeting" convened in Atlanta to again demand the governor's impeachment. About fifty people showed up. Some of those few were members of the state's General Assembly. Still incensed about *The Negro in Georgia*, Ridley charged that Dorsey compiled it with the help of Black researchers trained by the Young Men's Christian Association— yes, the YMCA—whom he had dispatched throughout the state. These researchers, he claimed, did not rely on court records for their case descriptions, but on Black informants and "sore heads." That amounted to official misconduct, Ridley reckoned, and such misconduct presented grounds for Dorsey's removal.

The organizers had little real hope of seeing Dorsey deposed—he had all of forty hours left in his term—so they directed most of their ire at his allies. The keynote speaker was one Miss Alief Benton, "representing patriotic societies" in Macon, according to the *Constitution*. She attacked the Commission on Interracial Cooperation for its efforts to "break down the color line," and the Catholic church for its missions in the South. She urged legislators to quash the "vicious propaganda" calling for full and equal rights for all—to, as she said, "expose the Negro in the woodpile in Georgia."

Hugh Dorsey's final message to the Georgia legislature, delivered on the morning of Saturday, June 25, defied these critics. After reviewing the state's troubled finances and failing educational system, he launched into a lengthy discussion of mob violence, again warning legislators that if they did not take action to suppress lynching, the federal government would do it for them. Then, in a dramatic departure from his past comments on the subject, Dorsey recited the names of the men and women lynched since he had taken office four years before. The list included Jesse Slater of Brooks County, killed in November 1917 for writing an insulting letter to a young woman; two residents of Mitchell County murdered eight days later for disputing the word of whites; and a man who died for "making remarks about [a] Chicago race riot." He named Hayes and Mary Turner, another man lynched for "alleged incendiary talk," and yet another for "making boastful remarks about another Negro shooting [an] officer of law." He mentioned William Anderson of Baker County, killed because he was kin to a man suspected of shooting a policeman.

"This makes a total of fifty-eight, all Negroes," Dorsey told the lawmakers. "Less than one-third of those put to death were charged with rape or attempted rape." And these were the lynchings reported by the newspapers, he hastened to add. The list might well be incomplete, because "the influence of the mob in some instances has been such as to prevent any information of these occurrences being given to the world. . . .

"Georgia sometimes stands at the head, and always high, on the list among the states of the Union in this practice," he said. "While we have had fifty-eight victims of mob violence who were not accorded a trial under the law or lynched after trial, we have hundreds who participated in these murders who have never been brought to justice, and in many cases no effort whatsoever made to apprehend or punish them.

"There are many instances of outrageous lynchings that could be prevented. Certainly there are instances where the perpetrators of such crimes could be, if the matter were properly investigated, brought to justice."

As he had in past messages to the General Assembly, Dorsey urged the creation of a statewide constabulary, or police force. "Much could be done by a governor through this agency to check all forms of crime," he argued. "The law establishing such a police force, should, of course, guard against its becoming a political machine in the hands of the Executive, but this can be easily accomplished. Many of the other states have already established such constabularies and where so established they have been found efficient and wonderfully helpful."

He advocated the creation of a grand jury with membership drawn from throughout the state and free from local influence, explaining: "I have concluded that there is little reason to expect county grand juries and local officers to adequately deal with the mob murderers of their communities." The cash-strapped state could pay for these innovations either from its general treasury, or—if state officials found that the counties in which mob action took place had not done their utmost to protect the victims—by billing the localities involved.

He must have known, given his audience, that these proposals would go absolutely nowhere.

The close of Dorsey's last speech as governor was typically ungilded. "During the two terms which I have had the honor to hold a commission as Georgia's chief executive," he told the legislators, "I have endeavored to serve the interests of all Georgia and all Georgians to the best of my ability."

A short while later, he listened on the capitol lawn as his successor, Thomas Hardwick, tore into *The Negro in Georgia* during his inaugural address. "The Georgia farmer bravely and manfully has gone energetically about his business and is now cultivating a crop to help clothe the world—a crop that may cost him twice as much as it brings on the market," Hardwick declaimed. "He has taken care of the Negro, fed him, clothed him, sheltered him, doctored him, and now, in a year like this, when he has made every imaginable sacrifice to help the Negro, to be charged on high authority with holding the Negro in peonage is almost more than he can bear.

"Such a burden, at this particular time, above all others, should not have been imposed upon him," the new governor groused. "It is an outrageous, unjustified and unjustifiable proceeding." From there, Hardwick plunged into fantasy, insisting that "there is no state in this Union, and no country in this world, having within its limits anything like an even division of its population between the white and Black races in which the relations between the two races are more harmonious than right here in the state of Georgia. There is no state or country in the world in which a good, law-abiding, peaceable Negro can live with more security to his life, his property, or his rights than the state of Georgia.

"The indictment brought against the state is untrue," he said, "and it is a matter of deep regret to me that such a monstrous charge should have been circulated just at this juncture, so calculated to impair the friendly relations between the races in our state and so calculated to prejudice the good name of the state of Georgia in other sections of the country."

While he was governor, Hardwick promised, he would write no pamphlets.

35

ALL THROUGH THE SUMMER AND FALL of 1921, Jasper County officials and the Macon federal court stood ready to take Williams and his family to trial, pending the arrest of his sons. The three stayed out of sight, despite the generous rewards for their capture.

E. Marvin Underwood appeared before Judge Hutcheson in a bid for a new trial for Clyde Manning. The judge denied his motion, so Underwood, like Greene Johnson, filed an appeal to the Georgia Supreme Court. Both men's appeals were laundry lists of complaints about Hutcheson's decisions from the bench. Johnson listed twenty-two grounds for a new Williams trial, most of them arguing the judge should have refused Manning's testimony about the deaths of the peons not thrown from Allen's Bridge.

Come January 1922, the justices ruled that Hutcheson had not erred in that decision, or any others he made during Williams's trial. With all concurring, they affirmed the verdict and sentence. Johnson mulled what to do next. "The Supreme Court is the highest tribunal which can pass upon the case," he said. "It cannot be appealed to the federal courts, for there is no question of constitutionality involved. The only further recourse is to appeal for a new hearing, and I cannot say whether this will be our course until I study the text of the decision."

Ultimately, he decided there was little to gain in pushing the matter further. If he won a new trial, Williams might be acquitted. But that was a long shot, and he stood just as good a chance of having exactly the same verdict and sentence imposed. Worse, there was a risk, however small, that a new jury might make no recommendation for mercy. The murder charges Williams still faced in Jasper pretty much rendered the decision moot, anyway. If Doyle Campbell brought him to trial there, it would be to see him hang. He'd have eight shots at it.

There was also this: John S. Williams was tapped out. Even before Johnson filed his appeal, Williams had appeared before a notary public at the Tower to swear, under oath, that "because of his poverty" he could not pay the court costs involved. The news made the papers, without explanation. His puzzled neighbors, having long viewed him as well-to-do, need only to have ventured to the Monticello courthouse to find the plantation's transfer to his lawyers and his unsettled $6,000 loan from the bank.

Williams no longer had land. He no longer owned a house. He had no income, and no prospect of earning any. He was now as poor as his former peons. "His home, which Williams had dreamed of gradually developing into a vast estate . . . is wrecked," the *Macon Telegraph* told its readers, in a report that smacked of lament. "John S. Williams' dream of a little kingdom in Georgia, where he would be law and lord has crumbled, and over his family doorstep there will forever hover an indispersable shadow." Early on the morning of February 1, 1922, Williams made his rounds of the Tower, bidding farewell to guards and fellow prisoners with whom he had grown friendly over the previous ten months, and was driven to the state penal farm at Milledgeville.

Manning's appeal, meanwhile, also faulted Judge Hutcheson for allowing the state's use of evidence regarding murders besides Lindsey Peterson's—evidence introduced when Lonnie Brand read Manning's own testimony from the Williams trial into the record. The Supreme Court rejected that complaint out of hand. But Underwood also found fault in the judge's charge to the jury, which he believed had not been sufficiently explicit. The lawyer had asked, in writing, that Hutcheson advise jurors that murder does not arise solely from the killing of another human being, but from killing done with malice. The judge had declined Underwood's request.

And on that point, the court found that Hutcheson had erred. If it was true that Manning had participated in the killings because he feared for his own life, he was "entitled to an instruction which presented this matter clearly and fully to the jury," Justice James K. Hines wrote for the majority. The judge should have stressed that malice could not be assumed just because other elements of murder (i.e., lack of provocation and evidence of an "abandoned and malignant heart") were present; it had to be proved, and it was the state's burden to prove it.

And so, on April 11, 1922, Clyde Manning's conviction was reversed. Underwood chose not to seek a change of venue for his new trial, saying he was satisfied that his client would get a fair shake in Newton County.

When the Stone Mountain Circuit convened its next Superior Court session in Covington, in late July 1922, Manning appeared again before Judge Hutcheson. Even by the standards of his largely overlooked first trial, this was a quiet affair. Few spectators, white or Black, showed up in the second-floor courtroom. Most newspapers gave the trial a pass. The prosecution, too, seemed eager to be done with the case. It called few witnesses. Special Agent Wismer was absent; Lonnie Brand read his testimony from the first trial into the record. Special Agent Brown was unavailable, as well. He'd left the government's service before Manning's first trial, and was now said to be living in Birmingham. The state didn't bother to track him down.

Once again, Sheriff Johnson testified for the prosecution and once again, Underwood's cross-examination turned the lawman into a seemingly willing defense witness. The lawyer reminded Johnson he had testified at the first trial that Manning "said he participated . . . because, he said, he was afraid not to do so—he was afraid Mr. Williams would kill him."

"Yes, sir," the sheriff said. "I testified to that."

"And that is true, is it?"

"Yes, sir. That is true."

"That on each and every time he made a statement to any one of this killing, he said he did it on account of fear of his life, from Mr. John S. Williams?"

"Yes, sir. He always said that."

"And that was the sole reason why he killed them?"

"That is what he told us." Manning had provided his account of the killings, Johnson said, only when convinced that Williams could not hurt him anymore.

Underwood: "And when he got under your protection in the jail, where he didn't think he was in danger, he told you all about it, and his connection with it and Mr. Williams's connection?"

"Yes, sir."

"And all those details have been verified?"

"Yes," Johnson replied. "All of them."

"And he has said substantially the same thing each time?"

"Yes, absolutely."

"You have never had any trouble with Manning?" Underwood asked.

"Not any in the world."

"He has made a good prisoner?"

The sheriff: "One of the best I ever saw."

The state wrapped up its presentation of evidence and the defense took over. As he had at the first trial, Underwood called numerous witnesses to establish that a climate of fear permeated every aspect of life on the plantation. Clyde Freeman, now living on a dairy farm northwest of Atlanta, described the deaths of Will Napier, Robert Nathaniel "Blackstrap" Williams, and John "Iron Jaw" Davis. He testified that the Williamses whipped the hands without pity, and that they and their field bosses carried revolvers. "What effect did the having of those pistols and the whippings, et cetera, have on the Negroes on the plantation there?" Underwood asked him.

"It kept them scared," Freeman answered. "It kept them cowered all the while."

"Were they very much afraid?"

"Yes, sir," he said. "They sure was."

On cross-examination, Lonnie Brand asked Freeman whether he spoke with the federal agents during their February 1921 visit. He had told them nothing, Freeman said, and offered a bit of news by way of explanation: Mr. Johnny had spotted the agents shortly after their arrival at his home place that day, and had driven to the river tracts to tell the hands there not to say a word. Then he'd doubled back to his house to introduce himself to the visitors. "He told me not to tell them anything and I wouldn't tell them anything," Freeman said. "I was scared."

"Scared of Mr. John S. Williams?"

"Yes, sir," he answered. "I was scared of him and the boys, too."

Clyde Freeman's younger brother, Claude, testified that when he was made a field boss up on the river tracts, Mr. Hulon had given him a handgun, along with instructions: "He said if any of the hands got away or tried to get away, or did anything to me, to kill them. And he said if I let anyone get away, I would know what was coming to me."

"What did he mean by that?" Underwood asked. "What did you understand him to mean?"

"I thought he meant I was going to be whipped—he would whip me if I let anyone get away."

"Did they have any whippings on the farm?"

"Yes, sir."

"Who did they whip?" Underwood asked.

"They whipped about all of them that has ever been there," Claude Freeman told him.

"How often did they whip?"

"They whipped some every day, near about."

"Did they whip them hard, or not?"

"Yes, sir," the witness said. "It was hard."

"How hard would they whip them? Would they bring the blood?"

"Yes, sir," Claude Freeman said. "Sometimes they would."

The defense next called B. B. Bohannon, Covington's police chief. Judge A. D. Meador, serving once more as Underwood's second, took a

turn at direct examination, asking the chief whether he recalled any dealings with the Williamses after Frank Dozier, Robert Nathaniel "Blackstrap" Williams, and John "Little Bit" Benford fled the farm in 1920.

Bohannon replied that "two of Mr. Williams's sons" approached him
in Covington. "They come to me and said they had three Negroes to run
away that day, and asked me if I had seen anything of them, and I told
them that I had not. And they said, 'Let us go over in Negro Town and
see if we can't find them.'

"I says, 'Have you any warrant for them?' And they said, 'No,' and I told
them that I would not go, that I would not fool with it if they didn't have
any warrant. I told them if they had a right to hunt them, they should
have warrants.

"They said, 'You don't object to our going over there and see if we can
find them? If we see them, we will come back.' They went over there and
in a short time they come back and said they would give me twenty-five
dollars' reward for each of those three Negroes . . . if I could arrest them.
And if I could catch them, to put them in the station house and they
would come with warrants and carry them back."

"Offered you twenty-five dollars' reward for capturing them?" Meador
asked.

"Yes," Bohannon replied.

"Do you remember the names of the darkies?" Once again, this was an
officer of the court talking. A former judge, no less.

"I don't recollect," the chief told him.

The trial's most chilling moment might have come when the defense recalled Sheriff Johnson to the stand. When Manning was first taken into
custody, and before he was indicted, John S. Williams had approached
him, Johnson testified, "and asked me to let him take [Manning] back
with him, and said if we needed him, he would bring him back the
next day."

"Asked you to let him take him home?"

"He asked me to let him take him back home that night, and he would bring him back the next day."

"Had Clyde then given testimony before the grand jury?" Meador asked.

"I don't think he had at that time," Johnson replied. "No, sir."

The exchange raised a terrible prospect: Had Manning been released to Williams's custody for the night, it seems a safe bet that he'd have been executed and buried somewhere on the plantation before the sun went down. The grand jury would never have heard the testimony that implicated Williams. It would have had no evidence to justify an indictment of the farmer or anyone else. The killings might still be unsolved today.

"State if any time later than that, anybody else made the same request," Meador instructed. "And, if so, who it was."

"Yes, sir," Johnson said. The next day, one of Williams's sons—he did not specify which—"asked me to let him take him back with him, and he would bring him back the next morning." By that time, Manning would have confessed to the sheriff and the federal agents. Johnson would have recognized what the family had in mind.

"Did you let him do it?" Meador asked.

"No, sir," the sheriff said. "I did not."

Finally came the defense's last witness: Clyde Manning, making another unsworn statement to the jury. It was a marked improvement over the meandering monologue at his first trial—more focused, more direct, more eloquent in its construction. He got right to the point: "Gentlemen of the jury, and Judge, your honor," he began, "I am not guilty of murder. The crime what I have done, I done it to save my own life."

He recounted Williams's order that he participate in killing his fellow peons a few days after the federal agents' visit. He had no choice but to obey. "I didn't do what I done of my own free will," he said. "And I will tell you, gentlemen, before God, if I done that of my own free will I hope this minute I will drop dead.

"It was against my will to do it, but it was against my power not to do it and live."

Manning and his lawyers had seen the prosecution emphasize his failure to flee at his first trial. Now, he bore down on his reasons for staying put, noting that others who had tried to run had been caught, to fatal effect. "There was Blackstrap: He run away and he had been more over the world than I had. I was raised around there and been kept right there, and never been away, never had been but a little ways from the farm. Never had been up here to Covington. And Blackstrap, he had been more over the world than I had. He had done more traveling than I had, and he run away and was gone two or three days and they caught him."

The same went for John "Little Bit" Benford. And Gus Chapman, who "had been out of the United States two or three times, and he run away and they caught him, and I seen what they done with him. And if he couldn't get away, I knowed I didn't have any chance." Almost surely, what with their nonexistent resources, Robert Nathaniel "Blackstrap" Williams had not been "over the world" and Gus Chapman had never been out of the country. Manning might have been trying to say they'd left the state. As he had barely left Jasper County, himself, a person need not have traveled far to seem a globe-trotter.

"If I had had some white man to speak to, someone I knowed, then I could have gone to him and told him and would have saved myself. But you know how it was: I didn't have nobody to say nothing to. The only white man I was with was Mr. Johnny there, and I would have disappeared, been killed just like these other boys." The "natural facts," Manning said, were that any person in his place would have done as he did. There was no refusing the Williamses. There was no escaping them. And on top of fear for himself, he had other worries. "I had a family," he said. "I had a wife and my baby and there was my mother and sister and brothers. I couldn't run off with my whole family. If I had got off and told this, my wife and sister and mother would all have been killed right there. I was not just like a loose man down there.

"I studied about leaving every day. I studied about leaving and how to get away. And I didn't know how," he said. "I figured out if them men"—the federal agents—"ever come back there, I would slip off with them. I would take a chance and tell them exactly what was going on. When they come back I didn't know they were back until they had a subpoena for me—when they came back and brought me up here and I asked them and the sheriff for protection. I asked them for protection if they would have me tell it. I didn't tell it until Mr. Sheriff here told me he would protect me. He said to tell it and he wouldn't let anybody hurt me, if I would tell it. And then, when he told me he would give me protection, so then I up and told them.

"I didn't do this of my free will," he stressed again. "I hope if I did this of my own free will that God will show it to you by killing me right here. I hope he will strike me dead if I ain't telling the truth, this minute."

Manning closed with an elegant flourish. "They are trying me for murder," he said. "That is a crime I am not guilty of, and God in heaven knows I am not guilty. And you, judge and jury, all I ask of you is to give me justice. I am not crying for mercy. Just give me justice.

"And if you do, God in heaven knows I will be a free man, because it was against my will, and this is a thing that God will not hold me accountable for, because I had to do just as he said to do."

This time, Judge Hutcheson's charge to the jury included an expansive discussion of malice. He also gave the panel the option to find Manning guilty of voluntary manslaughter, if it believed he had killed Lindsey Peterson unlawfully, but without malice. Such a verdict would send the defendant away for up to twenty years.

The second trial of Clyde Manning went to the jury at 11:08 a.m. on July 27, 1922. This panel returned with a verdict two hours and forty minutes later. Once more, he was found guilty of murder, with a recommendation for life in prison. Judge Hutcheson had him stand, declared that the verdict of the jury was the sentence of the court, and sent him away to the penitentiary for the rest of his life.

36

AND SO, IN LATE JULY 1922, Clyde Manning and John S. Williams again found themselves working on the same farm, this one the state's four-thousand-acre prison spread outside Milledgeville, the same facility that had briefly housed Leo Frank. Williams was now the farm's most notorious inmate. He was also a favorite of the prison administration: the superintendent, B. H. Dunaway, recognized that a lifelong planter, reputed to be among the most successful in central Georgia, brought valuable know-how to Milledgeville and its crops and livestock. Never mind that farmers and farm laborers constituted the bulk of the prison's inmate population; Williams was viewed as a special talent. Less than six months into his sentence, he was already a trusty.

Three days after Manning's conviction, in fact, Dunaway allowed Williams to leave the prison farm for a visit to Jasper County. The press in Covington caught wind of the excursion, and in early August 1922, published a report that the prisoner had been allowed to attend a family reunion and barbecue at his home place. A scandal erupted, the *Macon News* roaring that "one of the most revolting monsters in human form this state has ever produced" was hardly worthy to receive such treatment—that it was "a veritable mockery of the law to inflict upon a convicted murderer punishment so mild that he hardly realizes he is being punished at all."

Dunaway insisted that Williams had merely acted as a chauffeur when the superintendent went to Monticello to exchange some hogs and pick up seed for the prison farm. It was nothing but a business trip and entirely legal, he said, and the barbecue story was rubbish. That version of events didn't last long. On August 15, Dunaway admitted to the state prison commission that Williams had, in fact, been allowed to go home. The prisoner had been acting as Dunaway's chauffeur—itself a violation of prison policy, which dictated that no inmate could leave the farm without the commission's okay—and had been allowed to make a brief stop to see his wife, Lucy. But neither the barbecue nor a reunion had occurred: Williams saw only Lucy Williams and one of the couple's daughters, and he never left the superintendent's sight. Besides which, Dunaway said, Williams had proven himself trustworthy—he took a "personal interest" in the prison farm, and his contributions were "of the highest order." He spent most of his days guiding a plow.

Dunaway's testimony satisfied the commission, which took no action against him. A candidate for the prison commission named W. C. Bryant fastened on Williams's supposed "personal interest," however. What with "his past record for wholesale killing and the usual liberties allowed him as a trusty," Bryant declared, the inmate might be encouraged "to become entirely too personal for the safety of other prisoners who might be personally objectionable to him," and "some fine morning Superintendent Dunaway might wake up to find the whole farm depopulated."

The scandal only added to Williams's notoriety. When he was transferred to the chain gang in Colquitt County that November, officials reported he was drawing crowds of the curious, some of whom made trips from beyond the county's lines just for a glimpse of him. The officer who drove him to Colquitt reported that when they stopped in a small town for gasoline, half of the population massed around the car.

Three years passed, with little further news of Williams or his former field boss leaking from the prison complex. It is known that the murderer's youngest boy, Edward Dozier Williams, was allowed to spend parts of the summers living with the prison superintendent so that he could be near his father. Williams served on another chain gang, out of Fayetteville, during which he again demonstrated himself a model prisoner, but eventually returned to the penal farm. Lucy Williams and her younger children apparently continued living at the old home place. The fugitive sons remained on the lam.

Then, out of the blue, on a Monday in early February 1925, LeRoy Williams appeared in Monticello to turn himself in. He refused to divulge where he had been hiding since his father's trial, and would say nothing of his brothers' whereabouts. He simply presented himself to Sheriff Persons and posted a $3,000 bond.

Before he walked back out, LeRoy demanded that he stand trial during the ongoing term of the Jasper Superior Court. That was unlikely to happen. The Black families of the old Williams place, whose testimony would have been crucial to any prosecution in the murder of John "Iron Jaw" Davis, had scattered. It would take a while to round them up, a task complicated by the loss of institutional memory in the county courthouses. Doyle Campbell had been defeated for reelection the previous fall and was preparing to leave the state. Lonnie Brand and Greene Johnson had both died in 1923. Jasper's new solicitor general, J. B. Duke, asked that the case be continued until the Superior Court's August session.

Two days later, and in the company of a delegation of his Jasper County friends, LeRoy Williams appeared before the clerk of the U.S. District Court in Macon to post $1,000 bond against his federal peonage and conspiracy charges. Once released, he went into seclusion to await his day in court. But August 1925 came and went without LeRoy Williams summoned for trial in Monticello. Apparently hoping the other two sons would emerge from hiding and that he could try all three at once, Solicitor Duke sat on the case. No news came out of the federal courthouse in Macon, either. LeRoy quietly left the county. Word was that he had a home in Florida.

Another sixteen months passed. In February 1927, officials in Milledgeville went public with the news that Clyde Manning had contracted tuberculosis at some point in his past, that he had been in steady decline for months, and that he had succumbed to the disease on January 19. His death certificate listed no next of kin. Presumably, he was buried in the prison farm's graveyard, the place marked with a license plate pressed by one of his fellow inmates.

So ended a life that, by any measure, was miserable at its start and just got worse as the years passed. And so exited a major player in the Murder Farm affair, who remains as enigmatic a figure today as he was a century ago. The Bureau of Investigation would capture the odd dynamic that sealed Manning's fate in its 1932 summary of the case. "Worthy of emphasis," it decided, were "the peculiar characters of Williams and Manning, as disclosed by Williams' nonchalance and utter disregard for the life of a negro, although otherwise he was a law-abiding, prosperous farmer, who was kind to his family and neighbors, while Manning was noted for his simplicity and lack of criminal impulses, but was absolute clay in the hands of his lord and master."

Clyde Manning was survived by Rena—his ex-wife by then—and their daughter, Essie Mae, who was little more than a toddler when he confessed to the Murder Farm killings. He was thirty-two years old.

Manning's death had one predictable and almost immediate effect. Confident that a key witness against them could speak no more, Hulon and Marvin Williams showed up in Jasper County to turn themselves in. They spent the night in the Monticello jail, then were hauled before Judge Park. Prosecutor Duke told the judge he was not prepared to proceed to trial. "I wrote the clerk of Jasper Superior Court, asking that he subpoena all witnesses whose names appeared on the indictment," he said. "It appears that several of them are dead and a number of them are out of the state and only one witness was brought back. I talked with him this morning, questioned him thoroughly."

That one witness was John Freeman, father of Clyde and Claude. "We can't proceed to trial on his testimony," Duke said. "Now, just when the other witnesses will be available or when they will be within the jurisdiction of this court, of course I have no way of saying, nor have I any way of saying what their testimony would show if they were present."

Judge Park looked over the indictments, then read from one of them—the charge against Marvin Williams for killing John Singleton. "I see," he said, "the witnesses on this indictment are Clyde Manning—"

"Clyde Manning is dead," Duke told him.

"Then Mary Benton." Meaning Lula Benton, apparently.

"Mary Benton is dead," Duke said. "So this witness tells me who is here today. Says she was found dead in Atlanta last year." In fact, Lula Benton had been discovered with her skull fractured by blows "from some blunt instrument," according to her death certificate. The case had been ruled a homicide.

"Clyde Freeman?" the judge asked.

"Clyde Freeman, the last report they had on him, he was going to Florida, is probably in Florida now."

"You don't know where he is?"

"No, sir," Duke replied. "They looked all day yesterday, I understand, looked all over Atlanta. His father tried to help the officers find him and they couldn't locate him."

"Claude Freeman?"

"We don't know where he is."

And so on. The Williams brothers were represented in the hearing by William H. Key, a veteran of their father's defense team, and Florida lawyer E. M. Baynes. Key assured the judge that his clients were eager to cooperate and asked him to set their bail within easy reach. Baynes declared that he was "absolutely morally certain" that they had taken no part in the murders at the farm, and that they had fled the county out of fear of federal prosecution for peonage. With Duke's assent, the judge ordered the pair to pony up $2,500 apiece in bail. They were released later that day, Duke promising the public that he fully intended to prosecute them, despite Manning's death—which, he said, they obviously knew about before they surrendered. He planned to bring them to trial in six months.

Manning's death also spurred a second development. A few weeks later, on April 4, 1927, lawyer Key, also the attorney of record for John S. Williams, petitioned the state to give the planter a pardon or grant his parole. Williams had been the picture of a perfect inmate throughout his incarceration, Key argued, and he had the paperwork to prove it. Officials in Atlanta, including the Fulton County sheriff, four deputies, and the Tower's jailer, had written in support of his release. Officials at the prison farm and with the Colquitt County and Fayetteville chain gangs had done the same.

"Your petitioner shows that he denied and still denies any participation or knowledge of the crime, the murder of Lindsey Peterson, for which he was indicted and is now confined," Williams's petition read, "but inasmuch as the constituted authorities found otherwise . . . he prays that the time he has served and the punishment he has received be accepted as atonement for the crime, accepting his guilt as being true, which is denied."

So much for remorse. The prison commission agreed to consider the petition, and in early May convened a hearing in Atlanta. Lucy Williams attended, as did her oldest son, Gus, and several former neighbors. Attorney Key hammered on Williams's excellent behavior while locked up, his high standing in Jasper County society before his arrest, his mounting health issues, and his age—he was sixty, considered elderly at the time. Key offered up more testimonials, including one signed by some of the jurors at Williams's Newton County trial. Two high-ranking Methodist church elders objected to any change in the prisoner's sentence, as did a representative of the Christian Council of Atlanta. Still, when the session ended, it looked as if Williams just might find himself a free man after serving six years.

But it turned out that justice caught a break. John S. Williams did not get a pardon or parole. The commission offered no public explanation. The inmate remained at Milledgeville to pursue his personal interest in the prison farm. Justice was a bit harder to detect three months later, when the Jasper County Superior Court began its August 1927 session. Despite his assurances to the press, Solicitor Duke brought no case against any of Williams's sons.

With Hulon, LeRoy, and Marvin found, federal officials turned to tracking down the witnesses they needed to press their peonage and conspiracy cases. In the summer of 1928, the U.S. attorney at Macon asked the Bureau of Investigation to locate the Black workers present when the Williams place was shut down seven years before. The initial inquiry by the Bureau's Atlanta office located a handful of the thirty-nine potential witnesses on the list, and achieved an interview with just one—John Freeman, once again, who was living with his wife, Addie, in Marietta. Freeman told agents that he had not spoken with his sons in a year or more, did not know where they were, and had only sketchy information on a few of the others who survived the Murder Farm with him.

Undaunted, agents developed leads that, by November 1928, led them to sixteen witnesses, all but a few of them living in Atlanta. They found Clyde and Emma Freeman, and Clyde's brother Clifford, living together. They found Clyde Manning's brothers Gladdis and Julius sharing an address; their sister Grace, now remarried; and Hulon Williams's cook, the former Lessie May Benton, remarried and using the surname Whitlow. The agents discovered, too, that the women closest to Clyde Manning had struck up new relationships. Manning's widow, Rena, had married Claude Freeman and was living with him in Atlanta. Manning's mother, India, had married his Uncle Rufus, his father's brother; the couple lived in Charlotte, North Carolina.

With Clyde Manning dead and John S. Williams already serving a life sentence, it surprised no one that Jasper County chose not to press murder charges against the planter. After all, Greene Johnson had predicted as much even before Manning stood trial. But for whatever reason, the county had no stomach for taking Williams's sons to trial, and bringing to a just conclusion the most celebrated criminal case on Georgia soil since the death of Mary Phagan. By the time the feds found the sixteen witnesses, prosecutor Duke had quietly closed the books on the trio's murder charges.

Neither did the Department of Justice put its pool of witnesses to use. In January 1929, the Bureau learned that the case had been transferred from the federal court's new Middle District of Georgia, in Macon, to its redrawn Southern District, in Savannah. Five months later, agents were informed that the matter had been transferred back, on a motion by attorneys for the defendants. In July 1929, the U.S. attorney in Macon, W. A. Bootle, told the Bureau that he would review the case and advise it on what action he decided to take. There the matter sat until October, when Bootle wrote that while the federal case consisted of two indictments—one for peonage and the other for conspiracy—only one of them had been transferred from Savannah. He would get it sorted out and be in touch.

These delays claimed two of the newfound witnesses. Rena Manning Freeman fell ill with pellagra, a gruesome form of malnutrition caused by a deficiency of niacin in the diet, and died at home in May 1929. Three months later, Clyde Freeman apparently broke into a Marietta barbecue joint and did battle with the family living there. He was said to be using a shotgun as a club, swinging it by the barrel, when the weapon discharged into his abdomen. He died at the scene. Within months, Bootle's list of potential witnesses would again shrink. Lessie May Whitlow, Hulon's former cook, would be shot in the stomach in Atlanta. She would survive an operation and hang on for eleven days after, only to succumb to a perforated intestine at thirty-five.

On June 10, 1930, the prosecutor wrote again to the Bureau, this time to say he was seeking permission to drop the charges. He made the formal request later that month, in a letter to the attorney general in Washington. A "careful review of this case" had led Bootle to believe that John S. Williams "was the real moving spirit of the entire offense," and that the conviction of his sons "cannot be had because of the disappearance and absence of so many of the material witnesses.

"It is also my opinion that even if all of the witnesses were present and available," he wrote, "it would be a hopeless task to try this case because of the fact that all of the transactions occurred approximately ten years ago; and because of the further fact that the main defendant, John S. Williams, has already been convicted of murder and is now serving his life sentence."

The attorney general concurred. By month's end, the cases were no more.

———

By then, Lucy Williams had been dislodged from the plantation. She and her three youngest children lived in Monticello, where she rented a place for $12.50 a month. John S. Williams lived on at Milledgeville in relative comfort. Ten years into his sentence, he was even more well-liked by the prison farm's superintendent, warden, and guards—enough so that they called him "Uncle John" and entrusted him with a duty for which he was amply qualified: caring for and training the dogs kept on the grounds to track runaway inmates. He was, as a member of the prison commission described him, "one of the most trusted and faithful prisoners" there.

This lofty position put him at odds with his fellow guests of the state, who failed to appreciate his lust for catching escapees. Which he was called upon to do a lot: Breakouts were common. Antiquated, underfunded, and woefully understaffed, the farm was as poor at keeping prisoners locked in as it was at keeping lynch mobs locked out. Uncle John and his dogs stayed busy.

The resentment of his fellow inmates brought Williams no real trouble until January 25, 1932. Late that night, three prisoners in the farm's tuberculosis camp—a colony separated from the general population, and at least partly housed in crude outdoor cages—tore through the wooden floor of their enclosure and slipped past the lone guard on duty. They were led by Aubrey Smith, a stickup artist, car thief, and the mastermind of two previous escapes from Milledgeville, who was serving 145 years for an array of past misdeeds. The three stole a Cadillac from the garage of the prison's doctor and took off.

Prison bosses discovered the escape and dispatched guards and trusties to stand lookout on area highways. Williams was stationed on a road at the Milledgeville city limits—and, it turned out, in the path of the speeding Caddie. When it approached, he apparently tried to flag the car down—"waving frantically in an effort to deter the fleeing trio," according to the *Constitution*. The car swerved straight into him.

The prison's leadership honored the slain trusty as one of its own, decreeing that he had died in the "line of duty." The camp's chaplain led a prayer at Williams's funeral, which drew hundreds to the Monticello Baptist Church; the building was so stuffed with flowers from well-wishers, the *Constitution* reported, that they "literally hid the casket."

When Smith was captured in Florida five months later, state officials promised to seek an indictment against him for Williams's murder. But once again, they failed to back up their words with action, and chose not to submit the case to the grand jury in the summer of 1932—the Baldwin County solicitor reckoned he lacked evidence sufficient to get a conviction. Insofar as Smith was already facing 145 years behind bars, anyway, prosecuting him seemed a waste of the state's money and manpower.

So ended, after eleven years, the legal saga of John S. Williams. With the state unwilling to expend the effort to punish his accused killer. With the implicit message that perhaps a mass murderer was not all that sympathetic a victim.

With a decision that was its own form of justice.

PART SIX

Legacy

37

—

THE GREATEST TRAGEDY IN THIS STORY RIFE WITH IT is that peonage did not end
with the trials of John S. Williams and Clyde Manning. Despite the uni-
versal horror the case inspired, despite vows from officials to root out
the practice and end it, and despite the oft-voiced hope that the Murder
Farm's victims would not have died in vain, debt slavery survived. In fact,
it survives to this day.

But the case did have its effect. Williams unwittingly introduced many
of his countrymen to both the word and the practice, and his prosecution chased away the shadows that had long kept it from public attention.
Rural southerners now understood that some of their neighbors were not
only cruel, but criminal. Victims came to see that their plight was not
"just the way things were" but a violation of their rights, and that they had
the Constitution, federal law, and the courts on their side.

This new awareness was further heightened in February 1922, when
a young North Dakotan named Martin Tabert was arrested in Tallahas-
see, Florida, leased out by county authorities to a rural lumber camp, and
beaten to death by an overseer there. The public outcry that greeted the
incident—sparked by the fact that this peon was a white Yankee of comfortable upbringing—led Florida to outlaw convict leasing by the state's
counties.

All through the 1920s, the Department of Justice chased peonage cases
with a new resolve. Arrests became almost commonplace throughout the
South, netting public officials as well as prominent planters. In May 1925,
five men in Calhoun County, Florida, stood trial for debt slavery. Among
them: two members of the county board of commissioners, who were

both convicted and sentenced to the federal penitentiary in Atlanta. Also implicated were the local sheriff, a deputy, the county attorney, and a sitting judge. In September 1926, a federal peonage investigation in Amite County, Mississippi, ended with the indictment of the county sheriff, two deputy sheriffs from a neighboring Louisiana parish, and a justice of the peace. Another probe snared the sheriff of Willacy County, Texas, who was sentenced to hard labor at Leavenworth in March 1927.

Not all of the government's inquiries brought convictions. White juries acquitted many of the accused, evidence and the law be damned. In one celebrated 1929 case, a Georgia peanut planter was accused of holding both white and Black men prisoner and killing one of them. The case against the defendant looked to be solid. A jury dominated by other planters took just over an hour to set him free.

But many other defendants pled guilty. In March 1930, prominent Louisiana planter James E. Piggott admitted that he locked his workers up at night, chased down runaway peons, and chained one man to a tree. His defense recalled Williams's: "I handled niggers in the way every other planter handles them," he told the federal judge hearing his case. He was sentenced to eighteen months behind bars.

The drumbeat of prosecutions was fostered all along by the NAACP. In the years after the Murder Farm case, James Weldon Johnson spent a large share of his time and energy in Washington, D.C., lobbying Congress to adopt a federal law against lynching and pushing officials to hunt down and prosecute peonage wherever they found it. "I tramped the corridors of the Capitol and the two office buildings so constantly that toward the end, I could, I think, have been able to find my way about blindfolded," Johnson recalled. "My experience as a lobbyist brought me into personal contact with almost every outstanding man in both branches of Congress, and with a great many who were not outstanding."

Walter White continued showering Justice officials with tips the NAACP received about peonage. In 1927, he investigated reports that Black refugees and workers recruited to build levees after that year's calamitous Mississippi River floods were locked up in camps near Vicksburg, Mississippi, in a state of debt servitude. His report earned head-lines, government inquiries, and, he would later boast, the wrath of future president Herbert Hoover.

Throughout, the pair stayed true to the principles that, in Johnson's words, had guided the Association and would continue to do so. The group "is determined the Negro shall have not favor but opportunity," he said in a 1928 speech. "It wants him physically free from peonage, socially free from insult, mentally free from ignorance; and it will fight for his citizenship rights until he is fully, in the complete sense of the word in America, a man."

Change was slow to come. Even as bailing prisoners out of back-woods jails and enslaving them into peonage grew risky, white planters throughout the South continued to create de facto slaves of their share-croppers. The practice only grew more attractive when the price of cotton nose-dived, as it did in 1931. By late that year it had dropped to five or six cents a pound, its lowest level since 1898 even without adjusting for inflation. A bale that brought $215 "during the flush years following the War," the New Republic noted, now earned less than $28. Large land-owners struggled to make their mortgages. Banks stopped loaning them money, after their collateral—land—became virtually worthless. Share-croppers didn't have a hope of breaking even. Spurred by an acute need for cheap or free labor, their landlords were not inclined to let them go.

So the cases kept coming. In the summer of 1931, gunfire erupted between white lawmen and Black sharecroppers attempting to union-ize with the help of Communist organizers in Camp Hill, Alabama. In a scenario reminiscent of the 1919 massacre in Phillips County, Arkansas, the Black farmers sought financial transparency and fairness from their landlords, whose accounting tricks held them in peonage. What they got instead, the New Republic reported, was "an exciting two-day nigger hunt which filled the county jail at Dadeville with frightened and often wounded Negroes and put the little town on the front pages of the met-ropolitan press."

Debt slavery remained enough of a public scourge in 1939 that the all-white Georgia Baptist Association adopted a resolution declaring that peonage "has by no means disappeared from our land," and that it involved a shocking number of both victims and perpetrators. "There are more white people affected by this diabolical practice than there were slave holders," the group averred. "There are more Negroes held by these debt slavers than were actually owned as slaves before the war between the states. The method is the only thing that has changed." Whether or not the problem was really as widespread and severe as that, the group made a valid point: peonage had survived despite the shock of the Williams case, the publicity generated by scores of prosecutions since, and tireless lobbying by the NAACP.

The ground finally began to shift during the war years. Black peons and sharecroppers were drafted into the military. The mechanization of American agriculture was underway, which would eventually eliminate the need for vast pools of field laborers. At the same time, the federal government shifted tactics in fighting the peonage blight. Five days after the Japanese attack on Pearl Harbor, Attorney General Francis Biddle issued a circular titled "Involuntary Servitude, Slavery, and Peonage" in which he instructed U.S. attorneys throughout the country to flush out and prosecute compulsory labor, regardless of whether debt figured in the crime; the key was to use other existing statutes, such as that against kidnapping into slavery, in pursuing modern-day Simon Legrees. Biddle directed his people to spread the word that the Department of Justice was taking a bead on those who held or helped to hold anyone in captivity, or who returned anyone who escaped such a state. Moreover, the feds were to notify law enforcement and court officials that all contract laws enabling peonage were "repugnant to the provisions of the Thirteenth Amendment," and that enforcing those laws might get *them* locked up.

The FBI, Biddle added, would now title its peonage reports *Involuntary Servitude and Slavery*. "Henceforth," he wrote, "peonage will be considered as secondary to involuntary servitude and slavery investigations." With that, the attorney general smoothed the way for federal prosecutors to put slavers out of business: U.S. attorneys could still charge a defendant with violation of the 1867 peonage statute if they found evidence that debt was a factor in keeping a victim prisoner. But peonage would now be an additional charge, rather than a mandatory element of all prosecutions.

In short order the U.S. Supreme Court took aim at specific state laws that continued to enable debt slavery. In *Taylor v. Georgia*, decided in January 1942, the justices found that the prima facie clause in Georgia's contract law was unconstitutional and violated the 1867 peonage law. Their decision came twenty years after Hugh Dorsey had urged legislators to do away with his state's errant statutes, and more than thirty years after the court first attacked prima facie clauses as unlawful. Two years later, in April 1944, the court struck down Florida's latest prima facie contract law, and chastised its legislature for acting "with almost certain knowledge" of the court's past decisions in continually fine-tuning its statutes to sidestep federal interference.

A 1948 rewrite of the federal criminal code further bolstered the government's new approach. Southern farmers had demonstrated for nearly half a century that they didn't pay much mind to Supreme Court decisions or congressional acts. But the combined weight of those rulings, more aggressive federal investigations, and the morphing economics of agriculture finally crushed peonage as a viable business strategy. For a while, anyway.

It is a testament to James Weldon Johnson's indefatigable industry, not to mention his seemingly limitless talents, that throughout his overtasked years as secretary of the NAACP, he somehow found time to continue his artistic pursuits. He wrote poetry, publishing several well-reviewed collections, chief among them *God's Trombones*, a reimagining of seven Negro sermons in verse. He gathered the work of other Black poets, publishing a compilation in 1922. He and his brother collaborated on two anthologies of Negro spiritual music that still stand as classics. He encouraged up-and-coming Black writers, musicians, and artists who flocked to New York in the early twenties, and in the process helped midwife a movement.

In an August 1920 speech, Johnson worried that while African Americans "have this indescribable thing called soul," and were a "people not only of laughter and of song but of deep emotional [and] spiritual endowment," they were wasting it. He likened their gifts to a bottle of gas—with its stopper removed, the gas would escape to fill the universe, and "gas flying around does not light any streets, does not heat any houses, does not turn any machinery.

"But some day," he said, "we are going to channel it down; we are going to harness it, as it were; we are going to run it through a tube; and that very emotional endowment is going to break down any opposition. It is not only going to do that, but this overflow of soul which the Negro has, some day when it is compressed it is going to give America its greatest artists, its greatest writers, its greatest singers, its greatest musicians, its greatest poets."

Even as he spoke those words, such a compression of artistic talent was taking place in a vibrant and growing Black district at the north end of Manhattan. To the men and women who produced the explosion of work known since as the Harlem Renaissance, Johnson was a world-wise senior statesman, a model of probity, an accomplished artist, and an exemplar of both easy elegance and blazing intelligence. To Johnson, the Renaissance offered a test of his long-standing belief that Black artistry complemented the Association's legal and political campaigns for racial equality.

He had "good reason for gratification and pride" in this flowering, the *New York Times* observed. "Before his eyes and in the course of a few years he saw men and women of his race distinguish themselves in all the arts. Actors, singers, musicians, dancers, painters, sculptors, poets, novelists won their way to fame. All the world danced to Negro music."

But Johnson had reason to feel frustrated, too. In 1927, his *Autobiography of an Ex-Colored Man* was republished, this time with his name on the cover. It remained depressingly relevant fifteen years after its initial appearance. "We light upon one evil and hit it with all the might of our civilization, but only succeed in scattering it into a dozen of other forms," a central character declares in one memorable scene. "We hit slavery through a great civil war. Did we destroy it? No, we only changed it into hatred between sections of the country: in the South, into political corruption and chicanery, the degradation of the blacks through peonage, unjust laws, unfair and cruel treatment; and the degradation of the whites by their resorting to these practices; the paralyzation of the public conscience, and the ever overhanging dread of what the future may bring."

After a decade as the NAACP's secretary, an exhausted Johnson resigned to devote more of his time to writing and study at Nashville's Fisk University. He continued to craft poetry and turned out a nonfiction study of the Renaissance, *Black Manhattan*. He wrote an autobiography, *Along This Way*, that offered a wry and modest account of his remarkable life and achievements. Named to the NAACP's board of directors, he remained devoted to the organization and civil rights until the day he died, at sixty-seven, when his car was struck by a train in coastal Maine. More than 2,500 people attended his Harlem funeral. His honorary pallbearers included composers W. C. Handy, Eubie Blake, and Deems Taylor. Eleanor Roosevelt sent flowers. So many mourners congregated outside that mounted police were called in to clear the surrounding streets for traffic.

Johnson "found new frontiers of the heart and mind," eulogized Gene Buck, the president of the American Society of Composers, Authors and Publishers. "His contributions left an indelible impression on the nation. He had nobility, culture, infinite taste, and a burning desire for learning and tolerance that would not cease." His achievements, Buck said, eclipsed those of Booker T. Washington.

As that scene unfolded in Harlem, the NAACP held its annual conference in Columbus, Ohio. A memorial service was added to the agenda. It ended with those gathered reciting a passage from Johnson's 1934 book-length essay, *Negro Americans, What Now?*

"I will not allow one prejudiced person or one million or one hundred million to blight my life," he had written. "I will not let prejudice or any of its attendant humiliations and injustices bear me down to spiritual defeat.

My inner life is mine, and I shall defend and maintain its integrity against all the powers of hell."

Walter White, too, became a major player in the Harlem Renaissance. Following Johnson's example, he produced two novels in the mid-twenties while elbows-deep in the NAACP's campaigns—the well-received *The Fire in the Flint* of 1924, and *Flight*, in 1926—as well as a nonfiction study of lynching, *Rope and Faggot: A Biography of Judge Lynch*. He promoted his fellow Renaissance writers and artists with zeal.

On his mentor's resignation, White was named the NAACP's executive secretary. He would hold the position for twenty-four years. Under his leadership, the Association continued to lobby the Department of Justice on peonage, as well as Congress for a federal antilynching bill. It also waged long campaigns against segregated schools, Jim Crow seating on public transportation, and myriad obstacles to Black voting rights.

White and the NAACP won more often than they lost. In 1930, he helped block the confirmation of John J. Parker, a North Carolina judge who favored segregation, as President Herbert Hoover's appointee to the U.S. Supreme Court. A decade later, he was widely credited with authoring President Franklin D. Roosevelt's executive order erasing discriminatory hiring in wartime industries. After bumping heads with FDR over integrating the armed forces, he found a receptive ear in President Harry Truman, and saw the process begin in 1948. Racist housing covenants began to crumble the same year, when the Supreme Court ruled they could not be legally enforced. Most memorably, the NAACP's crusade against racially "separate but equal" public schools reached the court, culminating in its 1954 decision in *Brown v. Board of Education*.

Like Johnson before him, however, White was denied a federal law against lynching. Their early ally in the fight was Missouri representative Leonidas C. Dyer, a Republican who represented a largely Black district in St. Louis that had been flooded with refugees during the East St. Louis massacre of 1917. The congressman emerged from that experience with a passion to end mob violence, and with the help of the NAACP and legal experts, fashioned a bill that he introduced in the House in April 1918.

The Democratic majority marooned the bill in committee. It wasn't until Dyer reintroduced it on April 11, 1921—the day that the Jasper County grand jury indicted John S. Williams and his sons for murder—that the measure gained traction. Thanks, in part, to fierce lobbying from Johnson and White, the bill made it to the House floor and, in January 1922, was approved by a large majority. It did not fare so well in the Senate: southern Democrats threatened a filibuster that would have blocked other urgent legislation, and Senate Republicans eventually abandoned the fight. Dyer reintroduced the bill year after year through the twenties, but it never came close to passage. In fact, despite the efforts of generations of lawmakers after Dyer, no antilynching bill fared better for a century, and only twice—in 1937 and 1940—did one again pass the House. In 2005, the Senate adopted a resolution expressing its remorse for this failure—but wasn't feeling contrite enough, it seems, to pass a bill even then.

Only in 2022 did the Emmett Till Antilynching Act remedy the situation. Introduced by Representative Bobby Rush, a Democrat from Illinois, the bill expanded the definition of lynching and made it a federal hate crime. It passed the House by a vote of 422–3, and the Senate approved it by unanimous consent. "All right. It's the law," President Joseph R. Biden Jr. said after signing the bill. "Thank you for never giving up—for never, ever giving up."

By then, the Montgomery, Alabama–based Equal Justice Initiative had documented 6,500 examples of what it termed racial terror lynchings in the United States. And Walter White, the longest-serving executive secretary of the NAACP, had faded into the mists of history.

When White died at sixty-one, in March 1955, the *New York Age* predicted he was bound for immortality. "Fifty years from today when the rivers flowing in the democracies have eddied into every area barren of democracy," the paper said in editorial tribute, "men the world over will still be acknowledging Walter White as a poet of freedom, an author of justice." It seemed a safe bet. As the *New York Times* reckoned, "a great deal" of the progress in race relations could be "directly traced to his influence."

"He could easily have joined the 12,000 Negroes who pass the color-line and disappear into the white majority every year in this country," the *Times* observed. "But he deliberately sacrificed his comfort to publicize himself as a Negro and to devote his entire adult life to completing the emancipation of his people." And indeed, White laid the groundwork for the modern civil rights movement. Nine months after his death, Rosa Parks, the secretary of the NAACP's chapter in Montgomery, refused to give up her seat on a city bus to white passengers, igniting a Black boycott of the transit system that propelled a young preacher named Martin Luther King Jr. into the national spotlight.

Therein might lie a partial explanation for why White vanished from the public consciousness within a very few years. His leadership was top-down. Delighting in his status as a Washington insider, he argued the NAACP's positions behind the scenes, in the courts and halls of power, and relied on his personal relationships with white politicians to effect change. The Association's "quiet, bloodless revolution," as he once called it, often went unseen until its victories or defeats were in hand.

In contrast, the new movement was grassroots, built on public demonstration, and piloted by charismatic leaders who inspired, as well as organized. It offered every man, woman, and child in America a piece of the fight. And in contrast to White, the NAACP's new executive secretary, Roy Wilkins, did not hesitate to share or surrender credit for the movement's successes.

On top of that, White could be his own worst enemy. In 1949, he ended his marriage of twenty-seven years to a former NAACP secretary, Leah Gladys Powell—a Black woman with whom he had two children—to take up with a white magazine editor. Her name was Poppy Cannon, and he married her a short time later. It was a disastrous move. Whether he knew it or not, his first wife supplied White with an important bona fide, both as a Black man and the NAACP's leader. Dumping her for a white woman provoked confusion and charges of betrayal. His talk of identifying as African American suddenly seemed just that, an identity he could assume or discard at whim. The Association was dumbstruck. Fearful that he had squandered his moral authority, the board debated whether to let him return from a medical leave he'd taken after a couple of heart attacks.

Then, just a few weeks after the marriage, *Look* magazine ran a story under his byline that lauded the possible uses of a chemical bleach to lighten skin. Headlined "Has Science Conquered the Color Line?," the article suggested that an industrial solvent could strip melanin from epidermal cells, and enable its Black users to "live like other Americans and be judged on their own merits." The piece was apparently edited to make it more of a sales job than White intended, but the damage was done. At best, the story puzzled its readers. At worst, it further eroded confidence in White's fitness for leadership.

He did return to the NAACP, albeit in a diminished role: Roy Wilkins assumed the organization's day-to-day administration, leaving White to serve as its public face. But the man behind that face no longer inspired the same trust or reverence. And after he died and Wilkins rose to secretary, his name—associated with the NAACP's greatest successes to date, including his death-cheating probes of forty-one lynchings and eight race riots—began a quick slide into oblivion.

Down in Atlanta, Hugh Dorsey adjusted to a self-imposed exile. Since the first days of the Frank case, in 1913, he had been a prominent figure in Georgia's affairs. Now the former governor led a quiet life as an attorney in private practice, rarely stepping into the public eye and never assuming an obvious role in politics.

But behind the scenes, Dorsey continued to push the race envelope. In May 1922, for example, he joined the battle against white men who had terrorized Asbury McClusky, forty-seven years old and the owner of a farm in Barrow County, northeast of Atlanta. As Black men went,

McClusky was well respected in the area, having hoisted himself up from tenant farming to substantial landownership. But he ran afoul of his white supremacist neighbors, who showed up at his house and axed down his front door. He opened fire with a shotgun, ending the assault, but then had to flee to Atlanta.

There he sought help from the Commission on Interracial Cooperation. Its secretary, Thomas Jackson "Jack" Woofter Jr., in turn sought out Dorsey, who had promised his services to the commission, free of charge, on legal challenges to the Klan and mob rule. Per Dorsey's advice, they surprised McClusky's tormentors with a counterattack. First, they sought indictments against those they could name—intending, as Dorsey put it, to "get these men in open court out from under their hoods so the law abiding people could get a good look at the sorry specimens of whom they had been afraid." They also pursued a suit for $50,000 in damages against the mob, and a restraining order safeguarding McClusky from any further molestation. A Barrow County judge promptly granted the latter.

Woofter supplied Walter White with a running account of this campaign. White praised "the splendid way" the team had pitched its fight, adding: "The situation is far from being hopeless when men like yourself can reach such results in a community like Barrow County." The experience energized Woofter to keep swinging. As he wrote the commission's chairman: "The Williams case was only the opening gun in a long fight."

The judge convened a grand jury, which indicted eight white men for violence against McClusky and his neighbors. When the first of the cases came to trial in July 1923, Dorsey joined the team of prosecutors. No white witnesses appeared for the state, and an all-white jury acquitted the defendant; charges against the others were dropped. Even so, the affair signaled progress: it had exposed McClusky's tormentors to the world.

The state's response to lynching began to evolve, too. In answer to at least 430 mob murders between 1884 and 1921, Georgia had indicted precious few participants and convicted none. In 1922 alone, its grand juries indicted twenty-two accused lynchers, and the courts sent four of them to the penitentiary. That's not to say that mob killing had run its course in the Peach State: the last known mass lynching in the United States claimed two Black Georgia couples in 1946, and individuals have been targeted since—the killing of Ahmaud Arbery, attacked by three men in February 2020 while jogging in Brunswick, Georgia, stands as an example. But the heyday of the lynching party was coming to an end. In 1927, 1928, and 1929, the state reported none. And in the 1930s, Georgia slipped from first to second place among the states in its number of known lynchings. Mississippi took the lead, and holds it still.

When a judge of Atlanta's City Court died in September 1926, Governor Clifford Walker asked whether Dorsey might replace him. It was the same post Dorsey's father had held for a year after moving his family to Atlanta. Though it promised a paycheck only until the general election two months later, he accepted. "Judge Dorsey will reflect outstanding credit upon the bench," cheered the *Constitution*, ever his supporter. "He is a good lawyer, fair and honorable and will make a great jurist—as did his father before him."

That November, Atlantans voted to keep Dorsey for the rest of the departed judge's term. He heard cases ranging from damage suits to public corruption inquiries, dispatching most with speed and efficiency, and won election to his own four-year terms in 1928 and 1932. Flush enough to send his two sons to a tony boarding school in Virginia, Dorsey nonetheless found his judge's salary forced him to live modestly. When Georgia's historian asked that he donate photographic miniatures of himself and his wife to the state museum in 1931, he replied that his "financial condition since I left the Governor's office has been such that I have not been able to comply with your request."

But in 1935, the legislature abolished the city court and transferred its docket to a new division of the Fulton County Superior Court, with

Dorsey at its head. It was a step up in both pay and prestige. He won the unanimous backing of the Atlanta bar in his 1936 reelection bid, the city's lawyers citing "his courage, ability and fearless administration of justice and failure to allow political considerations to influence decisions."

As luck would have it, just as he breezed to an easy victory in that contest, Dorsey found his past resurrected in fiction and film. Former *Atlanta Journal* reporter Ward Greene published a novel, *Death in the Deep South*, that offered up a thinly veiled account of the Frank trial and its aftermath. A year later, in 1937, the novel was rejiggered for the screen as *They Won't Forget*, a Mervyn LeRoy picture that erased Frank's Judaism as a factor in his persecution, instead reducing the affair to a sectional tussle between Yankees and southerners. Both book and movie depicted the prosecutor, Andrew J. Griffin, as a vile opportunist who knowingly convicted an innocent man to further his political hopes, and reviewers were not bashful about citing the real-life inspiration for the tale. About the only positive for Dorsey was that his cinematic counterpart was played by Claude Rains.

The Frank case, and his role in it, would generate many a dramatic reinterpretation after that, none flattering. Dorsey did not suffer them, however. After winning reelection in 1940 and again in 1944, his health began to fail. By February 1947, he was taking lengthy medical leaves from the bench, and in March 1948, he was forced to retire.

Dorsey died three months later, at seventy-seven. The fierce passion with which the Georgia press had ravaged him in his final days as governor was forgotten—as was pretty much everything else about him. The *Macon Telegraph* called him "a man of magnetic personality, scholarly attainments and an essentially judicial mind." But that kind of praise stood apart; most papers relied on short wire service notices. Predictably, they told of his role in the Frank case, and little more. Once so popular that white Georgians named their children for him—late in the twentieth century, it was not uncommon to encounter Hugh Dorsey so-and-so in newspaper obituaries—he was remembered in death, when he was remembered at all, for the darkest chapter of his life, and one of the darkest in his state's history.

It would no doubt distress Johnson, White, and Dorsey to find that peonage, despite its apparent eradication a lifetime ago, endures in the United States. It no longer specifically targets African Americans. Modern victims tend to be immigrants from Mexico and Central America—easily held hostage by their visa status and their distance from home—or indigent U.S. citizens plucked from homeless shelters. It no longer enables the cheap production of cotton, either. Nowadays, peons are more likely to harvest fruits and vegetables. One more difference: these are now bigger operations, and even more brazen than those of old.

Over the past thirty years, federal investigators have uncovered one example after another. Take, for instance, the 2001 case of a Florida orange harvester who earned a four-year prison sentence for forcing his mostly homeless American workers to pay for food, rent, and drugs at his on-site company store, then leveraging that debt to keep them from leaving. Or the three members of one family who operated a debt slavery operation in Florida and North Carolina, and who recruited the homeless and drug-addicted from Miami, Tampa, and New Orleans into involuntary servitude in the fields. Those defendants received sentences running from ten to thirty years in 2007. Consider, as well, the case of two members of another family imprisoned in 2008 for practicing peonage in Florida and South Carolina: they forced dozens of tomato pickers into debt, then threatened them with violence if they tried to leave before settling up.

In 2010, a federal grand jury indicted eight people for holding hundreds of Thai guest workers in bondage on farms from Florida to Hawaii. In what prosecutors called the largest human trafficking case in U.S. history, the defendants—all associated with an American labor recruiting outfit—were alleged to have lured the workers into the country, confiscated their passports, then parlayed their helplessness in a strange land into forced labor. They also charged the impoverished workers high recruitment fees, the government said; some victims paid the fees with loans from their traffickers, secured by land owned by the victims' kin.

Once in the States, the indictment charged, the defendants kept the workers shackled by threatening to have them arrested or deported, "knowing the workers could not pay off their debts if sent home, thus subjecting the workers to serious economic harm including loss of their family property." Four of the eight defendants pled guilty. The feds eventually dropped charges against the company's executives.

And in 2021 came Operation Blooming Onion, for which a stew of federal agencies spent years investigating a transnational gang that allegedly defrauded the U.S. visa system to smuggle workers from Mexico, Guatemala, and Honduras into the United States. The conspirators required the workers "to pay for their border crossing fees, transportation fees, lodging fees, and food expenses," the indictment charged. "It was further part of the conspiracy that if a foreign worker could not afford the unlawful fees, conspirators would unlawfully require the worker to pay back a smuggling debt, resulting in debt-bondage."

Transported to farms in Georgia, Florida, and Texas, the government alleged, these victims were stripped of their passports and visa documents, forced to perform work for little or no pay, housed in wretched, overcrowded trailers and fenced work camps, and threatened with violence. Some victims were raped, the indictment asserted. Two died.

All of which is to say that peonage today has morphed into a complex international undertaking. If recent cases are a guide, it can involve extravagant organization, millions of dollars in loot, and large numbers of victims. Fraud and money laundering often figure in the crime.

That said, Johnson, White, and Dorsey would recognize it, and the same goes for John S. Williams. It remains an almost inconceivably cruel, brutal enterprise. It continues to prey on the poor, the disadvantaged, the downtrodden. It reduces its victims to the status of livestock.

And most of those victims have dark skin.

38

THE CROOKED ROAD THROUGH THE WILLIAMS HOME PLACE has not much changed in the past century. It remains narrow and unpaved, its red-clay bed dressed with crushed stone that coughs up great opaque clouds of gray dust when churned by the pickups and SUVs that account for most of its traffic.

Not that it sees much. The land through which it passes is as empty of people as it was in John S. Williams's time, if not more so. A dozen or so houses stand well off the road at its eastern end, nearest Monticello, but for most of its length it feels isolated from the surrounding county, left behind by the modern world, the province of ghosts. Not much imagination is required to picture peons driving hogs down its middle.

I explored it one afternoon in the fall of 2021 with Georgia historian Timothy Pitts, who grew up in Jasper and devoted his master's thesis to the Murder Farm. We were armed with contemporary newspaper descriptions of the place—of the simple farmhouse at the crown of a high knoll, its porch offering majestic views of the surrounding acreage, and of fields sloping downhill and treeless to the lower pasture where Johnnie Williams, Johnnie Green, and Willie Givens met the axe. I had a 1909 map of Jasper County's road system, annotated at some point with the hand-lettered names of early twentieth-century property owners—a map I found and copied at the University of Georgia, and which bore the label "John S. Williams" beside the road at one of its many twists. When we neared the spot, however, we found the ground beyond the sunken shoulders inscrutable. Dense forest had colonized the old cotton fields and meadows. Some was managed woodland—tree farms of southern yellow pine, which has replaced cotton as Jasper County's principal crop. The rest was a primeval tangle of white oak, sweetgum, and sourwood, of Brandywine maple and tulip tree, cedar and sassafras. The road's edges were choked with beautyberry, saber-toothed greenbrier, and thick drapes of kudzu.

Pitts braked his pickup, and we idled there for a while, peering into the jungle. If there was anything left of the farm, even twenty feet from where we sat, we couldn't see it. We couldn't read the shape of the land, either. We were in a green tunnel, the only clues to the terrain the rises and falls of the road itself. "You can tell, even now," Pitts said, "that if you're living out here, you're hell and gone from anyone else."

Therein lay one of the quandaries facing any peon tempted to run. He would have known that his only chance was to make for the Waters Bridge, roughly seven miles away, avoiding roads all the while, and that once across the Alcovy he had to keep pushing north and west to Atlanta. Reaching the bridge meant navigating fields and pastures patrolled by unsympathetic whites, and braving woods dark and disorienting, and racing breakneck across a vast quilt of lookalike spreads.

He would strike out on this journey with only the vaguest sense of the landscape. Even the Mannings, the Freemans, and the Williamses' paid servants, some of whom had passed much of their lives on the farm, knew little of the world beyond the fields they worked. Lessie May Whitlow, the cook, brought that truth home when she testified at Clyde Manning's second trial.

"How far is it from the Campbell place to Jackson?" she was asked.

"I don't know," she replied.

"How far is it from the Campbell place to Polk's store?"

"I don't know, sir, where Polk's store is at," she said.

"How far is it to Waters Bridge?"

"I don't know, sir, how far it is to Waters Bridge."

"It is not as far as to go down to Mr. Johnny's house, is it?"

"I don't know," she answered. This, from a woman who had lived on the plantation for eight years.

The cruel truth was that if a runaway peon beat the odds and found the Waters Bridge, the boss might well be there, waiting for him. John S. Williams knew that the crossing offered the only practical route out of Jasper County, that to flee elsewhere posed greater risk of exposure on a longer course to freedom. On discovering an escape, he needed only to position one of his sons at the bridge, then use the dogs to herd the desperate fugitive that way.

It seemed obvious, there at the remote, overgrown site of the home place, that the odds against successful escape were steep. Gus Chapman and James Strickland had been exceptionally lucky.

And Clyde Manning's decision to stay put made perfect sense.

I returned to the road a year later for a closer look. By then, some of the woods to the north had been replaced by a postapocalyptic wasteland: acres by the score were clear-cut, their red mud floors stirred into chaotic heaps, crisscrossed by dozer tracks, and piled with splintered trunks and exhumed roots. Hellscape though it was, it did reveal the rolling character of the ground that the Williams family once cultivated. This was difficult terrain, of swells and hollows and steep-sided gulleys.

I detected no clues to the past in that ravaged landscape. But I was parked on the road beside a couple of mailboxes, double-checking my location on my maps, when a car pulled up and a young woman stepped out to retrieve her mail. "You need help?" she asked.

"Maybe," I told her. "I'm looking for signs of a farm that used to be right around here. A place that was owned by a guy who killed eleven of his farmhands a hundred years ago."

"Around *here?*" Stephanie Pittman asked.

"Yes, ma'am."

Her expression made plain that this was news to her. "You need to talk to my husband," she said. "He'd probably know all about it. He grew up here." No sooner had she promised to fetch him from their house, unseen up an unpaved drive across the road, than Rusty Pittman pulled up aboard an ATV. I explained that I was looking for a farm that had been owned by a man named Williams.

He nodded. "The bad Williams."

"You know about it?" his wife asked, then glanced my way. "Told you."

"Oh, yeah," he replied. "Killed a bunch of people."

"Do you happen to know exactly where the farm was?" I asked him.

Rusty shrugged. "Right about here, I think." He looked back up the drive. "Who'd really know is my dad." As if summoned, a meaty old-timer in T-shirt and shorts chugged down the drive on a bigger, two-seat four-wheeler. Mike Pittman, seventy-two years old, had occupied his property alongside the road since the early 1970s, and had been collecting pieces of the Murder Farm legend ever since. I asked him whether anything remained of the old Williams farmhouse or any of the plantation's other buildings. Mike said he had never found a trace, save for some rosebushes among the trees that you could see from the road, on a neighboring property to the west. "Now, over there, there's an old slave burial ground," he said, pointing across the clear-cut to a stand of pines rising high above the surrounding woods. "That could have been part of the place." At that, we set off in the ATVs, but after thumping into the forest and splitting up to scour its pine-straw floor—eyes peeled for copperheads, ducking enormous spiders in webs the size of bedsheets—we found no sign of the cemetery. "Well," Mike sighed, "I remember it being right around here, within a few yards of these pines. But I ain't been back here in thirty-five years."

We doubled back to the driveway, where Mike invited me to follow him onto the family spread. Rusty, Stephanie, and their children lived in a fine-looking modern house surrounded by parked vehicles and yard toys. Mike's place was a humble and far more rustic trailer closer to the road. We stepped inside. The trailer was filled with treasures Mike had scavenged on his explorations of the place: arrowheads by the hundreds, stone axe heads, the bowls of ancient clay pipes. Some were displayed in frames that covered the walls. Others filled bowl after bowl on the tables and cabinets.

This was a man who paid attention to his surroundings, who studied the ground he walked. When he said he'd found no trace of the Williams home place, I was inclined to believe there was no trace left to be found.

The Williams family has vanished from Jasper County, as well. Of John S. Williams's twelve children, just one—his sixth-born, Ivah Sue—put down stakes near the plantation, on a farm she ran with her husband. The rest dispersed. The oldest son, Gus, moved to Macon after his father's trial and practiced medicine in the city for more than forty years. The planter's oldest daughter, Mary, lived for many years in Atlanta before moving out of state. His youngest, Lucy Claire—who broke down at Williams's trial, and who her nieces and nephews told me was "never quite right"—was committed by her mother to the Georgia Lunatic Asylum in Milledgeville in 1923, at age thirteen, and spent the rest of her life there.

The other eight left Georgia, half bound for East Texas, the others for Florida. They prospered, for the most part, and won places of honor and respect in their new communities. And wherever they settled, the Williams siblings kept a tight lid on the family's Georgia past. "All of the stuff about the peonage and the killings was not shared with anyone," recalled John Edward Williams, whose father—Edward, the youngest of the siblings—was just two years old when John S. Williams stood trial. "And I mean anyone. Not even their wives. So growing up, we had no awareness of that at all."

"They didn't say a thing about it," Kendall Wayne Williams, LeRoy's grandson, told me. "Well, of course, it's nothing to be very proud of. I mean, great-grandpa kept slaves and killed a bunch of them fifty years after the Civil War.

"They didn't have a name for it then, but that's mass murder," he said. "I didn't find out about this until the nineties. We had always known coming up that great-grandpa had died in a prison break, but we didn't know why he was in prison. Finally, my dad sat us down when we were fishing, and he said, 'Well, I have something to tell you about your great-grandpa.'"

I heard much the same from Glenn Raymond Brooks Jr., grandson of the ninth-born Williams child, Julian. "The subject was not ever brought up to our family, to anyone in the family," he said. "The brothers kept this an extremely tight secret until I was probably in my forties. My mother didn't even know. It was definitely something that was kept from the younger generations."

Susan Burnore, granddaughter of Ivah Sue, the one sibling who stayed in Jasper, was likewise oblivious, despite growing up just outside Monticello. "I don't think any of our generation of cousins knew," she said. "When I came of age, I guess, my mother thought I needed to know a little bit of the story." That little bit was "that my grandfather was a great guy, who worked hard and had a big farm. And they worked hardened criminals on the farm, and one night these prisoners escaped. John S. Williams and his sons and a lot of other white farmers tracked them down through the forest, and in the process some of them died." Williams, she was told, took responsibility for the deaths. "So it was kind of cast to me that he was a real good guy—that he had taken the blame to protect his neighbors. I knew that he had gone to prison and he had died in prison, and that he was a trusty in prison and was allowed a lot of privileges because he was such a good guy."

This was apparently the tale as her mother understood it. As Burnore got older, "a lot of the pieces of the story didn't make sense," she told me. "Why would he take the blame? And if they were escaped prisoners, why would he be sent to prison? But it didn't come up, because no one talked about it."

The secret survived for decades despite regular family reunions, some of which drew eighty or ninety Williamses. At each, the surviving siblings would meet behind closed doors. "No wives, no husbands, just the brothers and sisters," John Edward said. "And I have no idea what was said at those meetings. There was no expectation that there was something they needed to hide, in part because they were all such upstanding citizens."

John Edward, who was born in 1950, recalled that he caught his first whiff of the truth in the mid-1970s, when he and his sister, Jo Ann, embarked on a cross-country drive and called on their older cousin Mary June in Denver. "We just got to thinking about how the family never talked about what happened back in Georgia," he said. "By the time dad came along, there wasn't money to do much, and we wondered how that happened. We knew about the boll weevil. We knew about the Depression. We assumed those kinds of issues caused the younger brothers to all leave there. So we thought June might be able to tell us. We had a great meal and we started asking questions: What changed for the family between the time the older boys grew up and the younger boys grew up?"

Mary June became "very distressed," Jo Ann recalled.

"It was a very physical reaction, a kind of closing down," John Edward agreed. "She said, 'You're going to have to ask your father about that. I can't talk to you about that.' We went on with the rest of our trip, all the time wondering in the car what it could be that was so bad that she couldn't talk about it.

"We came back to Texas. We sat down one evening with dad when we were both at home, and asked, 'What the heck is it that we don't know about?' He said, 'Well, y'all probably need to know this, because depending on how your career paths go, you might run into an issue with this.'" Their father was too young to remember the killings or trial. "He knew only what he'd been told—that eleven Black men had been murdered, and his dad was convicted of those murders."

At a later family reunion, John Edward said, he broached the subject with his cousin Curtis Williams Jr., son of the tenth-born Williams sibling, Curtis, who was seven years old when his father was prosecuted. Curtis Jr. had never heard about it. But he "had an interest in genealogy, and he started to dig," and turned up transcripts of the trial. John Edward and Jo Ann were flabbergasted by the emerging narrative, and especially that three of their uncles—two of whom they thought they knew well—were indicted for murder. "This is such a paradox, but this was a very tight-knit, very loving family," Jo Ann said. "I can't overstate how loving this family was. Which is what made this story so unbelievable.

"I pulled away from the family for several years. I just couldn't reconcile it," she said. "The horror—I still have trouble."

It was not until the 1990s that the full story made itself known to the descendants of John S. Williams. By the time that happened, the three siblings implicated in murders at the plantation—Hulon, LeRoy, and Marvin—were dead. The trio had made for Florida during or after their father's trial, Marvin and Hulon settling in Tampa, and LeRoy to the east, on the outskirts of Orlando. And from the moment they arrived, it seems, they threw themselves into starting their lives anew.

Marvin married and had three children. He supervised Tampa's road paving operations before opening the M. H. Williams Tire and Battery Service in 1932. He twice sought public office: on the school board in 1936 (he dropped out of the running before the vote), and in an eight-way race for district constable four years later (he finished in the middle of the pack). He had a run-in with the law, too—he was arrested in April 1937 for conspiring with five other gas station owners to fix prices—but the charges were dropped.

Shortly after the attack on Pearl Harbor, wartime tire rationing compelled Marvin to shut down his service station and return to construction. One afternoon in late May 1942, he was working for a contractor installing city water lines when he noticed the ground at the work site had turned spongy. Worried that a cave-in was imminent, he ordered the hasty placement of another section of pipe. As a crane positioned it overhead, a cable snapped. The load fell. Twenty-four years after he allegedly murdered peon John Singleton, and twenty-two after the plantation's Black workers saw him dispose of the body of John "Iron Jaw" Davis, Marvin Williams was crushed to death. He was forty-three.

Hulon Williams set up house with his wife, Catholine, and their three children, and found that Florida agreed with him. After working in construction for five years, he bought a service station, did well with it, then bought two more. He operated them until 1935, when he cashed out his retail business to become the Tampa branch manager for the Seaboard Oil Company, a division of Pure Oil.

In 1945, he formed a partnership with his son, John Hulon Jr. They presided over one of the biggest oil distributorships in Florida, and—by reputation, at least—the largest Pure Oil wholesaler in the United States. Success made Hulon an important man. The governor appointed him to the county port authority; he served as a director of the Central Bank of Tampa; and he chaired the region's oil industry trade organization. In 1963, Hulon was the first recipient of an annual award bestowed by the Tampa Oil Men's Club for his "outstanding leadership and contributions to the petroleum industry since 1928."

He died in 1966, at seventy-three. The man indicted for killing Robert Nathaniel "Blackstrap" Williams, and named as Will Napier's slayer, had also once served as a juror in a Tampa murder trial. The panel found the white defendant guilty.

LeRoy Williams took a different, more isolated path. For his first several years in Florida he bounced around Lake County, in the state's interior, working at least part of the time as a grocer. He and his wife had two children. Sometime in the 1930s, he moved the family north, to Cross City, the biggest and most prosperous town in Dixie County—which wasn't saying much, in that Dixie was the poorest, least populated county in the state. There, in an unassuming settlement devoted to logging cypress and yellow pine, he worked as an agent for Pure Oil, served as mayor, and ran the local Lions Club.

"Once a year we loaded up the car and drove down to Cross City to see him," Kendall Wayne Williams recalled. "He was well respected by everybody. I loved him to pieces. He put me on his knee all the time. I had no idea he'd murdered anyone."

LeRoy Williams did not come across as a racist, John Edward recalled. On the contrary, at one family reunion, his uncle overheard a young relative make a disparaging comment about someone "based on their race or nationality." Then in his eighties, LeRoy "simply held a finger up, and told that family member that he could not know what that person was like, simply based on his race or nationality. It was much more meaningful than him saying, 'Don't use that word.'"

In 1986, sixty-six years after he allegedly killed John "Iron Jaw" Davis, LeRoy Williams died of natural causes. He was ninety.

39

FOR MORE THAN TWO MONTHS after the trial of John S. Williams, state and federal officials kept ten of the plantation's former workers under lock and key in the Fulton County Tower, wanting them safe and ready for duty as witnesses in the Clyde Manning and federal peonage prosecutions. Manning's wife, Rena, was among the detainees, along with his uncle Rufus, his brother Julius, his sister Grace, and Grace's second husband, Will Johnson. Clyde Freeman was held, too, with his wife, Emma, his brother Claude, and Hulon Williams's cook, Lessie May Whitlow. Their time behind bars marked the last gathering of Black principals from the Murder Farm.

The *Constitution* complained, with racist condescension shocking even for the times, that they were freeloaders living high on the hog at taxpayer expense—"Singing 'Swing Low, Sweet Chariot,' at intervals, partaking regularly of goodly portions of side meat and corn pone and other cotton field delicacies and enjoying a long, sweet rest, free from the arduous duties of 'working the new ground,' while the government of the United States pays them $1 a day each."

Insulting though the story was, its subjects might have laughed. Damn right, they were comfortable. They could breathe. They could sleep without fear for the first time in years. Their days posed no danger of lashings, beatings, or random cruelty. They were free of the terror they'd felt at the approach of the Chandler or the sound of that man's voice. They would never again face the long, hard, and often dangerous labor they'd endured as de facto slaves. They had outlived hell together, and now these siblings and cousins were together for this last little while to dream and talk about whatever came next. To savor their freedom—even locked up, it must have felt like that. They had it better in the bowels of the Atlanta jail than they'd ever had it in Jasper County.

And rightly so. They had put Williams away, and earned a place in history doing it. While still in the Tower, they provided the evidence that saw his sons indicted for murder. Then, after the federal grand jury finished its work in Macon, the government was done with them, and they wandered into the world with more money in their pockets than they'd ever known in their lives.

Most melted into vast, anonymous Atlanta. A few struck off for more distant locales. Wherever they went, they found that past hardship implied nothing of future happiness: that life was better than it had been—of course—but it was hard, just the same. Some of them saw that lesson play out into their old age. Others did not have much time to absorb it. Still others simply dropped out of sight.

Those who died first are most readily accounted for. Lula Benton and Lessie May Whitlow, as mentioned earlier, were victims of homicide, and Clyde Manning's former wife, Rena, died of natural (but wholly preventable) causes. Clyde and Claude Freeman's family suffered one loss after another: Their younger brother J. B. died of pneumonia at nineteen. Their brother Clifford fell to heat prostration. Their stepmother, Addie Jo—once married to Rufus Manning, and apparently shared by Uncle Rufus and the Freemans' father, John, before she left the former and married the latter—succumbed to colon cancer in February 1929. Six months later, Clyde Freeman himself died in the mayhem at the barbecue stand outside Marietta.

Tracking those who lived longer poses greater challenges—Black births, marriages, and other news went largely unreported in southern newspapers, and were even overlooked in state and local records. Beyond that, many a Black citizen chose to avoid notice. The "system" had done them no favors: Their families had been wrenched apart, terrorized, and abused by officialdom since 1619. Those born after slavery's reign of nearly 250 years still had to contend with mass incarceration, peonage, and convict leasing, and if they managed to dodge those traps, they nonetheless faced the burdens and uncertainties of poverty and discrimination—and the agents of their despair in Jim Crow America were, all too often, white people in suits or uniforms. So no wonder that Black Georgians of the period were not keen to intersect with census enumerators, marriage commissioners, city police, county sheriffs, or anyone else whose records have come to comprise the usual data points of history and genealogy. They knew to steer clear of bureaucrats.

They might appear in one census, only to never reappear under the same name. They might pick up and move without leaving documentary breadcrumbs between old home and new. They might choose to jump the broom in lieu of vows before a preacher or justice of the peace, or ask relatives to raise their children—and, in the process, snap the chain of facts, dates, and places that historians rely on, today, in tracing one generation to the next.

No surprise, then, that after Clyde Freeman's death, his widow, Emma, vanished from the record, along with his baby, Rufus. Clyde Manning's brother Julius disappeared. Before she died, Lessie May Whitlow told Bureau of Investigation agents she could not account for her teenage son, Howard—she had last heard of him "as being in Buffalo, N.Y., one year ago." Every now and then, former hands would spot James Strickland on the streets of Atlanta, but the encounters were fleeting and unpredictable, and no one seemed to know where he lived.

Government men found Clyde Manning's mother, India, in Charlotte only because she had written to her daughter back in Georgia. She was not in hiding: she and her new husband, Rufus Manning, made no attempt to duck the census or mention in the city directory; it's thus known that in 1930, Uncle Rufus was working as a carpenter and the couple was caring for a five-year-old grandson. But without the return address on her letter, the agents might have known neither where to look, nor when they'd found her, because she rarely used her real name; she preferred a

variation of Indy—"Endie"—which even appeared on papers document-
ing her death in 1935.

In contrast, Clyde Manning's brother Gladdis made a conscious effort to disappear. When the feds went looking for witnesses in 1928, its
agents found that he had adopted the surname Smith. Two years later,
he was calling himself "Gladie Smith." He never reclaimed his identity
as a Manning and continued to tweak his first name; when he died of an
infection, at thirty-six, he was going by "Gladys Willie Smith." Mindful
that the name might confuse, an official scrawled on his death certificate:
"The sex on this is correct."

Despite shoddy record-keeping and their distrust of authority, some of
the plantation's survivors left a trail. Clyde Freeman's half sister Mattie,
for example, married twice, had at least two children, and doted on a large
cast of grandchildren and great-grandchildren. His half sister Beauty
married and lived the rest of her long life in Atlanta, dying in 1982. His
half sister Emma settled in Detroit. Yet another half sister, Oma, died in
December 1960, barely into her fifties, but with a wealth of descendants.
And his half brother, Hollis—a preschooler during the trials—lived with
Oma in the 1930s, had four children with his second wife, and survived
well into the twenty-first century.

Clyde Manning's sister Grace—who, as a teenager, witnessed the
murder of her first husband, Will Napier—settled in Atlanta with her
second husband, Will Johnson, after both were released from the Tower.
They moved into an apartment near the railroad tracks east of downtown.
Grace would live there for forty years; when she died in July 1968, she
was survived by two of her three sons, eight grandchildren, and eleven
great-grandchildren. How much they knew of her traumatic youth is
a question. "Grace didn't do a lot of talking about her past," as Chessie
Dumas, the daughter-in-law of her middle son, Jimmie Lee Johnson Sr.,
told me. "She was kind of a quiet lady. She was keeping all that on the
inside."

And Grace Johnson was not the only former plantation worker who, like the Williams siblings, apparently chose not to speak of Jasper County. Rena Manning waited just a few months after Clyde Manning was imprisoned before leaving him to marry Claude Freeman in February 1923. In their six years together, she bore two sons, Claude Jr. and Henry. After her death, father and sons lived together in Atlanta for at least a decade, part of that time with Claude's half sister Mattie. As adults, both sons moved to Ohio, Claude Jr. for work as a crane operator, Henry for a career in industrial metal plating. Each had several children. Among Claude Jr.'s was the Reverend Kenneth J. Freeman of Akron.

Reverend Freeman grew up knowing nothing of his family's Georgia past. He had no notion of his grandfather's travails on the plantation. He heard no mention of the killings there. He was never told of his grandmother's central role in convicting Williams, let alone that she had been married at the time to Clyde Manning. "I met my grandfather just twice," he said. "My dad, he came [to Ohio] in 1949 or 1950, and he hardly ever took us back to Atlanta. And the way I found out most of what I know is from going to family reunions." There, he met the Kimballs, descendants of Rena's brothers and sisters, and "learned a lot."

The upshot of which was that a lifetime before, his family had been key players in a racial atrocity that horrified the country. The truth stunned him. "Just being amongst my grandmother's family, her immediate family, and listening to their stories, I was quite overwhelmed," he told me. "I was angered. I was almost trembling with tears, I was so overwhelmed by it—and I couldn't understand why my father and uncle never said a word about it. Unless they didn't know."

One of his rare trips to Atlanta came in January 1969, to attend Claude Sr.'s memorial service. His grandfather died, at seventy, without divulging his experiences on the farm. The reverend went down again in August 1997, to attend the funeral of a woman who had always been described to him as his aunt, his father's older sister.

That is not who she was. Essie Mae Pinkston was his father's half sister—the daughter of Rena and Clyde Manning. At some point before or during the trials, Rena sent the little girl to live with her sister Marietta, or "Etta." Essie stayed with her aunt through her seven years of school and into adulthood—and, in fact, continued to live with Etta Henderson after marrying a plasterer from Covington named Lewis Pinkston. Eventually, the couple moved into a little bungalow in Center Hill, on Atlanta's west side, and stayed put. Claude Sr., meanwhile, took to calling and treating Essie as his daughter.

"She was a wonderful, wonderful person, saved and sanctified," Reverend Freeman recalled. "What she talked about, mostly, when I went down there, was her granddad"—that is, Rena's father—"and about how he'd get so excited when he preached that the spit would be flying around. That would be Henry Kimball. He was a preacher, and she was so funny, talking about him.

"She kind of put you in the mind of Mahalia Jackson. She had that voice, that presence."

Alas, Essie Mae Pinkston died childless.

Which is to say that, unless he fathered children outside his marriage, Clyde Manning has no living descendants.

Three generations have come and gone since the Murder Farm earned headlines the country over. In Jasper and Newton Counties, the years have worn away much trace of the affair. Today, both trade on their latter-day renown as locations for big-budget films and TV shows: In the 1990s, Monticello's courthouse earned immortality as the outdoor backdrop to Hollywood's *My Cousin Vinny*. On summertime weekends, pilgrims descend on Covington's courthouse square to experience the fictional Mystic Falls, the setting for TV's *The Vampire Diaries*. The town's picturesque heart so often stands in for cinematic small-town Anywhere that its streets are stripped of signage, the better to preserve their anonymity.

Neither county acknowledges, in any public way, the events of 1921. They have moved on so thoroughly that the uninformed would be hard-pressed to catch a whisper of their shared past. In the process, they have been careless with the Murder Farm's victims. They have misplaced every last one of them.

Paying respects to the eight men slain on Williams land and at the Waters Bridge should be a simple matter. After their bodies were examined by the coroner's jury, the eight were piled onto a mule-drawn wagon and hauled to the cemetery at the Jasper County paupers farm. There, the three men axed at the Williams home place, the two murdered on the river tracts, and the three drowned in the Alcovy were placed in simple pine coffins and dropped into the ground.

The graveyard was substantial, it seems, as it served not only Jasper's dispossessed, but prisoners who died in the county's custody and unidentified strangers who expired while visiting Monticello and the surrounding countryside. It likely contained dozens of graves. Be that as it may, Jasper County has lost track of the burial ground. No surviving maps depict its precise location—none that I've been able to find, at any rate. No modern inventory of Jasper cemeteries lists its location. Not a single living soul I met in the county could pinpoint where it was.

The 1909 map of Jasper depicted the "Poor Farm" beside the road linking Monticello and the Waters Bridge—today a highway, straightened and widened and busy with traffic, known as Georgia Route 212. A 2010 column in the *Monticello News* mentioned that before it shut down in the 1930s, the paupers farm was "next door" to the county jail, or "convict camp." That camp, updated after World War II, remained in service long enough that officials at the county courthouse remembered it and could place it behind the present-day sheriff's office, about a mile from town on Route 212, or right where the map suggested it should be.

But today that spot is a jumble of modern county activities: near the road, the sheriff's office and a senior citizens center; behind them, the kennels of the county's animal control operation and a depot of tractors, trucks, and heaped sand and gravel used by public works crews; and behind that, a wooded swamp, the county landfill, and a cluster of baseball diamonds. The only seemingly undisturbed piece of the property, a dense forest of cedars, sweetgums, and pines, edges up to the senior center and stretches away to the north.

When I visited the complex early in 2023, a few clients at the senior center recalled talk of the county warehousing its poor "in olden times," as one put it, but had never seen the place themselves, and had no inkling as to where its dead might rest. Sheriff Donnie Pope, an affable Jasper native born more than forty years after the Williams trial, could offer little insight into the cemetery's location, either. "Never heard of one around here," he told me. "I know there's no caretaking being done there, because my inmates take care of cutting the county's grass." I polled longtime public works veterans on the subject. They professed ignorance, too, but reckoned there was only one place it could be: those woods.

I spent the better part of two days exploring them. The forest floor was snarled with blowdowns and greenbrier, heaped with fallen leaves and needles. Here and there I came upon animal bones—deer skulls, a spine, pieces of leg, all picked clean—but in miles of hiking, intersecting with my own path three and four times over, I saw neither makeshift headstones, nor depressions in the soil, nor anything else to signal the presence of graves. The forest seemed in close to a primeval state, untrammeled and wild.

A few days later, I received an email from the Jasper County surveyor, Robert Jordan. He had attached a series of aerial photographs of the county complex taken every few years, the oldest dating to 1951, and I was shocked to see that the woods I'd crisscrossed were open fields until just thirty years before. If a cemetery existed on that land before the trees took over, it should have been apparent in the images. They betrayed nothing.

But they did hint at another, long-shot possibility. Behind the senior center was a square of ground, perhaps thirty yards on a side, that looked to be largely unchanged in each of the pictures; from the earliest aerial to the most recent, taken in 2015, it appeared to have been spared the disruption that had occurred all around it. When I ran the idea past Sheriff Pope that this might be the cemetery, hiding in plain sight, he had doubts—it was his understanding that the plot was underlain by a septic system, and construction crews had dug back there in the course of building additions to the senior center. Surely, if they had stumbled upon graves, they'd have halted work.

Still, he agreed to give it a once-over, and in mid-February 2023 he examined the lawn with a deputy and two trusties from the county jail. They paced the square's edges first, then crossed back and forth over the grass, from one end of the plot to the other. They came across nothing to suggest that Johnnie Williams, John Will "Big John" Gaither, Johnnie Green, or Will Givens were buried there. They found no sign that under their feet lay John "Red" Brown, John "Little Bit" Benford, Charlie Chisholm, or Fletcher Smith. "I [am] afraid we came up empty," the sheriff reported in a text at day's end. "There are just no indications of a cemetery." He found it impossible "to tell if there was ever something there."

It could be that the sheriff and his team trod right over the graves without knowing it, that enough time has passed that all vestiges of the old burial ground have faded to nothing. It might be that the eight lie under the woods, that their graves had worn smooth and undetectable even before the forest erupted around and through them—and that I tramped over them without a clue.

They're lost, either way. John S. Williams's victims have suffered a final indignity.

And distressing though that thought might be, there's another, far less agreeable possibility: that the county has put a building or parking lot smack on top of them.

A few miles to the west, the river tracts are unrecognizable as cropland. The ground that Hulon, LeRoy, and Marvin Williams farmed for their father is now a wooded sanctuary of lakefront homes, meandering lanes, a nine-hole golf course. Turtle Cove, the place is called. Snaking among its dense stands of hardwood and pine, on roads that dive into darkened hollows and climb up and over high knolls, inspires wonder: How in God's name did anyone think this steep, corduroy terrain was suited to cotton or corn? How could a mule pull a plow here?

The trees make it almost impossible to imagine the place as it was. But on the crown of a high hill near Turtle Cove's middle stands the golf course clubhouse. It overlooks a carefully groomed fairway, as Hulon Williams's house commanded the shallow valley where the red house stood, and that lookout offers a glimpse—a sliver of an impression—of the place as a farm: Even cleared of trees, the river tracts were not wide-open spaces. This was deeply wrinkled land that defied prying eyes. Land suited to keeping secrets. ·

Not far from the clubhouse, one of the development's roads falls from a high bluff to the water's edge, dead-ending at a small private beach. Its sand, at the tip of a point reaching for the lake's middle, provides clear vantage of a two-pronged cove to the south. It is one of many such inlets—Jackson Lake has a convoluted edge, 135 miles of fingers and clefts, so these backwaters abound. Only a couple on the old river tracts, though, venture deep enough into the shoreline to qualify as the "pond." This is one of them.

In November 1921, Jasper County officials announced that a skeleton had been discovered in the lake's shallows—a drought that fall had seen the reservoir's level drop and its edges recede, exposing a set of remains on the muddy shore "with iron chains and weights attached." The bones, the officials decided, were likely those of John "Iron Jaw" Davis; forensic science being as it was at the time, there was no way to be certain. The county buried the scant remnants, presumably in the since-misplaced paupers cemetery.

In reporting the find, the *Constitution* noted that another body, believed to be that of John Singleton, had been pulled from the lake months before. This earlier discovery had been mentioned in passing in news stories during the Jasper County grand jury's April 1921 investigation of charges against the three Williams sons. Assuming the reports were accurate—and that comes with no guarantee—they raised as many questions as they answered: Who determined the remains were Singleton's, and how? And what became of them—were they, too, interred in the paupers cemetery?

Whatever the case, Jasper County officials told the *Constitution* that they had no plans to search for the third body they believed to be down on the bottom. And, indeed, nothing in the record suggests that they ever dragged the pond for the remains of Robert Nathaniel "Blackstrap" Williams. Whatever is left of him is likely still down there.

On sunny days, the view from the beach is lovely. The inlet's waters shimmer. Its shore is clustered with boathouses and pontoon rigs. Flags snap in the breeze. Beyond, the ground rises steeply to fine waterfront homes tucked among the trees.

Farther west, across Jackson Lake, the bodies of the three men killed in Newton County are probably long gone. Their death certificates note they were entombed in the banks of the South and Yellow Rivers, and make no reference to their being moved later on. The county appears to have no record of their reburial. All three graves were shallow, dug when the rivers ran low, and in the years since, the South and Yellow have swollen with flood too many times to count. High water has clawed at their banks, sweeping clay and vegetation downstream into the lake's wide impoundment. So it follows, sadly, that if the bodies of Lindsey Peterson, Will Preston, and Harry "Foots" Price were still in place when the Murder Farm trials ended, they did not stay that way for long.

All that remains of Allen's Bridge is a pair of rusted piers rising from the Yellow River's middle and crumbling abutments in the shadows on its banks. The old crossing is a still, quiet place, save for birdsong and the splashes of leaping fish. Nature has reclaimed it: weed and vine have overtaken old Route 36's approaches to the water. Dense brush has colonized the river's edges, cocooning the spot from its modern surroundings, erasing any sense of its past. It defies imagination that a vicious double murder unfolded there, or that hundreds of people gathered in this swampy, isolated place to witness the coroner's inquest. As for graves: if they survive, they're invisible.

On the South, Mann's Bridge stands rusted and spindly, glowing red in the early evening light. It meets the ghost of Route 36 on the river's east side, and local lore holds that Harry Price's body might rest in the woods a short distance down the old road, beneath the scant ruins of a long-abandoned homestead. No evidence supports such a notion. One can hope, however, because there's no hint of a burial in the eroded riverbank.

From under the span, one can look up among girders that cradled Mann's wooden roadbed—and, beyond them, to a surviving section of banister. Somewhere along that railing, the bound and weighted Foots struggled to balance himself as he peered into the river's dark water.

He must have despaired at his fate, though he might not have been surprised by it. His twenty-five or twenty-six years had brought little but poverty, pain, and heartache. As a Black man in Jim Crow Georgia, he'd have suffered a steady diet of insult and injustice, culminating in his term as a twentieth-century slave.

He might have realized, perched there, that he would be missed by few.

He might have understood he would be as overlooked in death as he was as a peon.

The shame of it—one of so many shames—is that he would have been right.

Acknowledgments

Back in 2007, as I reviewed old newspapers on microfilm for a book on the history of American highways, I came upon a front-page headline in the March 27, 1921, *New York Times*: "Find Nine Bodies in Georgia Peonage Murder Inquiry." I had never seen the word *peonage* and had no clue what it meant. But the headline drew me into the story, which detailed the gruesome Easter weekend dig for bodies on the Williams plantation and spurred me to scan the succeeding days' editions for follow-ups.

When I stepped away from the microfilm reader, I was staggered not only by the revelation that slavery had endured beyond the Civil War, but that a terrible affair that had so gripped the country had faded to historical footnote. Here, I thought, was a tale worth retelling. Between other projects, I started digging for details about what happened in Jasper and Newton Counties. You're holding the result.

Seventeen years of start-and-stop reporting has left me indebted to a lot of people, and to name names is risky; I'm bound to overlook more than a few. So know, up front, that this is an incomplete account of the knowledge, know-how, and kindness that others have bestowed upon me and this story—and that I will be forever indebted to everyone, named or not, who has made the time and effort to lend me a hand.

I'm grateful, first, to historian and Jasper County native Tim Pitts, whose scholarship laid the groundwork for much of my own research. This is a guy who makes an adventure out of history for his students, and who brought that same smart, playful spirit to our many conversations and a memorable day spent exploring his home turf. His generosity and humor have marked our every interaction.

I can say the same of Robert Thurston, professor emeritus of Miami

University of Ohio, who has been wonderfully generous in sharing his insights into Hugh Dorsey's upbringing, career, and motivations. Bob has put up with my questions for a dozen years or more, and has always been enthusiastic with his guidance.

In Jasper County, I found officials willing to help me nail down myriad details of this story, despite its describing their community's darkest chapter. I thank Superior Court Clerk LeAnn Airington and her staff, especially Deputy Clerk Chrissy Mason, for their hospitality during my many visits to the courthouse in Monticello; Sheriff Donnie Pope, who joined in my search for the elusive paupers cemetery; Robert Jordan, the county surveyor; Judy Johnson, director of planning and zoning; Mike Walsh, director of public works; the county tax assessor's office; the Probate Court staff; and retired county employees Kenneth and Tom Tillman.

I was also fortunate to encounter Mike, Rusty, and Stephanie Pittman, who live on a lovely spread that a century ago was the eastern edge of the Williams home place, and whose good cheer has no doubt diminished any bad juju lingering there.

In Newton County, I owe thanks to Superior Court Deputy Clerk Anne Jones; former deputy sheriff Doug Kitchens; County Clerk Jackie Smith; and LaTonja Hamp, executive assistant to the county's Board of Commissioners. Local mercantile legend Johnny Potts helped me crack a stubborn historical mystery—the location of Polk's store—and resident Terry L. Hall responded to a knock on his door by leading this complete stranger on hikes along old Route 36, a kayak paddle to Mann's Bridge, then a voyage by pontoon boat to Allen's. Brent Springfield and Christopher Jordan of Athens smoothed my numerous research expeditions to Georgia.

The bones of the narrative lay in correspondence, speeches, court and DOJ papers, photographs, and newspaper reports. Helping me chase down these documents were Allison Hudgins and the staff of the Georgia Archives; Serena McCracken, Jena Jones, and their colleagues at the Atlanta History Center's Kenan Research Center; Shane Bell of the National Archives in Atlanta; the staff of the Manuscripts Division at the Library of Congress; and library staffs at the University of Georgia and the University of Virginia. I first read the DOJ's 1932 case summary thanks to Georgia journalist Gregory A. Freeman, whose own book on the subject—*Lay This Body Down*—was published in 1999. Michelle Asci of Georgia State University, the repository of the *Atlanta Constitution*'s old photo morgue, was indispensable in my quest for images.

The descendants of John S. Williams were unfailingly gracious and wonderfully candid about their family's past. I thank John Edward Williams, Jo Ann Williams, Kendall Wayne Williams, Susan Burnore, Glenn Raymond Brooks Jr., Rodney Lee Williams, and Donna Gayle Williams Coleman.

My search for descendants of the plantation's Black workers was helped along immeasurably by Rev. Kenneth J. Freeman of Akron, Ohio, and by Trevor Marks and Chessie Dumas of Atlanta. Thank you, guys.

To this point, I've singled out people for their contributions to this specific story. Alongside them, I thank a cadre of friends who have sustained my writing, and me, for years. Maria Carrillo, my former editor at Norfolk's *Virginian-Pilot*, has been a font of encouragement from the start. I thank, too, fellow journalist and author Bill Morris; Ian "Hammer" Martin of Carmel, California; historian Joe "He Gets All the Facts In" Jackson of Virginia Beach; and Dean Strang of Madison, Wisconsin, himself the author of two first-rate explorations of all-but-forgotten legal dramas. Dick Todd, Jacob Levenson, Patsy Sims, Tom French, and Suzannah Lessard of Goucher College's Nonfiction MFA faculty applied their big brains to helping me shape this idea, but were enthusiastic backers of earlier books, too. My Virginia Humanities fellowship at the University of Virginia has been critical; I thank Matthew Gibson, Kevin McFadden, and the foundation's other leaders for putting up with me these past dozen years.

This is the fourth book I've written in partnership with Peter Hubbard, my editor at HarperCollins. Each has been as rewarding a collaboration as a writer could hope for, and this one especially so: Peter's intelligence, patience, advocacy, and good taste have permeated every step of the long and painstaking process of taking this story from concept to print. I pity writers who work with anyone else.

My agent, David Black, has looked out for me for more than twenty years. He's not only the best there is at what he does, but my trusted friend and mentor—and a big part of why I'm the luckiest guy on the planet.

My family, blood and otherwise, has buoyed my spirits and kept me on task while I reported and wrote. Mark Mobley, a native Georgian, took charge of my trips to his home state, put me up on several of those visits, gave the manuscript its first close read, and talked to me virtually every day I worked on it. He's been my smart, generous, and wildly entertaining tether to sanity.

My stepmom, Gerry Swift, has always been bullish on this story and has had my back for way longer. My brother Kevin Swift drew the lovely map that accompanies the text, contributed to the cover, cleaned up many photographs I could find only on blotchy microfilm images of old newspaper pages, read an early draft of the manuscript—and has kept me laughing since we were in diapers.

My heart's desire, Amy Walton, has been a passionate advocate for this story since my fateful day at the microfilm reader. Her belief in its importance has kept me from shelving it for easier subjects; her faith in me has been unflagging; and her love has spiced my solitary days at the keyboard, on this book and seven others.

My daughter, Saylor, saw her high school vacations hijacked for trips to the Georgia Archives, spent long days in the car with me exploring Jasper and Newton Counties, and suffered incessant talk from her father about a long-ago race massacre that, I'm sure, was pretty hard to grasp for a suburban teenager. In the years since, as my travels have taken me down yonder on a regular basis, she's minded my place and kept the home office running. If I play it right, it won't be long before she'll let my new grandson, Dawson, go off on reporting trips with me.

Finally, I thank my dear friend Laura LaFay, to whom this book is dedicated. As she has for several books now, Laura served as my first reader—a combination of story doctor, fact-checker, and literary critic of the manuscript in its rough and embryonic state. She is fierce in the role, and deserves a great share of the credit for the finished product.

The good parts of it, that is.

Any weaknesses it suffers are all on me.

Notes

This story is a work of nonfiction. All of it, sad to say, really happened, and the narrative is supported throughout by court documents, Department of Justice files, correspondence to and from the principals, contemporary press accounts, census and other public records, and my own interviews and on-site reporting. A wealth of academic scholarship further informed my understanding of peonage, lynching, and the context of what transpired in Jasper and Newton Counties in the spring of 1921.

As many of these sources are more than a century old, I have relied on accounts written or delivered when the style of expression was markedly different from today's. Nowhere are these differences more jarring than in use of the N-word: I was shocked by how casually it seeped into press coverage of the Murder Farm case, and even more by its utterance at the resulting three trials. Whether to substitute a less offensive term was a question I wrestled with as I wrote this book, and that I debated with my editor and early readers of the manuscript. I eventually concluded that the story had to be true to its time, that I was duty bound to err on the side of authenticity; it makes no sense, I reasoned, to chronicle a racially driven series of murders in the Jim Crow era while sanitizing the language used by the players. Some readers will disagree. I regret their discomfort, but trust they will understand my decision.

Other issues of language cropped up, as well. Early twentieth-century punctuation and capitalization did not follow the rules we use today—it sometimes seems they followed no rules at all—so I tried to develop a consistent approach in my handling of quoted material. The general rule I followed was this: If I quoted a piece of writing, I offered up its punctuation and capitalization as it originally appeared. If, however, I plucked a spoken remark from a news report or other document—that is, I took the quote and ditched the rest—I altered the punctuation and capitalization within that remark to meet modern standards. People don't generally speak in capital letters, and unless they're dictating a text message they don't assign punctuation to their remarks, so this presented no qualms; I second-guessed not what was said, but merely the mechanics of how it was presented on the page.

Thus, when I quote a 1920s news article referring to "negroes," I leave the word as is. When I quote a person using the word in speech, I capitalize it, just as I do whenever I use the word myself. The same goes for 1921 references to "Yellow river," "Newton county," "Allen's bridge," and such—if taken from a written passage they stand unchanged, but if spoken, the "River," "County," and "Bridge" get capped, per modern style.

I have chosen to capitalize *Black* throughout the book, while not capping *white*. This admitted inconsistency reflects my own preference, though it's also the standard used by many newspapers and magazines, and hews to the strictures of *The Chicago Manual of Style*, the rulebook followed by the book publishing industry. Again, I anticipate that some readers will differ with my decision.

My treatment of courtroom testimony deserves special attention. I have not changed a word of what witnesses said at the trials. But their statements were often rendered nearly impenetrable by errant punctuation in transcripts and court briefs, so I've repunctuated them to meet modern standards.

That brings us to subtle but important differences in how quoted speech is treated throughout the text. Where I have placed quote marks around a comment, I'm confident that it reflects, to the greatest degree possible, exactly what was said. In many passages I've recounted exchanges without the use of quote marks, which you should interpret as capturing the gist of what was said, rather than the exact phrasing. In some cases I've chosen this device to distill a long back-and-forth into its essence; in others, I've done so because no verbatim record exists, though reliable sources do capture the character of what was said.

NOTES

You'll note, for instance, that conversation during the federal agents' February 18, 1921, visit to the Williams plantation is presented in chapter 1 largely without quotes. That's because the agents' field notes have not been preserved; both the FBI and the National Archives report that they do not possess them. I've instead relied on trial testimony and a 1932 Bureau of Investigation summary of the case to reconstruct the dialogue.

Throughout part 3, covering the John S. Williams trial, you'll see I've placed quote marks around the witnesses' testimony, but not around the questions put to them by prosecutors and defense attorneys. That is because the full transcript of the Williams trial went missing from the Newton County Superior Court clerk's office years ago. In its place, I consulted a "Brief of Evidence" prepared by the court for use in Williams's appeal to the Georgia Supreme Court later in 1921. The brief includes all or most of the actual testimony, but with the questions removed. In the main, it requires little effort to deduce the question that produced an answer; in places, the court even folded the question into the answer to make its meaning clear. I am confident that, quote marks or no, my reconstruction of the trial accurately captures the event. For more on this point, see the notes for page 157.

The transcript of Clyde Manning's first trial is missing, as well. But, again, a Brief of Evidence was prepared for his appeal. What's more, the transcript of his second trial is intact, and includes long passages of his first trial—the testimony of multiple witnesses who appeared at the first was simply read into the record at the second. I was therefore able to reconstruct the first Manning trial in much the same manner I did the Williams proceedings, and quote the lawyers' questions verbatim in my reconstruction of the second.

In my handling of all three trials, I was able to augment the official record with an avalanche of newspaper reporting. Where they diverged from the court's version of events, I favored the latter.

A number of the photographs accompanying the text were pulled from newspapers covering the case. These were often in rough shape, and were digitally cleaned by my brother, St. Louis artist and designer Kevin Swift, in June and July 2023. These refinements removed chaff from the images (halftone clotting, smudges, microfilm flaws, and the like), and in one case added information: the photo of Lonnie Brand and Greene Johnson was originally two separate photos published to appear as one; we completed the effect by removing the seam between the images and adding an extension to Johnson's right shoulder.

A final note: the book's title was inspired by a headline—"Hell Put to an Open Shame"—over an editorial about the Williams case on page 4 of the Oklahoma City *Black Dispatch* of April 8, 1921.

What follows is my sourcing for the story, along with sideline observations, a few speculations, and stray tidbits of information that did not fit comfortably within the narrative.

Abbreviations

AC: *Atlanta Constitution*, the only big morning daily operating in Atlanta in 1921, and a forerunner of today's *Atlanta Journal-Constitution*. A consistent backer of Hugh Dorsey as prosecutor, governor, and Senate candidate.

AG: *Atlanta Georgian*, the city's third-largest daily paper. Staunchly southern Democratic and slow to evolve on subjects of race, the paper's sensationalist and specious reporting was at least partly to blame for touching off the 1906 riot. It had calmed down significantly by 1921.

Age: *New York Age*, an influential Black weekly newspaper published in New York, for which James Weldon Johnson wrote an editorial column from 1914 to 1924.

AJ: *Atlanta Journal*, an afternoon competitor to the *Georgian* and the city's most popular newspaper in 1921. It came under common ownership with the *Constitution* in 1950.

BOE: Briefs of the evidence presented at the Williams and first Manning trials, prepared by the Newton County Superior Court for the defendants' appeals. Both briefs are included in the DOJ Files. The Williams brief is also partially preserved in "Williams v. State," *The Southeastern Reporter*, vol. 110 (St. Paul: West Publishing Co., 1922), 286–300. I obtained a copy of the Williams brief from Georgia journalist and author Gregory A. Freeman in 2010, and a copy of the Manning brief from Georgia historian Timothy J. Pitts in 2021.

DOJ Files: *Peonage Files of the U.S. Department of Justice, 1901–1945*, a collection of documents culled from the National Archives and other sources by historian Pete Daniel and published on microfilm by University Publications of America in 1989; it's available from numerous college libraries around the country. Daniel appended the Williams and Manning trial briefs, along with the transcript of the second Manning trial, to the end of Reel 26.

FBI File: A 1932 Bureau of Investigation summary of the case, along with a hodgepodge of correspondence and field reports associated with the search for witnesses in 1928 and beyond. It includes a fairly comprehensive account of Clyde Manning's confession, but contains no field notes, interview transcripts, or other papers original to the 1921 investigation. The file, labeled Case 50-HQ-43, is available via Freedom of Information Act request from the National Archives and Records Administration at College Park, Maryland.

NAACP Papers: The collected papers of the National Association for the Advancement of Colored People, preserved at the Manuscript Division, Library of Congress. The papers include correspondence, meeting minutes, and speeches that provide valuable insight into the day-to-day workings of the NAACP, as well as files directly associated with peonage and the Murder Farm case.

NYT: *New York Times.*

Part One: Wire and Chain

Prelude

3 *The road beyond:* I walked the abandoned Route 36 and kayaked under and around Mann's Bridge with Newton County resident Terry L. Hall on September 16, 2022. We revisited the bridge by pontoon boat on July 26, 2023.

Chapter 1

7 *A January weekday:* The Bureau of Investigation's location is listed in the 1921 Atlanta city directory, available from the Internet Archive at https://archive.org/details/atlantacitydirec 1921atla (accessed February 24, 2023).

7 *Thirty-nine years old:* Gus Chapman's visit is detailed in the 1932 Bureau of Investigation case summary, FBI File. I fleshed out that account with Chapman's testimony at the first trial of Clyde Manning.

7 *That word has fallen:* My brief discussion of peonage here was informed by Pete Daniel, *The Shadow of Slavery: Peonage in the South, 1901–1969* (Urbana: University of Illinois Press, 1972); and Douglas A. Blackmon, *Slavery By Another Name: The Re-Enslavement of Black Americans from the Civil War to World War II* (New York: Doubleday, 2008).

9 *It so happened:* James Strickland's report to the Bureau is described in the 1932 Bureau summary, FBI File.

Chapter 2

11 *The John S. Williams home place:* My description of the property is drawn from Williams's deeds and mortgages, which are filed with the Jasper County Superior Court clerk; see Deed Book Y, pages 402–3, for a description of the tract when it left Williams's hands. A few of the documents create the impression that the home place measured 355 acres. I'm confident that is an arithmetical error.

My description of the Williams house was informed by "Trial of Williams Begins Tuesday," *Covington News*, March 31, 1921, 1; and "Dr. Gus Williams Makes Statement," *Savannah Morning News*, March 31, 1921, 1.

11 *Early in 1921:* Re the drop in cotton prices, see Mark Ellis, "Racial Unrest and White Liberalism in Rural Georgia: Barrow and Oconee Counties in the Early 1920s," *Georgia Historical Quarterly* 97, no. 1 (Spring 2013): 29–60.

12 *So it was no picture:* The agents' visit, described here and over the next several pages, is drawn from the case summary, FBI File; and the testimony of Wismer and Brown in the Williams BOE, DOJ Files.

15 *Away to the west:* For a detailed description of the waterways, see George Hatcher, ed., *Georgia Rivers* (Athens, GA: University of Georgia Press, 1962).

15 *In 1911:* The dam's construction is explained in an April 2020 archaeological assessment prepared for Georgia Power by TRC Environmental Corp., and available online at https://www.georgiapower.com/content/dam/georgia-power/pdfs/company-pdfs/lloyd-shoals-dam/ls-study-vol-3-of-4-public.pdf (accessed March 18, 2023).

15 *John S. Williams had done:* The lakefront purchases are chronicled in Jasper County's deed books. For Williams's acquisition of the Leverett property, see Book R, page 535; of the Steele place, Book S, page 104; of the Stone place, Book S, page 149; and of the Campbell place, Book T, page 373.

17 *The agents could see:* My account of the agents' confrontation with LeRoy Williams relies on their testimony and John S. Williams's unsworn statement at trial, both in the Williams BOE, DOJ Files. For the record, this was the only sliver of Williams's account of the visit that I found credible.

18 *One of the Williamses:* The agents described the fear they detected in their trial testimony, Williams BOE; the Bureau makes a point of it in its 1932 summary, FBI File. Clyde Freeman, Claude Freeman, and other plantation field hands confirmed their fear at both Manning trials.

18 *Arriving back:* Williams's case summary, FBI File; Wismer and Brown testimony, Williams BOE, DOJ Files.

Chapter 3

20 *Those officials were protected:* My passage on the Black Codes was informed by William Cohen, "Negro Involuntary Servitude in the South, 1865–1940: A Preliminary Analysis," *Journal of Southern History* 42, no. 1 (February 1976): 31–60; N. Gordon Carper, "Slavery Revisited: Peonage in the South," *Phylon* 37, no. 1 (1st Qtr, 1976): 85–99; Daniel A. Novak, *The Wheel of Servitude: Black Forced Labor after Slavery* (Lexington: University Press of Kentucky, 1978); Pete Daniel, "The Metamorphosis of Slavery, 1865–1900," *Journal of American History* 66, no. 1 (June 1979): 88–99; Daniel, *The Shadow of Slavery*; Donald L. Grant, *The Way It Was in the South: The Black Experience in Georgia* (New York: Birch Lane Press, 1993); Aziz Z. Huq, "Peonage and Contractual Liberty," *Columbia Law Review* 101, no. 2 (March 2001): 351–91; and Timothy J. Pitts, "Murder Farm: The 1921 Trials of John S. Williams and Clyde Manning" (master's thesis, Jacksonville State University, 2000).

20 *Vagrancy laws were so broadly:* The Florida vagrancy statute's unabridged wording targeted "rogues and vagabonds, idle or dissolute persons who go about begging, common gamblers, persons who use juggling or unlawful games or plays, common pipers and fiddlers, common drunkards, common night walkers, thiefs, pilferers, traders in stolen property, lewd, wanton, and lascivious persons in speech or behavior, keepers of gambling houses, common railers and brawlers, persons who neglect their calling or employment and misspend what they earn and do not provide for themselves or for the support of their families, persons wandering from place to place able to work and who are without means and who neglect to earn their support and live by pilfering or begging, idle and disorderly persons, including therein those who neglect all lawful business and habitually misspend their time by frequenting houses of ill fame, gaming houses, or tippling shops, persons able to work but are habitually idle and live upon the earnings of their wives or minor children, and all able-bodied male persons over eighteen years of age who are without means of support, and whose parents or guardians are unable to support them, and who are not usually in attendance upon some school or educational establishment, but who live in habitual idleness. . . ." See "Report of Hon. Charles W. Russell, Assistant Attorney General, Relative to Peonage Matters," *Annual Report of the Attorney General of the United States* (Washington, D.C.: U.S. Department of Justice, 1907).

21 *In Georgia, vagrancy:* Cohen, "Negro Involuntary Servitude in the South."

21 *Contract laws grew sharper:* Florida's overreaching statute is ibid.

22 *With the arrival:* The Du Bois quote is from his *Black Reconstruction in America, 1860–1880* (New York: Free Press, 1999).

22 *The form of peonage:* My description of convict leasing relies on ibid.; on Cohen, "Negro Involuntary Servitude in the South"; and on Blackmon, *Slavery By Another Name.*

24 *How many victims:* The NAACP's Walter White frequently asserted that peonage was rampant throughout the South, and especially in the Mississippi Delta. See "Peonage Common, Says Investigator," *New York Evening Post,* March 28, 1921 ("Jasper Peonage Clippings" file, Box I:C388, NAACP Papers).

24 *Other forms of debt:* On the abuses of the Keys railroad, see Charles W. Russell, *Report on Peonage* (Washington, D.C.: Government Printing Office, 1908).

24 *Meanwhile, untold numbers:* On turpentine camps, see Carper, "Slavery Revisited." The passage on the pants is ibid.

25 *Trouble was:* I quote J. D. Sayers, "Allowing Negroes to Purchase Goods on Landlord's Account Makes Debts Which Create a Virtual Slavery," reprinted in *New York Age,* April 23, 1921, 2. See also Roger L. Ransom and Richard Sutch, "Debt Peonage in the Cotton South After the Civil War," *Journal of Economic History* 32, no. 3 (September 1972): 641–69; and Daniel, "The Metamorphosis of Slavery."

25 *Landlords often shortchanged:* The NAACP investigator is Walter F. White, in "'Massacring Whites' in Arkansas," *The Nation,* Dec. 6, 1919, 715–16.

26 *So indebted:* The Pete Daniel quote is from "The Metamorphosis of Slavery."

27 *In 1907:* The quote is ibid. See also John Dittmer, *Black Georgia in the Progressive Era, 1900–1920* (Urbana: University of Illinois Press, 1977).

27 *Having invented this system:* My discussion of the origins of peonage legislation was informed by Alan Knight, "Mexican Peonage: What Was It and Why Was It?," *Journal of Latin American Studies* 18, no. 1 (May 1986), 41–74; Aviam Soifer, "Federal Protection, Paternalism, and the Virtually Forgotten Prohibition of Voluntary Peonage," *Columbia Law Review* 112, no. 7 (November 2012): 1607–39; William S. Kiser, "A 'Charming Name for a Species of Slavery': Political Debate on Debt Peonage in the Southwest, 1840s–1860s," *Western Historical Quarterly* 45, no. 2 (Summer 2014): 169–89; Andrés Reséndez, "North American Peonage," *Journal of the Civil War Era* 7, no. 4 (December 2017): 597–619; Huq, "Peonage and Contractual Liberty"; and Cohen, "Negro Involuntary Servitude in the South."

27 *Which might explain:* For more on the Eberhart case, see "Blacks Held in Bondage," *Savannah Morning News,* April 21, 1898, 2 (this story was the source of the quote); and "The Peonage Cases," *Savannah Morning News,* Jan. 10, 1899, 2. See also Benno C. Schmidt Jr., "Principle and Prejudice: The Supreme Court and Race in the Progressive Era, Part 2: The 'Peonage Cases,'" *Columbia Law Review* 82, no. 4 (May 1982): 646–718, footnotes 48 and 53.

28 *Despite that disappointing outcome:* My description of the 1901 case draws from Daniel, *The Shadow of Slavery.*

28 *In the midst:* My passage on Quackenbos was informed by Jerrell H. Shofner, "Mary Grace Quackenbos, a Visitor Florida Did Not Want," *Florida Historical Quarterly* 58, no. 3 (January 1980): 273–90; and Randolph H. Boehm, "Mary Grace Quackenbos and the Federal Campaign against Peonage: The Case of Sunnyside Plantation," *Arkansas Historical Quarterly* 50, no. 1 (Spring 1991): 40–59.

28 *Her findings prompted:* See "Report of Hon. Charles W. Russell, Assistant Attorney General, Relative to Peonage Matters." See also Russell, *Report on Peonage;* Carper, "Slavery Revisited"; and Cohen, "Negro Involuntary Servitude in the South."

29 *Russell recommended:* See "Report of Hon. Charles W. Russell, Assistant Attorney General, Relative to Peonage Matters."

30 *Then, in 1911:* My discussion of the Alonzo Bailey case was informed by Carper, "Slavery Revisited"; Cohen, "Negro Involuntary Servitude in the South"; and Daniel, *The Shadow of Slavery.*

Chapter 4

31 *That Sunday morning:* The discovery in the Yellow River was described in the 1932 Bureau summary, FBI File; and in "Chained Bodies of Negroes Found in Yellow River," *AC,* March 14, 1921, 2; "Mystery Shrouds Identity of Drowned Negros," *Covington News,* March 17, 1921, 1; and "Gruesome Find in Yellow River," *Monticello News,* March 18, 1921, 1. See also the testimony of B. L. Johnson and C. T. Hardeman at the Williams trial, Williams BOE, DOJ Files; and the testimony of Carl Wheeler at Manning's first trial, Manning BOE, DOJ Files.

33 *Little chance existed:* I quote "Chained Bodies of Negroes Found in Yellow River," *AC*, March 14.

Chapter 5

34 *But journalists had reason:* The wire report I mention was picked up by numerous papers on March 14, among them the *State* (Columbia, SC), *Tampa Tribune, Chattanooga Daily Times, Knoxville Sentinel, Wilmington* (NC) *Morning Star,* and *Tennessean* (Nashville).

34 *It was no secret:* The Persons case was described in "U.S. May Probe Negroes' Death," *Macon News*, March 19, 1921, 1. For more on the lynching of Eugene Hamilton, see "Convicted Negro Slain By Mob of Jasper Countians," *Macon Telegraph*, Oct. 8, 1919, 1; "Jasper Sheriff Probes Lynching," *Macon News*, Oct. 8, 1919, 1; and "Dorsey to Take Action Against Lynchers of Hamilton in Jasper," *Macon Telegraph*, Oct. 9, 1919, 1.

35 *Agents Wismer and Brown:* "Sensations Seen in Federal Probe of Peonage Here," *AC*, March 19, 1921, 1; and "Plans to Put Williams On Trial on Thursday Defeated by Defense," *AC*, March 29, 1921, 1.

36 *The agents' concerns:* Campbell described the exchange in Marion Kendrick, "Bodies Dragged Chained Together from Wet Grave," *AC*, March 28, 1921, 1; Brown testified that the agents visited Campbell "before and after" their visit to the plantation, Williams BOE, DOJ Files.

36 *Governor Dorsey:* The quote is from the Bureau's 1932 summary, FBI File.

37 *Meanwhile, business leaders:* The petition and Dorsey's reward are reported in "Mystery Shrouds Identity of Drowned Negros," *Covington News*, March 17.

37 *The development was overshadowed:* The discovery at Mann's Bridge was detailed in ibid.; "Body of Negro Chained to Rocks Found in River," *Macon News*, March 18, 1921, 1; and "Body of Third Negro Is Found Chained in River," *AC*, March 18, 1921, 12. See also "Drowned Man Was on Newton Side River," *Jackson Progress-Argus*, March 25, 1921, 8.

37 *Except, perhaps:* "Body of Third Negro Is Found Chained in River," *AC*, March 18.

38 *This body, like:* That the agents overlooked the detail about the dead men's shoes is suggested in the Bureau's 1932 summary, which makes the point that they learned of that detail during Eberhardt Crawford's visit. At the least, they didn't react to the information until then.

38 *The Justice Department official:* Alexander's remarks and the dustup that followed were reported in "U.S. May Probe Negroes' Death," *Macon News*, March 19; "District Attorney Asked to Appear Before Newton County Grand Jury," *Savannah Morning News*, March 21, 1921, 1; "Sensations Seen in Federal Probe of Peonage Here," *AC*, March 19; and "Urges Protection of Negroes Here," *AC*, March 20, 1921, 6. See also "Serious Charges Made Against Ku Klux Klan," *Macon News*, March 22, 1921, 10.

38 *Meanwhile, Sheriff Johnson:* The shoot-out tip was detailed in "Sensations Seen in Federal Probe of Peonage Here," *AC*, March 19. Dorsey's KKK tip was reported in "Serious Charges Made Against Ku Klux Klan," *Macon News*, March 22.

38 *It arrived in much:* My description of Crawford's visit in this and the following paragraphs was informed by the 1932 case summary, FBI File. It was reported in general terms in "Mystery Murder Witness Is Found," *AC*, March 24, 1921, 12.

39 *It was an innocent comment:* The Bureau's commentary is from its 1932 case summary, FBI File.

39 *Crawford offered another:* See the first note for page 38.

40 *The press caught wind:* The stories I quote are "Mystery Murder Witness Is Found," *AC*, March 24; and "Drastic Action in Defense of Negroes," *Savannah Morning News*, March 23, 1921.

Chapter 6

41 *Eight years before:* The Frank case has been the subject of intense scrutiny for more than a century, and has been the subject of books and articles of varying quality. Readers seeking to dive deeper into the affair would do well to start with Steve Oney's *And the Dead Shall Rise: The Murder of Mary Phagan and the Lynching of Leo Frank* (New York: Vintage, 2004), which offers the most complete and evenhanded account of the affair that I've encountered; Oney even names those in the lynching party.

Other summaries can be found in Jeffrey Melnick, "'The Night Witch Did It': Villainy and Narrative in the Leo Frank Case," *American Literary History* 12, nos. 1/2 (Spring–Summer 2000): 113–29; Stephen J. Goldfarb, "The Slaton Memorandum: A Governor Looks Back at His Decision to Commute the Death Sentence of Leo Frank," *American Jewish History* 88, no. 3 (September 2000): 235–339; and Nancy MacLean, "The Leo

Frank Case Reconsidered: Gender and Sexual Politics in the Making of Reactionary Populism," *Journal of American History* 78, no. 3 (December 1991): 917–48.

41 *"If Leo Frank"*: The quote is from Frank defense attorney Reuben Arnold, during a hearing on Frank's petition for a new trial. See Oney, *And the Dead Shall Rise*, 359.

41 *Dorsey was born*: The most complete scholarship into Hugh Dorsey's life and career, to date—in truth, the only real scholarship—can be found in Robert W. Thurston's *Lynching: American Mob Murder in Global Perspective* (Farnham, England: Ashgate Publishing Ltd., 2011). The chapters Thurston devotes to the governor are surprisingly lush, given the paucity of records held by the Georgia Archives and other depositories. I highly recommend the book, which also frames lynching in contrarian and thought-provoking style.

42 *He continued his*: Ibid. Dorsey's sideline activities were reported frequently in the Atlanta papers. See, for example, "Hugh Dorsey Was Orator," brief, *AC*, April 27, 1901, 2; "Parker Club Formed by Fulton Democrats," *AC*, March 13, 1904, 7; and "Hugh Dorsey Won't Run For the Senate," *AC*, July 22, 1910, 5.

42 *In short, Hugh Dorsey*: Dorsey's appointment was reported in "Solicitor's Place Is Sought by Many," *AC*, Oct. 25, 1910, 14; and "Hugh Dorsey Made Solicitor Fulton Court," *AC*, Oct. 26, 1910, 1. The latter story underlines just how small a legal community Atlanta was at the time: it notes that among Dorsey's examiners when he sat for the bar was Judge Leonard Roan, who was destined to preside over the Frank case.

Dorsey's reelection to the post was covered in "Hugh M. Dorsey Announces Candidacy for Solicitor," *AC*, July 21, 1912, 10; and "Solicitor Hugh Dorsey Praised by *Atlantan*," *AC*, Sept. 2, 1912, 7.

42 *But however adept*: The Grace case earned prominent headlines for months, in and out of Atlanta. See, for example, "Mrs. Daisy Grace Is Rearrested on Shooting Charge," *Daily Press* (Newport News, VA), March 8, 1912, 1; "Birth of Child May Complicate Mrs. Grace Case," *AC*, May 7, 1912, 1; "'She's a D—n Liar,' Hisses Eugene Grace as Wife Charges He Squandered Her Money and Attempted to Murder Her," *AC*, Aug. 2, 1912, 1; and "Mrs. Daisy Opie Grace Given Liberty By Jury Verdict; 'Thank God, My Name Is Freed from Stigma,' She Cries," *AC*, Aug. 3, 1912, 1. See also "Solicitor Hugh Dorsey is Highly Praised for His Strong Speech in the Grace Case," *AC*, Aug. 3, 1912, 1.

43 *Not long after*: The Appelbaum case was covered with gusto. See "Wives and Sweethearts Galore, Had Appelbaum Who Was Shot to Death," *AC*, Feb. 26, 1913, 1; "Appelbaum Trial Is Halted When Prisoner Faints," *AC*, April 25, 1913, 1; and "Mrs. J. A. Appelbaum Acquitted of Charge of Husband's Murder," *AC*, April 26, 1913, 1.

43 *So much has been written*: In this and the succeeding paragraphs, I was informed by Oney, *And the Dead Shall Rise*; Thurston, *Lynching*; Melnick, "'The Night Witch Did It'"; and MacLean, "The Leo Frank Case Reconsidered"; see also Douglas O. Linder's "Famous Trials" entry on the case, at https://www.famous-trials.com/leo-frank/27-home (accessed Feb. 25, 2023).

46 *Finally came Dorsey's*: For more on Dorsey's closing argument, see "As Bells Tolled, Dorsey Closed Magnificent Argument Which Fastened Crime on Frank," *AC*, Aug. 26, 1913, 2; and Sidney Ormand, "Hugh Dorsey's Great Speech Feature of Frank Trial," *AC*, Aug. 27, 1913, 2. The entire speech, published as a book in 1914 by N. Christophulos of Macon, GA, can be found at https://www.leofrank.org/library/arguments-of-hugh-dorsey-in-leo-frank-case.pdf (accessed Feb. 25, 2023).

46 *The jury was out*: For my account of the verdict, I relied on Oney, *And the Dead Shall Rise*; and "Frank Convicted, Asserts Innocence," *AC*, Aug. 26, 1913, 1. The quote is from the latter.

46 *The next day*: See "Frank Sentenced on Murder Charge to Hang Oct. 10," *AC*, Aug. 27, 1912, 1.

47 *The defendant immediately*: For a detailed account of Frank's appeals, see Oney, *And the Dead Shall Rise*. The quotes from Frank's attorney are from *The Trial of Leo Frank: Reuben R. Arnold's Address to the Court in His Behalf* (Baxley, GA: Classic Publishing Co., 1915). For purported accounts of Frank's state of mind, see "Frank Plans New Fight for Life," *AG*, Feb. 18, 1914, 1; and "How I Feel in Shadow of Gallows! Leo Frank Bares Soul," *Sunday American* [*AG*], March 1, 1914, 1.

47 *A sharp-eyed lawyer*: The *Journal's* editorial appeared under the headline "Frank Should Have a New Trial" in the edition of March 10, 1914.

48 *Ah, but the editorial*: Here and throughout my discussion of Watson, my primary source was C. Vann Woodward, *Tom Watson: Agrarian Rebel* (New York: Oxford University Press,

1963). I think the book cuts its subject far too much slack, but it's the most complete treatment of Watson yet published. The "blast" quote is from "The Frank Case: When and Where Shall Rich Criminals Be Tried?," *Jeffersonian*, March 19, 1914, 1.

48 *Watson opened a sustained:* The "pure little Gentile" quote is from "The Frank Case Brings in Another Horse—A Smaller One Than Usual," *Jeffersonian*, Oct. 15, 1914, 1. The "Frank's rich connections" warning is from "The Leo Frank Case Still Raging in Northern Papers," *Jeffersonian*, March 25, 1915, 1. The "fearless, honest" and "dignified, thorough" quotes are from "The Doleful Downfall of Hugh Dorsey!," *Jeffersonian*, Aug. 6, 1914, 11. "The sort of Georgian" is from "Nobody Wants To Drag the Frank Case Into Politics. But—," *Jeffersonian*, June 11, 1914, 1.

48 *"Honor to Hugh Dorsey!":* The quote is from "The Leo Frank Case," *Watson's Magazine*, January 1915, 139–64.

48 *Frank's appeals:* Judge Roan's quote is from Gov. John Slaton's commutation of Frank's sentence, available at https://vault.georgiaarchives.org/digital/collection/frankclem/id/44/rec/2 (accessed Feb. 25, 2023). For details of the closing rounds of Frank's appeals, see Oney, *And the Dead Shall Rise*. For more on the Prison Commission's action, see Frank's "Application for Executive Clemency," available from the Georgia Archives at https://vault.georgiaarchives.org/digital/collection/frankclem/id/13/rec/1 (accessed Feb. 25, 2023); "That Leo Frank Should Be Hanged Is the Prison Commission's Decision," *Macon News*, June 9, 1915, 1; "Frank Decision to Be Made Public Today," *AC*, June 9, 1915, 1; and "Case of Leo Frank Is Up to Governor for Final Decision," *AC*, June 10, 1915, 1.

49 *But Governor John M. Slaton:* The remarkable hearing in the governor's office was described in Oney, *And the Dead Shall Rise;* "Governor Hears Plea for Mercy Made for Frank," *Macon News*, June 12, 1915, 1; "Slaton to Spend Today in Study of Frank Appeal," *AC*, June 13, 1915, 1; "Slaton Expected to Inspect Scene of Murder Today," *AC*, June 14, 1915, 1; "Dorsey Claims Frank Guilty of Phagan Murder," *Macon News*, June 14, 1915, 1; "Howard to Finish Appeal for Frank Early Wednesday," *AC*, June 15, 1915, 1; and "Frank Hearing to Be Concluded This Afternoon," *Macon News*, June 16, 1915, 1.

Dorsey's lengthy speech is preserved in his meager collection of papers at the Atlanta History Center.

Slaton's commutation is available online, as noted above. See also Goldfarb, "The Slaton Memorandum"; "Frank's Sentence Is Commuted by Slaton," *AC*, June 21, 1915, 1; and "Governor J. M. Slaton Explains Why He at Last Determined to Commute Frank's Sentence," *Macon News*, June 21, 1915, 1.

49 *The news did not go down:* The violent public reaction is described in Oney, *And the Dead Shall Rise;* "State Capital Wildly Excited Over Frank Case," *Macon News*, June 21, 1915, 1; "Frank Starts Prison Work; Noisy Crowd at Governor's Home Dispersed by Militia," *AC*, June 22, 1915, 1; "Atlanta Quiet After Frank Stir," *AG*, June 23, 1915, 1; and "Excitement Continues," *Alexandria Gazette*, June 24, 1915, 1.

49 *Slaton explained:* Slaton made the remarks in a speech marking Gov. Nathaniel E. Harris's inauguration. See Oney, *And the Dead Shall Rise*.

49 *His critics were unswayed:* Harris offered a fascinating account of the pipe attack in his *Autobiography: The Story of an Old Man's Life, with Reminiscences of Seventy-five Years* (Macon, GA: J. W. Burke Company, 1925). See also "26 Men Arrested Near Slaton Home," *Macon News*, June 29, 1915, 1; and "Leo Frank," *New Republic*, July 24, 1915, 300, which declared, all too presciently: "Leaving out Governor Slaton, who risked his future and his life to uphold a civilization better than Georgia has yet attained, the treatment of Frank was one prolonged lynching."

49 *Tom Watson's reaction:* The quote is from "The Old Paths—and the New Path Taken By the Frank Case," *Jeffersonian*, June 24, 1915.

50 *If the system:* The quote is from "Do the Jew Business Men Want to Provoke Us Into a General Boycott?," *Jeffersonian*, Aug. 12, 1915, 9.

50 *A few days later:* For more on the lynching, see Oney, *And the Dead Shall Rise;* "Posses Chase Frank Mob," *AC*, Aug. 17, 1915, 1; "Harris to Head Probe of Mob," *AG*, Aug. 17, 1915, 1; "Great Throngs Assemble at Marietta," *AG*, Aug. 17, 1915, 2; and "Mob's Own Story in Detail," *AC*, Aug. 18, 1915, 1.

50 *A thousand or more:* The quote is from "Harris to Head Probe of Mob," *AG*, Aug. 17.

Chapter 7

51 *Hugh Dorsey revealed:* The first quote is from "Governor Probes Negroes' Death," *Macon News*, March 22, 1921, 1. The second quote, continuing in the next paragraph, is from "Mystery Murder Witness Is Found," *AC*, March 24.

51 *Eager to make good:* "Drastic Action in Defense of Negroes," *Savannah Morning News*, March 23. For more on the Commission, see William E. Cole, "The Role of the Commission on Interracial Cooperation in War and Peace," *Social Forces* 21, no. 4 (May 1943): 456–63; and Edward Flud Burrows, "The Commission on Interracial Cooperation, 1919–1944: A Case Study in the History of the Interracial Movement in the South" (doctoral dissertation, University of Wisconsin, 1954). Wilmer's advocacy on Frank's behalf are described in "Ministers Aid Frank: Organization Formed at Atlanta to Urge Commutation," *NYT*, May 24, 1915, 8; and MacLean, "The Leo Frank Case Reconsidered."

52 *The other citizens:* This and the balance of the chapter draw from the Bureau of Investigation's 1932 case summary, FBI File.

55 *Evening settled:* Johnson described the condition of the bodies in his testimony at Williams's trial. See his cross-examination by Greene Johnson, Williams BOE, DOJ Files.

56 *As a matter of fact, Sheriff Johnson:* My characterization of the interrogation draws from Johnson's testimony at trial. See Williams BOE, Manning BOE, and the transcript of Manning's second trial.

Chapter 8

57 *Whatever the agents:* This chapter relies, in its entirety, on the 1932 case summary, with additional sources as noted.

60 *Manning knew little:* The 1920 census was invaluable in establishing who among the plantation's peons had been there for more than a few months, and which of the properties they lived on. I chose to access the census (and the peons' death certificates, which was often the only other documentation I could find) via FamilySearch, a genealogical search engine offered to the public without charge by the Church of Jesus Christ of Latter-day Saints, at familysearch.org. I found it a touch less user-friendly than Ancestry.com, but also found that it sometimes yielded more information.

61 *As the session continued:* My account of Johnnie Williams's murder relied on Manning's confession to the agents and the Williams BOE, DOJ Files.

62 *Artis Freeman really had:* In his many tellings of the triple murder of that Saturday night, Manning consistently said that Williams pulled the car over halfway between Polk's store and the Waters Bridge. The fact that he put it that way—with the store named first—led me to believe that Polk's was somewhere on what's now Georgia Route 212 in Jasper County, not far from the Williams home place, and that one would reach it well before reaching the bridge. I could find no mention of the store in any Jasper County records, however, or anyone who recalled it on that stretch of highway. Eventually, I realized I was looking in the wrong county—that Manning listed it and the bridge out of order, and that the store was in Newton, some distance beyond the crossing. I interviewed Johnny Potts, the recently retired owner of the Potts store at Newton (established before World War II), who recalled it well and directed me to its precise location: on the west side of Route 36 about a half-mile south of the fork, and roughly one hundred yards past the highway's intersection with Campbell Road. This might seem trivial, but it clarifies that Williams pulled the car over between the bridge and Stewart.

64 *This, after all, was:* Williams's role in his church congregation was described by his pastor, James J. Winburn, in "Thorough Probe Is Wanted by Citizens, Says Minister," *Monticello News*, April 8, 1921, 1. Mention of the Williams sons' wartime service is ibid.; see also "Trial of Williams Begins Tuesday," *Covington News*, March 31. The twelve Williams children are listed in various censuses (the 1900 and 1910 editions for the older siblings, the 1920 for the younger).

For the record, here are the twelve, from oldest to youngest, and their ages on March 13, 1921, the date of the discovery at Allen's Bridge: William Augustus, or "Gus," 30; John Hulon, 28; LeRoy Lane, 25; Marvin Harris, 22; Mary Surfronia, 20; Ivah Sue, 17; James Luke, 15; Lucy Claire, 11; Julian Sims, 10; Curtis Compton, 7; Robert Wheeler, 5; and Edward Dozier, 2.

65 *He was a successful:* Press reports typically pegged Williams's holdings at 2,000 acres (see, for example, "Jackson County Farm Was Veritable Slaughter Pen," *Jackson Progress-Argus,* April 1, 1921, 1); some put it as high as 4,000 acres (e.g., "Fresh Evidence Is Given Jasper Jury; More Bills Found," *AJ,* April 12, 1921, 1). My exploration of the deed books at the Jasper County Courthouse indicated he actually owned 325 acres at the home place and 750 at the river tracts; he might have owned an additional thirty acres adjacent to the home place (see notes for p. 11) and leased some other lakeside property.

Part Two: The Murder Farm

Chapter 9

69 *The vast majority of Americans:* The Richmond quote is from "Lynched!," editorial, *Richmond Times-Dispatch,* Aug. 18, 1915, 6. The Louisville charge is from "Will Georgia Stand For It?," editorial, *Louisville Courier-Journal,* Aug. 18, 1915, 4. The *Birmingham News* quote is from "The Murder of Frank; An Unprecedented Horror," editorial, Aug. 17, 1915, 4.

69 *The New York Age:* The quote is from none other than James Weldon Johnson (whom I did not identify only because I've yet to introduce him) in "Once More Georgia," Views and Reviews, *Age,* Aug. 26, 1915, 4.

69 *Outrage ran high:* Harris made his comment in "Harris to Head Probe of Mob," *AG,* Aug. 17. Slaton's quote is from "Mob Hanging Better than Judicial Murder Says John M. Slaton," *AC,* Aug. 18, 1915, 1. The Watson quote is from a front-page brief in the *Jeffersonian* of Aug. 26, 1915.

70 *And in that response:* Thurston discusses Dorsey's pilgrimage to Hickory Hill in *Lynching.* Dorsey's resignation, dated June 24, 1916, and effective on July 1, is preserved in the Georgia Archives.

70 *His platform consisted:* See Britt Craig, "Dorsey's Plea for Courts Attracts Great Following," *AC,* July 18, 1916, 1.

70 *While hardly a racial:* For a thorough discussion of Dorsey's upbringing and influences, see Thurston, *Lynching.* The Northen quote is ibid. See also T. J. Woofter Jr., "Progress in Race Relations in Georgia," *Advocate of Peace through Justice* 85, no. 8 (August 1923): 297–302.

71 *That would have been hard:* Ibid.

71 *Beyond that, Dorsey:* Ibid. For more on the 1906 riot, see Dominic J. Capeci Jr. and Jack C. Knight, "Reckoning with Violence: W. E. B. Du Bois and the 1906 Atlanta Race Riot," *Journal of Southern History* 62, no. 4 (November 1996): 727–66. See also Oney, *And The Dead Shall Rise;* and Walter F. White, *A Man Called White: The Autobiography of Walter White* (Athens, GA: University of Georgia Press, 1995).

71 *So Dorsey knew better:* Watson's quote is from "Notes on Georgia Politics," *Jeffersonian,* Aug. 24, 1916, 6.

72 *That resonated:* The quote is from Britt Craig, "Hugh M. Dorsey, on the Stump, Is Making the Voters Think," *AC,* July 20, 1916, 1. See also "In Ringing Speech, Hugh Dorsey Nails Unfounded Charge," *AC,* July 28, 1916, 1.

72 *The masses didn't seem:* The quote and letter are contained in Britt Craig, "Slush Fund to Debauch Politics of the State Is Charged to Conspiracy," *AC,* Sept. 1, 1916, 1.

73 *Dorsey insisted:* Dorsey's comments are ibid. Slaton's response is from his letter to the editor, headlined "The Georgia Campaign," in the *NYT* of Sept. 16, 1916.

Chapter 10

74 *March 24, 1921:* The scene at the bridges is drawn from the 1932 Bureau summary, FBI File.

74 *Up in Atlanta:* The letter was quoted in "Dorsey Urges Constabulary," *AG,* March 24, 1921 ("Jasper Peonage Clippings" file, Box I:C388, NAACP Papers).

74 *The signature of one:* Williams's testimony was described in "Plans to Put Williams On Trial on Thursday Defeated by Defense," *AC,* March 29, 1.

75 *He begged the grand jury:* Ibid.

75 *The rest of the world:* The *NYT* story, headlined "Eleven Negroes Slain; White Farmer Accused," appeared on page 3 of the March 25, 1921 edition.

75 *The story took fuller:* Manning's jailhouse interview was reported in "Williams Taken to Fulton County Tower Following Confession of Negro Laborer," *Savannah Morning News*, March 26, 1921, 1.

76 *To the* Atlanta Georgian: "Peonage Case Toll Expected to be Fifteen," *AG*, March 27, 1921, 1.

76 *The Georgian's reporter:* Ibid.

77 *Williams, meanwhile:* The Leverett tale is quoted in "Accused Man Held Prisoner in Fulton Jail," *AG*, March 26, 1921, 8; and "'Frame-up,' Says Williams," *NYT*, March 27, 1921.

Incidentally, the record is unclear on the spelling of Leverett's surname—many sources list it with an "e" on the end. Census records are inconsistent. Some documents spell it both ways within a few paragraphs. I've gone with the simpler.

78 *In conversation with:* "Williams Denies He Ordered Death of His Employees," *AC*, March 26, 1921, 1.

78 *Asked about:* "Peonage Case Toll Expected to be Fifteen," *AG*, March 27.

78 *That same afternoon:* The meeting in Dorsey's office is described in the Bureau's 1932 case summary, and mentioned in "Williams Denies He Ordered Death of His Employees," *AC*, March 26; and "Tells How He Killed Five Negroes and Helped to Drown Six Others," *Macon News*, March 25, 1921, 1.

78 *Dorsey suggested:* The trip to Jasper was recounted in "Will Call Special Grand Jury," *Macon Telegraph*, March 27, 1921, 1.

78 *Newspapers reported:* The national guard's readiness was reported in Marion Kendrick, "Rivers and Graves Give Up Negro Bodies," *AC*, March 27, 1921, 1. Manning's quote on the bridge is from "Find Nine Bodies in Georgia Peonage Murder Inquiry," *NYT*, March 27, 1921, 1.

79 *They left a few:* The party's arrival was described in "Negro Digs Up Six Men He Says He Killed," *Macon Telegraph*, March 27, 1921, 1. The "gourd" quote is from "Will Call Special Grand Jury," *Macon Telegraph*, March 27. The scene in the pasture is from the *Telegraph's* "Negro Digs Up Six Men He Says He Killed." The *AC* quote is from "Rivers and Graves Give Up Negro Bodies," March 27.

79 *As the posse exhumed:* The Manning quote is from the *NYT's* "Find Nine Bodies in Georgia Peonage Murder Inquiry," and the *Telegraph's* "Negro Digs Up Six Men He Says He Killed," both of March 27. Wismer described viewing Johnnie Williams's body in his testimony at the Williams trial; see Williams BOE, DOJ Files. The *AC* quote is from "Rivers and Graves Give Up Negro Bodies," March 27.

79 *Once Manning identified:* The events at the river tracts are described in the Bureau's 1932 case summary and in "Rivers and Graves Give Up Negro Bodies," *AC*, March 27.

80 *Fletcher Smith:* Manning's quotes are from the 1932 case summary.

80 *Sheriff Johnson confirmed:* Johnson's quote is from "Will Call Special Grand Jury," *Macon Telegraph*, March 27.

81 *"Now, boss":* The quote is from "Find Nine Bodies in Georgia Peonage Murder Inquiry," *NYT*, March 27. The frenzy in Monticello is described in "Negro Digs Up Six Men He Says He Killed," *Macon Telegraph*, March 27.

81 *At the Waters Bridge:* The recovery efforts in the Alcovy were described in the *Telegraph's* "Negro Digs Up Six Men He Says He Killed," and the *AC's* "Rivers and Graves Give Up Negro Bodies," both March 27.

81 *The recovered body:* The quote is from "Find Nine Bodies in Georgia Peonage Murder Inquiry," *NYT*, March 27.

81 *Sheriff Johnson called a halt:* The quote is from the *Telegraph's* "Will Call Special Grand Jury," March 27.

Chapter 11

82 *But the forty-year-old:* Campbell's dealings with Williams were explored in "Jury Holds Farmer and Negro Hand," *AG*, March 28, 1921, 1; the *AC's* "Rivers and Graves Give Up Negro Bodies," March 27; Marion Kendrick, "Alleged Plot to Incite Whites Against Negroes Laid to Williams' Sons," *AC*, March 31, 1921, 2; and Marion Kendrick, "Bodies Dragged Chained Together from Wet Grave," *AC*, March 28. The quote is from the last.

82 *Truth was, though:* Dorsey's warrant and Judge Park's refusal to honor it were explored in "Rivers and Graves Give Up Negro Bodies," *AC*, March 27; "Jury Holds Farmer and Negro Hand," *AG*, March 28; and "Justice J. B. Park Issues Statement," *Monticello News*, April 1, 1921, 1.

83 *That ran counter*: Dorsey's letter to the attorney general, and Graham Wright's response, are part of the Governor's Incoming Correspondence file, DOC 3133, Georgia Archives.

83 *To the newspapers*: See "Justice J. B. Park Issues Statement," *Monticello News*, April 1.

83 *Prosecutor Campbell*: The quotes are from the *AC*'s "Bodies Dragged Chained Together from Wet Grave," March 28.

84 *Early that Easter*: Ibid.

84 *For five hours*: Ibid.

84 *A few miles away*: Ibid, and "Jury Holds Farmer and Negro Hand," *AG*, March 28.

85 *When the jury finished*: See the *AC*'s "Bodies Dragged Chained Together from Wet Grave," March 28; and "Developments in Peonage Case," March 28.

85 *And a new chapter*: The *Kansas City Star* quote is from "Seek Ten More 'Slave' Victims," March 28, 1921, 1.

86 *The case laid bare*: The stories cited are "Barbarous Butchery Demands Relentless Punishment," editorial, *Cincinnati Commercial Tribune*, misdated; and "Georgia Peonage Horror Rivals Turk Atrocities," *Knoxville Sentinel*, March 28, 1921 (both from "Jasper Peonage Clippings" file, Box I:C388, NAACP Papers).

86 *Georgia's newspapers*: The first quote is from "A Job For the Courts!," editorial, *AC*, March 28, 1921, 4. James B. Nevin's quote is from "Caught in the Current," column, *AG*, March 31, 1921.

86 *"It hurts us to think"*: "The Jasper Disgrace," editorial, *Macon Telegraph*, March 26, 1921, 4.

86 *"The fact that the men"*: "For Right and Georgia's Name," editorial, *Savannah Morning News*, March 27, 1921.

Chapter 12

88 *If he wasn't aware*: The best place to start exploring the accomplishments of the amazing James Weldon Johnson is probably his memoir, *Along This Way: The Autobiography of James Weldon Johnson* (New York: Viking Penguin, 1933). See also Lynn Adelman, "A Study of James Weldon Johnson," *Journal of Negro History* 52, no. 2 (April 1967): 128–45; and "James Weldon Johnson: A Chronology," *Langston Hughes Review* 8, nos. 1/2 (Spring/Fall 1989): 1–3.

88 *Later in Johnson's life*: Robert Wohlforth, "Dark Leader," *New Yorker*, Sept. 30, 1933.

89 *That Easter Monday*: Johnson telegram to George Towns of Atlanta University, March 28, 1921 ("Peonage, Jasper County, Ga., March 29–April 7, 1921" file, Box I:C388, NAACP Papers). Johnson's telegrams to the officials were reported in "Efforts to Cause Race Trouble Fail While Plans Are Made to Try Planter," *Savannah Morning News*, March 29, 1921, 1.

90 *"I assure you"*: Dorsey's reply was quoted in "Georgia Governor Promises Punishment of Peonage," NAACP press release, April 2, 1921 ("Peonage, Jasper County, Ga., March 29-April 7, 1921" file, Box I:C388, NAACP Papers). See also Hastings H. Hart, "Peonage and the Public," *The Survey*, April 9, 1921, 43. The *Macon Telegraph* waved off Dorsey's reply as much ado about nothing, judging in an editorial ("Convict Laws," April 5, 1921) that he sent it "out of Southern courtesy and to avoid an incorrect impression."

90 *Johnson's biography*: See Johnson, *Along This Way*; Adelman, "A Study of James Weldon Johnson"; and Clarence A. Bacote, "James Weldon Johnson and Atlanta University," *Phylon* 32, no. 4 (Fourth Qtr., 1971): 333–43.

90 *Graduating in 1894*: Ibid.

91 *His school duties failed*: Johnson, *Along This Way*.

91 *Undaunted, Johnson*: Ibid., and Wohlforth, "Dark Leader."

91 *He did not practice*: Ibid.; and James Robert Saunders, "The Dilemma of Double Identity: James Weldon Johnson's Artistic Acknowledgement," *Langston Hughes Review* 8, nos. 1/2 (Spring/Fall 1989): 68–75.

91 *Back running his school*: Ibid.; Adelman, "A Study of James Weldon Johnson"; and Imani Perry, "School Bell Song: 'Lift Every Voice and Sing' in the Lives of Children in the Segregated South," *May We Forever Stand: A History of the Black National Anthem* (Chapel Hill: University of North Carolina Press, 2018).

92 *But "Lift Every Voice"*: The quote is from Johnson, *Along This Way*.

92 *Returning to New York*: Ibid.

92 *In 1904, while accepting*: Ibid.

93 *Easier to like*: Ibid.; Johnson found Du Bois "abundantly endowed with the gift of laughter," but acknowledged his reputation. See also Claude McKay, *A Long Way From Home*, as excerpted in David Levering Lewis, ed., *The Portable Harlem Renaissance Reader* (New York:

Penguin Books, 1994); and Charles S. Johnson, "The Negro Renaissance and Its Significance," in the same anthology. By the way, if you've not read *The Souls of Black Folk*, you owe it to yourself to get busy.

93 *Du Bois considered him:* Ibid.

93 *Their differences:* The NAACP's creation was described in Mary White Ovington, "The National Association for the Advancement of Colored People," *Journal of Negro History* 9, no. 2 (April 1924): 107–16; and William F. Pinar, "The NAACP and the Struggle for Antilynching Legislation, 1897–1917," *Counterpoints* 163 (2001): 623–82.

93 *But first, in that summer:* Johnson describes his foreign service career in *Along This Way*; see also Adelman, "A Study of James Weldon Johnson."

94 *Johnson was promised:* My passages on Johnson's arrival and work at the *New York Age* were informed by his own writing in *Along This Way*; by Sondra K. Wilson, in the book's introduction; and in Fred R. Moore, "Our New Acquisition," *Age*, Oct. 15, 1914, 4.

94 *Taken together:* The quote is from Wilson, introduction, *Along This Way*.

94 *Johnson campaigned:* The first quote, re Wilson, is from "Negro Democraes [sic] and President Wilson," Views and Reviews, *Age*, Sept. 7, 1916, 4. The second quote is from "The Reason and the Remedy," Views and Reviews, *Age*, Aug. 24, 1916, 4.

95 *Georgia consistently:* The quote is from "Tom Watson, Apostle of Prejudice," Views and Reviews, *Age*, Sept. 2, 1915, 4.

95 *Alongside Du Bois's:* The Du Bois quote is from his "Criteria of Negro Art," in Lewis, *The Portable Harlem Renaissance Reader*. The Johnson quote is from the introduction of the same volume.

96 *It so happened:* Johnson, *Along This Way*. See also Bernard Eisenberg, "Only for the Bourgeois? James Weldon Johnson and the NAACP, 1916–1930," *Phylon* 43, no. 2 (Second Qtr., 1982): 110–24.

96 *And so James Weldon Johnson:* Johnson, *Along This Way*.

96 *That was partly:* Ibid.

96 *Besides expansion:* Ibid., and Eisenberg, "Only for the Bourgeois?"

97 *The new Atlanta branch:* Johnson, *Along This Way*. For an exploration of the branch's activities prior to Johnson's arrival, see "Walter White and the Atlanta NAACP's Fight for Equal Schools, 1916–1917," *History of Education Quarterly* 7, no. 1 (Spring 1967): 3–21.

97 *Shortly after Johnson:* Ibid.

97 *Detectives disinterred:* The newspaper is quoted in "The Lynching at Memphis," *The Crisis*, August 1917, 185–86.

97 *In an all-too-common:* Johnson, *Along This Way*. His report appeared in the August 1917 issue of *The Crisis*, pages 185–88.

98 *The Association did not:* Ibid.; "The Riot in East St. Louis," *The Crisis*, August 1917, 175–78; "The Massacre of East St. Louis," *The Crisis*, September 1917, 219–38; Edgar A. Schuler, "Race Riots During and After the First World War," *Negro History Bulletin* 7, no. 7 (April 1944): 155–56.

98 *While Du Bois investigated:* Johnson, *Along This Way*; "The Negro Silent Parade," *The Crisis*, September 1917, 241.

98 *It was the largest:* Johnson wrote about the Houston affair in *Along This Way*. See also Schuler, "Race Riots During and After the First World War."

99 *All of which is to say:* Johnson, *Along This Way*; White, *A Man Called White*; A. J. Baime, *White Lies: The Double Life of Walter F. White and America's Darkest Secret* (New York: Mariner Books, 2022).

99 *Walter White's racial makeup:* The McKay quote is from his *A Long Way From Home*, as excerpted in *The Portable Harlem Renaissance Reader*. White's genetic makeup is noted in "Walter White, 61, Dies in Home Here," *NYT*, March 22, 1955, 30.

99 *He had always identified:* White, *A Man Called White*; Baime, *White Lies*.

99 *He first put his complexion:* Ibid. The quote is from White's autobiography.

100 *But it was his next:* My account of the violence in Brooks and Lowndes Counties was informed by Julie Buckner Armstrong, "'The people . . . took exception to her remarks': Meta Warrick Fuller, Angelina Weld Grimke, and the Lynching of Mary Turner," *Mississippi Quarterly* 61, nos. 1–2 (Winter–Spring 2008): 113–41; Christopher C. Meyers, "Killing Them by the Wholesale: A Lynching Rampage in South Georgia," *Georgia Historical Quarterly* 90, no. 2 (Summer 2006): 214–35; Walter F. White, "The Work of a Mob," *The Crisis*, September 1918, 221–23; Walter F. White, "I Investigate Lynchings," originally published in *American Mercury* and anthologized

in Sondra Kathryn Wilson, ed., *In Search of Democracy: The NAACP Writings of James Weldon Johnson, Walter White, and Roy Wilkins (1920–1977)* (New York and Oxford: Oxford University Press, 1999); and Walter F. White, memo to Governor Hugh Dorsey, July 10, 1918 (Box I:C337, NAACP Papers).

100 *The next victim:* The quoted story was "4 Negroes Strung Up Since Tragedy in Brooks County," *Macon Telegraph*, May 20, 1918, 1.

101 *Walter White arrived:* The quote is from White, "I Investigate Lynchings."

101 *From White's report:* White, "The Work of a Mob."

102 *In a story he wrote:* White, "I Investigate Lynchings."

102 *White found no evidence:* White, "The Work of a Mob"; White memo to Dorsey of July 10, 1918.

Chapter 13

104 *The new governor:* Dorsey's June 30, 1917, inaugural address was published by the Index Printing Company of Atlanta in 1917. His first *Governor's Message to the General Assembly of Georgia*, delivered on July 25, 1917—less than a month after his inaugural—was likewise published by Index. That speech is also detailed in Edgar A. Toppin, "Walter White and the Atlanta NAACP's Fight for Equal Schools, 1916–1917," *History of Education Quarterly* 7, no. 1 (Spring 1967): 3–21. He delivered his second "State of the State" on July 3, 1918; it, too, was published by Index.

104 *His meeting with White:* The quotes are from White's memo to Dorsey of July 10, 1918.

105 *White also named:* Ibid.

105 *Dorsey's reaction:* The quote is from White, "I Investigate Lynchings." Dorsey's rewards and declaration of martial law were covered in "Johnson Is Killed; Crisp Jail Stormed," *Macon Telegraph*, May 23, 1918, 1; see also "Governor Dorsey Hits Mob Rule," editorial, *Atlanta Independent*, May 25, 1918, 4.

106 *Alas, Dorsey's determination:* The Augusta group's resolution was included in "Negro Johnson Is Shot to Death," *Macon Telegraph*, May 23, 1918, 4. Dorsey's response was reported in "Gov. Dorsey Gives Anti-Lynching Doctrine," *Macon Telegraph*, May 24, 1918, 1.

107 *The essential point:* Letter from Shillady to Dorsey of Sept. 11, 1918, included in NAACP press release of Sept. 12, 1918 (DOC 3118, September 1918 file, Georgia Archives).

107 *Dorsey doubled down:* Dorsey letter to Shillady of Nov. 30, 1918 (Box I:C337, NAACP papers).

Chapter 14

108 *Dorsey wondered:* The Williams case, important though it was, has been repeatedly varnished over the years: I've read in seemingly respectable and well-researched publications, for example, that it marked the only time a white defendant was convicted of murdering a Black victim in Georgia between 1877 and 1966. I've even read that it was the only time a white man was *indicted* for such a crime during the same period. In fact, indictments did occur on rare occasion, and though the subsequent trials routinely ended in acquittals, there were exceptions. In Columbus, Georgia, for example, seven white men were convicted in the January 1901 home invasion and shooting death of Sterling Thompson, a Black man. Two of the seven were sentenced to life in prison, and all did time. For more, see "Law and Order Upheld by Citizens of Campbell; Blow Struck at Terrorists," *AC*, Aug. 10, 1901, 9; and "Seven Mob Leaders Sentenced to Pen," *AJ*, Aug. 8, 1901, 2.

108 *Dorsey conferred with:* The governor's study of options was detailed in "Williams' Sons Accused of Plotting to Cause Riots in Two Counties," *Macon News*, March 30, 1921, 1.

109 *While Dorsey pondered:* "Plans to Put Williams On Trial on Thursday Defeated by Defense," *AC*, March 29.

109 *If he misread:* Greene's track record was described in Hubert F. Baughn, "Attorney Howard Flays 'Death Farm' as a 'Plague Spot,'" *AJ*, April 8, 1921, 1. His stretch without a client locked up was lauded in Albert G. Foster, "Memorial of Greene F. Johnson," *Report of the Forty-first Annual Session of the Georgia Bar Association, May 29–31, 1924* (Macon, GA: J.W. Burke Co., 1924), 291–97.

109 *Although he had passed:* Williams's land transfers are recorded at the Jasper County Courthouse. See Deed Book U, pages 318–19.

110 *The transaction:* The mortgage against the river tracts was recorded in Deed Book U, page 225.

110 *On that same Easter:* The response to a supposed Black insurrection was reported in "Armed Men Rush to Peonage Murder Farm at Rumor of Intended Negro Reprisal," *NYT*,

March 29, 1921, 1; and "Efforts to Cause Race Trouble Fail While Plans Are Made to Try Planter," *Savannah Morning News*, March 29.

111 *Alerted to rumors:* The Black prayer meeting was reported in "Efforts to Cause Race Trouble Fail While Plans Are Made to Try Planter," *Savannah Morning News*, March 29; and Marion Kendrick, "Plans to Put Williams On Trial on Thursday Defeated by Defense," *AC*, March 29.

111 *That term shortchanges:* The "hoax" was outlined in "Jasper County Also Plans to Try Planters," *AG*, March 31, 1921, 1; and in Marion Kendrick, "Alleged Plot to Incite Whites Against Negroes Laid to Williams' Sons," *AC*, March 31.

111 *Called to testify:* Floyd Johnson's story, which unspools over the next several paragraphs, was contained in an affidavit he filed with the Newton County court clerk on March 30, 1921.

113 *The Williams brothers:* The *NYT* story was "Armed Men Rush to Peonage Murder Farm at Rumor of Intended Negro Reprisal," March 29; the notes were also reported in Marion Kendrick, "Peonage Conditions Given as the Cause of Killings," *AC*, March 28, 1921, 2. The plan to dispatch runners was explained in Marion Kendrick, "Alleged Plot to Incite Whites Against Negroes Laid to Williams' Sons," *AC*, March 31. The brothers' plan to stage raids was noted in "Williams' Sons Accused of Plotting to Cause Riots in Two Counties," *Macon News*, March 30; and "Negroes Flee as Whites Plot Peon Race War," *New York Call*, March 31, 1921 ("Jasper Peonage Clippings" file, Box I:C388, NAACP Papers).

113 *With Floyd Johnson's:* That the grand jury found the Williams brothers culpable was reported in "Georgia Governor Asks Early Trial of Planter and Negro for Peonage Murders," *NYT*, March 30, 1921.

113 *The family countered:* "Dr. Gus Williams Makes Statement," *Savannah Morning News*, March 31.

114 *While the Newton County:* "Asks Early Trial of Jasper Planter," *Savannah Morning News*, March 30, 1921, 1.

114 *The conference, which went on:* See "John Williams May Be Tried in Bibb County," *Macon News*, March 29, 1921, 1; and "New Witness in Jasper Case; Probe Goes On," *AG*, March 29, 1921. The "earliest possible moment" quote is from "Williams' Sons Accused of Plotting to Cause Riots in Two Counties," *Macon News*, March 30.

114 *That was no hyperbole:* "Asks Early Trial of Jasper Planter," *Savannah Morning News*, March 30; "April 11 Date Asked to Open Jasper Trial," *AG*, March 30, 1921, 1. The "governor is acting" quote is from "Williams' Sons Accused of Plotting to Cause Riots in Two Counties," *Macon News*, March 30.

115 *The News offered:* "Federal Agents Continue Probe of Peonage Case," *Macon News*, March 31, 1921, 1.

115 *That evening:* "Plan to Sever Cases and Force Williams to Trial in Newton County on April 4," *Savannah Morning News*, March 31, 1921, 1. See also "Georgia Joins Prosecution in Peon Murders," *New York Tribune*, March 30, 1921 ("Jasper Peonage Clippings" file, Box I:C388, NAACP Papers).

115 *Judge Hutcheson apparently:* Details of the judge's decision can be found in "Trial of Williams Begins Tuesday," *Covington News*, March 31. See also "U.S. Agents Raid Death Farm for Peon Witnesses," *New York Tribune*, March 31, 1921 ("Jasper Peonage Clippings" file, Box I:C388, NAACP Papers).

116 *Within hours:* The raid is discussed in "Trial of Williams Begins Tuesday," *Covington News*, March 31; and in Marion Kendrick, "Son of John Williams, Hero of Somme Retreat, Says Father Is Innocent," *AC*, March 31, 1921, 1.

116 *They brought the five:* "Protection for Manning Urged," *AG*, April 1, 1921, 1. The disrobing of the Black witnesses was reported in Marion Kendrick, "Planter Asserts Killing Was Done in Self-Defense," *AC*, April 3, 1921, 1.

116 *In New York:* The Association's letter-writing campaign is described in "Peonage," a brief in *The Crisis* of June 1921, page 68. Letters to several NAACP branches—including the April 1, 1921, letter to the Los Angeles branch—are available from the NAACP Papers ("Peonage, Jasper County, Ga., March 29-April 7" file, Box I:C388).

117 *To that end:* Ibid.

117 *Johnson also prepared:* The Association's letters to labor unions and legislators, and letters in reply, are in the "Peonage, Jasper County, Ga., March 29–April 7" file, Box I:C388, NAACP Papers. See also correspondence in Box I:C386 (Peonage, general).

117 *Newspaper reporters down:* Marion Kendrick, "Planter Asserts Killing Was Done in Self-Defense," *AC*, April 3.

117 *In her first comments:* Both quotes are from "Sure Her Husband Didn't Kill Blacks," *New York World*, April 1, 1921 ("Jasper Peonage Clippings" file, Box I:C388, NAACP Papers).

118 *Dr. Gus Williams:* "Son of John Williams, Hero of Somme Retreat, Says Father Is Innocent," *AC*, March 31.

118 *Had reporters inspected:* The *NYT* story was "Slain Negro Peons Dug Their Graves as Killer Watched," March 28, 1921, 1. Though unsupported, the number doesn't seem far-fetched, in retrospect. As Tim Pitts told me: "If you've done eighteen, there's not much of a line left for you to cross—between eighteen, and thirty-six, or whatever. It wouldn't surprise me if there are dozens more bodies on the property."

119 *The Savannah Morning News:* The quoted story was "Two More Negroes Found in River; Some of the Dead Dug Own Graves," *Savannah Morning News*, March 28, 1921, 1.

119 *The New York Call:* The quote is from "Alleged Slayer of Many Peons Whines in Cell," *New York Call*, March 29, 1921 ("Jasper Peonage Clippings" file, Box I:C388, NAACP Papers).

Chapter 15

120 *The NAACP had come far:* The membership numbers are from "The Battle of 1920 and Before," Eleventh Annual Report (abridged), *The Crisis*, March 1921.

120 *Shillady's most dramatic: Thirty Years of Lynching* is available from the Internet Archive at https://archive.org/details/thirtyyearsoflyn00nati (accessed March 20, 2023).

121 *The NAACP spread the news:* "The Battle of 1920 and Before," *The Crisis*, March 1921.

122 *"People used to say":* James Weldon Johnson speech to the NAACP Annual Meeting of January 3, 1923, included in Wilson, *In Search of Democracy*.

122 *That campaign grew:* Du Bois, "Returning Soldiers," *The Crisis*, May 1919. The essay is available online from *The American Yawp* at https://www.americanyawp.com/reader/21-world-war-i/w-e-b-dubois-returning-soldiers-may-1919/ (accessed March 20, 2023).

123 *All the while:* The best place to start for insight into the Great Migration is Isabel Wilkerson's remarkable *The Warmth of Other Suns: The Epic Story of America's Great Migration* (New York: Random House, 2010).

123 *Black migration had no less:* Alan D. DeSantis, "Selling the American Dream Myth to Black Southerners: The *Chicago Defender* and the Great Migration of 1915–1919," *Western Journal of Communication* 62, no. 4 (Fall 1998): 474–511.

124 *So tensions mounted:* Johnson's quote is from *Along This Way.*

124 *In early May:* The Charleston riot is described in Nic Butler, "The Charleston Riot of 1919," at https://www.ccpl.org/charleston-time-machine/charleston-riot-1919 (accessed March 20, 2023). The Texas riot was the subject of "The Riot at Longview, Texas," *The Crisis*, October 1919; and William M. Tuttle Jr., "Violence in a 'Heathen' Land: The Longview Race Riot of 1919," *Phylon* 33, no. 4 (Fourth Qtr. 1972): 324–33. The Washington riot is explored in Schuler, "Race Riots During and After the First World War." The Norfolk disturbance is detailed in "Riot Staged Upon Arrest of Negro Soldier," *Virginian-Pilot*, July 22, 1919, 1.

124 *At July's end:* For more on the Chicago riot, see Schuler, "Race Riots During and After the First World War"; and William M. Tuttle Jr., "Contested Neighborhoods and Racial Violence: Prelude to the Chicago Riot of 1919," *Journal of Negro History* 55, no. 4 (October 1970): 266–88.

124 *Then, in Omaha:* For reporting from the paper that reputedly fanned race hatred into the eventual riot, see "Omaha Mob Hangs and Burns Negro Who Assaulted Girl," *Omaha Daily Bee*, Sept. 29, 1919, 1. See also "U.S. Soldiers Guarding the City," *Evening World-Herald*, Sept. 29, 1919, 1; and, from the same Omaha paper, "Wood Asks Parade Called Off," Sept. 30, 1919, 1.

125 *As alarming as these:* The origins of the trouble in Phillips County are explained in "The Real Causes of Two Race Riots," *The Crisis*, December 1919, 56–62.

125 *In swooped Walter White:* White's exposé was "'Massacring Whites' in Arkansas," *The Nation*, Dec. 6, 1919.

126 *His time in Elaine:* White's close call is quoted from "I Investigate Lynchings."

126 *The Red Summer claimed:* Shillady's reasons for traveling to Austin were detailed in Johnson, *Along This Way*; Pinar, "The NAACP and the Struggle for Antilynching Legislation, 1897–1917"; NAACP Board of Directors Minutes, Aug. 26, 1919 (Box I:A1, NAACP Papers); and in *Mobbing of John R. Shillady*, a booklet published by the NAACP in October 1919 and available from the Internet Archive at https://archive.org/details/mobbingofjohnrsh00nati

(accessed March 2, 2023). The size of the NAACP's Texas membership is from James Weldon Johnson, "In Texas," Views and Reviews, *Age*, Aug. 30, 1919, 4.

127 *On arriving: Mobbing of John R. Shillady.* The secretary's failure to meet with high state officials was also reported in Pinar, "The NAACP and the Struggle for Antilynching Legislation, 1897–1917." See also "White Secretary Negro Society Chased Out of City," *Austin Statesman*, Aug. 22, 1919, 1, and Johnson, *Along This Way*.

127 *The next day:* Ibid. The quotes are from "Austin Beating Sends Shillady on North Trail," *Austin American*, Aug. 23, 1919, 1.

127 *Shocked and battered:* The response from Travis County Deputy Sheriff Gene Barbisch is ibid.

127 *Hobby's response:* The governor's answer to Ovington was reported in "White Negro Advancement Society Men Advised to Stay Out of Texas by Hobby," *Austin American*, Aug. 24, 1919, 1. His comments a few days later—in a September 4 speech in Fort Worth—were quoted in "Party Critics Are Scored by Hobby in Speech," *San Angelo Weekly Standard*, Sept. 5, 1919, 1.

128 *One of Houston's:* I'm referring to William P. Hobby Airport, otherwise known as HOU.

128 *"What democracy":* Johnson, "In Texas," *Age*, Aug. 30.

128 *Johnson met Shillady's:* Johnson, *Along This Way*.

128 *To Walter White:* White, *A Man Called White*. White wrote that Shillady died shortly after resigning from the NAACP, "a victim of lynching as surely as any Negro who had been strung up to a tree or burned at the stake." In truth, Shillady lived until 1943.

128 *While the NAACP:* The board's campaign for redress is detailed in its minutes of Aug. 26, Sept. 8, and Nov. 10, 1919, and Feb. 9, 1920. Shillady's leave was approved at the Nov. 10 meeting. His resignation was acknowledged in the minutes of April 12, 1920, and accepted in the minutes of May 10, 1920. The search for a new secretary is recorded in the minutes of June 14 and Sept. 13, 1920. (All from Board of Directors 1919 minutes from Box I:A1, and 1920 minutes from Box I:A2, NAACP Papers.)

129 *Not until November:* See Board of Directors minutes for Nov. 6, 1920, ibid. Johnson's column appeared as "A Greeting from the New Secretary," *The Crisis*, January 1921, 116.

129 *Hugh Dorsey, meanwhile:* Dorsey's second inaugural, delivered on June 28, 1919, is available at http://dlg.galileo.usg.edu/ggpd/docs/1919/ga/g600/_ps1/m4/1919_sjune_b28.con/1.pdf (accessed March 3, 2023). The governor's invitation to Black leaders was described in "Montgomery of Mississippi Writes Governor of Georgia," *Age*, Jan. 17, 1920, 5.

129 *It's possible that:* Thurston, *Lynching*; and author interviews with Thurston in Oxford, Ohio, June 28 and 29, 2021.

130 *If so, it was a metamorphosis:* Dorsey's eager anticipation of private life was alluded to in "Governor's Fee Wired Gardner," *AC*, July 30, 1920, 1; and "Dorsey Will Make Race For Senate," *AC*, Aug. 1, 1920, 1.

130 *But another political:* The shortcomings of Hoke Smith and Tom Watson were spelled out in "Entry of Dorsey Expected Sunday," *AC*, July 31, 1920, 1; and "Governor's Fee Wired Gardner," *AC*, July 30.

130 *The former kingmaker:* The split came within days of Dorsey's election, apparently because Watson demanded the governor-elect block an endorsement of President Woodrow Wilson at the 1916 state Democratic convention in Macon; Dorsey refused. See "Watson Fighting Wilson," *NYT*, Sept. 21, 1916, 1; and Watson, "Notes on Georgia Politics," *Jeffersonian*, Sept. 21, 1916, 1. Watson's loss of the *Jeffersonian* was the subject of several angry columns in the paper. His children's deaths and his decline were described by C. Vann Woodward in *Tom Watson: Agrarian Rebel*.

130 *Unless, that is:* The summit was reported in "Dorsey Will Make Race For Senate," *AC*, Aug. 1; and "Governor Enters Senatorial Race After Conference," *Atlanta Tri-Weekly Journal*, Aug. 3, 1920, 1.

130 *Hoke Smith called:* The "flank attack" quote is from "Governor Enters Senatorial Race After Conference," *Atlanta Tri-Weekly Journal*, Aug. 3. Watson's quote is from "Watson Makes Last Appeal to Georgia Voters," *AG*, Sept. 7, 1920, 1.

131 *Stumping across the state:* Dorsey's boastful comments are from "Victory Assured, Governor Tells Cheering Crowd," *AC*, Sept. 5, 1920, 1.

131 *He was mistaken:* According to a front-page chart in the *AC* of Sept. 10, 1920, Watson won 105,400 votes to Dorsey's 71,097; Hoke Smith got 59,425.

131 *He was now officially:* Dorsey described the Gwinnett County affair, his letter, and the sheriff's reply in his booklet, *A Statement from Governor Hugh M. Dorsey As to the Negro in*

Georgia. The case was also reported in Pitts, "Murder Farm"; and "Intimidation of Negroes Charged in Six Counties," *AC*, Jan. 16, 1921, 1. The affidavits of the victims are filed in the Georgia Archives (Governor's Incoming Correspondence, DOC 3133).

Chapter 16

133 *Come Thursday, March 31:* "Dorsey Seeks Attorney for Newton Trial," *AG*, April 2, 1921, 1.

133 *When reporters caught wind:* Official denial of Howard's retainer was voiced in "Graham Wright Named to Assist Solicitor Brand," *AC*, April 2, 1921, 1.

    Howard's career is summarized in the *Biographical Directory of the United States Congress*, available online at https://bioguide.congress.gov/search/bio/H000848 (accessed March 3, 2023). His 1910 defeat was covered in "Ten Counties for Tribble in Race for Congress," *Americus Times-Recorder*, Nov. 11, 1910, 1; and "Howard to Practice Law in Lexington," *Columbus (GA) Ledger*, Dec. 5, 1910, 6.

133 *On Howard's departure:* My passage on Howard's post-Congress life was informed by "Howard Named on Tariff Board," *AC*, March 5, 1911, 6; "William Howard Is on Tariff Board," *Macon News*, April 3, 1911, 1; "Ten Millions to Prevent War Among Nations," *Macon Telegraph*, Dec. 15, 1910, 1; and "W. M. Howard, 75, Dies in Augusta," *AC*, July 6, 1932, 1. The Taft quote is from "President Taft Addresses the Southern Commercial Congress; Royally Welcomed in Georgia," *Macon Telegraph*, March 11, 1911, 1. The "no superior" quote is from "Williams Trial at Covington Tuesday," *Savannah Morning News*, April 3, 1921, 1.

133 *He and Dorsey had:* Howard's argument for Frank was covered in "Frank Hearing to Be Concluded This Afternoon," *Macon News*, June 16; and "More Interest in Frank Case Now than at Trial," *Macon Telegraph*, June 16, 1915, 1.

134 *At one point:* Slaton's interruption of Dorsey's speech was reported in "Dorsey Claims Frank Guilty of Phagan Murder," *Macon News*, June 14, 1915, 1; and "Frank Case Presented to Governor Yesterday from Three Different Angles," *Macon Telegraph*, June 15, 1915, 1.

134 *When he announced:* See "Williams Trial Scheduled to Begin Monday," *Macon News*, April 3, 1921, 1. Brand's quote is from "Planter Asserts Killing Was Done in Self-Defense," *AC*, April 3.

134 *Dorsey's intervention:* Dorsey's worries about Manning's safety were noted in "Protection for Manning Urged," *AG*, April 1. His request to have India Manning rescued is from Marion Kendrick, "Planter Asserts Killing Was Done in Self-Defense," *AC*, April 3. Her rescue was reported in "No Peonage Found in Newton County," *Savannah Morning News*, April 3, 1921, 1.

135 *Most memorably:* Dorsey's maneuverings to hire Underwood were reported in "Noted Attorney Is Retained to Defend Manning," *Macon News*, April 2, 1921, 1. The quote is from "'Murder Farm' Trial Promises Big Legal Fight," *AG*, April 3, 1921, 1.

135 *That load was bound:* The lawyer's bona fides and hiring are described in "Underwood Will Represent Negro in Peonage Case," *AC*, April 3, 1921, 1; "'Murder Farm' Trial Promises Big Legal Fight," *AG*, April 3. Underwood's later ascension to the U.S. District Court for the Northern District of Georgia (and his dealings on the bench with Chicago mobster Al Capone) is described in Luther D. Thomas, *Do Equal Right: The History of the United States District Court, Northern District of Georgia, 1849–2013*, published by the Clerk of the District Court in 2014 and available online at https://issuu.com/bookhouse1/docs/usdc_for_issuu (accessed March 20, 2023).

135 *In the last few days:* The feds' interviews with Manning were reported in "Dorsey Seeks Attorney for Newton Trial," *AG*, April 2; Johnson's sit-down with Williams in "Graham Wright Named to Assist Solicitor Brand," *AC*, April 2; Johnson's application for (and withdrawal of) a change of venue in Marion Kendrick, "Son of Williams Ordered Slaying, Is Declaration," *AC*, April 2, 1921, 1; and his plantation tour in "Prosecutors in Williams Case in Final Talk," *AG*, April 5, 1921, 1.

136 *The Constitution offered:* "Planter Asserts Killing Was Done in Self-Defense," *AC*, April 3.

136 *When asked directly:* "Son of Williams Ordered Slaying, Is Declaration," *AC*, April 2.

137 *He made these remarks:* Blackstrap's murder was reported in "Dorsey Seeks Attorney for Newton Trial," *AG*, April 2. That and a second earlier murder, and the origin of the information, was part of "Son of Williams Ordered Slaying, Is Declaration," *AC*, April 2. Johnson's quote is from the same story.

137 *Lonnie Brand, meanwhile:* The Atlanta powwow was described in "Extra Deputies Are Sworn In for Williams Trial," *Macon News*, April 4, 1921, 1; and "Prosecutors in Williams Case in Final Talk," *AG*, April 5. Brand's quotes were from "Planter Asserts Killing Was Done in Self-Defense," *AC*, April 3.

137 *The same day:* Johnson's meeting at the White House was reported in "Secretary Johnson Confers with President," *The (Birmingham, AL) Voice of the People,* April 9, 1921, 4; "Weldon Johnson Confers with President Harding," *Chicago Defender,* April 9, 1921, 2; and Richard B. Sherman, "The Harding Administration and the Negro: An Opportunity Lost," *Journal of Negro History* 49, no. 3 (July 1964): 151–68. Johnson's meeting with Harding before the election draws from "Report of the Field Secretary on Interview with Senator Warren G. Harding, Marion, Ohio, August 9, 1920" ("Special Correspondence—Warren G. Harding, 1920–21" file, Box I:C64, NAACP Papers). His Jan. 15, 1921, meeting with President-elect Harding was detailed in "Report of the Secretary's Visit to Senator Harding" (in the same NAACP Papers file) and Pinar, "The NAACP and the Struggle for Antilynching Legislation, 1897–1917."

137 *Harding had expressed:* The NAACP memo is included in the Association's "Special Correspondence—Warren G. Harding, 1920–21" file (Box I:C64, NAACP Papers).

138 *Johnson's lobbying:* "President Harding Discusses Negro Needs with Congress," *Dallas Express,* April 16, 1921, 1. See also Sherman, "The Harding Administration and the Negro: An Opportunity Lost."

138 *As for a Justice probe:* White described the visit in an April 19, 1921, letter to Mrs. Ludie Andrews of Atlanta ("Peonage, Jasper County, Ga., April 8–May 24, 1921" file, Box I:C388, NAACP Papers).

139 *Herron, looking over:* The Zebulon case might well be that of Cornelius Alexander, whose fate was described by James Weldon Johnson in "Slavery in Georgia," Views and Reviews, *Age,* Aug. 7, 1920, 4:

> Some weeks ago a colored man named Cornelius Alexander mysteriously disappeared in Pike County, Georgia. Federal investigators of the Department of Justice exhumed a body in a badly decomposed condition near Hollinsville in the same county, which was identified as that of the missing man.
>
> A year ago this same Cornelius Alexander had gone to Atlanta with a badly bruised head, and appealed to the district attorney for protection against Beecher Connell, a white plantation owner, who according to Alexander, had beaten him because he refused to obey an order of Willard Connell, a brother of Beecher. Alexander was advised not to return to his Pike County employers, and he went to Douglasville, where he got a job in a garage.
>
> Last February Alexander was arrested in Douglasville by Willard Connell and the sheriff of Pike County. He was placed in the Zebulon jail, where he remained until Philip Moore, a tenant on the Connell plantation, secured his release and took him to work for him. Moore stated that he paid Robert Connell, father of the Connell brothers, $22.50 a month for Alexander's services, while the colored man received no wages at all.
>
> It is brought out that in 1918 Alexander was working for Matt Bottom, a white farmer of Concord, in order to pay an indebtedness of $40, and in November of that year was turned over to Frank Huff, who assumed a debt of $175 which Bottom claimed Alexander owed him. In December of 1918 Huff turned Alexander over to Robert Connell, who now assumed the continually accumulating debt and agreed to pay Alexander $20 a month, provided it was applied in payment of the debt. It was from Robert Connell's plantation that Alexander ran away in August of last year.
>
> Here we have the case of an able-bodied man working a couple of years at forced labor to pay off an indebtedness of $40, a sum which ought to have been liquidated in a couple of months. But even at the end of a couple of years the original debt was not only not liquidated, but had continued to increase. But the shocking thing about the whole matter is that in the supposedly enlightened state of Georgia a man can still be held in bondage and confined in jail on a charge of debt.

Alexander's headless corpse was found on property owned by a Hollinsville storekeeper; the nearby store was later dynamited. Willard Connell was indicted for the killing in June 1920, went to trial concurrent with the John S. Williams trial in 1921, and was acquitted by an all-white jury after five minutes of deliberation.

139 *In January 1921:* The quote is from "Peonage Again," editorial, *NYT*, March 29, 1921, 14.

139 *From all indications:* James Weldon Johnson March 28, 1921, telegram to Ovington ("Peonage, Jasper County, Ga., March 29–April 7, 1921" file, Box I:C388, NAACP Papers).

139 *White was especially:* White's March 29, 1921 letter is in the "Peonage, Jasper County, Ga., March 29–April 7, 1921" file, Box I:C388, NAACP Papers. The DOJ's March 31, 1921, reply from Assistant Attorney General R. P. Stewart is preserved in the same file.

140 *White nonetheless came:* White made the claim in an April 2, 1921, letter to Ernest H. Gruening, managing editor of *The Nation* ("Peonage, Jasper County, Ga., March 29–April 7, 1921" file, Box I:C388, NAACP Papers); and an April 4, 1921, letter to Nathan B. Young, president of Florida A&M University (same NAACP Papers file). The Atlanta branch claimed its role in the Williams case in an annual report to the NAACP's national office, dated June 20, 1921 ("Atlanta, Ga., Branch, 1919–21" file, Box I:G43, NAACP Papers).

140 *Inevitably, Johnson's visit:* "Harding's Negro Adviser," editorial, *Cordele Dispatch*, April 5, 1921, 4.

141 *Johnson caught wind:* James Weldon Johnson, "The Voice of a Southern Bully," Views and Reviews, *Age*, April 23, 1921, 4.

Part Three: The Majesty of the Law

Chapter 17

145 *The first Tuesday:* The scene in and outside the courthouse was described in Marion Kendrick, "Preliminaries Are Finished in Williams Trial; Manning to Tell Jury of 'Death Farm' Today," *AC*, April 6, 1921, 1. Kendrick wrote that "the weather bordered on that of a midsummer day."

145 *In Judge Hutcheson's:* "Williams Trial at Covington Tuesday," *Savannah Morning News*, April 3; "John S. Williams On Trial Charged with Murder," *Covington News*, April 7, 1921, 1; "Preliminaries Are Finished in Williams Trial; Manning to Tell Jury of 'Death Farm' Today," *AC*, April 6. The orderliness of the proceedings was also noted in Rowland Thomas, "Draw Jury Quickly in Williams Trial for Negro's Death," *New York World*, April 6, 1921, 1; and Paul Stevenson, "Mostly Farmers on Williams Case Panel; State Scores Point," *AG*, April 6, 1921, 1.

145 *Up in Atlanta:* "Preliminaries Are Finished in Williams Trial; Manning to Tell Jury of 'Death Farm' Today," *AC*, April 6.

146 *When the train arrived:* Ibid.

146 *Packed as the courtroom was:* Ibid.

146 *Judge Hutcheson assumed:* See "Judge Hutcheson Dies at Jonesboro," *AC*, May 22, 1939, 1.

147 *With that, the first group:* "Mostly Farmers on Williams Case Panel; State Scores Point," *AG*, April 6.

147 *The first panel:* "Another Atlanta Sensation: The Mayor of Lithonia, Ga., Stabbed by J.B. Cowan," *Brunswick News*, Dec. 3, 1908, 5.

147 *Instead, he was being asked:* Pitts, "Murder Farm."

148 *Brand was unmoved:* "Mostly Farmers on Williams Case Panel; State Scores Point," *AG*, April 6.

148 *Rebuffed in his bid:* Ibid.; Hubert S. Baughn, "John S. Williams, of 'Death Farm,' On Trial for Life," *Atlanta Tri-Weekly Journal*, April 7, 1921, 1; and Pitts, "Murder Farm."

148 *"Were the names of any":* "Mostly Farmers on Williams Case Panel; State Scores Point," *AG*, April 6; Pitts, "Murder Farm."

149 *Johnson took his implication:* Ibid.

149 *Johnson next called:* Ibid.

149 *Lonnie Brand spoke up:* Ibid. Reporters differed on the judge's exact words. The *AJ*, for instance, quoted him as saying the proceedings were not "a circus or a moving picture show."

149 *Johnson turned now:* The quote is from "Mostly Farmers on Williams Case Panel; State Scores Point," *AG*, April 6.

149 *Sworn in, Underwood:* Ibid., and Pitts, "Murder Farm."

150 *Johnson questioned:* Ibid.

150 *"That's all"*: Ibid.

150 *While his lawyers huddled*: Pitts, "Murder Farm."

150 *When the judge gaveled*: The jury was named in "John S. Williams, of 'Death Farm,' On Trial for Life," *Atlanta Tri-Weekly Journal*, April 7; "Mostly Farmers on Williams Case Panel; State Scores Point," *AG*, April 6; and "Preliminaries Are Finished in Williams Trial; Manning to Tell Jury of 'Death Farm' Today," *AC*, April 6. Pitts made the point about the preponderance of farmers in "Murder Farm."

    The jurors selected from the first group of twelve were T. L. Hill, a farmer who lived on the east side of Newton County, not far from its border with Jasper; and G. W. Gober, who ran a successful farm northeast of Covington. Those from the second group were Robert Stanton, a young farmer, and W. A. Pate, a merchant from the small college town of Oxford. From the third were Charles A. Cason, who worked land in the county's north end; T. R. Starr, whose place was just outside Covington; and W. C. Moore, a planter who had once lived not far from Williams and who now lived at the southern edge of Newton, near the bridges over the Yellow and South Rivers. Finally, from the fourth group, were Byron Thacker, a grocery store clerk in Covington; F. G. Crowley, an automobile dealer; J. T. Dennard, a farmer with a spread near Oxford; J. E. Rawlins, a barber; and William Reginald Robinson, a drugstore employee.

151 *Of the original*: The quote is from "John S. Williams On Trial Charged with Murder," *Covington News*, April 7.

151 *That evening, Gus Williams*: Marion Kendrick, "Dr. Gus Williams Admits Brother Killed Negro," *AC*, April 6, 1921, 1.

Chapter 18

153 *The trial's second day*: See "Slayer's Graphic Story of Wholesale Murders Unshaken by Withering Fire of Cross-Examiners," *AC*, April 7, 1921, 1; Hubert F. Baughn, "Federal Agents First Witnesses in Williams Trial," *AJ*, April 6, 1921, 1; Paul Stevenson, "Negro's Testimony of Wholesale Killings Starts Legal Battle," *AG*, April 6, 1921, 1.

153 *Judge Hutcheson gaveled*: "Federal Agents First Witnesses in Williams Trial," *AJ*, April 6; Pitts, "Murder Farm." The quote describing Manning is from Rowland Thomas, "Tossed Shackled Peons Off Bridge, Swears Manning," *New York World*, April 7, 1921 ("Jasper Peonage Clippings" file, Box I:C388, NAACP Papers). Thomas was describing Manning on the stand; I've repurposed his passage.

153 *With the witnesses sequestered*: "Negro's Testimony of Wholesale Killings Starts Legal Battle," *AG*, April 6; ". John S Williams On Trial Charged with Murder," *Covington News*, April 7.

154 *So began a long series*: Marion Kendrick, "Death Roll Call Gives Dramatic Touch to Trial," *AC*, April 7, 1921, 1.

154 *With Howard guiding him*: All of Brown's quoted testimony throughout this chapter is drawn from the Williams BOE.

155 *Whether Brown knew of it*: Manning's cover story came fully to light during grand jury testimony in Jasper County. See "Fresh Evidence Is Given Jasper Jury; More Bills Found," *AJ*, April 12; and Pitts, "Murder Farm."

155 *Greene Johnson rose*: "Negro's Testimony of Wholesale Killings Starts Legal Battle," *AG*, April 6.

156 *The judge divided*: Ibid.

157 *Greene Johnson began*: Here, as elsewhere throughout the trial, I have surmised the lawyer's questions from the phrasing of the Williams BOE. In preparing the brief, court reporter D. O. Smith eliminated all of the questions put to the witnesses, and merged the actual testimony into long paragraphs of monologue. As Smith testified in the second Manning trial: "I wrote out the evidence in narrative form, made a brief of it, and as far as possible in making the brief, I used the language of the witness."

    Where necessary to clarify the meaning of a passage, Smith folded the lawyer's question—or a piece of it—into the answer. In this section of Brown's testimony, for instance, the BOE reads: "I then told Clyde Manning that he had lied to me, I don't think I pointed my finger in his face and called him a scoundrel, but I told him he had lied about it, I told him that in the presence of Mr. Williams." In the context of Brown's testimony, it is clear to me that "I don't think I pointed my finger in his face and called him a scoundrel" is either (a) a response to a question phrased just that way, or, more likely, (b) the question itself, inserted into the answer so that the rest of Brown's comments make sense.

With either of these interpretations in mind, I worded this portion of the testimony as: "When Williams told a different story, [Johnson] asked, hadn't Brown pointed a finger in Manning's face, and called him a lying scoundrel? No, Brown replied, 'but I told him he had lied about it. I told him that in the presence of Mr. Williams.'"

This is the approach I've used throughout my reconstruction of the Williams and first Manning trials. I have been careful to preserve the meaning of what was said by the witnesses, and—as I explained in the headnotes—have left the lawyers' questions without quote marks to signal that they approximate the wording used.

You'll notice that I have also corrected the punctuation in what, in the original, was a single run-on sentence. As the BOE was a transcription of speech, rather than a piece of writing in any traditional sense, I judged court reporter Smith's shortcomings as a grammarian as fair game for editing.

159 *Next to take the stand*: All of Wismer's quoted testimony is taken from the Williams BOE.

Chapter 19

163 *The* Atlanta Constitution: The photo appeared on the front page of the April 7, 1921, edition. I visited the courtroom in February 2023, and was surprised to find that it was enormous—the size of a college lecture hall—which underlined just how many people were crammed into the space for the trial. The room is now used as a meeting place by Newton County commissioners; Judge Hutcheson's bench has been replaced by a horseshoe-shaped table for the governing panel, and the jury box by a wheelchair ramp. Still, one can sit in the spot Clyde Manning occupied while he delivered his story, and appreciate both the closeness of the jury and the crush of humanity he braved.

163 *Every other square foot*: Manning's testimony was pulled from the Williams BOE. Howard's eyeglass leash was mentioned in Rowland Thomas, "Tossed Shackled Peons Off Bridge, Swears Manning," *New York World*, April 7 ("Jasper Peonage Clippings" file, Box I:C388, NAACP Papers).

168 *Greene Johnson jumped*: The lawyer's objection was not included in the BOE. I relied on Paul Stevenson, "Negro's Testimony of Wholesale Killings Starts Legal Battle," *AG*, April 6.

168 *"The indictment on which"*: The arguments held while the jury was out of the courtroom were, likewise, not recorded in the BOE. This part of Johnson's objection is drawn from "Federal Agents First Witnesses in Williams Trial," *AJ*, April 6.

168 *"It makes no difference"*: Marion Kendrick, "Death Roll Call Gives Dramatic Touch to Trial," *AC*, April 7.

168 *Johnson ran through*: "Federal Agents First Witnesses in Williams Trial," *AJ*, April 6; Pitts, "Murder Farm."

168 *When William Howard's*: Ibid.

169 *Lucy Williams wept*: Ibid. The detail about Manning dozing in the witness chair is from Hubert F. Baughn, "Manning Tells Jury Story of Jasper Death Farm," *AJ*, April 6, 1921, 1.

169 *The jury returned*: The quote is from "Negro's Testimony of Wholesale Killings Starts Legal Battle," *AG*, April 6.

Chapter 20

179 *Johnson's cross-examination*: Manning's testimony throughout this chapter is drawn from the Williams BOE.

191 *Johnson was just about out*: All three quotes are from Hubert F. Baughn, "No Limit Placed on Arguments by Judge Hutcheson," *AJ*, April 7, 1921, 1.

Chapter 21

192 *Now taking the oath*: The testimonies of Lessie May Benton and Clyde Freeman in this chapter were pulled from the Williams BOE.

193 *Greene Johnson objected*: "Death Roll Call Gives Dramatic Touch to Trial," *AC*, April 7.

Chapter 22

197 *Williams, wearing an air*: The defendant's wardrobe was detailed in Rowland Thomas, "Williams Defense Rests on His Own Plea of Innocence," *New York World*, April 8, 1921 ("Jasper Peonage Clippings" file, Box I:C388, NAACP Papers).

197 *Lonnie Brand called:* The testimonies of Rena Manning and Sheriff Johnson were drawn from the Williams BOE. The detail about Rena Manning's gum chewing is from Paul Stevenson, "Death Farm Trial Moves with Speed," *AJ*, April 7, 1921, 1.

200 *Who told her:* The defense attorney's "Who told you?" questioning was reported in "Death Farm Trial Moves with Speed," *AJ*, April 7.

202 *Judge Hutcheson paused:* Ibid.

Chapter 23

205 *The defense team:* The quote is from Marion Kendrick, "Numerous Tilts Mark Progress of Famous Trial," *AC*, April 9, 1921, 1.

205 *The conventional wisdom:* Ibid.

205 *He walked to the witness chair:* Marion Kendrick's observations are ibid. Rowland Thomas's account is from "Williams Defense Rests on His Own Plea of Innocence," *New York World*, April 8.

206 *Whatever the case:* Williams's unsworn statement is pulled from the Williams BOE. The newspaper reporters in the room offered variations on the official transcript, most of them significantly shorter. Several, however, included remarks that did not appear in the court document. One, for example, came at the opening of his statement—

From Hubert F. Baughn, "Williams' Statement," *AJ*, April 7, 1921, 1: "There are two sides to every question. You have heard the other side of this case, and now I want to tell you mine. And I want to start by telling you that I am an innocent man."

From "John S. Williams On Trial Charged with Murder," *Covington News*, April 7: "Gentlemen, there are two sides to every question. In this case you have heard the other side. Now I want to tell you mine, and I want to begin by telling you I am an innocent man."

What to make of this? In an age when trials were transcribed by shorthand note-taking, it could be that the court reporter simply failed to capture that passage. In the main, however, the official version of Williams's statement is far more comprehensive than any of those reported by the press. And as it *is* the official version, I've stuck with it.

206 *In truth, remember:* The quote is from "Williams Defense Rests on His Own Plea of Innocence," *New York World*, April 8.

207 *"He walked up to me":* Note the "tell" in Williams's account of the conversation—his use of the phrase "ought to have your neck broke." This was a favorite expression of his, if his quoted speech in the press is any indication—and a signal that he is not quoting Brown accurately.

208 *Presumably, Williams was quoting:* The quote is from the *AJ*'s front-page "Williams' Statement" story of April 7.

211 *The balance of Williams's:* My description of Williams's body language and the jury's behavior relies on "Numerous Tilts Mark Progress of Famous Trial," *AC*, April 9.

211 *"I heard down there":* According to the official version of his statement, Williams did not use Eberhardt Crawford's surname. Newspaper versions included it. See, for instance, "Williams' Statement," *AJ*, April 7.

212 *Now Williams turned:* Lucy Williams's behavior is recounted in "Numerous Tilts Mark Progress of Famous Trial," *AC*, April 9.

214 *Williams stepped down:* Greene Johnson is quoted in "Williams' Statement," *AJ*, April 7.

214 *The defense team:* The quote is from "Death Farm Trial Moves with Speed," *AJ*, April 7.

Chapter 24

216 *King revisited the case law:* Paul Stevenson, "Howard Falls at Close of Powerful Plea," *AG*, April 8, 1921, 1.

216 *Those formalities complete:* The first quote was pulled from "Numerous Tilts Mark Progress of Famous Trial," *AC*, April 9. The "schemed to destroy" quote is from "Overseer Not Ordered to Kill Negroes, Is Plea," *New York Call*, April 8, 1921 ("Jasper Peonage Clippings" file, Box I:C388, NAACP Papers). The "motive he had" quote is from "Howard Falls at Close of Powerful Plea," *AG*, April 8. The "cunning Negro" quote is from "Overseer Not Ordered to Kill Negroes, Is Plea," *New York Call*, April 8.

217 *The courtroom, which:* The heat in the room was referenced in "Howard Falls at Close of Powerful Plea," *AG*, April 8. The quote is from "Numerous Tilts Mark Progress of Famous Trial," *AC*, April 9.

217 *Besides, both of the Mannings:* The "well trained" quote is from "Howard Falls at Close of Powerful Plea," *AG*, April 8. The "one statement alone" comment was quoted in "Numerous Tilts Mark Progress of Famous Trial," *AC*, April 9.
217 *"We say, gentlemen":* "Howard Falls at Close of Powerful Plea," *AG*, April 8.
218 *He opened, as had King:* Ibid.
218 *Williams fanned himself:* Ibid.
218 *Came now William Hicks Key:* Ibid., and "Numerous Tilts Mark Progress of Famous Trial," *AC*, April 9.
218 *Brand objected:* Ibid.
219 *Key pivoted to mocking:* The "able and eloquent" quote is from "Howard Falls at Close of Powerful Plea," *AG*, April 8. The later quotes, and that of the following two paragraphs, are drawn from "Numerous Tilts Mark Progress of Famous Trial," *AC*, April 9.
219 *Key's "grandstanding":* "Howard Falls at Close of Powerful Plea," *AG*, April 8.
219 *That Peterson and the other:* Ibid.
220 *This was a case:* Ibid.

Chapter 25

221 *Thronged as it was:* The students were mentioned in "Manning Flayed by Counsel for Jasper Farmer," *Macon News*, April 8, 1921, 1.
   AC reporter Marion Kendrick noted the presence of women in "Judge Is Asked for Instructions After Midnight," April 9, 1921, 1.
221 *"There are before you":* The quote here, and continuing over the succeeding two paragraphs, is from Paul Stevenson, "Howard Falls at Close of Powerful Plea," *AG*, April 8.
222 *With the reference:* The bulk of the paragraph is ibid. The final quote is from "Williams' Jury Is Up All Night," *Miami Herald*, April 9, 1921, 1.
222 *The temperature:* Howard's review of peonage was described in Hubert F. Baughn, "Attorney Howard Flays 'Death Farm' as a 'Plague Spot,'" *AJ*, April 8. Howard's quote about Williams's fear is from "Howard Falls at Close of Powerful Plea," *AG*, April 8.
222 *Howard held up a stenographic copy:* Ibid.
222 *Howard derided the defense:* The "Who leased" quote is ibid. The "willing to kill" quote was reported in "Attorney Howard Flays 'Death Farm' as a 'Plague Spot,'" *AJ*, April 8.
223 *As for Manning:* The quote and that of the following paragraph were contained in "Howard Falls at Close of Powerful Plea," *AG*, April 8.
223 *The temperature in the room:* The quote here, continuing through the next three paragraphs, is from "Attorney Howard Flays 'Death Farm' as a 'Plague Spot,'" *AJ*, April 8.
224 *"Could the man live":* "Judge Is Asked for Instructions After Midnight," *AC*, April 9.
224 *"You can't bring back":* The quote here, and continuing through the following paragraph, is ibid.
224 *At that moment:* Ibid., and "Howard Falls at Close of Powerful Plea," *AG*, April 8.
224 *Few spectators left:* "Attorney Howard Flays 'Death Farm' as a 'Plague Spot,'" *AJ*, April 8.
224 *Hutcheson pounded his gavel:* Ibid.
225 *Was that a not-so-subtle dig:* The quote here, and continuing through the next paragraph, is ibid.
225 *"I suggest that the Atlanta":* "Jury Recommends Mercy for Planter Who Killed Negro," *AG*, April 9, 1921, 1.
225 *This was, after all:* The quote here and extending through the next paragraph was reported in "Peonage Murder Case Goes to Jury; Mistrial Forecast," *New York Tribune*, April 9, 1921 ("Jasper Peonage Clippings" file, Box I:C388, NAACP Papers).
225 *Johnson shifted his:* The quote before the attribution is from "Attorney Howard Flays 'Death Farm' as a 'Plague Spot,'" *AJ*, April 8; the following quote is from "Jury Recommends Mercy for Planter Who Killed Negro," *AG*, April 9.
226 *He had plenty:* This quote, continuing through the succeeding paragraph, was reported in "Attorney Howard Flays 'Death Farm' as a 'Plague Spot,'" *AJ*, April 8.
226 *Johnson paced in front:* Most of the paragraph's quotes are ibid.; the final sentence is drawn from "Jury Recommends Mercy for Planter Who Killed Negro," *AG*, April 9.
226 *It's worth noting:* The first two quotes are from "Jury Recommends Mercy for Planter Who Killed Negro," *AG*, April 9. The quote beginning "Manning tells you" is from "Attorney Howard Flays 'Death Farm' as a 'Plague Spot,'" *AJ*, April 8.

227 *"Deeply seeped":* "Jury Still Out in 'Death Farm' Murder Trial, *New York Call,* April 9, 1921 ("Jasper Peonage Clippings" file, Box I:C388, NAACP Papers).

227 *Johnson added one more:* "Judge Is Asked for Instructions After Midnight," *AC,* April 9.

227 *Williams dined:* The defendant's sober air was reported in "Attorney Howard Flays 'Death Farm' as a 'Plague Spot,'" *AJ,* April 8.

227 *Williams clapped Johnson:* Ibid.

227 *Hutcheson directed Johnson:* Ibid.

228 *That was but one of many:* The quote here, and continuing through the next three paragraphs, was reported in "Judge Is Asked for Instructions After Midnight," *AC,* April 9.

228 *Johnson moved into:* The *New York Call* story I cite is "Jury Still Out in 'Death Farm' Murder Trial," April 9. The *Broad Ax* story I quote is Charles E. Stump, "Charles E. Stump, the Headlight Traveling Correspondent for *The Broad Ax,* has been Walking About in Savannah and Covington, Ga.," a front-page report in the edition of April 16, 1921.

229 *Johnson told the jury:* The cannibal quote is from "Attorney Howard Flays 'Death Farm' as a 'Plague Spot,'" *AJ,* April 8 . The "Negro like Manning" quote was drawn from "Jury Still Out in 'Death Farm' Murder Trial, *New York Call,* April 9. The "must have confidence" remark, which continues through the end of lawyer Johnson's argument, is from "Judge Is Asked for Instructions After Midnight," *AC,* April 9.

230 *Johnson retreated:* The scene at argument's end relies on "Judge Is Asked for Instructions After Midnight," *AC,* April 9.

230 *Rowland Thomas:* The story I quote is "Williams Murder Jury Is Locked Up After Nine Hours," *New York World,* April 9, 1921 ("Jasper Peonage Clippings" file, Box I:C388, NAACP Papers).

Chapter 26

231 *Late in the afternoon:* The judge's charge is included in the Williams BOE.

232 *The jury left the room:* The quote is from "Williams Murder Jury Is Locked Up After Nine Hours," *New York World,* April 9. The *New York Tribune* headline is from the paper's April 9 edition ("Jasper Peonage Clippings" file, Box I:C388, NAACP Papers).

Just how unlikely a conviction seemed is put into perspective by a *New York World* story of March 30, 1921, reprinted as "Deaths of 11 Negroes Charged to Employer" in the *Age* of April 2, 1921: "A substantial citizen of Covington told the *World* correspondent today that for a Negro to testify against a white in Jasper County ordinarily would mean one more dead Negro, and that conviction of a white man by a jury of friends and neighbors for the killing of a Negro is impossible there unless the circumstances are extraordinarily atrocious and the evidence practically flawless."

233 *For an hour:* "Jury Recommends Mercy for Planter Who Killed Negro," *AG,* April 9.

233 *The jury broke:* The doctor's session with reporters was described in Rowland Thomas, "Will Come Clean on Second Trial, Asserts Planter," *AC,* April 10, 1921, 1. For whatever reason, the *AC* ran a story by the *New York World's* correspondent, rather than its own.

233 *Seeing as how virtually:* The quote is from "Planter Asserts Killing Was Done in Self-Defense," *AC,* April 3.

233 *Gus Williams might:* The quote here, and continuing through the next three paragraphs, is from Rev. James J. Winburn, "Thorough Probe Is Wanted by Citizens, Says Minister," *Monticello News,* April 8.

234 *Late that night:* "Jury Recommends Mercy for Planter Who Killed Negro," *AG,* April 9. The subsequent back-and-forth between judge and jury foreman is included in the Williams BOE.

235 *The answer came soon:* "Jury Recommends Mercy for Planter Who Killed Negro," *AG,* April 9.

235 *"Have you reached":* "Will Come Clean on Second Trial, Asserts Planter," *AC,* April 10.

235 *Williams met the news:* The family's reaction was detailed in "Jury Recommends Mercy for Planter Who Killed Negro," *AG,* April 9. The *Minutes of the Newton County Superior Court, 1919–1927,* available at the clerk's office, shows the verdicts in both the Williams and first Manning trials on page 169. Manning's jury apparently followed the proper form, recommending "that his punishment be life imprisonment," rather than simply recommending "mercy."

235 *From Rowland Thomas:* The story I quote is "Will Come Clean on Second Trial, Asserts Planter," *AC,* April 10.

235 *"The jury has found you"*: The judge's comments are ibid. The family's breakdown is detailed in "Hearing for New Trial to Be Held in Decatur April 30," *AJ*, April 9, 1921, 1. This story identified the youngest Williams daughter—Lucy Claire—as "Tillie."

236 *Williams kissed his family*: The convict's encounter with his neighbor is recounted in "Will Come Clean on Second Trial, Asserts Planter," *AC*, April 10.

Part Four: American Congo

Chapter 27

239 *So it was*: The "horse sense" assessment is ibid.

239 *Beyond the Newton County*: Dorsey's quote, which continues through the next paragraph, is ibid.

240 *In the main*: The quoted *AJ* editorial was reprinted as "Justice in Georgia" in the *Covington News*, April 14, 1921. The *Tribune* editorial was reprinted as "The New South" in the *Age* of April 23, 1921. The *Broad Ax* quote is from "Charles E. Stump, the Headlight Traveling Correspondent for *The Broad Ax*, has been Walking About in Savannah and Covington, Ga.," April 16.

240 *The New York World*: The quoted editorial is "Georgia Upsets a Precedent," in the *World's* edition of April 11, 1921 ("Jasper Peonage Clippings" file, Box I:C388, NAACP Papers). Johnson's *Age* column appeared under the headline "An Epoch-Making Trial" in the April 16, 1921, edition, 4. The *Chattanooga Times* quote is from "Georgia Justice," editorial, April 11, 1921, 4. The Columbus editorial was quoted in "Jury of Georgia Farmers Asks Mercy For Slayer of 11," *Chicago Whip*, April 16, 1921, 1.

240 *Dorsey, in New York*: "Governor Says Public Disapproves Verdict," *Age*, April 16, 1921, 1.

241 *"I want you gentlemen"*: "Roll Away the Stone Down in Jasper," editorial, *Madisonian* (Madison, GA), April 15, 1921 ("Jasper Peonage Clippings" file, Box I:C388, NAACP Papers).

242 *He ended his charge*: Hubert F. Baughn, "Findings Will Be Reported Monday; Lynching Inquiry," *AJ*, April 11, 1921, 1.

242 *The first witness*: Ibid.

242 *Gus Chapman did just that*: Chapman's account of his escapes is from Hubert F. Baughn, "Fresh Evidence Is Given Jasper Jury; More Bills Found," *AJ*, April 12. See also Marion Kendrick, "Three Sons of Williams Indicted in Jasper," *AC*, April 12, 1921, 1.

242 *Manning was recalled*: The quote is from "Fresh Evidence Is Given Jasper Jury; More Bills Found," *AJ*, April 12.

243 *The grand jury made*: "Three Sons of Williams Indicted in Jasper," *AC*, April 12.

243 *At that point*: See "Williams Boys Still at Liberty," *AC*, April 16, 1921, 1.

243 *Hugh Dorsey, who had*: "Negro Farm 'Boss' to Go on Trial for Life in May," *Atlanta Tri-Weekly Journal*, April 14, 1921, 1.

243 *No sooner had word*: "Alleged Cruel Treatment of Negroes on Williams Farm Will Be Probed Here," *Macon News*, April 15, 1921, 1; "Peonage Murders Are Now Put at 18," *NYT*, April 15, 1921, 17; and "Ex-Peons Testify to Killings in 1910," *New York World*, April 15, 1921 ("Jasper Peonage Clippings" file, Box I:C388, NAACP Papers).

244 *The witnesses reported*: The baby's death was reported in "Tells About Conditions on the Williams Farm; Death List Increased," *Macon News*, April 17, 1921, 1.

244 *The agents allowed*: The quote is from "Peonage Murders Are Now Put at 18," *NYT*, April 15.

Chapter 28

245 *It was in the flush*: Johnson's telegram, dated April 11, 1921, is included in the NAACP Papers ("Peonage, Jasper County, Ga., April 8–May 24, 1921" file, Box I:C388). Dorsey's telegram in reply, dated April 14, is in the same file.

245 *And so, two principals*: The diary entry is filed in the NAACP Papers in the "James Weldon Johnson Office Diaries, 1921" file, Box I:C111. The NAACP statement was reported in "NAACP Thanks Governor Dorsey," *Philadelphia American*, April 16, 1921 ("Jasper Peonage Clippings" file, Box I:C388, NAACP Papers).

245 *The day after that*: "An Epoch-Making Trial," *Age*, April 16.

246 *That was an oft-voiced:* The quote is from Rowland Thomas, "Peonage Admitted; Georgia Governor Says It Must End," *New York World*, April 2, 1921 ("Jasper Peonage Clippings" file, Box I:C388, NAACP Papers).

246 *And indeed:* Ibid.

246 *That commitment translated:* Hughes's remarks are quoted in "Extra Deputies Are Sworn In for Williams Trial," *Macon News*, April 4.

247 *According to the Bureau:* Hughes's quotes are ibid. Dorsey's is from "Governor Says Public Disapproves Verdict," *Age*, April 16.

247 *This marked a sudden:* The *Washington Star* quote is from the editorial "Governor Dorsey and Peonage," May 17, 1921, 6. The Madison paper's quote is from "Let Up on Jasper," editorial, *Madisonian*, April 22, 1921.

248 *The NAACP sounded:* The editorial was "Slavery," *The Crisis*, May 1921, 6.

248 *Du Bois detected:* The "ray of hope" quote is ibid. Johnson's comments are from "'The Birth of a Nation'—Again," Views and Reviews, *Age*, May 14, 1921, 4.

249 *While Dorsey wrapped:* The episode involving the old woman in the creek is explored in "Probe Is Planned of Race Trouble in South Georgia," AC, April 28, 1921, 1. See also "Dorsey Presses Inquiry," NYT, April 29, 1921, 26.

250 *Business as usual:* The quote is from John Dittmer's *Black Georgia in the Progressive Era 1900–1920.*

250 *On the evening of Friday:* All quotes are from the booklet, available from the Library of Congress at https://www.loc.gov/resource/gdcmassbookdig.statementfromgov01geor/?st=gallery (accessed March 10, 2023).

251 *The next category:* Pitts's quote is from "Hugh M. Dorsey and 'The Negro in Georgia,'" *Georgia Historical Quarterly* 89, no. 2 (Summer 2005): 185–212.

255 *When he finished:* The resolution is included as the last page of the booklet in the version cited above.

255 *Wilmer saw particular merit:* The reverend is quoted in "Georgians to Air Race Problems," *New York World*, April 24, 1921 ("Jasper Peonage Clippings" file, Box I:C388, NAACP Papers).

256 *It is difficult to overstate:* For further speculation on Dorsey's possible motivations, see Pitts, "Hugh M. Dorsey and 'The Negro in Georgia'"; and Thurston, *Lynching.*

256 *Beyond that, the governor:* Dorsey's comment early in the Murder Farm inquiry was mentioned in "Governor Probes Negroes' Death," *Macon News*, March 22. The later quote is from "Peonage Admitted; Georgia Governor Says It Must End," *New York World*, April 2.

257 *Last, but certainly:* The absence of a useful Dorsey archive is vexing. At the Atlanta History Center, his papers consist of a personal letter, his lengthy final argument to John Slaton on Frank's clemency petition, several scrapbooks of newspaper clippings, and not much else of interest. His administration's papers at the Georgia Archives are all business. His grandson Rufus Dorsey II told me that the family had held on to few, if any, of his records.

Chapter 29

258 *In New York:* White's letter of April 23, 1921, is part of the NAACP Papers' "Peonage, Jasper County, Ga., April 8–Mary 24, 1921" file, Box I:C388.

258 *White immediately became:* White's April 27, 1921, press release is included in the same file cited above, NAACP Papers.

258 *At first, the speech:* The quote is from "135 Cases Cited of Mistreatment to Negroes Here," AC, April 24, 1921, 1.

258 *"Governor Dorsey has been":* The editorial I cite is "Courts Get Busy," *Macon News*, May 5, 1921, 6.

259 *Out-of-state reaction:* "The South Proposes," editorial, *New York Globe*, April 27, 1921 ("Jasper Peonage Clippings" file, Box I:C388, NAACP Papers).

259 *"Georgia is most fortunate":* "Georgia Makes Plans to Clean House," editorial, *New York World*, April 28, 1921 (in the same NAACP Papers file as cited above).

259 *The New York Times:* The quoted NYT editorial was "Specific Charges Are Best," in the "Topics of the Times" column, April 29, 1921, 14.

259 *Still, for a full two weeks:* Here, and in the following several paragraphs, I quote from James Weldon Johnson, "Governor Dorsey's Statement," Views and Reviews, *Age*, May 7, 1921, 4.

260 *As if on cue:* See "U.S. Grand Jury Will Take Up Peon Charges," *Macon Telegraph*, May 1, 1921, 1; "Hogan's Trial for Peonage Set for May 23," *Macon Telegraph*, May 11, 1921, 1.

"Governor Urges Halt of 'Riders' in Taliaferro," *AC*, April 29, 1921, 1; "Another Peonage Arrest," *Macon News*, April 26, 1921, 1.

261 *These revelations:* "Says State Should Ask U.S. to Take Charge Of Peonage Situation," *Atlanta Tri-Weekly Constitution*, April 28, 1921, 1; "Federal Aid in Race Crisis Seen in Georgia," *NYT*, April 26, 1921, 9. See also, "Federal Government Will Not Be Asked to Protect Lives of Blacks in State," *Macon News*, April 26, 1921, 1. Dorsey's quote is from "Dorsey to Aid in Peonage Crusade, *Atlanta Tri-Weekly Journal*, April 28, 1921, 2.

261 *James Weldon Johnson:* Johnson, "The Awakening of Georgia," Views and Reviews, *Age*, April 30, 1921, 4.

261 *Down in central Georgia:* The postponement was reported in "Lawyer Will Ask Delay in Hearing of Williams Case," *AC*, April 30, 1921, 1; and "Johnson to Offer Plea of Jeopardy," *AC*, May 1, 1921, 12.

261 *The session would have been:* Greene Johnson's quote was drawn from "Williams Hearing Postponed a Week," *AJ*, April 30, 1921, 7. See also "May Be No Trial in Jasper County," *Atlanta Tri-Weekly Journal*, May 3, 1921, 1.

262 *Although the eight:* Ibid.

262 *Court officials declined:* "Johnson to Offer Plea of Jeopardy," *AC*, May 1.

262 *While that might have:* The federal grand jury's action was described in "South Georgia Federal Court Will Soon Probe 'Murder Farm' Cases," *AC*, April 16, 1921, 1; "Manning Testifies in Peonage Probe," *AC*, May 3, 1921; "Negro Farm 'Boss' Gives Testimony, *Atlanta Tri-Weekly Journal*, May 5, 1921, 1; "Planter and Sons Indicted in Bibb," *AC*, May 5, 1921, 1; and "Nation-Wide Hunt Started for Sons of John Williams," *AC*, May 6, 1921, 1.

The indictments are on file at the National Archives in Atlanta. See Federal Conspiracy Indictment, Case 2296 (Records of the Federal District Courts, Macon Criminal Case Files, 1882–1926, Box 53); and Federal Peonage Indictment, Case 2297 (Records of the Federal District Courts, Macon Criminal Case Files, 1882–1926, Box 53).

263 *With those indictments:* "Nation-Wide Hunt Started for Sons of John Williams," *AC*, May 6; and "Georgia Jury Returns Indictments for Peonage," *NYT*, May 5, 1921, 19.

263 *This drew closer:* "Williams' Motion for New Trial Is Denied by Court," *Atlanta Tri-Weekly Journal*, May 10, 1921, 1.

Chapter 30

264 *Soon enough came:* Searcy's letter was reprinted in its entirety in "Judge W. E. H. Searcy, Jr., in Severe Arraignment of Dorsey for His Indictment of Georgia," *Macon Telegraph*, May 11, 1921, 1.

265 *Asked about the letter:* "Dorsey to Reply to Searcy Attack," *AC*, May 11, 1921, 1.

265 *"I do not personally vouch":* Ibid.

265 *Dorsey had made:* The new charges were reported in "'Ugly Record,' Dorsey Says to Georgia," *Chicago Defender*, May 21, 1921, 1. Hardwick's "infamous slander" quote is from "'Three Georgians Assail Pamphlet on Peonage Cases," *AC*, May 15, 1921, 1. Searcy's second letter is ibid., as is the comment from Sam Olive.

266 *In Macon, an outfit:* The Guardians of Liberty resolution was covered in "Dorsey's Negro Appeal Raises Cry to Impeach," *New York Tribune*, May 16, 1921 ("Jasper Peonage Clippings" file, Box I:C388, NAACP Papers). See also "Rhetoric Out of Georgia," a *New York World* editorial reprinted in the *Age*, May 21, 1921, 2.

266 *As the Black-owned:* "'Ugly Record,' Dorsey Says to Georgia," *Chicago Defender*, May 21.

Chapter 31

267 *Hugh Dorsey did not:* Dorsey's reply to Searcy was reprinted in whole in "Governor Replies to Letters of Judges Searcy and Shurley," *AC*, May 13, 1921, 8.

268 *To the judge and solicitor:* Ibid.

268 *This response only:* The *Macon Telegraph* editorial was reprinted as "An Explanation" in the *Monticello News* of May 13, 1921.

269 *This radical shift:* The *Madisonian* editorial, "Burdening the Farmer," appeared in the edition of May 6, 1921. The *Americus Times-Recorder* comment appeared in "Observations," an editorial in the May 6, 1921, paper. The *Griffin Daily News* was quoted in Pitts, "Hugh M. Dorsey and The Negro in Georgia.'"

269 *One critic, Baptist preacher:* Caleb A. Ridley, *The Negro in Georgia: Another "Pamphlet" Called Forth by Governor Hugh M. Dorsey's Slanderous Document, Scattered Broadcast over the Coun-*

try, and in Which He Purported to Set Forth the Brutal Treatment Accorded the Negro by White Citizens of Georgia—The "American Belgian Congo" (Dixie Defense Committee [Georgia Division], 1921). See also Ridley: "Pastor Attacks Peonage Booklet," AC, May 16, 1921, 1.

270 The NAACP's officers: James Weldon Johnson, "Governor Dorsey Under Attack," Views and Reviews, Age, May 21, 1921, 4.

271 In The Crisis: "The Rising Truth," editorial, The Crisis, June 1921, 53.

271 In late May, The Nation: The editorial appears in the magazine's May 25, 1921, edition, page 727.

271 Dorsey had other allies: The quoted "Topics of the Times" commentary is from "Much Denial but No Disproof," NYT, May 17, 1921, 16.

272 Three days later: "Such Charges Easy to Answer," editorial, NYT, May 20, 1921, 14.

272 Closer to home: "Co-operation Pledged to Governor Dorsey," AC, May 24, 1921, 8.

272 U.S. Attorney: "Federal District Attorney Defense Charges Preferred by Governor in Pamphlet on Negro," AC, May 27, 1921; "U.S. Attorney Comes to Gov. Dorsey's Defense," Richmond Planet, June 4, 1921, 3. Alexander had been at odds with Dorsey at least since the Frank case, when he came out in support of the accused man and declared Jim Conley the real killer. See "Leo M. Frank Is Innocent and Jim Conley Is Guilty, Asserts Hooper Alexander," AC, May 30, 1915, 1.

272 His critics were eager: The quote is from "Dorsey Launches Publicity Drive," Macon Telegraph, Sept. 15, 1920, 7. See also "Will Use $300,000 To Boost Georgia," AC, July 25, 1920, 1; "Georgia Ad Men to Hear Dorsey," Macon Telegraph, Sept. 10, 1920, 13; and "Ten Counties Are Represented at 'Advertise Georgia' Meeting Here When Governor Explains Project," Macon Telegraph, Sept. 23, 1920, 1.

273 "The discussions over peonage": The quote is from "Tearing Georgia Asunder," an editorial in the Progress-Argus's June 3, 1921, edition.

273 As May closed: Watson's diatribe was reported in "Senator Watson Takes Issue with Gov. Hugh Dorsey," Macon News, May 30, 1921, 3.

274 In the face of the continuing: See "Committee Backs Peonage Booklet," AC, May 26, 1921, 1; "Defend Pamphlet Issued by Dorsey," AC, May 29, 1921, 3; and "Race Relations Committee Backs Dorsey Charges," AC, May 30, 1921, 1.

Part Five: "Give Me Justice"

Chapter 32

279 By the time: The most complete coverage of Manning's first trial was served up in Marion Kendrick, "Clyde Manning Convicted and Given Life Term," AC, June 1, 1921, 1; and Hubert Baughn, "Manning Declared He Was Forced to Kill, Witnesses Say," Atlanta Tri-Weekly Journal, May 31, 1921, 1.

279 Brand kept everyone: Ibid., and the Manning BOE, DOJ Files. Actually, he tipped his hand just a bit during jury selection, when he objected to a defense motion that prospective jurors be disqualified if they were related to John S. Williams. Judge Hutcheson overruled Brand.

280 On cross-examination: The sheriff's quotes are from the Manning BOE.

280 Wismer testified: Ibid.

281 Some of the farm's other: Ibid., and "Clyde Manning Convicted and Given Life Term," AC, June 1.

281 James Strickland, who: Manning BOE.

281 Last came Claude Freeman: Ibid.

282 The first described: Will Napier's killing was described by multiple witnesses, here and in the succeeding paragraphs, in the Manning BOE.

283 The witnesses detailed: The killing of John "Iron Jaw" Davis was, likewise, detailed by multiple witnesses in the Manning BOE.

284 About the death of Robert: Ibid.

284 Emma Freeman described: Ibid.

285 The highlight of the trial's: Manning's unsworn statement is included, in its entirety, in the Manning BOE.

286 *Now Manning did something:* The defendant's breakdowns during his statement were noted in both the BOE and "Clyde Manning Convicted and Gets Life Term," *AC,* June 2.

289 *Manning fell silent:* Underwood's intervention is quoted in the Manning BOE.

Chapter 33

291 *William Howard offered:* "Clyde Manning Convicted and Gets Life Term," *AC,* June 2.

292 *Rising for the defense:* Ibid. Meador was often misidentified in press coverage (and even some court documents) as "A. D. Meadows." Hard to imagine how that happened, given that he was a former judge and a courthouse regular, but, in any event, my spelling is correct. For more, see Lucian Lamar Knight, *A Standard History of Georgia and Georgians, Vol. 4* (Chicago and New York: Lewis Publishing Co., 1917), 2282–83.

292 *At this trial:* Underwood's closing argument was drawn from "Clyde Manning Convicted and Gets Life Term," *AC,* June 2.

293 *Lonnie Brand, playing the lead:* Brand's closing statement is ibid.

294 *Judge Hutcheson's charge:* The charge was included in the Manning BOE in its entirety.

294 *At that, the panel:* The quote is from "Manning Convicted; Draws Life Sentence," *Macon Telegraph,* June 1, 1921, 1.

295 *Granted, it's easy to judge:* One such previous case is *State v. Nargashian* (Rhode Island, 1904), summarized at https://casetext.com/case/state-v-nargashian. Another, *People v. Martin* (California, 1910) is summarized at https://casetext.com/case/people-v-martin-218. Blackstone's relevant passages are quoted in the *Martin* decision, but I've used a version with slightly different punctuation, at https://lonang.com/library/reference/blackstone-commentaries-law-england/bla-402/; see Part VI, section 2 (all accessed March 21, 2023).

295 *As Manning said:* Manning's quote is from "Race Question in Dramatic Setting in Georgia Case," *St. Louis Post-Dispatch,* April 3, 1921, 4.

296 *The jury took just forty:* "Clyde Manning Convicted and Given Life Term," *AC,* June 1; "Manning Convicted; Draws Life Sentence," *Macon Telegraph,* June 1.

296 *To the editorial writers:* "A Just Verdict," *AC,* June 2, 1921, 8.

Chapter 34

297 *That same day:* White's account of his investigation is from "I Investigate Lynchings."

297 *While being deputized:* NAACP board meeting minutes of June 13, 1921 ("BOD minutes 1921" file, Box I:A2, NAACP Papers).

298 *Even as James Weldon Johnson:* Ridley's charges are folded into Johnson's response, which appeared as "Defenseless Dixie," Views and Reviews, *Age,* June 25, 1921, 4.

298 *Meanwhile, in Atlanta:* Hoke Smith's remarks are from "Hoke Smith Says Georgia Unjustly Held Up to Scorn," *Daily News* (Palata, FL), June 19, 1921, 1.

299 *On Dorsey's penultimate:* My account of the meeting was drawn from "Ask Impeachment of Hugh Dorsey," *AC,* June 24, 1921, 3.

299 *Hugh Dorsey's final message:* The governor's address is preserved as *Message of Governor Hugh M. Dorsey to the General Assembly of Georgia, June 25, 1921* (Atlanta: Index Printing Co., 1921). See also "Text of Final Message of Former Governor Dorsey," *AC,* June 26, 1921, 6; "Dorsey, In Last Message, Urges Taxation Reform," *Atlanta Tri-Weekly Journal,* June 28, 1921, 2; and "Dorsey Cites 58 Georgia Lynchings," *NYT,* June 26, 1921, 25.

301 *A short while later:* Hardwick's inaugural address was reported in "Hardwick Sounds Policies in Inaugural Address," *AC,* June 26, 1921, 7. His attack on Dorsey's *Statement* was also detailed in "Hardwick Takes Oath of Office as State Leader," *AC,* June 26, 1921, 1; and "Dorsey Cites 58 Georgia Lynchings," *NYT,* June 26.

Chapter 35

303 *E. Marvin Underwood:* Manning's petition for a new trial was reported in "Clyde Manning's Appeal for New Trial Denied," *Columbus (GA) Enquirer-Sun,* July 31, 1921, 1. The appeals were recounted in the Georgia Supreme Court rulings on each, both of which are available online from Harvard Law School's Caselaw Access Project. For the Williams appeal, see https://cite.case.law/ga/152/498/; for *Manning v. Georgia,* see https://cite.case.law/ga/153/184/ (both accessed March 12, 2023).

303 *Come January 1922:* The quote is from "John S. Williams Denied New Trial," *AC,* Jan. 13, 1922, 12.

304 *There was also this:* Williams's plea of poverty was filed in Fulton County on May 12, 1921. See Williams BOE, DOJ Files. See also "Williams Takes Oath of Pauper in Filing Appeal," *AC,* June 1, 1921, 16.

304 *Williams no longer had land:* "Owner of Jasper Horror Farm Begins Life Sentence in Pen," *Macon Telegraph,* Feb. 2, 1922, 2.

304 *Manning's appeal, meanwhile:* See the Manning appeal, at https://cite.case.law/ga/153/184/.

304 *And on that point:* Ibid.

305 *And so, on April 11:* The Georgia Supreme Court's decision is available for review at https:// cite.case.law/ga/153/184/ (accessed March 21, 2023).

305 *When the Stone Mountain Circuit:* Transcript, *State of Georgia v. Clyde Manning,* July 26–27, 1922 (Reel 26, slides 955–1113, DOJ Files).

305 *Once again, Sheriff:* Johnson's testimony occupies Reel 26, slides 964–977, DOJ Files.

306 *The state wrapped up:* Clyde Freeman's testimony is preserved in the DOJ Files, on Reel 26, slides 1015–1041.

307 *Clyde Freeman's younger brother:* Claude Freeman's testimony is preserved on Reel 26, slides 1041–1051 and 1053–1064, DOJ Files.

307 *The defense next called:* Bohannon's testimony is archived on Reel 26, slides 1064–1066, DOJ Files.

308 *The trial's most chilling:* Johnson's return to the stand is documented on Reel 26, slides 1066–1067, DOJ Files.

309 *Finally came the defense's last:* Manning's unsworn statement is preserved on Reel 26, slides 1097–1101, DOJ Files.

311 *This time, Judge Hutcheson's:* The charge to the jury is preserved on Reel 26, slides 1102–1113, DOJ Files.

311 *The second trial:* "Manning Convicted of Murders Again," *AC,* July 28, 1922, 14.

Chapter 36

312 *Three days after:* The scandal was covered in "Officials Probing Report Williams Visited His Home," *AC,* Aug. 13, 1922, 1; the *Macon News* quote is from "A Mockery of the Law," an editorial in the Aug. 15, 1922, edition, 6.

312 *Dunaway insisted:* "Dunaway Denies 'Murder Farm' Barbecue Story," *AC,* Aug. 14, 1922, 3. The superintendent's admission to the prison commission was reported in "Permitted Boss of Murder Farm To Visit Family," *AC,* Aug. 16, 1922, 1. The quotes are from the latter.

313 *Dunaway's testimony satisfied:* "Dunaway Scored by Dr. Bryant," *AC,* Aug. 21, 1922, 7.

313 *The scandal only added:* "'Murder Farm' Owner Taken to Colquitt Gang," *Macon News,* Nov. 27, 1922, 1.

313 *Three years passed:* Edward Dozier Williams's visits to the prison were reported by his son, John Edward Williams, in a Dec. 2, 2022, phone interview. Williams's activity in prison was summarized in "Parole Sought: Convicted Owner of 'Murder Farm' Wants His Freedom," *Macon Telegraph,* April 5, 1927, 10.

314 *Then, out of the blue:* "Famous 'Murder Farm' Case Again Gets Attention," *AC,* Feb. 4, 1925, 1.

314 *Before he walked back:* Ibid. Lonnie Brand died on March 5, 1923, at forty-six, prompting Judge Hutcheson to assign members of the Covington bar to draft a memorial. "We all loved him as a big brother," the lawyers wrote, going on to suggest that Brand had worked himself to death: "So earnest and diligent did he enter upon and perform his duties as Solicitor General of this circuit that it took less than two years to undermine his health and vitality and turn disease upon his robust form. . . ." Greene Johnson died on Nov. 29, 1923, at fifty.

314 *Two days later:* "LeRoy Williams Gives Bond Here," *Macon Telegraph,* Feb. 5, 1925, 7.

314 *Another sixteen months passed:* Manning's death certificate, available through FamilySearch, indicates he'd been living at the prison farm (having returned, presumably, from the chain gang) for about six months when he died. It also demonstrates just how lax the state was at record-keeping: in the spaces for Manning's marital status, spouse's name, and parents' names, officials wrote "don't know." His date of birth was left blank. So was the blank reserved for whether he had been breastfed.

315 *So ended a life:* The FBI file includes memos between Vincent Hughes, who led the Bureau's office in 1921, and agents writing the case summary ten years after the fact. Hughes's critique reflected his belief that, while the agents had nailed down the facts, they had not adequately captured the drama of the affair. He offered up the paragraph I quote here, which was subsequently stitched into the finished version of the summary.

315 *Clyde Manning was survived:* One of the weirdest footnotes to this story occurred a few months later, in November 1927, when a young Black man identifying himself as Clyde Manning turned up in New York City. To a reporter from the *Age,* he claimed to have helped a Georgia farmer and modern-day slave driver drown 313 of his Black farmhands. That number is no misprint: 313.

"Federal authorities recovered from the river scores and scores of skeletons which bore silent testimony to the wholesale slaughter done on the farm," read the resulting story— "Georgia Slave Farm Overseer Gains Liberty After Serving Six Years in Federal Penitentiary in Atlanta, Ga."—in the paper's Nov. 12, 1927, edition.

"A pardon let the white man off four weeks after his imprisonment. And just three weeks ago the colored man . . . was paroled. Friendless, penniless and with the terrible memory of his farm enslavement, he is in New York trying to forget and to get a new start in life."

James Weldon Johnson would have recognized immediately that it was a sham—but he had given up his column in 1924, after producing it for a decade, and no one else on staff, it seems, recalled that Clyde Manning went to *state* prison, not federal, or that John S. Williams remained a prisoner. A week later, after receiving word from Atlanta that Manning was dead and the visitor a fake, the *Age* announced it had been duped. "The public is warned against giving said Clyde Manning any financial assistance," the paper advised.

315 *Manning's death had one:* "Williams Boys Give Selves Up," *Monticello News,* Feb. 18, 1927, 1. That the county would press the case, and that it was plain the sons had come forward after learning of Manning's death, were reported in "Duke to Try Williams Boys," *Macon News,* Feb. 17, 1927, 11. The transcript of the hearing is filed at Jasper County Superior Court.

316 *Manning's death also spurred:* Williams's bid was reported in "Parole Sought: Convicted Owner of 'Murder Farm' Wants His Freedom," *Macon Telegraph,* April 5.

317 *"Your petitioner shows":* Ibid.

317 *So much for remorse:* Williams's hearing was covered in "Peonage Farm Head Plea Heard Today," AC, May 5, 1927, 3; and "'Death Farm' Head Plea Considered," AC, May 6, 1927, 5.

317 *With Hulon, LeRoy, and Marvin:* The search for witnesses is chronicled in the FBI File.

318 *With Clyde Manning dead:* The Bureau correspondence makes clear that Jasper County had turned away from any further state prosecution.

318 *Neither did the Department:* The correspondence I cite is included in the FBI File; additional documents are available in the DOJ Files, Reel 9 (beginning with slide 1055) and Reel 18 (beginning at slide 885). The conventional wisdom seems to be that the death of Manning and other witnesses led the feds to abandon the cases, but that doesn't really wash: Manning was an eyewitness to just one of the three killings for which the Williams sons were indicted. Other, more useful witnesses—brothers Clyde Freeman and Claude Freeman, among them—were alive and located. Tim Pitts, in his study of the matter, reckons that the feds simply lost interest in pressing what was, by then, a case that long predated most of the agents and prosecutors involved.

320 *By then, Lucy Williams:* Lucy's new address and the rent she paid are listed in the 1930 census. John S. Williams's vaunted status at Milledgeville was described in "Two Fugitives Face Charge of Murder," *Macon News,* Jan. 26, 1932, 1.

320 *This lofty position:* Ibid.

320 *The resentment of his fellow:* Smith's two earlier prison breaks are mentioned in "Murder Charge Confronts Bandit Caught in Florida," AC, June 25, 1932, 1. The breakout and Williams's death are chronicled in ibid.; "Two Fugitives Face Charge of Murder," *Macon News,* Jan. 26; "Three Escapes Make Clean Getaway," *Macon News,* Jan. 27, 1932, 1; "Jno. S. Williams Is Killed By Car," *Monticello News,* Jan. 28, 1932, 1; "Williams' Funeral Held in Monticello," *Macon News,* Jan. 28, 1932, 2; and "Dunaway Asserts Guards Underpaid," *Macon News,* Feb. 2, 1932, 7. Conditions at the prison are described in "Thorough Probe of Recent Escapes Promised by Prison Commissioners," *Macon News,* Jan. 27, 1932, 1.

320 *Prison bosses discovered:* The quote is from "Smith to Return to Prison Today," *AC,* June 26, 1932, 13. The detail that the car swerved into Williams is from "Three Escapes Make Clean Getaway," *Macon News,* Jan. 27.

320 *The prison's leadership:* The notation on Williams's death certificate is from "Two Fugitives John S Face Charge of Murder," *Macon News,* Jan. 26. The funeral was described in "Many Attend Funeral of Williams," *AC,* Jan. 29, 1932, 12.

Incidentally, the *Monticello News* story of Jan. 28, 1932, cited above, reports that the get-away car "mangled his body beneath the wheels"—a detail not reported in most accounts—but then chose to skip any mention of how Williams came to be standing on a road outside the prison farm when he died. "The deceased was a favorite among a wide circle of relatives and friends in Middle Georgia," the story read. "He was a devoted husband and father, loyal friend and neighbor, vigorous and untiring in his everyday duties. He was a member of the Bethel Baptist Church and a member of the Masonic lodge. Mr. Williams came to Jasper from Monroe County and at one time operated a large plantation." Not a word about his criminal history.

According to the records of the Jasper County Probate Court, Williams's estate consisted of just two shares of stock in the First National Bank of Monticello, valued at two hundred dollars. He left behind a life insurance policy that provided Lucy Williams, daughter Lucy Claire, and the three youngest Williams children "probably Three Hundred Dollars, each."

Part Six: Legacy

Chapter 37

325 *This new awareness:* For more on the Tabert killing, see Carper, "Slavery Revisited"; "The Whipping Boss," editorial, *Orlando Evening Reporter-Star,* March 27, 1923, 6; "Florida Senate Votes for Peonage Inquiry," *NYT,* April 6, 1923, 19; "This Civilized Land," editorial, *Age,* April 7, 1923, 4; "Grand Jury Begins Inquiry into Death of Martin Tabert," *Tampa Tribune,* April 10, 1923, 1; and "Indicts Gang Boss for Killing Tabert," *NYT,* April 12, 1923, 10.

325 *All through the 1920s:* The Calhoun County, FL, case is reported in "Sensations Seen in Pensacola Peonage Trials," *Miami Tribune,* May 19, 1925, 9; "Federal Court Hears Final Testimony in Peonage Trial," *Orlando Evening Reporter-Star,* May 22, 1925, 12; and "Floridians Found Guilty of Peonage," *Birmingham News,* May 23, 1925, 1. The Amite County, MS, case is detailed in "Deputies Named in Peonage Case," *Macon Telegraph,* Feb. 4, 1927, 12; and "Amite Farmers to Go On Trial," *Semi-Weekly Journal* (McComb, MS), Feb. 23, 1927, 5. The Willacy County, TX, case is laid out in "Sentences to Be Passed Saturday in Peonage Cases," *Corpus Christi Caller,* March 11, 1927, 1; "Prison Terms and Fines in Peonage Case," *Corpus Christi Caller,* March 13, 1927, 1; and "Willacy County Men Not to Appeal Peonage Conviction," *Brownsville Herald,* March 19, 1927, 1.

326 *Not all of the government's:* The case against Georgia planter W. D. Arnold was reported in "Lashed, Paid $2.50 Week, Man Alleges," *AC,* June 20, 1929, 1; "Peons Describe Flogging Parties in Federal Court," *Macon News,* July 3, 1929, 1; and "Deaver Recesses Trial of Arnold," *Macon Telegraph,* July 4, 1929, 1.

326 *But many other defendants:* The Piggott quote is from Renwick C. Kennedy, Walter Wilson, and Henry Fuller, "The Cotton Kingdom," *New Republic,* Dec. 16, 1931, 129–34.

326 *The drumbeat of prosecutions:* Johnson described his D.C. work in *Along This Way.*

326 *Walter White continued:* White's Mississippi levee investigation was reported in White, *A Man Called White;* and "Effort to Hush Inquiry Is Laid to Department," *Monroe (LA) News-Star,* Sept. 23, 1932, 1.

327 *Throughout, the pair:* The quote is from Johnson's speech titled "The Militant NAACP," delivered April 27, 1928 ("Speeches & Articles—James Weldon Johnson, 1920–28 and undated" file, Box I:C178, NAACP Papers).

327 *Change was slow to come:* Cotton's nosedive was described in Kennedy, Wilson, and Fuller, "The Cotton Kingdom."

327 *So the cases kept coming:* The quote is ibid. For more on the Camp Hill affair, see "Volleys Disperse Alabama Negroes," *NYT,* July 18, 1931, 30; and "In Tallapoosa," *Time,* July 27, 1931.

327 *Debt slavery remained:* The quote is from Dittmer, *Black Georgia in the Progressive Era, 1900–1920.*

328 *The ground finally began:* Pete Daniel makes the point about mechanization in "The Metamorphosis of Slavery." Biddle's Dec. 12, 1941, circular (No. 3591, titled "Involuntary Servitude, Slavery, and Peonage") is available online at https://en.wikisource.org/wiki/Circular_No._3591 (accessed March 14, 2023). The document is analyzed in Blackmon, *Slavery By Another Name;* and Novak, *The Wheel of Servitude.*

329 *In short order:* The Supreme Court's decision in *Taylor v. Georgia* can be reviewed online at https://supreme.justia.com/cases/federal/us/315/25/ (accessed March 20, 2023). See also a case summary at *George Washington Law Review* 10, No. 6 (April 1942): 748–50. The court's action in the Florida case, *Pollock v. Williams,* is reproduced and analyzed at https://supreme.justia.com/cases/federal/us/322/4/ (accessed March 14, 2023).

329 *A 1948 rewrite:* Blackmon offers up a nice summary of the postwar measures in *Slavery By Another Name.*

329 *It is a testament:* Johnson's literary output is cataloged in Adelman, "A Study of James Weldon Johnson"; and in Johnson, *Along This Way.*

330 *In an August 1920 speech:* The quotes are from "The Negro's Place in the New Civilization," a speech Johnson delivered at Bordentown, NJ, on Aug. 12, 1920 ("Speeches & Articles—James Weldon Johnson, 1920–28 and undated" file, Box I:C178, NAACP Papers).

330 *He had "good reason":* The quotes are from "James Weldon Johnson," editorial, *NYT,* June 28, 1938, 18.

330 *But Johnson had reason:* As noted in the text, the quote is from *Autobiography of an Ex-Colored Man.* The words belong to the narrator's white benefactor.

331 *After a decade:* Johnson's funeral was covered in "Thousands Attend Johnson Funeral," *NYT,* July 1, 1938, 19; and "2,500 Pay Final Tribute to James Weldon Johnson; Many Celebrities at Last Rites," *Age,* July 9, 1938, 1.

331 *As that scene unfolded:* "2,500 Pay Final Tribute to James Weldon Johnson; Many Celebrities at Last Rites," *Age,* July 9.

332 *Walter White, too, became:* White, *A Man Called White.*

332 *White and the NAACP:* Ibid.; Baime, *White Lies;* "Walter White's Death Shocks Nation," *Age,* March 26, 1955, 1; "Walter White, 61, Dies in Home Here," *NYT,* March 22.

332 *Like Johnson before him:* The bill's origins are explored in Schuler, "Race Riots During and After the First World War"; Pinar, "The NAACP and the Struggle for Antilynching Legislation, 1897–1917"; and Johnson, *Along This Way.*

333 *The Democratic majority:* The bill's 1921 fate was covered in Mary White Ovington, "The National Association for the Advancement of Colored People," *Journal of Negro History* 9, no. 2 (April 1924): 107–16; Robert L. Zangrando, "James Weldon Johnson and the Dyer Antilynching Bill," *Langston Hughes Review* 8, nos. 1/2 (Spring/Fall 1989): 76–79; and Johnson, *Along This Way.* The Senate's 2005 action was covered in Sheryl Gay Stolberg, "Senate Issues Apology Over Failure on Lynching Law," *NYT,* at https://www.nytimes.com/2005/06/14/politics/senate-issues-apology-over-failure-on-lynching-law.html (accessed March 20, 2023).

333 *Only in 2022:* The three dissenters to the act's passage were Republicans Andrew S. Clyde of Georgia, Thomas Massie of Kentucky, and Chip Roy of Texas.

333 *By then, the Montgomery:* The EJI offered the death toll in a 2020 report, *Reconstruction in America: Racial Violence after the Civil War,* available for download at https://eji.org/reports/reconstruction-in-america-overview/ (accessed March 14, 2023).

333 *When White died:* The *Age* quote is from "The Wind Still Rises," an editorial on page 10 of the paper's April 2, 1955, edition. The *NYT* editorial cited is "Walter White," March 23, 1955, 30.

334 *"He could easily have joined":* "Walter White, 61, Dies in Home Here," *NYT,* March 22.

334 *Therein might lie a partial:* White's leadership style is described in White, *A Man Called White;* and Beth Tompkins Bates, "A New Crowd Challenges the Agenda of the Old Guard in the NAACP, 1933–1941," *American Historical Review* 102, no. 2 (April 1997): 340–77. His egotism and delight at name-dropping were cited in "Some of His Best Friends Were Noted," *Age,* April 2, 1955, 12. White made his "quiet, bloodless revolution" comment in a June 29, 1947, speech at the Lincoln Memorial, at which President Harry S. Truman also spoke. It's preserved at Catherine Ellis and Stephen Drury Smith, eds., *Say It Plain: A Century of Great African American Speeches* (New York: The New Press, 2005).

334 *In contrast, the new:* White's reported self-centeredness was noted in "Walter White: NAACP Leader Influenced the Era in Which He Lived," *Age,* April 2, 1955, 11.

334 *On top of that:* Ibid.; Baime, *White Lies;* and the online Walter White Project, at https://scalar.usc.edu/nehvectors/stakeman/marriage-divorce-and-remarriage.

335 *Then, just a few weeks after:* The story is preserved at https://chawedrosin.wordpress.com/2012/04/21/1949-look-magazinearticle-on-skin-lightening/. For more on the resulting controversy, see Eric Porter, "'Black No More'? Walter White, Hydroquinone, and the 'Negro Problem,'" *American Studies* 47, no. 1 (Spring 2006): 5–30.

335 *He did return to the NAACP:* See Porter, "'Black No More?'"; and Baime, *White Lies.*

335 *But behind the scenes:* The McClusky affair is chronicled in Mark Ellis, *Race Harmony and Black Progress: Jack Woofter and the Interracial Cooperation Movement* (Bloomington and Indianapolis: Indiana University Press, 2013); Benjamin E. Mays, *Born to Rebel: An Autobiography* (Athens, GA: University of Georgia Press, 1971); and Wilma Dykeman and James Stokely, *Seeds of Southern Change: The Life of Will Alexander* (New York: W. W. Norton Inc., 1976).

336 *There he sought help:* The Dorsey quote is from Ellis, "Racial Unrest and White Liberalism in Rural Georgia: Barrow and Oconee Counties in the Early 1920s."

336 *Woofter supplied Walter White:* Both the White and Woofter quotes are ibid.

336 *The judge convened:* Ibid.

336 *The state's response:* For more on the decline of lynching, see ibid.; and "Take Steps to Curb Mob Rule," *Macon Telegraph,* Nov. 3, 1922, 9. The 1946 lynching is thoroughly explored in Laura Wexler, *Fire in a Canebrake: The Last Mass Lynching in America* (New York: Scribner, 2003). Georgia's improved record in lynching is reported in the online New Georgia Encyclopedia, at https://www.georgiaencyclopedia.org/articles/history-archaeology/lynching/ (accessed July 10, 2023).

337 *When a judge of Atlanta's:* Dorsey's appointment was reported in "Hugh M. Dorsey Named as Judge of City Court," *AC,* Sept. 12, 1926, 1; and "Dorsey Takes Oath of Office," *Macon Telegraph,* Sept. 14, 1926, 8. The quote is from "Judge Hugh M. Dorsey," editorial, *AC,* Sept. 14, 1926, 6.

When Dorsey's father, Rufus T. Dorsey, won his City Court post in 1884, judges were allowed to take private clients on the side. When that practice was abandoned after he had served a year, he quit the bench. Not, however, before achieving a rare distinction: not one of his decisions was reversed on appeal.

337 *That November, Atlantans:* The Dorsey children's schooling was reported in a brief in the *AC,* Sept. 24, 1927, 11. The quoted letter to state historian Ruth Blair, dated Sept. 11, 1931, is preserved in Dorsey's papers at the Georgia Archives.

337 *But in 1935:* Dorsey's move to the Superior Court was reported in "Dorsey Takes Oath as Judge for New Superior Court," *AC,* May 2, 1935, 7. His 1936 support is described in "Judge Dorsey Given Indorsement of Bar," *AC,* Aug. 6, 1936, 9.

338 *As luck would have it:* Ward Greene's *Death in the Deep South* is long out of print, but I found a used copy on Amazon. *They Won't Forget,* which is usually remembered for the debut of Lana Turner (and the scene that earned her the nickname "the Sweater Girl") is available on DVD.

338 *The Frank case, and his role:* Dorsey's declining health was noted in "Personals," *AC,* Feb. 26, 1947, 13; and in "Judge Dorsey Quits," *Macon News,* March 4, 1948, 16. His resignation was reported in "Dorsey Resigns; Pharr Successor," *AC,* March 4, 1948, 1.

Dorsey was frequently cast as a villain in dramatic revisits to the Frank case. In 1964, NBC devoted an hour-long episode of its *Profiles in Courage* television series to Governor Slaton's commutation of the sentence, with Walter Mathau in the principal role. Dorsey was represented, but as a minor and fairly benign character. Such was not the case in 1988, when the network aired a two-part miniseries written by novelist Larry McMurtry. *The Murder of Mary Phagan* depicted Dorsey as a weaselly schemer willing to do anything to earn political points, and Slaton—portrayed by Jack Lemmon—as an ace amateur detective who single-handedly cracks the case before saving Frank from the gallows.

In 1997 David Mamet released a novel, *The Old Religion,* that explored Frank's psychological torment during the trial. A year later, Frank's ordeal was repackaged as a Broadway musical titled *Parade.* The production, which won Tony Awards for best book and best original score, concentrated on the relationship between Frank and his wife, and offered up Dorsey as principal villain. The musical was revived in 2023 to intense and widespread acclaim.

338 *Dorsey died three months later:* The story I quote is "Death of Former Governor Dorsey," editorial, *Macon Telegraph,* June 14, 1948, 4.

339 *Over the past thirty years:* The cases I cite were described by the Anti-Slavery Program of the Florida-based Coalition of Immokalee Workers; summaries of the prosecutions are available at https://ciw-online.org/slavery/ (accessed March 15, 2023).

339 *In 2010, a federal grand jury:* Ibid. See also "Federal Agency Files Large Human-Trafficking Suit," an April 21, 2011, story on the CNN website, at http://www.cnn.com/2011/CRIME /04/21/farm.worker.trafficking/index.html (accessed March 15, 2023).

340 *And in 2021 came:* Operation Blooming Onion is detailed by the Justice Department at https://www.justice.gov/usao-sdga/pr/human-smuggling-forced-labor-among-allegations -south-georgia-federal-indictment/ (accessed March 15, 2023).

Chapter 38

341 *I explored it one afternoon:* Tim Pitts and I made our trip to the home place on Aug. 14, 2021. The 1909 map I mention is a Hudgins Co. map of Jasper County. While I found my copy at the University of Georgia, the Georgia Archives also holds one, and makes it available for download at https://vault.georgiaarchives.org/digital/collection/cmf/id/329/rec/2 (accessed March 16, 2023).

342 *He would strike out:* The testimony of Lessie May Whitlow is from the transcript of *Georgia v. Clyde Manning,* July 26–27, 1922, DOJ Files.

343 *The cruel truth:* This scenario was raised by Deputy U.S. Marshal C. H. Livsey in "Georgia's Governor Says Peonage Must Be Stopped," *Age,* April 9, 1921.

343 *I returned to the road:* The visit I describe occurred on Sept. 15, 2022.

345 *The Williams family:* I tracked Augustus "Gus" Williams's movements through his obituary, on page 2 of the Dec. 27, 1965, *Macon News;* and "Death Claims Dr. Williams; Rites Monday," the same paper's Dec. 25 front-page story reporting his passing. I traced Mary's presence in Atlanta—and later Tampa—through the U.S. censuses of 1930 and 1940 and her obituary, at "Mary W. Martin," *Tampa Tribune,* May 20, 1994, 20. Lucy Claire's commitment is documented in Jasper County Probate Court records (Jasper County Court of Ordinary Writ of Lunacy, Book B, 64).

345 *The other eight left Georgia:* Author telephone interview with John Edward Williams and Jo Ann Williams, Dec. 2, 2022.

345 *"They didn't say a thing":* Author telephone interview with Kendall Wayne Williams, Nov. 30, 2022.

346 *I heard much the same:* Author telephone interview with Glenn Raymond Brooks Jr., Nov. 21, 2022.

346 *Susan Burnore, granddaughter:* Author telephone interview with Susan Burnore, Nov. 21, 2022.

346 *The secret survived:* Dec. 2, 2022, interview with John Edward and Jo Ann Williams; Nov. 21, 2022, interview with Glenn Raymond Brooks Jr. The quote is from the former conversation.

346 *John Edward, who was born:* Dec. 2, 2022, author interview.

347 *Mary June became:* Ibid.

347 *"It was a very physical":* Ibid.

347 *At a later family reunion:* Ibid.

348 *It was not until the 1990s:* I heard from several Williams descendants that the event that brought the story to their attention was the publication of Gregory A. Freeman's *Lay This Body Down* (Chicago: Lawrence Hill Books, 1999). Freeman's interpretation of some events in the Murder Farm saga differs from my own, and I have thus not cited his book as a source. The longtime Georgia journalist was generous in sharing documents with me, however, and has put up with my questions since, and his work overall informed the story you now hold in your hands.

348 *Marvin married:* Marvin Williams's life in Florida is outlined in "M. H. Williams, Doing Good Job, Killed by Crane," *Tampa Tribune,* May 31, 1942, 2. His run for constable was reported in "Marvin H. Williams Becomes Candidate in Constable Race," *Tampa Tribune,* Feb. 18, 1940, 10. His legal trouble was detailed in "Filling Station Men Are Freed Without Trial," *Tampa Tribune,* May 15, 1937, 9.

348 *Shortly after the attack:* Marvin Williams's fatal accident was chronicled in "M. H. Williams, Doing Good Job, Killed by Crane," *Tampa Tribune*, May 31.

348 *Hulon Williams set up:* Hulon Williams's Florida career was described in "Oilman J. H. Williams Sr. Dies in Hospital at Age 73," *Tampa Tribune*, Feb. 10, 1966, 2.

349 *In 1945, he formed:* Ibid., and "Central Bank Reelects Officers and Directors," *Tampa Tribune*, Jan. 13, 1959, 21.

349 *He died in 1966:* "Jury Selected for Trial in Wife Murder," *Tampa Tribune*, Feb. 3, 1937, 4. The trial's outcome was reported in "R.C. Kimball Convicted Here," on page 2 of the next day's *Tribune*.

It's one of those improbable turns of nonfiction that the Williams sons were joined in the Tampa area by the man who led the search for them in Jasper County. After failing to win reelection as solicitor general of the Ocmulgee Circuit in 1924, Doyle Campbell sat for the Florida bar exam, earned his license there, and moved to Tampa a short time later.

In 1928, he was appointed assistant county solicitor. He held the post for just ten months before the appointment was revoked, for reasons that were kept under wraps. He made an unsuccessful run for county solicitor in 1932. After that, Campbell apparently devoted himself to a modest private practice in which he became expert at sniffing out real estate that he could acquire at a discount. He became a bit of a land baron.

Along the way, he handled some legal matters for the family of a Western Union telegraph supervisor named Rita C. Harnett. When he suffered a series of heart attacks in the early 1950s, Harnett became his caregiver, cooking his meals and minding his house and driving him around town. On his death in 1954, Campbell willed his estate to his friend. It consisted mostly of property valued, at the time, at half a million dollars.

At her own death in 1981, Harnett willed two hundred acres of mangrove forest and swampland south of Tampa to the county for the creation of a wildlife preserve that she wanted named for her benefactor. Today, that acreage—a refuge, as Harnett had instructed, for a dense population of waterfowl, amphibians, and swamp mammals—is known as Doyle Campbell Park.

349 *LeRoy Williams took a different:* LeRoy Williams's movements are reflected in the U.S. censuses of 1930, 1940, and 1950. His stints as mayor and president of the local Lions Club were reported in "Dixie County Lions Club Observes 'Ladies Night,'" *Tampa Tribune*, Aug. 5, 1948, 10.

349 *"Once a year we loaded":* Kendall Wayne Williams interview of Nov. 30, 2022.

349 *LeRoy Williams did not come across:* John Edward Williams interview of Dec. 2, 2022; John Edward Williams email to author of Feb. 9, 2023.

Chapter 39

351 *For more than two months:* The shockingly racist account of the group's time in the Tower is "Negroes Living on Fat of Land and Getting Paid," *AC*, May 26, 1921, 1. My account of the workers' movements on their release was informed by U.S. census records, death certificates, and newspaper obituaries.

352 *Those who died first:* The death certificates of those I mention are available through FamilySearch. For a handy clearinghouse of all things Jasper County, see the Jasper County Genealogy wiki at https://www.familysearch.org/en/wiki/Jasper_County,_Georgia_Genealogy (accessed March 16, 1993).

Addie Jo Phelps married Rufus Manning in 1900. At the time, John Freeman was married to the former Ida Maddox; she was gone from the household by the 1910 census. In the 1920 federal headcount, Addie Jo was listed as wife to both men, and several children were listed in both homes, as well. On her death certificate, John Freeman was listed as her husband.

353 *No surprise, then:* Lessie May Whitlow's comments to the Bureau are included in the FBI File. James Strickland's elusiveness is ibid.

353 *Government men found:* Ibid., and the 1930 census and Charlotte city directories.

354 *In contrast, Clyde Manning's:* That Gladdis Manning changed his name is reported in the FBI File. I also found him in the 1930 census, and located his death certificate via the FamilySearch website.

354 *Despite shoddy record-keeping:* I traced the descendants named in this paragraph through U.S. census records, newspaper obituaries, and death certificates, most gleaned through FamilySearch and Ancestry.com.

354 *Clyde Manning's sister:* I traced Grace Johnson's movements through U.S. census records, newspaper obituaries, and the help of her granddaughter-in-law, Chessie Dumas, in February and March 2023. At the time, Grace Johnson's daughter-in-law, Ada Johnson, was ninety-five and in assisted living in Atlanta; when it became clear that her health would not permit me to interview her, Ms. Dumas agreed to take my questions to her. Ms. Dumas's quote reflects her findings.

355 *And Grace Johnson:* I again used U.S. census records and newspaper obituaries to establish the outlines of Claude Freeman's life with Rena and his sons.

355 *Reverend Freeman grew up:* I interviewed Rev. Kenneth J. Freeman on Dec. 4, 2022, and Jan. 10, 2023. According to family lore, the reverend told me, the newborn baby that John S. Williams allegedly ordered killed was his grandmother's—that is, Rena Manning's.

355 *That is not who she was:* Kenneth J. Freeman interviews; U.S. census records.

356 *Three generations have come:* The Sac-O-Suds, scene of the robbery that launches the action in *My Cousin Vinny,* is a real-life convenience store near Jasper's Jackson Lake shoreline. Downtown Covington was taped off for a *Vampire Diaries* shoot when I first visited the town in the spring of 2010. The courthouse square has also served as a backdrop for TV's *In the Heat of the Night.*

357 *The 1909 map of Jasper:* The column I mention was J. S. "Chick" Wilson, "Poor Farm," a Jan. 14, 2010, *Monticello News* item that was anthologized in Wilson's *Museum Notes: History & Remembrances of Monticello and Jasper County[,] Georgia, Vol. II* (Monticello, GA: Museum of Jasper County Heritage, 2010).

358 *When I visited:* I visited the former paupers farm site on Jan. 31 and Feb. 1, 2023. Sheriff Donnie Pope offered the quote in a Jan. 31, 2023, interview in his office.

358 *A few days later:* Jasper County surveyor Robert Jordan shared the aerials with me in early February 2023.

359 *Still, he agreed:* As noted in the text, Sheriff Pope explored the ground behind the senior center on Feb. 14, 2023.

359 *A few miles to the west:* I visited Turtle Cove's clubhouse and private Parrot Beach on Sept. 16, 2022, and Feb. 1, 2023.

360 *In November 1921:* The discovery of the skeleton was reported in "Another Victim of 'Murder Farm['] Found in Pond," *AC,* Nov. 9, 1921, 1; and "Find More Bones on Murder Farm," *Macon News,* Nov. 9, 1921, 3. The quote is from "Skeleton of an Alleged Peon Found on J. S. Williams' Farm," *Macon Telegraph,* Nov. 9, 1921, 1.

360 *In reporting the find:* "Another Victim of 'Murder Farm['] Found in Pond," *AC,* Nov. 9. See also "Williams and Three Sons Indicted by Jasper Grand Jury," *Macon Telegraph,* April 12, 1921, 1.

361 *Whatever the case:* "Another Victim of 'Murder Farm['] Found in Pond," *AC,* Nov. 9.

361 *Farther west:* I spoke with Newton County Coroner Tommy Davis three times about the disposition of remains initially buried in the riverbanks. He told me he had found no paperwork suggesting the bodies had been exhumed and reburied.

361 *All that remains:* Local resident Terry L. Hall took me to Allen's Bridge by pontoon boat on July 26, 2023.

362 *On the South:* Hall and I explored Mann's Bridge on September 16, 2022, and July 26, 2023. On the latter trip, he pointed out the homestead off old Route 36, about one hundred yards from the bridge. His father told him, he said, that Harry Price lay beneath the ruins. We saw no sign of graves, and I have found no other evidence to back up the story.

Index

412

ABOUT
MARINER BOOKS

MARINER BOOKS traces its beginnings to 1832 when William Ticknor cofounded the Old Corner Bookstore in Boston, from which he would run the legendary firm Ticknor and Fields, publisher of Ralph Waldo Emerson, Harriet Beecher Stowe, Nathaniel Hawthorne, and Henry David Thoreau. Following Ticknor's death, Henry Oscar Houghton acquired Ticknor and Fields and, in 1880, formed Houghton Mifflin, which later merged with venerable Harcourt Publishing to form Houghton Mifflin Harcourt. HarperCollins purchased HMH's trade publishing business in 2021 and reestablished their storied lists and editorial team under the name Mariner Books.

Uniting the legacies of Houghton Mifflin, Harcourt Brace, and Ticknor and Fields, Mariner Books continues one of the great traditions in American bookselling. Our imprints have introduced an incomparable roster of enduring classics, including Hawthorne's *The Scarlet Letter*, Thoreau's *Walden*, Willa Cather's *O Pioneers!*, Virginia Woolf's *To the Lighthouse*, W. E. B. Du Bois's *Black Reconstruction*, J. R. R. Tolkien's *The Lord of the Rings*, Carson McCullers's *The Heart Is a Lonely Hunter*, Ann Petry's *The Narrows*, George Orwell's *Animal Farm* and *Nineteen Eighty-Four*, Rachel Carson's *Silent Spring*, Margaret Walker's *Jubilee*, Italo Calvino's *Invisible Cities*, Alice Walker's *The Color Purple*, Margaret Atwood's *The Handmaid's Tale*, Tim O'Brien's *The Things They Carried*, Philip Roth's *The Plot Against America*, Jhumpa Lahiri's *Interpreter of Maladies*, and many others. Today Mariner Books remains proudly committed to the craft of fine publishing established nearly two centuries ago at the Old Corner Bookstore.